DANCE ON THE RAZOR'S EDGE

Crime and Punishment in the Nazi Ghettos

Historians have mainly seen the ghettos established by the Nazis in German-occupied Eastern Europe as spaces marked by brutality, tyranny, and the systematic murder of the Jewish population. Drawing on examples from the Warsaw, Lodz, and Vilna ghettos, *Dance on the Razor's Edge* explores how, in fact, highly improvised legal spheres emerged in these coerced and heterogeneous ghetto communities.

Looking at sources from multiple archives and countries, Svenja Bethke investigates how the Jewish Councils, set up on German orders and composed of ghetto inhabitants, formulated new definitions of criminal offenses and established legal institutions on their own initiative, as a desperate attempt to ensure the survival of the ghetto communities. Bethke explores how people under these circumstances tried to make sense of everyday lives that had been turned upside down, bringing with them pre-war notions of justice and morality, and she considers the extent to which this rupture led to new judgments on human behaviour. In doing so, Bethke aims to understand how people attempted to use their very limited scope for action in order to survive. Set against the background of a Holocaust historiography that often still seeks clear categories of "good" and "bad" behaviours, *Dance on the Razor's Edge* calls for a new understanding of the ghettos as complex communities operating in an unprecedented emergency situation.

(German and European Studies)

SVENJA BETHKE is a lecturer in modern European history at the University of Leicester.

GERMAN AND EUROPEAN STUDIES

General Editor: Jennifer L. Jenkins

Dance on the Razor's Edge

*Crime and Punishment
in the Nazi Ghettos*

SVENJA BETHKE

TRANSLATED BY SHARON HOWE

UNIVERSITY OF TORONTO PRESS
Toronto Buffalo London

Originally published in German as: TANZ AUF MESSERS SCHNEIDE:
KRIMINALITÄT UND RECHT IN DEN GHETTOS WARSCHAU,
LITZMANNSTADT UND WILNA
© 2015 by Hamburger Edition HIS Verlagsges. mbH, Hamburg, Germany
This translation from German is published by arrangement with Hamburger
Edition.

ISBN 978-1-4875-0492-2 (cloth)   ISBN 978-1-4875-3117-1 (EPUB)
ISBN 978-1-4875-2354-1 (paper)   ISBN 978-1-4875-3116-4 (PDF)

German and European Studies

Publication cataloguing information is available from
Library and Archives Canada.

The translation of this work was funded by Geisteswissenschaften
International – Translation Funding for Work in the Humanities and Social
Sciences from Germany, a joint initiative of the Fritz Thyssen Foundation,
the German Federal Foreign Office, the collecting society VG WORT and the
Börsenverein des Deutschen Buchhandels (German Publishers & Booksellers
Association).

The German and European Studies series is funded by the DAAD with funds
from the German Federal Foreign Office

 Deutscher Akademischer Austauschdienst
German Academic Exchange Service

University of Toronto Press acknowledges the financial assistance to its
publishing program of the Canada Council for the Arts and the Ontario Arts
Council, an agency of the Government of Ontario.

 Canada Council   Conseil des Arts
for the Arts   du Canada

 ONTARIO ARTS COUNCIL
CONSEIL DES ARTS DE L'ONTARIO
an Ontario government agency
un organisme du gouvernement de l'Ontario

Funded by the   Financé par le
Government   gouvernement   Canada
of Canada   du Canada

Contents

Acknowledgments

This is a revised and updated version of my first book, which was published in German by Hamburger Edition in 2015. I finished this manuscript in Jerusalem in the late spring of 2020 during a month of almost complete lockdown because of the coronavirus crisis. I was only allowed to venture within a one-hundred-metre radius of the house while wearing a mask, and only permitted to meet those living in my immediate household. I am grateful to my friends and family for their love, support, and encouragement in what I sometimes found to be challenging times.

Although the work did not take up the past five years since the book was first published in German, this revised version feels like the result of a very inspiring and enriching period of my life and the end of a very steep learning curve to which many wonderful colleagues, friends, and family members have wittingly or unwittingly contributed.

I started to prepare the English publication after I was appointed Lecturer in Modern European History at the Stanley Burton Centre for Holocaust and Genocide Studies at the University of Leicester in 2016. My thanks go to my colleagues for their encouragement and support in this process. I am especially grateful to George Lewis, Paul Moore, Roey Sweet, Jo Story, Richard Butler, Deborah Toner, and Zoe Groves. I would also like to express my appreciation for the financial support that I received from the Stanley Burton Centre for Holocaust and Genocide Studies for this publication.

I am also grateful to the many students I have taught over the past years, who were open to learning about aspects of the Holocaust that they had not previously thought about, for their questions and ideas, and for reminding me how important it is to keep your audience in mind. I know that some of you will be pleased to see that this book is now finally available in English. I also thank my PhD students, who often helped me to rethink and explore further the intersection of legal norms and the (aftermath of the) Holocaust.

I am greatly obliged to the Institute for Contemporary History at the University of Vienna, the Austrian Society for Contemporary History, the Cultural Department of the City of Vienna, and the Austrian Federal Ministry of Science and Research for awarding the German book the Irma Rosenberg Prize in 2016.

I thank Paula Bradish from Hamburger Edition for her wonderful support and guidance in making this English publication happen. I am very grateful to the jury of the program Geisteswissenschaften International and the program's partners – the German Publishers and Booksellers Association, the Fritz Thyssen Foundation, VG Wort, and the German Federal Foreign Office – who generously funded the translation by awarding my German book that prize in 2017. I thank University of Toronto Press for accepting the German manuscript for translation and express my appreciation to Sharon Howe for an excellent translation and for her accuracy when checking and adjusting references. I am especially grateful to my editor, Stephen Shapiro from University of Toronto Press, for his help, expertise, knowledge, and sometimes the decisiveness that I needed. I would also like to express my gratitude to the anonymous peer reviewers and the committee members at UTP for their immensely helpful comments and suggestions on how to improve the manuscript. I am furthermore grateful to colleagues who kindly sent me their published and unpublished work before and during the coronavirus crisis. I finally thank the Hamburger Stiftung zur Förderung von Wissenschaft und Kultur, which funded the additional Polish-language editing and the indexing of the book, and Krzysztof Heymer and Lindsay Buckle, respectively, for doing such a fine job on these two tasks.

Publishing this book in English marks the end of a long process. My acknowledgments from the German version that I wrote five years ago, in May 2015, are therefore still equally relevant.

When I first conceived the idea for the project on which this study is based, many people were sceptical and doubted its feasibility. Considering the hard facts, I could hardly blame them: I spoke neither Yiddish nor Polish, the sources were spread around a number of international archives, there was no guarantee of funding, and the topic was regarded as highly sensitive. To all those who encouraged me to go ahead regardless, I am especially grateful.

First of all, I would like to thank Professor Frank Golczewski and Professor Stefanie Schüler-Springorum, who supported the project from the beginning and gave me invaluable guidance and assistance.

I would also like to thank Professor Michael Wildt, Professor Bernd Greiner, and Professor Jörg Baberowski, editors of the series Studies in the History of Violence, for their extremely helpful feedback on the first draft and for including my work in the Hamburger Edition series. Thanks go, furthermore, to Birgit Otte from Hamburger Edition and to Sigrid Weber for their professional editing and proofreading assistance – and their patience.

In terms of financial support, I would like to thank the Hans Böckler Foundation, which enabled me to carry out the research project promptly, including a number of archive visits abroad. I am also grateful for the further financial and technical support I received from the Hansen Foundation at the University of Passau, the Institute for Jewish Research, YIVO in New York, the Schroubek Fund for Eastern Europe, and the German Historical Institute in Warsaw. In September 2014, the project was awarded the Immanuel Kant Research Prize by the Federal Institute for Culture and History of the Germans in Eastern Europe, for which I am greatly obliged to the German Federal Government Commissioner for Culture and Media. I would also like to express my appreciation to the Polish Consulate-General in Hamburg for the award of its Research Prize in December 2014.

Further thanks go to the registrars who assisted me with my archive research in Germany, Israel, the USA, and Poland – even if they did not always understand what I was looking for. I am similarly grateful to the committed participants of the research colloquia where I presented my project for discussion, and especially the Colloquium of the Department of Eastern European History at the University of Hamburg.

A number of people assisted with the implementation of the project in a spirit of professionalism, cooperation, and cordiality, and I would like to take this opportunity to say a special thank you to them: Nele Haelbich, Jan-Hinnerk Antons, Henning Obens, Hanna Schmidt Holländer, Tanja Kinzel, Klaus Richter, Klaas Voß, and Gabriel Finder. I am also grateful to Katrin Stoll, Ingo Loose, and Stephan Lehnstaedt for their valuable assistance.

I am much obliged to Eva Karnowski and Ewa Wróblewska for their helpful clarifications regarding the translation of Polish sources, and to Laura Halm, Jule Böhmer, Philipp Dorestal, Anna Menny, and Ann-Katrin Braunmiller for proofreading the manuscript.

Further thanks go to Professor Tanja Penter – for whom I worked as a research assistant in the department of Eastern European History at the Helmut-Schmidt University in Hamburg – for her support and understanding. I am similarly obliged to Professor Miriam Rürup from the Institute for the History of German Jews – where I worked as a research associate from August 2013 until February 2015 – for granting me "writing space" in which to revise the manuscript in summer 2014. A special thank you also to Professor Marie-Elisabeth Hilger, who has mentored and supported my research work over the past years.

I am indebted to my "refectory tablemates" in Hamburg for the almost daily distraction they provided during lunch breaks, which, over the years, has amounted to so much more.

Heartfelt thanks to my sister Thyra Bethke: she knows what for. And, last but not least, to my mother, Marianne Bethke, who encouraged me to do a PhD, however alien the world of academic research may have seemed to her.

Note on Names and Places

The spelling of names and places in this book needs some clarification because many of them had multiple variants – Polish, Yiddish, German – and, for Lithuania, Lithuanian and Russian in addition. In a historical context in which belonging and exclusion were so closely linked to the use of language and in which the brutal enforcement of power by the Germans was associated with the appropriation of geographical space and the renaming of places, every decision regarding the use of certain terms and names bears meaning. I have nonetheless chosen a pragmatic approach.

For place names that are commonly used in English scholarly writings, anglicized versions are used without diacritical marks, such as Lodz, Warsaw, and Vilna. For other places, the general practice in this book is to spell them in accordance with pre-war official usage, although this should not distract from the fact that the introduction of German names marked a crucial step in the brutal occupation of Eastern Europe during the Second World War. Kulmhof is used for the German extermination camp in the city of Chełmno, and Auschwitz (not Oświęcim) as the commonly known name for the concentration camp complex. I also kept German terms that were newly introduced, such as those of the administrative districts Generalgouvernement, Reichsgau Wartheland, and Reichkommissariat Ostland. In the case of personal names with multiple versions, I stuck to those commonly used prior to the Second World War, which were in most cases Polish/Lithuanian adaptations of the Yiddish. When referring to primary sources, I tried to choose the version chosen by the authors (which can thus lead to different spellings for similar names). For Hebrew transliterations, I dropped the apostrophes in the main text for easier reading, but kept them in the bibliography.

Abbreviations

APŁ	Archiwum Państwowe w Łodzi, Lodz
AR	Archiwum Ringelbluma
FPO	Fareynigte Partizaner Organizatsie
GFH	Beit Lohamei Ha-Getaot/Ghetto Fighter House, Western Galilee
IPN	Instytut Pamięci Narodowej, Warsaw
OS	Order Service
PSŻ	Przełożony Starszeństwa Żydów w Getcie Łódzkim
USHMM	United States Holocaust Memorial Museum, Washington, DC
YIVO	Institute for Jewish Research, New York
YVA	Yad Vashem Archives, Jerusalem
ŻIH	Żydowski Instytut Historyczny, Warsaw
ŻOB	Żydowska Organizacja Bojowa
ŻZW	Żydowski Związek Wojskowy

DANCE ON THE RAZOR'S EDGE

Introduction

On 25 April 1941, Mordechaj Chaim Rumkowski, the Jewish Council chairman in Lodz, or Litzmannstadt, as it was then called,[1] used the columns of the *Geto-Tsaytung* (ghetto newspaper) to inform the ghetto population of the kind of activities that would, in future, be classed as vandalism, and hence as a crime:

> It appears that an exceptionally large number of lowlifes and vandals have reduced the ghetto to a state that is posing a risk to our health. Over the last few months, these unscrupulous individuals have, for example, dismantled most of the wooden and brick latrines and refuse pits, leaving not a trace behind. Such forms of vandalism are a daily occurrence ... The aforementioned criminals will stop at nothing, and are continuing to wreak havoc purely out of self-interest, in order to sell the stolen wood at extortionate prices.[2]

Ghetto residents guilty of such offences were arrested by the Jewish ghetto police and could be sentenced by internal courts to fines and imprisonment, or alternatively to sewage transportation duties, one of the most unpopular tasks in the ghetto. Offenders serving prison sentences in the ghetto jail were often the first to be deported.

In the Vilna ghetto, the Jewish Council chairman, Jakub Gens, made rumour-mongering one of a number of punishable offences, and in December 1942 a culprit was sentenced by the ghetto court to seven days' imprisonment.[3] The Jewish police in the Warsaw ghetto uncovered the case of a woman who had taken in a series of vulnerable residents under the pretext of looking after them, only to wait for them to die so that she could sell their clothes.[4] And in December 1941, the Jewish Council judicial panel in Lodz tried its first murder case.[5] Two years later, the Lodz ghetto chronicler drew a sobering conclusion: "Sadly, ethics are practically non-existent in the ghetto – for all its residents, food comes first, whatever the means used to obtain it."[6] In the Vilna ghetto, Herman Kruk noted similarly in his diary: "Ghetto is amoral, and ghetto life in Vilmen is the lawlessness of the borderland between life and death."[7]

This is a book about how people create notions of right and wrong and how such notions lead to definitions of crime and thence to prosecution and punishment. However, it considers these questions in the context of an unprecedented emergency situation, by focusing on the ghetto communities that the Germans set up by force following their attack on Poland on 1 September 1939. It is a book about rules, definitions of criminal behaviour, and legal norms in a coerced community: a community defined as "Jewish" by the Germans, and thus deprived of all legal rights and facing hunger, disease, tyranny, violence, and ultimately systematic murder. It explores how, under these circumstances, people tried to make sense of everyday lives that had been turned upside down, bringing with them pre-war notions of justice and morality, and it considers the extent to which this rupture led to new judgments of human behaviour. As such, the book's primary aim is to understand how people attempted to exploit the very limited scope for action allowed to them within a coerced situation in order to survive. More specifically, it looks at how and why the Jewish Councils – despite German arbitrariness, violence, and the erasure of pre-war legal standards – labelled numerous acts within the ghetto communities "criminal" and established internal legal institutions to prosecute and punish such offences. Based on these findings, it explores how ordinary ghetto inhabitants reacted to these new and unfamiliar definitions, and even made use of the relevant institutions to assert their own interests.[8]

The prosecution of criminal acts was high on the Jewish Councils' agenda in all three ghettos mentioned above, where such acts – ranging from vandalism to the spreading of rumours – took on specific forms. Indeed, the Jewish Councils had some room for manoeuvre, however limited and variable, in dealing with such offences within the ghetto walls.

The Germans set up Jewish Councils shortly after the occupation, later forcing them to carry out ever-changing German orders in the ghettos and ultimately to hand over ghetto inhabitants for deportation to extermination sites. Most famous among the numerous voices that have harshly criticized the Jewish Councils as "puppets of the Nazis," "traitors," and collaborators was Hannah Arendt, who, writing on the Eichmann trial in 1963, condemned their compliance "as the darkest chapter of the whole dark story."[9] Probing the Jewish Councils' role in defining and entrenching moral and legal standards may, therefore, appear somewhat provocative. As we will see, however, this topic touches upon the most troubling questions regarding Jewish survival, defiance, and resistance during the Holocaust.

Whose definitions of delinquent behaviour end up being enforced within a community always depends on the prevailing social power structure.[10] In Nazi-occupied Eastern Europe, it was the Germans who wielded the overwhelming power to define criminality and law. They denied the Jews any kind of legal status, stigmatized them as "born criminals," and created new legal norms in order to legitimize their own policies of anti-Jewish discrimination and persecution. In the context of the ghettos, however, they did grant the Jewish Councils certain limited powers to regulate internal affairs, and to that extent, the Councils had a degree of definitional authority.

Through their compliance, the Jewish Councils hoped to be able to secure the survival of the ghetto community, or at least part of it. As such, their definitions of criminality and law were crucial to the question of how to organize the inhabitants' enforced cohabitation, and to their ability to fulfil German demands and "keep the ghetto calm." In order to achieve a certain room for manoeuvre – however limited and volatile – the Jewish Councils attempted to interpret the German plans according to rational criteria, with the aim of capitalizing on perceived German interests such as labour power.[11]

It is the premise of this book that the desperate attempt to identify a certain rationality behind the Germans' behaviour so as to derive measures for survival – only to find that assumptions were constantly being overthrown and violated – found its most significant expression in the emerging ghetto-internal legal sphere. As historian Dan Diner writes, "However varied the councils' circumstances may have been, together they shared the experience of a borderline situation that renders null and void all anticipations of human behaviour ordinarily deemed to be universally valid."[12] Part of that experience was the knowledge that the Germans were murdering ghetto residents *in spite of* the Councils' compliance with German demands. Diner characterizes this as "counterrationality" – a symptom of the rupture of civilization represented by National Socialism.[13]

Against this background, I will examine how the Jewish Councils defined criminality and law within the coerced communities, how they went about enforcing those definitions, and the institutional structures that grew out of them. Here, as in the ghetto as a whole, the Councils walked a tightrope between the twin necessities of complying with German demands and ensuring the welfare of the ghetto community. Over time, these endeavours were to prove irreconcilable in the face of the German murder campaign.

The Councils' definitions of criminality and law were not static, but varied according to Germany's changing plans for the Jewish population. The Germans established the ghettos after the invasion of Poland in September 1939, and especially during the course of 1940, and conceived of them as "temporary measures" pending further, unspecified "resettlement arrangements." During the summer of 1941, they then decided on the systematic murder of Europe's entire Jewish population. As the Germans' plans evolved and their intentions became known in the ghettos, the Councils tried to identify German core interests in order to modify their survival strategies for the ghetto communities accordingly. In the following pages, I will demonstrate to what extent these perceived changes and anticipated German intentions were reflected in the Councils' conceptions of criminal conduct and the legal norms and sanctions they imposed on that basis.

The Jewish Councils' concepts of criminality and law are examined here as they existed in the ghettos of Warsaw, Lodz, and Vilna. These lay in different German administrative districts (Warsaw in the Generalgouvernement, Lodz in the Reichsgau Wartheland, and Vilna in the Reichskommissariat Ostland) and endured for different lengths of time: while the Warsaw ghetto lasted from October 1940 to May 1943, that of Lodz was sealed by the occupiers in April 1940 and the last residents murdered in August 1944. The Vilna ghetto was established in September 1941 and liquidated in September 1943.[14] The comparison between two ghetto communities in occupied Poland – set up when the Germans still regarded the ghettos as "temporary measures" – and the Vilna ghetto in the occupied Soviet Union – created once the German plan for a comprehensive annihilation of the Jewish population was already in place – is instructive on many levels. For one thing, it illustrates how the Germans' changing intentions, and the way these were perceived by the Jewish Councils, influenced ghetto-internal definitions of criminality, the organization of the legal sphere, and, consequently, people's values and expectations regarding communal life within the coerced communities. For another, it demonstrates how the different lifetimes of the ghettos affected the enshrinement of definitions of criminality and law and the institutionalization of legal authorities.[15]

This book will show that, despite the differences between the ghetto communities discussed here, all three exhibited similar generic categories of criminal behaviour:

1. Crimes that were to be prosecuted directly on German orders, such as illegal border crossing or smuggling.
2. Behaviour that was deemed by the Jewish Council to pose a danger to the ghetto in that it might trigger a brutal intervention by the

Germans. This covered a wide variety of activities such as unhygienic candy production, rumour-mongering, and labour offences.
3. Actions directed against ghetto institutions, whose efficient operation was regarded as essential to the survival of the ghetto community.
4. So-called classical crimes in which private individuals were the injured party, such as brawls, sexual abuse, or murders.

New types of ghetto-internal crime belonging to categories (2) and (3) were thematized notably in Lodz and Vilna, in keeping with the overarching survival strategy of "rescue through labour." In Warsaw, by contrast, the main focus was on crimes defined by the Germans (1) and attempts to uphold evaluation criteria from the pre-ghettoization period. From the second half of 1942 onwards, armed resistance groups gained more authority and asserted their own values and survival strategies. In terms of the "classical" crimes of category (4), we will see that the Jewish Councils increasingly reset their priorities after learning of the German murder plans. Pre-ghettoization evaluation criteria became less important, and attention switched to individual activities endangering the survival of the ghetto community as a whole.

Based on these new crime definitions, the Jewish Councils established a highly improvised ghetto-internal legal sphere. The resulting institutions and procedures were set up partly in response to German orders, especially by the Jewish police, and partly at their own initiative. In this way, the Councils attempted to exploit the evolving room for manoeuvre. Their overall aim was to assert their own evaluation and punishment criteria in order to avoid the threat of harsher punishment and brutal German intervention. At the same time, the scope for action within this sphere was unpredictable and constantly changing. This led to ad hoc procedures and often unexpected dynamics in terms of carving out limited room to manoeuvre – but it also led to German interference.

For the public they were addressing, however – the ordinary ghetto inhabitants, who did not play a part in the Jewish self-administration – it was a very different story. For them, the newly defined criminal acts were in many cases the only means of individual survival, and their values were therefore often diametrically opposed to the Councils' definitions. As we will see, however, this did not prevent them from making use of the ghetto-internal legal authorities where it was in their interests to do so.

To date, scholars have paid scant attention to the various offences committed by ghetto inhabitants, complaints of a high level of criminality and declining moral standards within these communities, and internal attempts by the Jewish Councils to deal with such offences. The absence of moral norms has primarily been discussed in connection with the German occupiers, who systematically deprived the Jews of all legal rights, were arbitrarily and institutionally violent towards them, and ultimately subjected them to systematic extermination. Given these constraints on the Jewish Councils, the prevailing opinion has been that there was no internal scope for action within the ghettos. When I presented my project at a research colloquium in Germany, a member of the audience argued that, faced with the German extermination plans, the Councils had had no choice but to implement German orders and enforcement measures as they stood.

Other voices in research literature, contemporary sources, and memoirs have asserted that the level of "criminality" among the Jewish ghetto inmates was relatively low, considering their catastrophic living conditions.[16] The Kovno ghetto survivor Samuel Gringauz, for example, writing retrospectively in 1949, attributed this to a "heightened Jewish morality."[17] Józef Rode, a Jewish police officer in Warsaw, noted in his diary that there had been neither murders nor violent robberies in the Warsaw ghetto,[18] and the Warsaw police functionary Stanisław Adler commented that "the general level of crime within the Quarter was not as large as might have been expected considering the utter poverty to be found there."[19] On the Lodz ghetto, Oskar Rosenfeld wrote: "Even if on occasion, driven by immense misery, a small theft occurs, a quick reach for somebody else's possessions, the ghetto is, nevertheless, free from violence or incrimination."[20] Similar attitudes are still encountered today. "Criminality? – There was no such thing in the ghettos!" was the incredulous response of one registrar when I asked her, during my first visit to the archives in Israel, where I might find sources for my research project on criminality and law in Nazi ghettos. And the most notorious offence of smuggling food into the ghettos has been widely interpreted in retrospect as an act of resistance in light of the German murder plans.

This book does not answer the question of whether or not there was criminality in the ghettos. Instead, it reconciles these apparently conflicting views by emphasizing that the perspectives of both the Jewish Councils and those who saw an absence of criminality demonstrate that definitions of criminal behaviour were – and are – highly subjective and susceptible to constant change. Inevitably, they are embedded in the communities and social context in which they are formulated.

The criticisms of the colloquium participant and the registrar noted above, as well as Arendt's harsh judgment of the Jewish Councils, thus point to crucial trends and shortcomings in Holocaust scholarship. What they have in common is that they present stereotypical images of active German perpetrators, puppet-like Jewish Councils, and essentially passive Jewish victims, ascribing specific patterns of behaviour to them and placing them in dualistic, black-and-white categories of "good" and "bad" that are presented as objective. This book will instead integrate ambivalences into the picture and emphasize the broad range of behaviours – and behavioural classifications – in the context of brutal German occupation and murder. In so doing, it seeks to significantly change our understanding of the internal dynamics that operated in the ghetto communities and the patterns of behaviour and resistance with which German mass murder was confronted.

State of Research

Research on ghettos in German-occupied Eastern Europe can be broadly divided into two overarching approaches.[21] The first has, at different times and with varying emphasis, concentrated on the internal life of the ghettos, while the second has focused more on the role of the ghettos within the Germans' overall plans.[22] Both are associated with certain concepts and expectations regarding the ghetto communities and the behavioural patterns of both the Jewish Councils and the ordinary ghetto inhabitants. In the immediate post-war years, before the emergence of institutionalized Holocaust research, a small number of sociologically motivated researchers from Israel and the USA, among them Holocaust survivors, published thought-provoking work on communal life and internal dynamics in the ghettos.[23] They understood these ghetto communities as "Jewish communities."[24] Samuel Gringauz, for instance, a social scientist and survivor of the Kovno ghetto, describes the history of the ghettos during the Second World War as a "sociologically relevant experiment of a *Jewish* community" under extraordinary living conditions. They were, he claims, the only instance of a "homogeneous Jewish community" outside the state of Israel.[25] This view was bound up with the expectation that the inhabitants behaved "morally well" and were community-minded. As such, it had important implications for the topic of criminal behaviour. Scholars and contemporary voices argued that, because of a "heightened *Jewish* morality," the level of criminality in the ghettos was very low, and criminal behaviour was imputed only to residents who had already committed crimes prior to ghettoization.[26]

Judgments of the Jewish Councils were made on a similar basis. Their conduct was described – not least, in many cases, because of the authors' personal experience – as "morally reprehensible," and the Council members themselves as dictators who had turned against "their own Jewish brothers and sisters."[27] Rumkowski, fiercely criticized as a "tyrant" who had betrayed his fellow Jews by ruthlessly enforcing

German decrees as chairman of the Jewish Council in Lodz, was often seen as archetypal.[28] In line with these severe judgments of the 1960s, scholars such as Hannah Arendt and Raul Hilberg applied very clear categories of morally good and bad behaviour – corresponding to the opposite poles of resistance and collaboration – to ghetto communities. This view reduced all Jewish resistance to armed resistance and saw any fulfilment of German demands, coerced or otherwise, as complicity or even collaboration.[29] Their criticism triggered an important shift in research on the Jewish Councils during the 1970s and 1980s. Scholars such as Isaiah Trunk, Jacob Robinson, and Aharon Weiss, who were mainly affiliated with the Institute for Jewish Research in New York, now emphasized the tragic dilemma of the Jewish Councils in light of the Germans' actions. Focusing mainly on the large ghettos in German-occupied Poland, they contributed to an important new understanding of the Councils' activities and their willingness to comply with German orders.[30]

During the 1960s, and importantly in the 1970s and 1980s, scholars also became increasingly concerned with the German perpetrators and sought to shed light on the role played by ghettoization in the systematic murder of European Jewry. Analysts of the German reasoning behind the establishment of ghettos now saw them primarily as a stepping stone to mass murder – or what historian Tim Cole later called "Holocaust places."[31] This often led to a polarized view of active German perpetrators versus passive Jewish victims, leaving little room for the question of how the victims classified by the Germans as "Jewish" conducted themselves in these coerced ghetto communities, or how they perceived and organized their day-to-day life.[32]

With the opening up of the Eastern European archives after 1991, scholarly interest in internal ghetto life gained in importance, with researchers now able to draw on a much broader range of sources. Increasingly, they aimed to write what historian Saul Friedländer had called an "integrative history" of the Holocaust, in which the perpetrators' actions and the victims' perspective and conduct could be illuminated side by side.[33] Based on the newly accessible ghetto-internal documents, pioneering studies appeared on the subject of everyday life in the ghetto communities, often building upon earlier instructive studies by Polish scholars.[34] With regard to the ghettos, an emphasis on ego-documents such as diaries and survivor testimonies allowed perspectives on the everyday life of the ghetto to be integrated into the picture. Within this framework, a broad range of ordinary activities, such as engagement in cultural pursuits, were classified as "resistance" based on the concept of *amidah* (Hebrew "to stand up"). This concept was first formulated by Meir Dworzecki in the 1950s and subsequently revived by Yehuda Bauer in the 1980s to classify retrospectively as an act of resistance any behaviour during the Holocaust that aimed to undermine the Germans' intentions.[35] Indirectly, studies that have applied this concept to research on ghettos, especially since the 2000s, also stress the "Jewish identity" of the actors, but with a greater emphasis on Jewishness as a construct based on German racial definitions. The notion of *amidah* also led to new studies, albeit few in number, revisiting the topic of criminality in the ghettos – most prominently smuggling – and reinterpreting it as "acts of resistance."[36] Jan Grabowski and Barbara Engelking have similarly argued that the inhabitants had to violate German norms in order to survive.[37] Yet these works fall short in two regards. First, they do not consider the variety of motivations that would have existed in the historical situation of the ghetto. To interpret every deed as an act of resistance is to overlook the range of intentions, not all of which were noble. Second, they appear at times to be seeking some kind of "objectively measurable" criminality within the ghetto.[38] Nevertheless, by sharpening our awareness of ambivalences and power ratios within the ghetto communities, these works are an important springboard for the observations in this book.[39]

The newly available archival sources and the exploration of internal ghetto life led researchers to reassess the role of the Jewish Councils and their institutions, now stressing the coercive nature of the ghetto communities over their "Jewishness."[40] Yet only a few studies have touched upon the internal legal authorities of the ghetto, focusing mostly on the organization and activities of the Jewish police, and less on the ghetto courts and prisons.[41] Research into the Jewish police has tended to concentrate on their ambivalent role in relation to smuggling and their involvement in the preparations for the German deportations.[42] Far less space has been devoted, by contrast, to the perspective of Jewish police officers themselves, their interaction with the Polish and German police organs, the way they dealt with new kinds of policing duties in the ghetto, and their approach to prosecuting unfamiliar offences.[43] Overall, the whole question of the perceptions and considerations that lay behind the Jewish Councils' ambivalent conduct – based on a reading of the available ghetto-internal sources – remains comparatively unexplored.[44] This has led to a focus – especially in large ghettos – on the hostile relationship between the Jewish Councils and ordinary ghetto inhabitants, while other, more ambivalent aspects of their mutual interaction have gained far less attention.[45]

Crucial inspiration can be drawn from studies on other coerced communities during National Socialism, which have increasingly focused on ambiguous patterns of behaviour that cannot be easily classified as morally "good" or "bad."[46] Building upon this approach, ground-breaking studies have focused on internal dynamics and hierarchies among inmates of concentration camps, while much remains to be done with regard to ghetto communities.[47] Where scholars have addressed related questions of inter-Jewish judgments and notions of morality, they have mainly done so with regard to post-war trials and honour courts.[48]

How can we explain this relatively limited state of research? Besides the fact that scholars need comprehensive language skills to work with the relevant primary sources, there seems to be another, more profound reason: partly rooted in the post-1945 desire to present Jewish history as the history of a nation, researchers still seem hesitant to question the assumption that the common experience of the ghetto led without exception to a sense of solidarity.[49] This ultimately touches upon the highly sensitive question of who survived the Holocaust and why. Which decisions and behaviours were more likely to guarantee collective or individual survival, and at whose expense? Admittedly, any analysis of the ghetto-internal legal sphere from this angle raises difficult issues. Jewish judges in the Vilna ghetto imposed death sentences, while the Jewish Council chairmen Rumkowski and Gens made ghetto prisoners their first resort when ordered to fill German quotas for deportation and shooting. Residents stole from one another and denounced each other to the Jewish police, and in some cases even to the Germans. To morally condemn such behaviour or deny its existence is, however, to misunderstand the perspective – and hence the dilemma – of the Jewish Councils. Besides, it ignores the nature of the ghetto as a heterogeneous, coerced community based on the Nazi definition of "Jewry" rather than on any voluntary decision. The people crammed together there in catastrophic conditions and in fear of their lives acted as any human beings would, exhibiting the whole range of human emotions from empathy and solidarity through egoism and envy to anger and revenge. The lesson here for the historian is to refrain from black-and-white depictions and leave room for ambivalence. To some extent, then, this study should be read as an anti-heroic history. It breaks with simplifying narratives of tyrannical Jewish Council chairmen and illustrious smugglers feted on all sides as resistance fighters, and rejects the theory of an inherently strong "Jewish" morality in the ghettos that precluded any form of criminality. This naturally complicates the picture: faced with the Germans' murderous intentions, people reacted in different ways, and their behaviour sprang from different motives.

Rupture, Criminality, and Law

Definitions of criminality and law entail perceptions of desirable and undesirable conduct within a community, accompanied by the attempt to fix them in the public consciousness. They permeate all areas of human coexistence and are the result of complex negotiation processes surrounding the question of how communities choose to organize their communal life, and the extent to which they are able to do so. The situation for the ghetto communities could not have been more different from that of any democratic society. However varied the individual experiences of the inmates, all of them found everyday life in the new coerced community of the ghetto unlike anything they had known before. Their ignorance of what awaited them is exemplified by the fact that some Jewish people initially supported ghettoization in the hope that segregation would bring protection from brutal attacks.[50] Writing retrospectively in June 1941, the Jewish Council chairman Rumkowski commented that the creation of the ghetto had confronted him with a totally unknown situation – a fact he used to justify the teething troubles of the administration: "It is true that mistakes were made at the time [following the ghetto's establishment]. That is – it must be said – an inevitable consequence when sudden changes occur in the entire life structure of a community or particular group of people."[51]

The forcibly created ghetto communities consisted of large numbers of individuals who came from different regions, spoke different languages, and were differently socialized – in short, they brought with them diverse experiences and "stocks of knowledge."[52] For all these people, ghettoization meant new, unfamiliar, and life-threatening conditions, in response to which their perception of their everyday tasks and their resulting decisions and behaviour drastically changed. At the same time, the personal and professional background and experiences of both the Jewish Council personnel and ordinary ghetto inhabitants were anchored in pre-war societies and their moral and legal values. On one hand, therefore, they tried to make sense of and cope with their daily life based on their pre-war experiences and knowledge. On the other, however, these soon proved to be of limited use, given the unprecedented emergency situation under German occupation. This was reflected in the perceptions and concepts of criminality and law within the coerced communities, and hence in the way people conducted themselves. In his memoirs of the Warsaw ghetto, the former Jewish police functionary Stanisław Adler writes of a "paradoxical situation" where "it was difficult to take action against the falsifiers of food products, or the sellers of rotten food, or all the other merchants who could be described in normal times as swindlers. In our jungle, everyone had to be the guardian of his own health and his own pocket, and had to make his own choice according to his personal means. The picture I describe here refers, of course, to the most frequent and most dangerous methods, that is, those which sat on the borderline between legality and criminality."[53]

His record provides an insight into the changing notions of what counted as criminal, morally reprehensible, just, unjust, or lawful within the ghetto, where contrasting evaluations of human behaviour were an ever-present theme. Sociologists Alfred Schütz and Thomas Luckmann introduced the term "lifeworld" to emphasize how people perceive their social surroundings based on previous experience, gathered knowledge, and classifications derived from such experience. As they point out, however, such classifications can change within a community when sudden shifts or ruptures occur.[54] Their approach can provide an insight into how definitions of "criminal behaviour" changed after enforced ghettoization.[55] To understand this shift and the resulting dilemma, it is useful to reflect on the relative nature of criminality.

The sociologist Emile Durkheim understood criminality as a "normal" social phenomenon delineating those actions that are offensive to certain "collective feelings" within a community.[56] The criminologist Fritz Sack argued similarly that definitions of criminality are a means by which members of a community consolidate and reinforce their shared values.[57] They are, he claims, contingent on the processes by which norms are formulated, established, and applied, and which are manifested in the form of social conflicts.[58] Fellow criminologist Howard Becker expresses this as follows: "The same behaviour may be an infraction of the rules at one time and not at another; may be an infraction when committed by one person but not when committed by another … deviance is not a quality that lies in behaviour itself, but in the interaction between the person who commits an act and those who respond to it."[59]

What we see in Adler's account is an attempt by a member of the legal personnel to evaluate certain acts by referring to pre-war judgment criteria. In the coerced community of the ghetto, however, Adler was now facing the dilemma of having to consider the dangers that certain modes of behaviour could pose to the ghetto community, while knowing at the same time that such behaviour was part of people's struggle for survival.

What purpose do definitions of criminal behaviour serve? From a criminological perspective, they are a means of asserting binding values and allowing people to live together without conflict.[60] In the coerced ghetto communities, by contrast, the Jewish Councils attempted to use their specific definitions of criminality to secure the survival of the ghetto population in the face of the German murder campaign. That meant classifying certain activities hitherto considered "normal" as dangerous and hence criminal. Yet the Councils could not know with any certainty which individual activities posed a genuine threat to the community's survival. Therefore their survival strategies were based on a constant endeavour to anticipate the Germans' actions and interpret them as being governed by rational criteria. The resulting definitions of criminality were then announced in the form of a set of rules, with penalties threatened and imposed for the "criminal behaviour" thus proscribed. In this way, legal norms and practices began to evolve within the ghettos.

This development, which effectively gave rise to an internal legal sphere, was described by Adler in his reflections on the Warsaw ghetto:

> Under these circumstances, it became imperative to establish law and legal sanctions without looking for the occupier's consent and to ensure our own means of compliance to our orders. This was an evolving process which developed by imposing penalties for particular offences. With the passage of time, when this means proved practical, we moved on to more general aspects of law.[61]

The science of law proceeds from the assumption that most legal orders evolve historically out of the social morality of a community.[62] As such, the legal norms in democratically legitimized communities derive their legitimation from the acceptance of the majority, which itself derives from a basic desire for "certainty of orientation."[63] In the ghettos, the Jewish Councils had to conform to the (legal) agenda of the German occupiers and comply with demands that ran counter to the welfare – and survival – of the ghetto community. The harsh judgments of Council measures by ghetto inhabitants, the voices identifying a "heightened Jewish morality," and the acts performed in the struggle for survival testify to the fact that legal norms in the forcibly ghettoized communities were *not* based on the moral values of the majority of the population. In other words, there was a mismatch between the norms formulated by the Jewish Councils and the social morality of the ghetto population. The aim of the Councils was to ensure the survival of the ghetto community using whatever strategies they felt had the best chance of success. This was particularly true of the ghettos in Lodz and Vilna, both of whose Council chairmen promoted the strategy of "rescue through labour." Exponents of a materialistic theory of law emphasize its "ideological" function: following on from philosopher Antonio Gramsci, they see it as part of a "hegemonic project" aimed at securing the continuation of a (capitalist) social order by enforcing a world view to which moral norms are ascribed. Political scientists Sonja Buckel and Andreas Fischer-Lescano define this as "a permanent practice, a world-view fought out in struggles for recognition, through which moral, political, and intellectual leadership is established."[64] My purpose here is not to propose a definitive concept of law, but to select definitions which can be used to highlight features specific to the organization of the ghetto-internal legal sphere. While the Jewish Councils' aim was not, of course, to uphold a capitalist social order, it was in a way an attempt by the internal ruling class to enforce a comprehensive "hegemonic project," often against the moral values of the majority of the ghetto population. Definitions of criminality and law, which the Councils sought to anchor within the ghetto communities, were part of this endeavour.

Their "hegemonic project" was not uncontested. An alternative to the Jewish Councils' survival strategies and associated notions of morality and justice was demonstrated by those ghetto residents who joined armed resistance groups. The Jewish Councils in Lodz and Vilna firmly rejected the option of armed resistance, fearing a brutal intervention by the German occupiers and hence a risk to the ghetto community as a whole. In the Warsaw ghetto, by contrast, some individual Council members lent financial support to the resistance.[65] And despite the disapproving stance of the Councils in Lodz and Vilna, no resident was ever prosecuted for "armed resistance" by a ghetto court.

At the same time, "resistance" was cited as an offence in many of the arrest warrants issued by the Jewish police authorities. Which specific actions belonged to this category cannot always be reconstructed, one exception being the large number of arrest warrants from the Vilna ghetto that were issued for behaviour such as insulting the ghetto police or striking a police officer. Even when ghetto residents in Vilna joined the Fareynigte Partizaner Organizatsie (FPO) and other armed resistance groups, however, such offences did not appear in the arrest warrants. This shows that the Jewish Councils' discussions and positioning with regard to armed resistance were not part of the ghetto-internal legal sphere, but primarily a matter of political debate. This assumption is borne out by a speech delivered by Jakub Gens in the Vilna ghetto on 15 May 1943, just a few months before its liquidation, in which he called on the ghetto population to denounce armed resistance fighters to the ghetto police.[66] The fact that – in the final months of the ghetto's existence, when the Germans had already murdered thousands of residents in Ponary – he needed to define Jewish police powers for dealing with this type of offence suggests that such crimes had not been dealt with previously within the ghetto. For these reasons, the attitudes of the armed resistance groups are only mentioned in this study where their beliefs and actions were in competition with the Jewish Councils' survival strategies, resulting – as in the Warsaw ghetto – in an undermining of Council institutions.

Amid all this, the pressing question remains as to why the Jewish Councils set up such complex legal institutions as courts and endeavoured to stick to established procedures – even after the German extermination plans became known. The sociology of law emphasizes the role of legal norms in (democratic) communities as a means of guaranteeing stability and thus contributing to the construction of social reality.[67] First, they offer regulated mechanisms for managing conflicts of interest within a community and curbing personal disputes.[68] And second, they help ensure stability not just at the level of society but in terms of individual psychology. As the social psychologist Arnold Gehlen writes, "Because many things are already predetermined by the behavioural norms of the community, the individual does not have to weigh up for himself, and choose between, all the possible courses of action in any given situation."[69] The third stabilizing force cited in this context is that of continuity: guaranteeing a measure of stability over time, it is argued, creates legal certainty.[70] Legal certainty derives in turn from certainty of orientation, i.e., the knowledge of how one is expected to behave, and from certainty of implementation, i.e., the knowledge that the defined norms will be observed and enforced.[71]

The reality of life in the ghettos was a far cry from this definition, precluding any kind of certainty of orientation. The Germans changed their plans at short notice and their behaviour was unpredictable and characteristically arbitrary. Despite this, we can assume that by formulating, anchoring, and enforcing legal norms and procedures, the Jewish Councils wanted to guarantee a minimum of social stability. To this end, they drew on experiences and familiar structures from the pre-war period in an attempt to create some kind of "normality"[72] – all the more so given that the Germans' actions were contrary to all previously valid conceptions of law and morality. Not least, the Councils were also anxious to prevent an outbreak of panic.

The necessity of responding quickly to German demands and to the unfamiliar and life-threatening living conditions was not, however, conducive to the emergence of an established canon of legal norms capable of guaranteeing stability. Crimes had to be evaluated differently from case to case and at different points in time. Moreover, the ghettos only existed for a relatively short period, and even then the Germans shifted the goal-posts. In this situation, there was no chance of developing any continuity in the legal practice of the ghettos.

In the ghettos, the Jewish Councils were the authorities invested with the (albeit limited) power to implement orders and legal norms by imposing sanctions on the ghetto inhabitants. In democratic societies, this role usually falls to the state, being the body endowed with supreme powers to guarantee the law. The necessity of such an institution is explained by legal scholar Reinhold Zippelius as follows: "The very fact that people differ in their views on justice and injustice, good and evil, renders it necessary to make binding decisions regarding the course of action."[73] Sanctions, exerted by the supreme powers within democratic communities, allow "socially compatible behaviour" to be instilled and pressure to be exerted in order to restore "normality" or make amends.[74] For the Jewish Councils, it was difficult to define what constituted sanctionable, "socially damaging" behaviour. The definitions they devised were based on previous experience and individual actions which they feared might trigger a brutal German intervention in the ghetto, and hence a danger to the community as a whole.

On the subject of sanctions, scholars differentiate between schools of thought. According to the "absolute theory of punishment," the reason for the punishment lies in the past; it is a form of atonement for disturbing the "public order" and the polity, even if no social benefit can be expected to come of it.[75] "Relative punishment theory," by contrast, is directed towards the future: punishments are inflicted in order to prevent further offences. Jurisprudence distinguishes here between "special prevention," which is intended to teach the perpetrator a lesson, and "general prevention," which seeks to deter other members of the community from committing criminal acts.[76] As we will see, in ghetto-internal punitive mechanisms, "general prevention" played an important role; the punishments were less concerned with individual atonement than with the collective deterrent effect. In this way, the Jewish Councils handed down their own oppression at the hands of the Germans to the ghetto population in the form of coercive measures.

Sources and Structure

The ghettos in Warsaw, Lodz, and Vilna were large, highly institution-alized communities. In smaller and so-called open ghettos, the orga-nization of legal authorities took different forms.[77] In small ghettos, particularly those in former Soviet territory, the legal sphere was less sophisticated. There, regulatory and judicial functions were assumed by the Jewish police as per German orders, with German legal defi-nitions being imposed more directly on the ghetto populations from the outset, in accordance with the occupiers' change of plan.[78] While a comparison with these would be illuminating, the emphasis here is on the complex negotiation processes conducted by the authorities of the Jewish self-administration bodies. These can only be studied in relation to the large ghettos because of their high degree of institutionalization and the resulting wealth of source material.

The central concern of this book is with definitions and regulations classically associated with criminal law: in other words, legal norms whose function is to prohibit certain behaviours and make them pun-ishable by law. The reason for this emphasis is that the Jewish Councils attached far more importance to these cases than to affairs of civil law: after all, issues such as divorce posed no threat to the ghetto community at large, whereas criminal matters were quite likely to do so. As such, the criminal law practised within the ghetto-internal legal sphere bore on the key questions of human existence under the life-threatening con-ditions of ghettoization.[79] As a result of this thematic focus on the legal authorities of the Jewish Council, parallel religious authorities that conducted dispute settlement procedures according to rabbinic law are only considered where they are identified as conflicting or overlapping with agencies of the Jewish self-administration.

The German occupiers' concepts of criminality and law are traced with the aid of reports and orders issued by the German functionaries responsible for the ghettos and by the German police agencies.[80] These are supplemented with rulings by the German Special Court in Lodz pertaining to tried "ghetto offences," and correspondence between the German occupiers and the ghetto-internal legal authorities.[81]

The bulk of the source material consists of documents produced by the Jewish self-administration bodies within the ghetto. A large volume of these has survived for all three ghettos because the respective Jewish Councils, as well as private individuals, kept and filed records of daily life, hiding some of the reports from the German occupiers in under-ground archives in order to document the experience of the ghetto for posterity.[82] In the Warsaw ghetto, the historian Emanuel Ringelblum began organizing an archive with the help of a few colleagues from October 1939 onwards. After the sealing of the ghetto in November 1940, his activities continued illegally under the cover name *Oneg Shabbat*.[83] The archive staff wrote accounts of everyday life in the ghetto, collected reports from ghetto residents, kept Jewish Council documents on file, and conducted their own research.[84] In Lodz, the Jewish Council created an archive in November 1940 in order to collate documents and materials for a future account of the ghetto's history.[85] Between January 1941 and July 1944, its team of staff – which included journalists and writers – wrote a chronicle, initially in Polish and later in German, consisting of news round-ups and feature articles on the main day-to-day events in the ghetto.[86] In the Vilna ghetto, the librarian Herman Kruk – with the aid of Rahel Mendelsund-Kavarski – collected reports, documented current affairs in the form of a chronicle, and organized a ghetto library.[87] These sources survived the liquidation of the ghettos because the personnel involved in collecting them managed to bury, hide, and preserve large parts of the documents, often only a few days before liquidation.[88]

When dealing with source material from the Jewish self-administration bodies, it is necessary to bear in mind that definitions of criminality and law in the ghetto were not generally uppermost in the archivists' minds, and that the relevant documents may therefore not have been preserved. In addition, the fear of discovery by the Germans may have led to a situation where German-defined criminal activities in particular were not always recorded in detail.

Other important sources are the ghetto newspapers: namely, the *Gazeta Żydowska* for Warsaw,[89] the *Geto-Tsaytung* for Lodz,[90] and the *Geto-Yedies* for Vilna.[91] Although these were subject to German control, they offer a unique insight into new definitions of criminality, regulations, incidences of crime, and imposed sentences. Valuable information can also be gleaned from the proclamations published by the Jewish Councils, which likewise served to announce new offences and regulations.[92]

The discussion of the Jewish police agencies draws on statistics, directives, activity reports, and arrest warrants.[93] In order to reflect the viewpoint of Jewish functionaries, I also cite their diaries and memoirs, which shed light on the changing definitions of criminality and law. An invaluable source of information on the Warsaw ghetto is the memoir of Stanisław Adler, written in a hideout on the "Aryan" side of the city in 1943.[94]

In terms of the judicial authorities, I analyse court rulings from the Lodz and Vilna ghettos which have barely featured in the research to date.[95] Information on the legal personnel of the Lodz ghetto is also drawn from an encyclopaedia compiled in the ghetto.[96] In the case of the Warsaw ghetto, the source material situation is particularly problematic. There, the Germans granted Jewish Council members only limited internal powers of prosecution; consequently, the Jewish functionaries conducted their proceedings in secret, and the verdicts were never recorded in writing. As a result, our impression of the judicial authorities in the Warsaw ghetto remains incomplete, resting solely on a few diaries.[97]

Studying the perspective of ordinary ghetto residents is similarly difficult, as their values were never captured in the form of binding written definitions or rules. The attitudes they expressed – if at all – towards their own criminal activities, the offences of other residents, or the Jewish Councils' definitions of criminality and law varied according to whom they were addressing and at what point in time. Relevant insights can be gained from ego-documents hitherto largely neglected by researchers: among these are numerous letters sent by residents to the Jewish Councils – and in some cases even to the German authorities – together with testimonies given before ghetto-internal and German courts.[98] The focus here is on contemporary sources, and particularly those in which residents refer explicitly to Jewish Council definitions, while diaries and survivor stories are only used in a supplementary capacity.[99] When considering post-war testimonies in particular, we are confronted with the question of which behaviours survivors were willing to reveal and which they kept to themselves. Ultimately, those who could bear witness after the war were the ones who had survived. In a historical context in which clear categories of "good" and "bad" behaviour prevailed for a long time, it is unlikely that survivors would reveal behaviours that may have guaranteed their own survival but would not be classified as heroic and community-minded by survivor communities and scholars. The source material examined here can, inevitably, only give a limited sense of the outlook of ghetto inhabitants, since only a small group of them were able to give (written) expression to their views. Among these were, first, members of the Jewish self-administration bodies, whose office gave them certain powers and, not least, the financial and material means to formulate their opinions on criminality and law. As such, they constituted a mostly male "ghetto elite" whose position came with power and privileges which they were afraid of losing. A second subgroup consisted of a small, well-educated class of people who decided, either as Council members or at their own initiative, to collect, archive, or write their own records of everyday life in the ghetto. In consequence, even the sources originating from ordinary residents have a limited representative value: they too only tell us about those who could read and write, or indeed chose to do so because they (still) believed that it would help their cause.

The book follows a thematic structure. I first focus on Nazi Jewish policy in occupied Eastern Europe and the resulting orders and demands, in order to trace the German ideological and legal parameters against which the Jewish Councils tried to develop their survival strategies and a ghetto-internal legal sphere. Second, I examine how Jewish Councils announced their new regulations and corresponding concepts of criminality through proclamations and newspapers in the ghetto, which effectively fulfilled the role of legal norms. Third, I consider the organization of the Jewish police as an internal executive organ and assess how far it was responsible for enforcing predefined concepts of criminality and law.

The fourth chapter discusses the ghetto courts as agencies of the "judiciary" and the attempt by their personnel to establish a legal practice balancing pre-war legal traditions against the unprecedented conditions of the ghetto. Besides the institutional framework, I consider the cases tried and the criteria applied by these agencies, in order to assess what functions their rulings served. Chapter 5 examines the ghetto penal system, considering its punitive mechanisms and ghetto prisons as places that were particularly vulnerable to access by the German authorities.

In the sixth chapter, I turn the spotlight on those at the receiving end by exploring their perspective and pragmatic struggle for survival in the face of the shifting concepts of criminality and law. In conclusion, I consolidate the findings of the study with the debate surrounding the theory of low ghetto criminality and place it in the wider context of Jewish legal history.

The focus of my analysis moves between the different ghettos according to the topic under discussion, whereby a comparatively large amount of space is devoted to the Lodz ghetto owing to the nature of the source material. This is justifiable in that Rumkowski's strategy of "rescue through labour" can be seen as epitomizing the outlook of the Jewish Councils.[100] Moreover, the Lodz ghetto – dating back to 1940 – was regarded by the Germans as a model for subsequent ghettos and can therefore be studied, so to speak, as an "ideal type."[101] By contrasting it with the Vilna ghetto in particular, which was not established until 1941, we can identify variations resulting from these chronological differences, while examples from the Warsaw ghetto show how the less autocratic leadership style of its Jewish Council and the tighter restrictions placed on it by the Germans impacted on the development of an internal legal sphere. Through this comparative approach, it is thus possible – despite differences of time and place – to highlight similarities of experience between the ghetto communities in the face of the German demands placed on their respective Jewish Councils.

Chapter One

Nazi Jewish Policy in Eastern Europe and the Perspective of the Jewish Councils

"As many as 250,000 Jews live in the ghetto, all of whom are more or less criminally inclined. The large number of reported incidents renders it necessary for Criminal Police officers to conduct an immediate investigation."[1] Such was the justification given by the occupiers in May 1940 for setting up a German Criminal Police force within the Lodz ghetto.[2] The "incidents" referred to were mainly smuggling offences. Nor was it long before the Germans saw their perceptions of Jewish "criminal inclinations" duly confirmed, as illustrated by the Criminal Police annual report of September 1942: "The long experience of Ghetto Commissariat officers and employees has given them extensive insights into the living habits of the Jews, and especially their criminal disposition ... The Jew will seize every available minute to enrich himself at the expense of others."[3]

The Ghettoization of the Jewish Population

Bogeyman images of the "criminal Jew" were firmly entrenched long before the ghettos were established. Central to the Nazi ideology, which was elevated to a state doctrine after 1933, was an anti-Semitism uniting the fear of a "racial degeneration" of the German people with the belief that salvation could be achieved by the "removal" of the Jews from the *Volksgemeinschaft* (German ethnic community).[4] The recourse to the topos of the "criminal Jew" lent a distinctive edge to the attempt to stigmatize "the Jews" as "foreign bodies."[5] Historian Michael Berkowitz sees this topos as instrumental in embedding anti-Semitic enemy stereotypes within German society under National Socialism: "The perception of Jews as criminals occupied a larger role – and was intertwined in other anti-Jewish efforts, political, economic and 'racial' – than has heretofore been acknowledged in the history of the Holocaust and anti-Semitism."[6] The propaganda campaign spread by the press and elsewhere was based on the idea of Jews as "born criminals."[7] Hence the headline on a poster advertising a special edition of the anti-Semitic newspaper *Der Stürmer* in September 1937: "Jewry is organized criminality ... the Jew is the founder, organizer and leader of *all professional criminality and the underworld* at large."[8]

At a legal level, the premise of the "criminal-born Jew" was enshrined in the Nuremberg Laws of September 1935. From then on, only German "citizens of the Reich" were "bearers of full political rights in accordance with law," not the Jewish population.[9] In order to legitimize the disenfranchisement and criminalization of the latter, the Nazis invoked newly created legal norms.[10] Anti-Jewish decrees were passed within a short space of time, and only rarely publicly announced. For the Jewish population, all sense of legal certainty vanished,[11] so that many had already emigrated by 1939. The exclusion of the Jews was now well under way within the territory of the German Reich.[12]

Following the invasion of Poland on 1 September 1939 and its subsequent occupation, the "Jewish question" acquired a new dimension in view of the 2.5 million Jews living in the new Nazi-ruled territory. The Germans were convinced of the need to "eliminate" the Jewish population in Eastern Europe from the surrounding communities and place it under surveillance. It was this belief that prompted the establishment of ghettos. Notions of the "criminal Jew" were consistently an issue:[13] besides the alleged threat of the spread of typhus, the main justification for the creation of ghettos in occupied Poland in 1939 and 1940 was that of "criminal machinations" on the part of the Jews, such as "hoarding of provisions" and black-marketeering.[14]

On 21 September 1939, the chief of the Security Police, Reinhard Heydrich, sent a dispatch (*Schnellbrief*) to the heads of the *Einsatzgruppen* (mobile killing units) in Poland ordering them to set up "Jewish" ghettos.[15] It was thought that the concentration of the Jewish population would provide a better "possibility of control and later of deportation" when it came to the planned "resettlements."[16] This measure envisaged wholesale "population transfers" in the eastern territories. The idea was that "ethnic Germans" would organize and inhabit the new *Lebensraum* in the east, while "undesirable" sections of the population – i.e., the majority of Poles and the entire Jewish population – would be expelled.[17] What form these resettlements were to take was not further specified, however. Measures discussed included a "Jewish reserve" near Lublin, the creation of a huge ghetto on Madagascar, and lastly, as preparations began for a war against the Soviet Union, the expulsion of the Jews to Siberia.[18]

The subsequent ghettoization process was a decentralized operation and varied from one administrative district to another, as the local

German authorities in Poland were not given any clear instructions from above, and a certain amount of local flexibility was, in any case, intentional.[19] Although compulsory labelling, movement restrictions on the Jewish population, and the installation of Jewish Councils had been enforced as "preparatory" measures directly upon creation of the German civil administrations in 1939, most of the ghettos in the Generalgouvernement were not established until 1940.[20]

These "Jewish Residential Districts" were meant to be a temporary solution, but since the planned population transfers turned out to be unachievable, the German authorities were faced with the prospect of maintaining the ghettos for longer than planned.[21] This was partly due to the impracticality of "removing" the Jews to the eastern territories, given the military situation. Nor was a resettlement within the Generalgouvernement possible because of an acute lack of housing. Moreover, Himmler's resettlement plans met with resistance in the shape of Göring, who wanted to maximize economic exploitation in view of the war, and the head of the German civil administration, Hans Frank, who objected to the unlimited deportation of Jews to the Generalgouvernement. Nevertheless, tens of thousands of Jews were expelled or murdered during the annexation of Eastern Europe.[22]

With the invasion of the Soviet Union on 22 June 1941, the situation changed fundamentally. Following the conquest of the Soviet territories, the expulsion of the Jewish population threatened to reach unmanageable proportions. This circumstance, compounded by the association of Bolshevism with Jewry, ushered in a change during the second half of 1941 whereby the idea of expelling the Jewish population evolved into a plan for their annihilation.[23] Consequently, many ghettos in the occupied Soviet Union were already established on the premise of an organized extermination program, and parallel mass shootings of Jewish people were duly carried out by SS and police units in June/July 1941.[24] Here, too, the notion of the "criminal Jew" played a role, as illustrated by the Jäger report, in which SS Colonel Karl Jäger gave an account of the systematic murder of Lithuanian Jews by the killing squad under his command, *Einsatzkommando* 3, between July and winter 1941. This was, he wrote, not so much a case of "racial cleansing" as a "police operation" against "criminal Jews."[25] After the invasion of the Soviet Union, the association of "Bolshevism" with "criminal Jews" was also integrated into the Nazi world view in occupied Poland. In an announcement of 13 May 1943 to the Warsaw ghetto, Governor Fischer warned that "Communist agents and Jews," who were blamed for a series of murder attempts, had taken refuge among the Jews in the ghetto: "Any Jew or Bolshevik who is still free today is the most dangerous enemy of the population."[26]

In his dispatch to the *Einsatzgruppen* in September 1939, Heydrich had ordered the creation of "Jewish Councils of Elders" (*Judenräte*),[27] which were to consist of up to twenty-four males according to the size of the Jewish community.[28] These Councils had to comply with the demands of the German occupiers and would be made "fully responsible in the literal sense of the word" for the execution of German orders.[29] This included enforcing German definitions of criminality and law vis-à-vis the Jewish population, which was bound, under the decree issued for the Generalgouvernement, to obey Council instructions.[30] The occupiers threatened the Jewish Councils with harsh sanctions in the event of non-compliance:[31] brutal bullying, arbitrary arrests, and the murder of Jewish Council members were the order of the day. Under the decree of 28 November 1939, the Jewish Councils in the Generalgouvernement were subject to state control and constituted public institutions.[32] The power of the regional authorities over the Jewish Councils was unlimited.

On 13 July 1941, General von Schenckendorff issued a decree similar in character to the *Schnellbrief* for the occupied Soviet territories. In it, he ordered the formation of Jewish Councils consisting of twelve to twenty-four members, to be selected by the Jewish communities from their own ranks. In contrast to the situation in occupied Poland, however, their appointment was no longer explicitly linked to the establishment of ghettos. Although Jews were to be "concentrated in a closed community in buildings occupied exclusively by Jews,"[33] this instruction was a response to Jewish "vagabondage"[34] and did not seek a fundamental geographical separation, unlike Heydrich's *Schnellbrief*. The Jewish Council was regarded as "useful," but not "essential" to the realization of the "Final Solution."[35] It was to receive the commands of the German army and police and implement them within the Jewish community, and would be held responsible for any incident "directed against the German army and police or their orders."[36] Depending on the gravity of the offence, the death penalty could be inflicted not just on the perpetrators but also on members of the Council.[37]

The responsibilities of the forcibly created Jewish Councils differed fundamentally from those of the self-administration bodies of the *kehilla*, the Jewish community that had existed before the war. Traditionally, the Jewish communities had assumed functions relating to religion, welfare, education, and political organization. They also enjoyed some legal powers, although these were mostly limited to matters of civil law.[38] "After the occupation of Warsaw, the Jewish community faced an entirely new set of tasks,"[39] wrote the local Jewish Council chairman Adam Czerniaków in spring 1940. Compliance with German demands was now its first priority, including the construction of an internal ghetto administration. The Jewish Councils created agencies which were designed, on one hand, to help meet German demands efficiently and, on the other, to regulate communal life in the ghetto and, as far as possible, compensate for the exclusion of Jews from state institutions by organizing the supply of provisions.[40]

Even if the Jewish Councils enjoyed no more than a "pseudo-autonomy,"[41] the question remains why the Germans gave them so much leeway in ghetto-internal affairs. Isaiah Trunk explains this in terms of a certain "tolerance,"[42] although "indifference" seems closer to the mark.[43] According to Trunk, the maintenance of a kind of "normality" also helped to conceal the German murder plans for as long as possible.[44] We should also bear in mind that well-functioning procedures and a degree of organization within the ghetto community were the best ways to ensure effective compliance with German demands. For reasons similar to those that had prompted their establishment in the first place, the German occupiers must have believed that the Jewish Councils knew best how to ensure "peace and order" within the ghetto community. The Councils played a key role in shaping this internal autonomy: in the larger ghettos in particular, they created complex administrative set-ups with numerous institutions, partly in accordance with German instructions, and partly at their own initiative. As Trunk writes, "the Nazi-created Jewish ghetto necessarily became a Jewish city sui generis."[45] The structures of these administrative bodies were rarely set in stone. Often, they were remodelled over time, and freedoms that had been granted initially by the Germans were later restricted, whether case by case or across the board, and usually by brutal means. One activity report by the Jewish Council in Warsaw reads, for example:

> The *organization committee* is working tirelessly to organize the departments, define their tasks, and split up larger departments into smaller or more viable cells which, in time, have to be subdivided again or dissolved. In this way, a succession of new committees is appointed and new departments and institutions created which cannot be covered in a condensed report.[46]

The legal institutions constituted only a fraction of this apparatus. Despite the large number of institutions and staff, it was the Council chairmen who were the key players, acting as decision-makers and liaising constantly with the Germans. In occupied Poland in particular, most of those forced by the German occupiers to act as Council chairmen had already been authority figures within the Jewish communities before the war.[47] In the Baltic states, too, the Germans were able to appropriate existing structures, however much they had changed over the previous two years of Soviet occupation.[48]

The Warsaw Ghetto

When the Germans occupied Warsaw on 28 September 1939, it was home to around 360,000 Jews, making it the largest Jewish community in Europe.[49] The city was assigned to the Generalgouvernement district, where the head of the German civil administration, Hans Frank, was in charge of all "Jewish affairs" from autumn 1939 to summer 1940.[50] The governor of the Warsaw district from the end of October 1939 was Dr Ludwig Fischer.[51] Waldemar Schön, head of the Resettlement Department under his governorship, was responsible for the ghetto from the beginning of 1940[52] until Heinz Auerswald replaced him as commissar for the Jewish Residential District on 15 May 1941.[53]

In the wake of the German invasion, members of the pre-war *kehilla* had fled Warsaw in large numbers.[54] On 4 October 1939, the Germans ordered the engineer Adam Czerniaków, who had assumed responsibility for Jewish affairs by default, to appoint a Jewish Council. Since he came from an assimilated Jewish family, the majority of the Jewish community did not recognize Czerniaków as an authority at the time of his appointment.[55] Despite their scepticism, many of the former *kehilla* members initially consented to join the Council, covering between them the broad political spectrum of the Jewish community, including Zionists, Bundists, and members of the Aguda.[56]

On 1 April 1940, the Germans began building a ghetto wall, which was completed in June of that year. In October, Ludwig Fischer announced the planned division of the city of Warsaw into a German, a Polish, and a Jewish sector.[57] On 12 October 1940, the entire Jewish population was ordered to move to the "Jewish Residential District" within six weeks.[58] This territory, which consisted of one small and one large ghetto, was sealed on 16 November 1940,[59] with 360,000 people now being confined within an area of 3.5 square kilometres.[60] By March 1941, following the arrival of large numbers of deportees from the surrounding municipalities, over 460,000 people from diverse social, economic, and religious backgrounds were living in a tiny space under catastrophic sanitary conditions and with insufficient food supplies.[61]

When the Germans ordered Czerniaków to enforce the resettlement to the ghetto, the Jewish Council head was often unclear about the exact course of the ghetto border and the scope of the Council's regulatory powers. Moreover, he struggled to find accommodation for the resettled people.[62] After the sealing of the ghetto territory, the Jewish Council – partly on German orders and partly on its own initiative – set up a complex administrative apparatus. Its purpose was, on one hand, to ensure effective compliance with German demands and, on the other, to regulate communal life in the exceptional living conditions of the ghetto.[63] On 23 September 1940, ghetto inhabitant Aron Kaplan wrote in his diary: "The *Judenrat* has turned into a Jewish government, and by order of the conqueror it must now perform governmental functions of a sort it was never prepared for."[64] In May 1941, the administration comprised twenty-six departments, which were repeatedly reorganized.[65] Among these institutions were the "Order Service" (OS) or Jewish police, a ghetto prison, and a legal department set up by the Jewish Council with its own disciplinary court. At the micro-level of apartment blocks, the administration was complemented by so-called house committees.[66] As we will see, in addition to providing neighbourhood assistance, they became important tools in the implementation of the Jewish Council's directives, but also in settling disputes among tenants.[67]

After the establishment of the ghetto, the German functionaries forced Czerniaków, while depriving him of any financial resources, to ensure the provisioning of the ghetto community and meet the Germans' financial demands.[68] From spring 1941 onwards, he was also required to supply quotas for the labour camps.[69] At first, men had signed up voluntarily because of financial hardship, but after 1941, following reports of the appalling working conditions and lack of food in the camps, the Jewish Council had to fill the required quotas by force.[70] As a result of the Council's compliance and the involvement of the Jewish police, the ghetto community increasingly rejected the Jewish Council personnel.[71]

The requirement to provide the Germans with a Jewish labour force gained in importance from May 1941 onwards, when Max Bischof, as head of the German Transfer Office, encouraged the use of Jewish labour in factories outside the ghetto and drove forward the establishment of ghetto "shops."[72] These were production facilities allowing German firms to exploit ghetto labour power for purposes such as textile manufacturing.[73] The Jewish Council's provisioning department used the pittance paid for this work to buy food supplies for the ghetto.[74] After January 1941, the Jewish Council began to organize the distribution of the scant provisions provided by the occupiers. Food ration cards – which were subject to taxation – could be used to purchase goods in authorized stores.[75] The Council also levied taxes in other areas in order to meet the financial demands of the occupiers and maintain institutions such as welfare and health care services.[76]

From July 1941, news of German massacres of the Jewish population reached the Warsaw ghetto via the Polish underground press.[77] At the beginning of February 1942, a Jew named Szlamek who had fled the Kulmhof extermination camp reported on the mass gassings taking place there.[78] Resistance fighter and ghetto survivor Marek Edelman writes that, at first, it was only supporters of the resistance who believed the news.[79] Then, in early June 1942, the underground press reported on a labour and death camp in Treblinka, rumours of the Sobibor extermination camp having already started circulating in April[80] – though it was several months before the Jewish Council functionaries began to take this seriously. After April 1942, Moritu Orzech, a member of the Bund, attempted to convince Czerniaków that the Germans intended to gradually exterminate the Jewish population.[81] The Council chairman had been uneasy since the beginning of the year and, on hearing that Auerswald had been summoned to Berlin, had noted in his diary: "I cannot shake off the fearful suspicion that the Jews of Warsaw may be threatened by mass resettlement."[82] On 20 July 1942, he obtained assurances from Auerswald that no deportations were planned.[83] Just one day later, members of the Jewish Council were taken hostage in order to pressurize Czerniaków into making all the necessary preparations for "resettlements to the East" that were to begin the next day. Initially exempted were Jewish Council employees, workers employed by German firms, and people potentially "fit for work." On 22 July, the Germans deported over 60,000 ghetto residents to Treblinka and murdered them in the extermination camp.[84] The following day, 23 July, Czerniaków committed suicide, after receiving German orders to prepare for further deportations.[85] His suicide note, in which he laments, "They are demanding that I kill the children of my people with my own hands," indicates that he knew the "resettled" Jews would be murdered by the Germans.[86] In a sense, Czerniaków's suicide can be regarded as an expression of his disillusionment with his own survival strategy. Up to July 1942, he had still hoped to be able to channel the Germans' arbitrariness and brutality through compliance, compromise, and negotiation.[87] Once he became aware of their calculated murder campaign in July 1942, however, he gave up any hope of securing the survival of the ghetto population by these means.[88]

After Czerniaków's death, the Germans replaced him with Marek Lichtenbaum, who, with the assistance of the Jewish police, was willing to participate in the preparations for the German deportations.[89] Perceiving the interest in a Jewish labour force, the Jewish Council established further workshops, in the hope that residents would be protected by having a job in the ghetto.[90] At the same time, however, alternative survival strategies gained momentum, with support growing for groups advocating armed resistance. On 28 July 1942, representatives of the youth organizations Hashomer Hatzair, Dror, and Akiva founded the Żydowska Organizacja Bojowa or Jewish Fighting Organization (ŻOB).[91]

From 31 July 1942, the deportations – which were now part of "Aktion Reinhardt"[92] – became even more brutal, with SS men, German police officers, and Ukrainian and Lithuanian auxiliaries participating in the ghetto arrests under the command of Hermann Hoefle. On 10 August 1942, the small ghetto was dissolved and the residents forced to move to the large one. During the period from 6 to 12 September, the Germans carried out mass deportations which also included members of the Jewish police and their families. Between 22 July and 21 September, 90 per cent of the population – approximately 265,000 people – were deported to Treblinka and murdered there. Left behind were 35,000 employed in the ghetto by German firms and around 20,000 in hiding.[93] The structures of the Jewish self-administration were shattered. After the deportations, only 2,500 out of a previous 9,000 people were still employed by the Jewish Council institutions. The survival strategies pursued by Council staff no longer centred on the ghetto community, but on individual welfare. According to the ghetto survivor and historian Israel Gutman, "Their greatest concern was for themselves and the members of their families."[94] The only Council department that remained functional was the supply authority.[95]

It was after the deportations that Zionist youth activist Mordechaj Anielewicz attempted to re-form the armed resistance groups within the ghetto, aided by outside contacts that made it possible to smuggle in weapons. Alongside the ŻOB, the Żydowski Związek Wojskowy or Jewish Military Union (ŻZW) was now also founded, born out of the Revisionist movement. These groups stood for survival strategies that were contrary to the former Jewish Council's compliance with German demands. From autumn 1942 onwards, these groups endeavoured to alert the remaining residents to the fate of the deportees. They also carried out attacks on people whose actions they deemed "contrary to the welfare of the ghetto community," executing members of the Jewish police such as Jakub Lejkin and other Jewish Council members.[96] During this time, the viewpoints of the resistance fighters, including their notions of "acceptable behaviour," morality, and justice in the ghetto, gained in influence.[97] Although their ideas did not lead to any legal norms, they did now find greater acceptance – in the wake of the mass deportations – among the ghetto community.[98]

In January 1943, Himmler ordered a further "reduction" of the ghetto community. When the occupiers entered the ghetto on 18 January 1943, many residents resisted the deportation order and went into hiding. Members of the armed group Hashomer Hatzair fired at the "intruders." Although the Germans were unable to carry out the deportation as planned, they removed 5,000 people from the ghetto and shot around 1,700 directly on the street.[99]

After this, the armed resistance groups gained new support within the ghetto community, to the detriment of the Jewish Council. As the historian Havi Dreifuss writes, "During this period, the Judenrat and Jewish Order Service altogether lost all their authority in the ghetto, and for the first time, the underground functioned as an alternative Jewish leadership."[100] Hiding also became more common as an individual survival strategy, whether in the ghetto or – for those with suitable connections – on the "Aryan" side.[101] At the beginning of February 1943, Hitler finally ordered the liquidation of the Warsaw ghetto. On 19 April, the eve of Passover, SS and German police units invaded the ghetto and a rebellion ensued. The ŻOB and ŻZW fired at the Germans with the few available weapons, and residents refused to obey the deportation orders. From 23 April – after having evacuated the "skilled labour" from the ghetto factories – the German occupiers began to set fire to central ghetto buildings and disconnect the electricity, gas, and water supplies, resulting in the death of large numbers of people in hiding. On 16 May, SS General Jürgen Stroop ordered the main synagogues to be blown up, and declared the "operation" complete. 30,000 out of approximately 40,000 remaining residents were then deported to the extermination camps in Majdanek, Poniatowa, Trawniki, and Treblinka to be murdered. A further 10,000 had either been executed in the ghetto during the uprising or fallen victim to the fire. Only a few survived in hiding, most of them on the "Aryan" side.[102]

The Lodz Ghetto

In Lodz, the Germans ordered the establishment of a Jewish Council on 13 October 1939, after taking control of the city on 8 September. They appointed the sixty-three-year-old Mordechaj Chaim Rumkowski, a former textile entrepreneur and insurance agent, as chairman. Rumkowski had already worked in the Jewish community before the war, on issues including child welfare.[103] He was a confirmed Zionist and known for his authoritarian leadership style.[104] On 11 November 1939, the Gestapo arrested the thirty-one members of the first Jewish Council and murdered most of them. Thereafter, Rumkowski was forced to assemble a new committee, which was not able to sit until 5 February 1940, now with twenty-one members.[105]

On 12 February 1940, the Germans issued a police regulation establishing a ghetto in the slum districts of the city.[106] Some 16,000 people were crammed together in an area of 4.13 square kilometres, where they suffered from overcrowding, hunger, disease, uncertainty, and fear.[107] They came from different regions, social strata, and political camps and included assimilated and Orthodox Jews.[108] Between 16 October and 4 November 1941, the ghetto community grew even more ethnically diverse as nearly 20,000 Jews from the "Old Reich," Vienna, Prague, and Luxembourg, along with 5,000 "gypsies," were deported there.[109] Among the new arrivals were large numbers of business people and pensioners unused to physical labour.[110] As in Warsaw, the Jewish Council chairman in Lodz hoped to be able to channel the Germans' arbitrary brutality by obeying their instructions. His duties in the initial phase included the registration of the Jewish population, the evacuation of housing in preparation for "resettlement measures," the provision of labour, and the confiscation of objects of value.[111] In addition, he was tasked with enforcing the newly drawn ghetto border with the aid of a Jewish police force.[112] In order to meet these demands and organize communal life in the ghetto, Rumkowski set about building a complex administrative apparatus, partly on explicit German orders, as in the case of the Jewish police, and partly at his own initiative. At the residential level, after March 1940 the Jewish Council took over self-organized house committees, initially set up by tenants, to organize food distribution and the maintenance of the buildings.[113] Central to Rumkowski's strategy was the attempt to harness the German interest in labour, in the hope that this would secure the survival of the ghetto community. To this end, he created numerous workshops and administrative authorities along with a central office responsible for the allocation of employees.[114]

Having deemed the "revenue" from confiscated valuables to be insufficient, the Germans changed their demands in August 1940, when the head of the German ghetto administration, Hans Biebow, called for a more organized exploitation of ghetto labour power. Once District Governor Friedrich Uebelhoer had approved this change of course in autumn 1940 and granted a loan for the provisioning of the ghetto, Biebow began issuing Rumkowski with production orders.[115] From then on, the workshop labour force was devoted primarily to fulfilling textile orders for the German army, toiling for more than ten hours a day, six days a week, without breaks or adequate food rations. The earnings from production went into the account of the German ghetto administration and were used chiefly for the purchase of food, while the Jewish Council paid workers in the ghetto currency.[116] In summer 1940, in order to be able to deliver "objects of value" to the German ghetto administration or use them to procure food supplies, Rumkowski also set up banks and purchasing agencies where residents could exchange their last possessions for a small sum.[117]

From 1941 onwards, the Germans confronted Rumkowski with new and drastically different demands. From summer 1941, Gauleiter Arthur Greiser declared his intention to reduce the number of Jews allegedly unfit for work.[118] In December 1941, Rumkowski received notification that 20,000 people would have to leave the ghetto owing to "supply shortages."[119] Among the first to be deported at the end of December 1941 were the "gypsies."[120] Between 16 January and May 1942, a further 55,000 people were deported and murdered at the Kulmhof extermination camp.[121] Rumkowski attempted to negotiate a reduction of the deportation quota demanded by the Germans and to influence the selection of residents via a resettlement commission he had set up in January 1942.[122] He then first selected the "offenders" who had violated his "order in the ghetto."[123]

At the end of August 1941, the Reich Security Main Office ordered the Jewish Council chairman to "weed out" all residents aged under ten or over sixty-five, along with all the sick and unemployed, the plan being to turn the ghetto into a straightforward labour camp. During this period, known as the "curfew," 15,885 people were murdered.[124] In June and July 1944, after a phase of relative calm, a further 7,000 residents were deported to Kulmhof. In August 1944, the Germans liquidated the ghetto and sent 72,000 people to Auschwitz-Birkenau.[125]

Owing to a postal ban, reports of systematic murders perpetrated on the Jewish population reached the Lodz ghetto relatively late. Rumkowski probably learned of the fate of the "labour transports" by the end of May 1942, as information to this effect from death camp escapees had reached the ghetto that month in the form of a letter carried by an "incomer" from Brzeziny.[126] Ghetto Chronicle entries for this period also testify to a general unease among the population with regard to the "resettlements."[127] From summer 1942, diaries show increasing signs of an awareness of "gassings" and fears of an intended "eradication" of the Jewish population.[128] Unlike Czerniaków in Warsaw, who had committed suicide on being forced to deliver up ghetto residents for deportation, Rumkowski agreed to carry out the "self-selection" process according to German "utility criteria." His willingness to cooperate with the Germans was already highly controversial during the ghetto's existence, as well as directly after the war. Rumkowski enjoyed a virtual monopoly of power within the ghetto. In the eyes of many, he acted like a self-aggrandizing "king," "tyrant," or even "Führer,"[129] handing down the bullying he received from the Germans to the ghetto population by exercising similarly brutal instruments of power. His solution, "work is our only way," was based on making the ghetto attractive to the Germans by raising "productivity." In so doing, he sought to secure the survival of the ghetto population.[130] Once Rumkowski learnt of the Germans' organized murder plans and was forced to provide them with quotas for the deportations, he attempted to save at least part of the community by "sacrificing" a large number of individuals. It was a race against time: all the while he was supplying the Germans with labour, he was probably hoping for a change in the course of the war in favour of the anti-Hitler coalition and the Red Army.[131]

The Vilna Ghetto

The ghetto in Vilna was established under very different circumstances, which affected the Jewish Council's survival strategies. The city of Vilna lay in the part of Eastern Europe that had been occupied by the Soviet Union at the end of September 1939 following the Ribbentrop-Molotov Pact. After the invasion of the Red Army, the city was initially part of Lithuania until a pro-Soviet government assumed control on 15 June 1940.[132] The subsequent Sovietization process had dramatic consequences for the previously active Jewish community: because all organizations and parties except the Communist Party were banned, Jewish institutions, organizations, and parties could no longer legally exist.[133]

Prior to the Second World War, around 55,000 Jewish people had lived in what was then Vilnius, with a further 12,000 to 15,000 refugees arriving following the invasion of Poland by the German Wehrmacht.[134] On 24 June 1941, two days after their attack on the Soviet Union, the Germans occupied the city. From July 1941, they enforced a series of anti-Jewish measures accompanied by random violence and murders.[135] Because of the previous Soviet ban on Jewish organizations, it was more difficult for the Germans to recruit a Jewish Council from among the pre-war community. On 4 July 1941, the German military administration ordered the synagogue sexton Chaim-Majer Gordon to appoint a Jewish Council. Seeing all too clearly by this time that the Germans would force the Council to turn on its own community, many of the candidates at first declined to be involved. In response, Dr Gershn Gershuni, a figure of authority within the Zionist movement, insisted at the election conference that the election would require the status of a Jewish commandment or *mitzvah*. Classing it as a *kiddush hashem* meant that those concerned now had to accept their appointment, as an expression of their devotion to God and reverence for the commandments.[136] In consequence, ten members from across the Jewish political spectrum of the pre-Soviet period were eventually elected by the Jewish community, to which a further twelve were added on German orders at the end of July.[137]

Since the establishment of a German civil administration after the end of July 1941, Vilna had been part of the Reichskommissariat Ostland, overseen by Reich Minister Alfred Rosenberg in Berlin.[138] The responsible local official was Reich Commissar Heinrich Lohse, who was in charge from the end of July 1941 to the end of July 1944.[139] The Vilna district commissar, Hans Hingst, dealt with Jewish affairs as part of the political department, while provisioning of the ghetto and supervision of the ghetto border were the responsibility of District Commissar Franz Murer.[140] Here, in contrast to Warsaw and Lodz, the establishment of a Jewish Council and the ghettoization process initiated in September 1941 were already characterized by systematic murder.[141] On 27 July 1941, at an initial meeting with the district commissars, Lohse had informed those present of the intended "Final Solution to the Jewish question," and on 13 August 1941, he announced that this would have consequences for the Jewish Councils.[142] From July 1941 onwards, *Einsatzkommando* 9, with Lithuanian help, had been carrying out mass shootings of Vilna's Jewish population in Ponary.[143] At first, this led to a clash of opposing German interests: while the German military administration demanded labour power from the Jewish Council in order to keep factories, railways, and so on running and support the military with the necessary resources, the killing squad was bent on murdering the Jewish population, starting with all male leadership figures as potential sources of resistance.[144] Between 31 August and 2 September 1941, the occupiers killed nearly 3,700 Jewish people during the so-called Great Provocation.[145] Here, too, the image of the "criminal Jew" served as a justification when District Commissar Hingst claimed that Jewish "bandits" had fired at German soldiers, an act for which the entire Jewish community would be held accountable.[146] On 1 and 2 September 1941, the Germans deported and murdered sixteen members of the Jewish Council, leaving Vilna's Jewish community with no means of communicating with the occupiers.[147] People living near Ponary had assumed that mass shootings of Jews had been taking place since July 1941, but it was only on 3 and 4 September 1941, when Jewish women fled Ponary, that reports of mass shootings reached the Jewish population of the city.[148] As Kruk recorded on 4 September 1941, "The dreadful thing is hard to describe. The hand trembles, and the ink is bloody. Is it possible that all those taken out of there have been murdered, shot in Ponar[y]?"[149]

It was under these circumstances that on 6 September, without warning, the Germans concentrated the Jewish population into two ghettos within the space of twenty-four hours.[150] Large numbers of Jews were deported to Ponary to be shot.[151] On 7 September 1941, the Germans gave orders for a new Jewish Council to be appointed in each ghetto. In the first ghetto, where nearly 30,000 people were interned, Murer installed the assimilated Jew and former bank manager Anatol Fried – who had already served on the first Jewish Council – as chairman, with orders to put together a five-strong assembly. The Council was composed of former public figures and representatives of different parties.[152] In the second, smaller ghetto, numbering around 10,000 people, SS Oberscharführer (Staff Sergeant) Horst Schweinberger ordered a tradesman named Isaak Lejbowicz to form a Jewish Council, along with four others plucked from the streets at random.[153] Faced with this experience of constant violence and murder, the Jewish Council members in both ghettos tried to comply with German orders by developing institutions through which to organize the necessary procedures in terms of food, health, housing, and employment, while Jewish police forces were established in accordance with German orders.

Between 15 September and 29 October 1941, the Germans wiped out the population of the second ghetto, most of whom were elderly, sick, or orphaned. Right at the outset, the occupiers had divided up the ghetto population, assigning those "fit for work" to the larger ghetto and those "unfit for work" to the smaller one, and the same principle was applied in the so-called operations (Aktionen).[154] It soon became clear that having a job was no guarantee of survival in either ghetto, however, as was demonstrated by another incident in the first ghetto on 1 October – Yom Kippur – when the Germans ordered the Jewish Council to hand over 1,000 residents. When the Jewish Council failed to surrender the required number, Germans and Lithuanians seized people at random, aided for the first time by the Jewish Police.[155]

Since the first Jewish Council had just been murdered, the new Council members in Ghetto I are likely to have learned of the killing operations between mid-September and early October 1941, when further escapees from Ponary reached the ghetto.[156] By this time, scarcely any information was getting through to Ghetto II.[157] After the liquidation of the latter, the Jewish Council in Ghetto I was able to keep its knowledge of the German murder plans secret in order to keep the ghetto community calm until 5 November 1941.[158] The occupiers had issued certificates of different colours according to the bearer's working status and movement restrictions, which made it seem that a certain work status could still serve as protection from deportation. Following the establishment of the ghetto, Himmler issued 3,000 yellow "skilled worker" certificates to the Jewish Council. These were known as "life certificates" because they had the power to protect workers and their families from German murder campaigns; everyone else had pink ones.[159] Over time, the Germans began to use the certificate colours as a basis for deciding who to murder.[160] It soon became tragically clear that not even the skilled worker certificates would provide protection. Between 3 and 5 November 1941, some 8,000 residents fell victim to the "yellow certificate campaign," with further massacres following in December.[161] It was after the November 1941 operations that knowledge of the systematic murder policy became more widely known in the ghetto. On 2 January 1942, Kruk wrote in the Chronicle that he had known of the Germans' objectives for six weeks.[162] The period between the end of December 1941 and summer 1943 then constituted a "phase of relative stability" in the history of the ghetto: for the time being, conflicts of interest between the German civil administration, the army, and the SS prevented the occurrence of large-scale killing sprees.[163]

As in the Lodz ghetto, the Jewish Council in Vilna pursued a strategy of "rescue through labour."[164] No one was more assiduous in enforcing this than Jakub Gens, who was initially chief of the ghetto police until July 1942, when Murer appointed him Council chairman in place of Anatol Fried.[165] Before the war, Gens had been an officer in the Lithuanian army and a member of Betar, a Zionist youth movement founded in Riga in 1923.[166] Gens declared "work, discipline, and order" the pillars of his survival strategy for the ghetto community.[167]

To meet the German demand for a labour force, the Jewish Council set up production facilities with workshops and tailoring factories in the ghetto. The workforce grew from 337 in June 1942 to 759 in December 1942, and by May/June 1943 there were 2,400 people working in thirty-three workshops. Some residents also worked outside the ghetto in labour camps, building roads and railways or cutting timber.[168] The profits from their labour swelled the coffers of the German District Commissariat, while the workers themselves received a mere pittance.[169] Here, too, the right to food rations was dependent on labour,[170] and the Jewish Council levied various taxes on the ghetto community in order to meet the financial demands of the German occupiers and maintain ghetto institutions.[171]

From summer 1942 onwards, the Germans delegated the task of "selection" to the Jewish Council and the Jewish Police in particular. On 17 July 1942, they ordered Gens to deliver up all those "unfit for work."

Unlike Rumkowski in Lodz, Gens knew early on that the deportees were being murdered. He was willing to "select" those unfit for work, at a time when information gleaned from newspapers and workers returning to the ghetto nourished hopes of a German defeat and the impending arrival of the Red Army.[172] During the "operation against the old," eighty-four elderly and weak residents were transported out of the ghetto by the Jewish Police and shot in Ponary on 23 July.[173] From October 1942, the occupiers also entrusted Gens with the administration of the surrounding ghettos. On 18 October, he was required to surrender 1,500 Jews from the ghetto in Oszmiana. Gens negotiated the initial figure down, so that the Jewish Police finally handed over 406 elderly Jews.[174] From autumn 1942 in particular, news of massacres in other areas reached the ghetto.[175] As the broader ghetto population became aware of the systematic extermination – and with it the Jewish Council's inability to protect them – alternative individual and communal survival strategies gained in importance. One way of trying to survive was to go into hiding. This had been going on since the beginning of German occupation, with people hiding in so-called *malines* to escape the Lithuanian "snatchers" and Germans hunting Jewish men for forced labour.[176] It was after the end of November 1942, however, when the ghetto inhabitants learned of Himmler's intention to annihilate the entire Jewish population, that the practice became more widespread.[177] Despair found further expression when residents heard about the liquidation of the Warsaw ghetto and the organized murder campaigns in Western and Eastern Europe in April 1943; around this time, Kruk reported that people drank as never before.[178]

In Vilna, as elsewhere, armed resistance groups challenged the survival strategies of the Jewish Council by calling for a communal struggle, while rejecting hiding as "individual" action.[179] Following initial dialogues between political youth groups directly after ghettoization, the Fareynigte Partizaner Organizatsie (FPO) was founded on 21 January 1942, drawing its membership from Hashomer Hatzair, Hanoar Hatzioni, Betar, and Communist groupings; the Bund joined in summer 1942.[180] Because people were aware of the mass shootings in Ponary, political differences were – unlike in Warsaw – set aside relatively early in favour of the common aim of carrying out acts of sabotage against German institutions and trains and procuring weapons and ammunition.[181] Since the constraints on the Council were more obvious to the ghetto population than in Warsaw, for instance, the campaigns in Vilna were not directed primarily at the Jewish Council and ghetto police.[182] Here, the groups' operations were strictly conspiratorial.[183] Initially, views on survival strategies varied among the different organizations.

While the FPO argued for resistance within the ghetto that should only result in fighting if *the whole ghetto* was in danger, the so-called Yechiel Group called for the establishment of partisan groups in the surrounding forests.[184] However, after 4,000 Jews from surrounding ghettos were murdered by the Gestapo in April 1943 and news of armed resistance in the Warsaw ghetto reached Vilna, the armed groups stepped up their activities.[185] In May 1943, the FPO and the partisans in the forest began to work together.[186]

The fact that their strategies challenged the Jewish Council's agenda was not without consequences. From May 1943, Gens attempted to take decisive action against the resistance fighters, rejecting their actions as a danger to the ghetto community.[187] Prior to this, the Gestapo had threatened him with the liquidation of the ghetto following a rise in weapon purchases in the surrounding area. He exhorted the ghetto population: "You will have to watch each other, and if there are any hot-heads then it is your duty to report it to the Police. That is not informing. It would be informing if you were to keep silent and the people were to suffer."[188]

Neither Gens's strategy of rescue through labour nor the armed resistance groups were able to stop the slaughter of the ghetto community: on 21 June 1943, Himmler ordered all ghettos in the occupied eastern territories to be liquidated or turned into concentration camps by 1 August.[189] Between 6 August and 5 September 1943, the Germans deported over 7,000 people from the ghetto.[190] Although the FPO had called for an armed rebellion on 1 September, most residents complied with the German deportation orders. After opening fire, some last remaining FPO members fled to the forest on 15 September 1943.[191] On 23 September 1943, the ghetto was completely liquidated, and its residents were deported to concentration camps in Estonia or to Kaiserwald near Riga, or they were shot in Ponary. Jakub Gens was shot on 14 September 1943 on the premises of the German Security Police.[192]

In all three ghettos, the Jewish Council leaders complied with changing German orders in the hope that this would increase the survival chances of the ghetto population, a prime example being the request for a labour force that led the Councils to try and optimize the ghetto-internal work sphere. Once they became aware of the Germans' murder campaign, however, they differed in the measures and strategies they adopted in response. While Czerniaków was not willing to hand over any ghetto inhabitants for deportation, both Rumkowski and Gens conformed to the German "selection criteria," hoping that their "rescue through work" strategy would at least save *part* of the ghetto population. In Warsaw and Vilna, as in most other ghettos, the Germans forcibly replaced Jewish Council leaders with figures who were willing to comply with their orders, especially after the decision to pursue a mass extermination policy.

At the heart of all the Jewish Councils' survival strategies lay the desperate attempt to identify a certain logic and rationality behind the Germans' actions.

German Core Interests

The German occupiers imposed ever-changing demands on the Jewish Councils and used brutal methods to enforce them. The nature of these demands depended on the Germans' prevailing "Jewish policies" and core interests in the ghettos, which evolved over time. Unfortunately for the Jewish Councils, local differences, conflicts of interest among German functionaries, and constant clashes between the Germans' ideological premises and their practices meant that the logic they were so desperately trying to identify hardly existed. Nonetheless, it was from these perceived and anticipated German interests that the Councils derived their concepts of crime and law.

After the creation of the ghettos – particularly in occupied Poland – the Germans' initial intention was to remove all "objects of value" from the Jewish population. The ground had already been prepared for this via measures such as the Decree on the Confiscation of Jewish Property (September 1939) and the freezing of all Jewish bank deposits and accounts (November 1939), which made it possible to "access" the alleged "wealth" of the Jewish population.[193] The looting that had begun immediately after the occupation of Poland continued with the establishment of the ghettos in Warsaw and Lodz, where a key role was assumed by so-called Trusteeship Offices.[194] Before long, however, the Germans found the confiscation policy to be insufficiently lucrative and ordered the Jewish police agencies to help track down supposedly hidden valuables in the ghetto alongside German police officers.[195]

In Vilna, too, the SS killing squads had already begun stealing cash and valuables by mid-July 1941. Even before the ghetto was set up, Franz Murer was extorting "contributions" and ransoms from the Jewish Council for detained hostages.[196] After ghettoization, the District Commissariat in Vilna organized the systematic confiscation of valuables and looted Jewish property left behind in the abandoned houses.[197] Before the creation of the ghettos, the German occupiers were already seizing Jews at random in the street in order to exploit their labour.[198] From spring 1940 onwards, as dissatisfaction with the poor yield from confiscated valuables grew, so did interest in "Jewish labour."[199] From summer 1940, this prompted a change of policy in Lodz, for example, where attention now switched to the organized exploitation of labour power.[200] Ghetto residents were forced to work and produce goods for the Germans, both in internal factories and outside the ghetto, in private firms or labour camps.[201] In Warsaw, Alexander Palfinger, the official in charge of the transfer station coordinating "economic cooperation" between the ghetto and the "Aryan" side, ordered the Jewish Council to organize internal production units from December 1940. This new interest was pursued consistently, especially after May 1941, with the appointment of Heinz Auerswald as commissar for the Jewish Residential District.[202] The workers' paltry wages had to be used by the Jewish Councils to pay the occupiers for the already scarce food supplies needed for the bare survival of the ghetto community.

Even after their decision to embark on the systematic murder of the Jewish population, the Germans still continued to exploit ghetto labour. The same applied to the ghettos established on Soviet territory – as in Vilna, for example – which the Germans now increasingly viewed as labour camps.[203] From now on, ghetto residents were selected or murdered according to their capacity or incapacity for work, and the Jewish Councils were forced to do the Germans' bidding. In occupied Poland, this was still happening covertly in the Warsaw and Lodz ghettos in late 1941 and the first half of 1942, in that the deportations – which effectively meant the murder of those concerned – were sold to the Jewish Councils as "labour transports."[204] With the dissolution of the ghettos and the extermination of the remaining inhabitants, the other, previously acute, German interests became less important. From now on, the all-out extinction of the Jewish population became – against all reason – the Germans' top priority.[205]

Because the anticipation of German core interests and corresponding demands offered a means of averting threats to the ghetto, they exerted a major influence on Jewish Council practice with regard to criminality and law. Disastrously for the Councils, however, those core interests were neither static nor easily discernible.

New Definitions of Criminality

Immediately after the occupation of Poland, the Germans had already begun to define new offences resulting from the anti-Jewish directives in the occupied territories. They also created a new judicial system: Polish courts were preserved at the local and district level and remained in charge of "classical" criminal cases. In addition, however, Hitler issued a decree ordering German Special Courts to be set up under the control of the civil administrations from 8 October 1939. These dealt with cases involving Germans or substantially affecting German interests.[206] The offences discussed below do not cover all criminal activities prosecuted by the German occupiers, but only those which the Jewish Councils deemed relevant to the ghetto-internal legal sphere.

Enforcement of the Ghetto Border

One of the Germans' key concerns was the enforcement of the ghetto border. The geographical separation of the Jewish population that ghettoization was designed to achieve had to be drummed into the ghetto population as well as into the communities living outside its confines.[207] Violations of the relevant regulations were subject to German jurisdiction. The Jewish Councils and the Jewish police agencies under their control were to prosecute all such acts and inform the Germans accordingly or refer the case to the German authority.

Following the establishment of the ghettos in Warsaw, Lodz, and Vilna, the occupiers issued decrees announcing the newly drawn borders and ordering Jewish people to move to the ghetto areas. Subsequent changes to the borders were publicized via posters or loudspeaker announcements.[208] The Germans' territorial ambitions were enforced with the threat of harsh sanctions. In May 1940, for example, SS Brigadier Johannes Schäfer of the German Criminal Police issued the following order in Lodz: "Any attempt by a ghetto resident to leave the ghetto without permission, in any way whatsoever, shall be [prevented] at once with the use of firearms."[209] After the sealing of the ghetto, the offence of "illegal border crossing" – that is, without the permission of the German authorities or the Jewish Council – became a live issue. It was forbidden, for instance, to work outside the ghetto without a pass. Not only "illegal border crossers" but also those aiding and abetting such offenders by failing to inform the German authorities risked severe punishment, as City Plenipotentiary Ludwig Leist made clear on 14 January 1941 in a penal decree regarding the Warsaw ghetto.[210] From 10 November 1941, "unauthorized leaving of the ghetto" became a capital offence in Warsaw.[211] In Lodz, attempts by Germans and Poles to enter the ghetto without permission were likewise to be punished explicitly as criminal acts.[212] These measures show how important it was to the occupiers to imprint the ghetto border on the minds of non-Jews. The geographical segregation of the Jewish and non-Jewish population had been "prepared for" by the Germans with the introduction of compulsory labelling. Thus, "violations of the labelling regulation" – that is, failure to wear the prescribed Star of David – were classed as criminal even before ghettoization. After segregation, less attention was devoted to the prosecution of this offence, although it did not disappear entirely from the agenda. Particularly in ghettos where compulsory labelling had only been introduced shortly before ghettoization, and where residents also had to leave the ghetto to get to work – as in Vilna, for instance – violations continued to be punished and had to be prosecuted by the Jewish police.[213]

Smuggling was probably the most prominent "ghetto offence" defined by the Germans. The common assumption is that they criminalized it because it hampered their plan to starve out the ghetto communities.[214] This was not the declared aim in 1940, however, when the ghettos were first created in occupied Poland. Rather, the Germans saw smuggling or "trafficking" as another threat to the borders of an institution which was initially designed to last for some time. In Lodz, for example, the crackdown on smuggling was often discussed in connection with the need for tighter border security. Moreover, the prevention strategy was directed not only at ghetto residents but also at Poles bringing goods into the ghetto.[215]

From the end of 1941 onwards, when plans were developed for the comprehensive extermination of the Jewish population, the suppression of supplementary food imports into the ghetto became another option for the Germans. The food supply was to be used as a means of retaining control over the ghetto community, and death by starvation was approved at least as a side-effect.[216] Starvation does not, however, appear to have been a primary motive for the prosecution of smuggling even in the Vilna ghetto, which was established as late as September 1941. Although the district commissar, Franz Murer, complained that the Jewish Council was not taking vigorous enough action against smuggling, there is no evidence of any murderous intentions behind this.[217]

The crimes of illegal border crossing and smuggling were especially prominent in the Warsaw and Lodz ghettos, which were set up in 1940. Such activities were also prosecuted by the German authorities in Vilna, but without assigning them to established categories. Thus, while a decree issued by Franz Murer made "bringing too much food into the ghetto" a punishable offence, there was no mention of smuggling.[218]

Compulsory Registration, Public Order, and Hygiene

With the creation of the ghettos, the German occupiers defined which other criminal acts they wanted to be notified of by the Jewish Councils. In Warsaw and Lodz, these included both "political offences" – such as the illegal receipt of messages and the reading and sale of newspapers prohibited in the ghetto, the prosecution of which was officially the business of the Gestapo – and "classical" crimes such as theft, robbery, and murder, which were dealt with by the German Criminal Police.[219]

In Lodz, the Criminal Police also demanded to be informed of suicides.[220] Presumably, the occupiers felt that this would give them an insight into the mood in the ghetto, as panic and unrest might have hindered their plans. In this respect, both internal murders and suicides could serve as a gauge. In the early stages, certain legal conventions seem to have played a role too, and may have led the Germans to reserve cases classified as "serious" for themselves. This situation was initially compounded by the curtailment of the Jewish Councils' criminal investigation powers, which made it impossible for such cases to be followed up within the ghetto. As we shall see, however, German interest in this aspect waned in the second half of 1941, thereby giving the Jewish Councils – officially or unofficially – greater scope for internal prosecutions.

In the case of Vilna, where ghettoization did not take place until 1941, less importance was attached to such an explicit demarcation of powers. By that time, Nazi concepts of "political criminals" such as Bolsheviks and partisans had come to be associated with the stereotype of the "criminal Jew," and, since all Jews were "criminal" in German eyes, it was evidently no longer deemed necessary to make this a dedicated area of responsibility.

Another key German concern was the maintenance of public order, for which the Jewish Councils were held responsible. This included the curfew periods when ghetto residents were not allowed on the streets, for example, along with the accompanying blackout regulations.[221] In the case of Warsaw, Lodz, and Vilna, residents also had to observe the correct greeting when encountering uniformed Germans in the ghetto.[222]

In addition, the German authorities ordered the Jewish Councils to implement measures for the "maintenance of hygiene"; this applied particularly to the period when the ghettos were expected to be in place for some time. Like the topos of the "criminal Jew," Nazi notions of the Jew as a "spreader of disease" capable of undermining the German ethnic community had accompanied the social exclusion of the Jewish population,[223] and signs proclaiming "Warning – danger of epidemics" were now erected at the ghetto borders in Warsaw and Vilna.[224] As Berkowitz has rightly pointed out, the German ghettoization policy created a self-fulfilling prophecy: cramming hundreds of thousands of people into a tiny space with insufficient food supplies and catastrophic hygiene conditions turned the prediction of epidemics and diseases into a reality.[225] In the Warsaw and Lodz ghettos in particular, the Jewish Councils were given concrete instructions for combating the outbreak of epidemics. These included vaccination, delousing of residents and their pets, and cleaning orders.[226] The Germans' overriding fear was that the epidemics might spread beyond the ghetto and infect the surrounding non-Jewish communities.[227] That said, the attitudes of the responsible Nazi functionaries were ambivalent on this point, depending on their respective interests. In September 1939 – that is, even before ghettoization – Himmler, as Reich Commissar for the Consolidation of German Nationhood, had declared that "the time has come to drive this rabble into ghettos, and then epidemics will erupt and they'll all croak."[228] In 1940, when it became clear in occupied Poland that the ghettos would continue to exist for some time, and interest in Jewish labour began to increase, the occupiers ordered the implementation of anti-epidemic measures.[229] This happened even after September 1941 in Vilna, owing to District Commissar Hingst's fears that "Jewish" epidemics might spread to the surrounding population.[230] The actual measures for preventing an outbreak became less explicit as time went on, however, apart from those that harked back to the early days of the ghetto's existence.[231] Nevertheless, as poet and ghetto survivor Abraham Sutzkever records, Gestapo chief August Hering made it abundantly clear from the start what the consequences of an outbreak would be for the ghetto community: "If he were to find even one person with scabies, or a single typhus victim, that would be the end of the ghetto."[232]

The Problem of Definitions

As already discussed, the Germans subscribed to the view that Jews were born criminal. In practice, however, it became apparent that the German concepts of criminality were based on new definitions of criminal behaviour not "naturally" rooted in the minds of the responsible German personnel. This is evident, for example, from an administrative meeting called by the district governor in Lodz in August 1940 regarding the confiscation of "Jewish objects of value." Attendees were reminded of the agreement to confiscate only goods "obtained through criminal activity," and the German Criminal Police were criticized for not adhering to this, as it left the ghetto administration unable to guarantee the food supply for the ghetto community.[233] This led to the identification of a fundamental problem: "At the meetings, the definition of criminal activity was never clarified. Probably, no such definition had ever existed. According to the special instruction of 10.5.1940 issued by the Chief of Police, Criminal Police officers in the 'ghetto' are to deal solely with smuggling, which is what they are there to prevent."[234]

In other cases, the German authorities were unsure whether to classify particular actions as criminal and, if so, which generic crime categories to assign them to. In June 1940, the case of a ghetto resident named Goldberg caused some ambiguity in the Lodz ghetto. The mayor of Lodz accused Goldberg of selling the banned newspaper *Litzmannstädter Zeitung* within the ghetto.[235] The accused objected that he had been unaware that this constituted a "forbidden activity," since even the German police officers had bought the paper from him.[236] The mayor had initially defined this activity as the sale of an illegal newspaper, and hence as a political offence, for which the Gestapo had been declared officially responsible. Now, however, it was to be classified on his instructions as a "smuggling matter" and referred accordingly to the German Criminal Police.[237] In Warsaw, too, the plethora of new German crime definitions and regulations led to a certain amount of confusion: at the beginning of 1942, a "News Gazette for the Jewish Residential District in Warsaw" was published summarizing all the orders and proclamations issued up to that point. This was considered necessary not just as a means of informing the ghetto population: as expressly stated, it had also "increasingly proved a shortcoming that not all interested authorities are aware of these publications and that, with the proliferation of announcements and proclamations, it has become progressively harder to collect and maintain an overview of them all. For this reason, the publication of a special bulletin proved indispensable."[238]

Arbitrary Actions and Paradoxical Developments

From a Jewish Council perspective, German demands, crime definitions, and consequent prosecutions were characterized by arbitrariness and brutality. Temporary insights into German core interests would be gleaned, only to be confounded again. Nowhere was this more apparent than in the context of smuggling. After the creation of the Warsaw and Lodz ghettos in 1940, smuggling cases were initially tried by German Special Courts. Officially, the Special Court judges were obliged to apply German law, but the sentences and judgment criteria were generally much more severe when Poles or Jews were in the dock, and death penalties were common.[239] After 1942 in particular, cases were only considered worth bringing before the Special Courts if they were deemed relevant to the *Volksgemeinschaft* (German ethnic community).[240] While a large number of smuggling offences were tried there initially, correspondence from the Lodz ghetto court from 1942 onwards makes frequent reference to cases dropped on the grounds that they were "not in the public interest," resulting in the punishment of the accused without trial. From thereon in, the Special Courts only had a role to play where Germans were involved as the "injured party."[241]

Outside the realms of criminal law practice, decisions and actions often proved dependent on the individual case or situation. For example, one report of 10 July 1940 by the German Criminal Police concerning a Jewish woman named Hala Schweizer states: "She left the ghetto having removed the Star of David for that purpose, in order to import food for her own use from the city centre into the ghetto ... The food was in a bag in a revolting condition, and was returned to her. The 1 RM was also returned."[242] Such reports exist for the early period in particular, when the ghetto border was officially enforced and smuggling was supposed to be rigorously pursued. As they demonstrate, however, food was also returned to residents when the quantities involved were small.[243] At the same time, German police officers in Lodz and Warsaw often shot smugglers directly at the ghetto border, and abuses were rife among German, Polish, and Lithuanian police, who routinely enriched themselves with smuggled goods and bribes.[244] After the Germans clamped down on smuggling and illegal border crossings in the Warsaw ghetto from autumn 1941 onwards, the number of residents executed for this reason rose significantly.[245]

The punishment of illegal border crossings could be equally brutal. Eight inmates of the ghetto prison on Gęsia Street were shot by the Germans on 17 November 1941, followed by a further twelve in December 1941.[246] By contrast, just a few months later, in March 1942, Heinz Auerswald – as commissar for the Jewish Residential District – declared an amnesty whereby 151 inmates held in the ghetto central prison for offences including "illegal border crossing" were spared the death penalty.[247] This action is likely to have been prompted by the declining relevance of such offences in light of the new plans for wholesale extermination.

Writing on German criminal procedure in his Warsaw ghetto diary, Ringelblum remarked: "It was believed that everything was permissible, that the Germans were not concerned about what Jews thought, but only went after illegal trading."[248] Engelking and Leociak conclude similarly that the German occupiers were more interested in illegal trade than political offences.[249] In fact, "political crimes," though classed as relevant, were actually pursued relatively rarely. Again, one reason for this may have been the occupiers' tendency – particularly after the invasion of the Soviet Union, and the association of Bolshevism with "Jewish criminals" – to regard ghetto residents per se as "political criminals." It is also conceivable that they underestimated the potential of underground activities inside the ghetto.[250] In the few cases where Germans intervened as a result of "political crimes," they did so with extreme brutality. In Warsaw, they executed 52 ghetto residents on 17/18 April 1942 – known as the "St Bartholomew's Day Massacre of the ghetto" – for the "political crime" of printing underground newspapers.[251] In June 1942, 110 inmates of the ghetto prison were shot for "resisting German orders."[252] In Vilna, the Witenberg affair sparked terror in the ghetto community: following a German raid, underground fighters from Vilna had revealed the name of the commander of the Fareynigte Partizaner Organizatsie (FPO), Yitzhak Witenberg. The Gestapo ordered Gens to hand him over on pain of liquidation of the ghetto. After several meetings between Gens and the FPO leadership, who called for armed rebellion, Witenberg was duly surrendered. The next day, he was found dead, with signs of torture on his body.[253] The case brought home vividly to Gens the reality of German punitive mechanisms, and his dilemma as chairman of the Jewish Council.

The German treatment of "classical" crimes such as murders within the ghetto was highly variable. In Lodz, they had tried the first internal murder case before the Special Court in April 1941.[254] Thereafter, as the jurisdiction of the ghetto court was extended, they delegated the task of sentencing to the Jewish Council. As we shall see, however, they often decided on a case-by-case basis whether to intervene in ghetto practice and deport prisoners convicted of murder by ghetto courts. In Warsaw and Lodz, by contrast, the Germans took very little interest in ghetto-internal murders and robberies, a fact which gave the Jewish Councils added room for manoeuvre in this area of criminal procedure.

Since the Germans regarded Jews per se as criminal, the same ideological premise could, in case of doubt, be used to justify despotism, brutality, and murder. As Jacob Robinson writes on this subject, "Law was of no practical value. Each German could break the law with impunity if, in his view, it was not in accordance with German interests."[255] This invites the question of why the Germans bothered to define crimes and legal norms at all. Berkowitz argues convincingly that it served as a means of self-assurance: "The Germans had to erect a veneer of legality not only for the sake of appearance to the Jews and the subject Polish population, but also to assure themselves that they were the supreme guardians of law and order."[256]

The German prosecution of criminal acts by ghetto residents continued to be based on German crime definitions for a relatively long period. Consequently, even when the German police shot people directly at the ghetto border, their written statements would describe this as a response to smuggling or illegal border crossing, for example. From the end of 1941, following the German decision to proceed with the organized murder of the Jewish population, it seems to have become increasingly irrelevant which offences ghetto residents had actually committed. As far as the Jewish Councils were concerned, the Germans' fading interest in criminal prosecution gave them, to some extent, a new freedom to define and enforce their own evaluation criteria within the ghetto. Where the Germans did intervene, on the other hand, their actions were even more arbitrary, ruthless, and far-reaching than before.

It was against this background that the Jewish Councils tried to identify German interests in order to react in a flexible and ad hoc manner to behaviours that could trigger brutal German intervention. This found specific expression in the way the Councils endeavoured to entrench and prosecute criminal offences. Despite their differences in terms of the period of ghettoization, the personnel involved, and the perceived scope for action in the face of fluctuating German plans, the Jewish Councils in all three ghettos established legal institutions and procedures at their own initiative as part of the ghetto-internal administration. These became crucial tools in the Councils' quest to "keep the ghetto calm" and their desperate attempt to prevent German intervention that could endanger the whole ghetto community.

Chapter Two

Jewish Council Proclamations:
Definitions of Criminal Activity

You don't know what you're allowed to do, and most often you find you're not allowed to do anything, and so all social activities, whether economic or cultural, are driven underground, into the realm of illegality.[1]

This comment on life in the Warsaw ghetto – written by Stanisław Różycki in December 1941 – was true of all ghetto communities. No one knew what constituted criminal activity. Therefore, it was up to the Jewish Councils to clarify which actions would, in the new reality of German occupation, pose a threat to peaceful coexistence and hence to life itself, and which would consequently be considered punishable offences.

The Jewish Councils in the Warsaw, Lodz, and Vilna ghettos differed in their approach to the communication of new offences and rules. In Lodz, Rumkowski professionalized this practice, publishing a raft of proclamations (*obwieszczenia*) concerning new crimes, regulations, and corresponding sanctions, only a few of which arose directly from German commands. Most served to introduce internal rules aimed at shoring up newly created ghetto institutions, or to highlight activities potentially harmful to the ghetto community. Proclamations were also published in the Warsaw and Vilna ghettos, but generally as a direct means of relaying German instructions.[2] As we shall see, similar offences to many of those defined by Rumkowski in relation to the Lodz ghetto were also defined in Warsaw and Vilna.

The majority of Rumkowski's proclamations were issued in 1940 and 1941, when he was setting up an internal administration and was still granted a certain amount of freedom by the Germans.[3] They were usually drawn up in three languages – German, Polish, and Yiddish – and displayed at central points in the ghetto.[4] An important supplementary role was played by the Council-initiated *Geto-Tsaytung*, which was published regularly from March to September 1941 in order to communicate and clarify the latest decrees.[5] Its declared purpose was to "keep residents informed of all ghetto affairs and explain exactly what is and is not allowed."[6]

Through his proclamations, Rumkowski sought to impose his rules – and hence his survival strategy – on the ghetto population. In autumn 1941, for instance, they were used to help integrate the 20,000 new arrivals from the west as quickly as possible into a coerced community of people who often had little in common except the German-defined label "Jewish." On 7 November 1941, Rumkowski warned that "newcomers" must adjust immediately to ghetto conditions and follow his instructions precisely or face sanctions. They had "no right to preferential treatment,"[7] but were to conform straightaway to existing ghetto regulations introduced during the previous months.[8]

New definitions of criminality were announced not only via billboards but also through internal newspapers. In Warsaw, for instance, ghetto residents turned to the dedicated columns of the *Gazeta Żydowska* to find out which activities were "permitted" or "prohibited," and which institutions were responsible for what. By printing both question and answer, the paper was able to make the information available to all.[9] On 6 June 1941, one reader asked the editors whether he had any legal means of accessing his bank balance, for example. The paper did not appear to be very well informed, however, advising him to try the Jewish Council legal department or, failing that, to take the matter to a Polish court.[10]

By reporting on incidents such as theft, ration card fraud, or confidence trickery[11] and publishing the verdicts of the ghetto courts,[12] the papers served to warn readers and alert them to what would henceforward be classified by the Jewish Council as a crime subject to prosecution and punishment. This was especially true of activities arising from the specific conditions of the "ghetto lifeworld," and which were not previously regarded as criminal. In Vilna, the *Geto-Yedies* of 14 March 1943 reported, for example, on a case in which a resident named Ema Z. had failed to appear for work and was consequently sentenced to imprisonment by the ghetto police. Another resident allowed himself to be arrested in her place, but the "fraud" was discovered when the responsible ghetto police officer queried the appearance of a woman's name on the arrest warrant. The matter was referred to the court, where both residents were sentenced to a week's detention and Ema Z. to an additional fine.[13]

German Demands and Their Assimilation
into Ghetto-Internal Jurisdiction

Separating German definitions of criminality from ghetto-internal ones is no easy feat, because the actions of the Jewish Council were premised on compliance with German demands as a strategy for saving the ghetto community. To this extent, the set of norms operating within the ghetto was inevitably influenced by those demands. Whether and how the Councils made this clear in their proclamations, for instance by prefacing them with "by order of the German authorities," tells us which German demands they adopted as their own at which point.[14]

The proclamations issued immediately after the creation of the ghetto in Lodz arose directly from German orders and related initially to the consolidation of the ghetto border. The proclamation of 8 May 1940, for example, read: "According to Section 2 of the Police Regulation issued by the District Governor for the Residential District of Lodz on 14.2.1940, it is a punishable offence for Jews to leave their place of residence. I hereby declare the ghetto district in Lodz a 'place of residence' for the purposes of this Police Regulation."[15] The document was signed jointly by Police Chief and SS Brigadier Johannes Schäfer and Rumkowski as Jewish Council chairman. In other words, German authorship was still explicitly acknowledged at this stage. On 9 July 1940, a further notice was displayed stating, "By order of the authorities, I hereby declare that it is *strictly* forbidden for those living inside the ghetto to *talk* with persons on the other side of the fence."[16]

Although the Germans expressly demanded that smuggling be prosecuted, Rumkowski seldom made a point of this in the proclamations. This reticence may have been due to his ambivalence on the subject: on one hand, smugglers brought precious foodstuffs into the ghetto, thereby helping to keep it supplied.[17] On the other, collective death penalties were a constant threat, and German guards regularly shot (alleged) smugglers at the ghetto border.[18] Accused by the German authorities of neglecting his duty to combat smuggling, Rumkowski addressed the ghetto population in spring 1941 via the *Geto-Tsaytung*: "Unnecessary walking along the fence provides ideal cover for irresponsible smugglers who will stop at nothing in order to line their own pockets, regardless of any mortal danger to innocent people."[19] Here, the chairman was not threatening smugglers directly with punishment, but appealing to residents who unwittingly facilitated the practice by hugging the perimeter fence.

In Vilna, the Jewish Council's attitude to smuggling was similarly ambivalent, but manifested itself less in proclamations than in ghetto police practice.[20] Here, in addition to the ban on leaving the ghetto, the Germans insisted on compulsory labelling. In this case, it was Jakub Gens, as ghetto police chief, who issued orders to this effect from December 1941, supported by the threat of internal sanctions: "Any persons found in the ghetto without the Star of David will be fined five roubles ... Going out of the gate of the ghetto without a yellow permit or special permission from the Chief of Police is strictly forbidden"; "those attempting to go through the gate of the ghetto will be sentenced to a fine of ten roubles."[21]

Although residents of the Lodz ghetto were also obliged to wear the "badge," there was no need for an explicit proclamation by the Jewish Council. In contrast to the situation in Vilna, where compulsory labelling was not introduced until shortly before ghettoization, the Jewish population of occupied Poland had already had similar legal requirements imposed on it by the Germans several months before.

German notions of public order – such as curfew and blackout regulations – also had to be implemented within the ghetto communities themselves. In this context, a certain evolution can be observed in Rumkowski's proclamations. For a short while after their introduction in October 1940, he continued to mention the original Gestapo order,[22] but dropped it in subsequent announcements concerning curfews and general curfews.[23] The same was true of blackout regulations for homes and factories during curfew hours. At first, Rumkowski continued to allude to the "order of the *authorities*,"[24] and the threatened penalties were couched in very general terms.[25] From 1941, the population was threatened with the withdrawal of its power supply,[26] and in 1944 we find: "Violators of home blackout regulations will be arrested and have their current cut off, while those responsible for blackout procedures in offices, workshops, and factories will be sentenced to detention."[27] This is a typical example of how German orders were assimilated into ghetto-internal jurisdiction. Since violations risked harming the ghetto community, Rumkowski made the cause of compliance his own. Similar blackout and curfew regulations were introduced in Vilna by police chief Gens, backed up by the threat of severe punishment by the ghetto police.[28]

By contrast, the "obligation to salute" was presented consistently across all ghettos as an explicitly German order. In May 1942, Rumkowski addressed a letter to the ghetto population stipulating that all German officials and persons in uniform were to be greeted with a salute.[29] Two weeks later, an emphatic reminder was issued because of lack of compliance.[30] The same obligation was introduced by the Jewish Council in Vilna, making reference to its originator both in a proclamation and in the ghetto newspaper.[31] Here too, the order was reiterated following a complaint by Murer that it was being ignored.[32]

Numerous other German orders governing areas irrelevant to German core interests were communicated by Vilna's Jewish Council via proclamations acknowledging German authorship. These included regulations forbidding women to use make-up or dress "elegantly,"[33] a ban on pregnancies,[34] and – at Murer's insistence – a ban on smoking on Jewish Council premises, which effectively outlawed the use of any combustible material.[35] Orders of this kind were issued far more frequently in Vilna than in Lodz or Warsaw, and were either proclaimed directly by the German occupiers or relayed via the Jewish Councils quoting the German text.

A whole cluster of proclamations arose surrounding the German core interest in objects of value and labour power. The Jewish Council in Lodz embraced the confiscation of valuables in the hope that this would help secure the provisioning and survival of the community – as is clear from the relevant orders, which were signed by Rumkowski without reference to their German origin.[36] Through a series of proclamations, he tried to persuade ghetto residents to surrender their valuables voluntarily by guaranteeing them immunity from punishment despite the fact that the possession of items such as gold or foreign currency was already forbidden.[37] In this case, he hoped to be able to further his cause not by threatening sanctions in the usual way but by offering "rewards."[38]

While Rumkowski issued an appeal in June 1942 urging residents of the Lodz ghetto to deposit furs at his ghetto banks,[39] the German commissar for the Jewish Residential District in Warsaw had ordered the surrender of furs, on pain of severe punishment, in a proclamation of December 1941: "Jews remaining in possession of surrenderable items after the allotted period of time will be shot."[40] And the warnings were no less harsh in Vilna, where the Jewish Council relayed a similar German order to ghetto residents on 28 December 1941, echoing the German threat of shooting in the event of non-compliance.[41]

In accordance with the high priority Rumkowski placed on "rescue through labour" in the Lodz ghetto, many of his proclamations related to the organization of the internal labour sphere. On 26 October 1940, for example, the following notice appeared in the ghetto: "Due to the large volume of orders for my tailoring and underwear workshops, *sewing machines* are needed most urgently. I therefore call on all those in possession of sewing machines – whether for work or private use – to loan them to the community. Those who refuse to make their sewing machines ... available voluntarily will be punished and their machines confiscated."[42] In addition to the surrender of necessary work tools, Rumkowski also ordered residents who were "fit for work" to register or risk sanctions.[43] When the Germans demanded quotas for "labour transports" at the beginning of 1942, Rumkowski appealed personally to residents earmarked for "resettlement" to appear punctually or be *"apprehended by force"* and compelled to leave their luggage behind.[44] In January 1942, he issued an emphatic warning to the community not to shelter those selected for deportation; otherwise the harbouring families and house watchmen would be "resettled" likewise.[45]

Unlike Rumkowski, the chairman of the Warsaw Jewish Council, Adam Czerniaków, had announced the forced labour policy introduced prior to ghettoization with clear reference to its German origin: "Pursuant to the order of 26 October 1939 issued by the Generalgouvernement regarding the introduction of compulsory labour for the Jewish population of the district, and pursuant to the second executive order of 12.XII.1939 and the instruction of 27.I.1940 issued by the acting Mayor of Warsaw, the Chairman of the Jewish Council hereby declares as follows: all Jewish men between the ages of twelve and sixty inclusive must appear in person on the following dates in order to be registered in the file of persons subject to compulsory labour."[46] During the preparations for the first "resettlements," Czerniaków subsequently announced on 22 July 1942 that residents employed in German enterprises were to continue their work,[47] threatening that "anyone failing to comply with this order will be punished most severely."[48] Here again, he made explicit reference to the German order. In Czerniaków's case, therefore, the German demands for Jewish labour and the surrender of "unproductive" residents were not assimilated unconditionally into a set of internal norms.

Like Rumkowski in Lodz, the Jewish Council in Vilna was consistent in declaring the assurance of "ghetto productivity" its central task. In January 1942, for example, the Council's labour department made the following announcement on its own behalf: "Workers are warned not to leave their workplaces, on pain of punishment. Should a worker be unable to report for work, he must submit a letter explaining the reason to the Labour Department."[49] The regulations did not appear to achieve the desired effect, however. In a proclamation of April 1942, District Commissar Murer personally reiterated that leaving one's workplace was a punishable offence.[50] The fact that people stayed away from work despite German and ghetto-internal orders to the contrary suggests that – in view of the thousands already shot in Ponary – they no longer believed in the strategy of "rescue through labour." After January 1943, Gens warned that "work deserters" would face flogging in future, as well as a spell in the ghetto prison. Repeat offenders would be turned over to the Lithuanians and Germans.[51]

Ghetto-Internal Regulations and Sanctions

Rumkowski's proclamations also served to govern areas of ghetto life which were not at first sight relevant to German core interests. He used them, for instance, to publicize newly created institutions and regulations and clarify the obligations arising from them, often accompanied by the threat of severe sanctions in the event of non-compliance. Typical examples were the organization of food distribution within the ghetto and the allocation of housing. One such proclamation, of 6 June 1940, required residents to register for rationing, adding: "Those who fail to register will not only lose their right to food rations but will also be *punished*."[52]

The Jewish Council had been entrusted with the resettlement arrangements via a German police regulation of February 1940.[53] When residents had to move to other parts of the ghetto at the beginning of 1941 to make way for the construction of a tramline,[54] Rumkowski ordered them to wait for instructions from his resettlement commission: "I must … forbid any unauthorized removals, as this is sure to be exploited by irresponsible people for their own ends, and the result would be pure chaos. Anyone moving to a new apartment in contravention of the above will be compulsorily resettled, together with all tenants of that apartment. Furthermore, food ration cards will *not* be reissued to the new address, meaning that they will receive *no food allocation*."[55] In Vilna, Gens – as head of the ghetto police – also used a proclamation in December 1941 in his attempt to enforce the relocation of residents through the housing department, warning that anyone occupying accommodation not officially allocated by the Jewish Council would be "banished" from the ghetto.[56]

Other proclamations were used by Rumkowski to regulate the registration of ghetto residents, including births, as well as the procedure for ghetto burials.[57] On 26 March 1940, he ordered the appointment of house committees within three days, accompanied by the threat: "those who fail to comply with my request will be punished most severely."[58] This was followed by a series of regulations defining the duties and responsibilities of the house committees and house managers, which involved overseeing the general cleanliness, order, and safety of the apartment buildings together with specific tasks such as snow clearing.[59] Failure to fulfil these obligations would result in the instant dismissal of the house manager without pay.

From spring 1941, the Jewish Council chairman made increasing appeals to the ghetto population to save electricity and limit their use of lighting and electric cooking appliances. On 3 March 1941, for instance, he stipulated that "bulbs above fifteen watts may not be used in any room," adding that checks would be carried out and the current cut off in case of non-compliance.[60] The reason for this measure was that the German ghetto administration charged Rumkowski for electricity used in the ghetto, and was constantly putting up the price.[61]

Rumkowski's aim in creating an internal administration was to meet German demands effectively and guarantee the provisioning of the ghetto community. Consequently, any actions directed against his institutions jeopardized the operation of the "ghetto system" and could, ultimately, lead the German occupiers to decide against the continued maintenance of the ghetto itself.

In addition, Rumkowski defined as criminal several activities which he saw as "harmful to the ghetto as a whole." After 1940, for example, he censured the "unjustified claiming of relief aid" by the unemployed since the previous September. This was notably the case directly after ghettoization, when many people had yet to be integrated into the work environment.[62] Untruthful statements were to be *"punished most severely,"* and any such application would be cancelled immediately, with those concerned being publicly named[63] and their right to payments withdrawn.[64] Anyone registering a claim for relief aid while still in possession of items of value was likewise deemed guilty of "fraud." Those who abused the system would have their valuables confiscated; moreover, they would have to pay back the entire sum and submit to drastic sanctions.[65] Writing in the *Geto-Tsaytung*, Rumkowski remonstrated: "Relief aid is for all those who have no other source of income, and not for layabouts or people with goods and valuables. Such people are under obligation to sell their property to my authorized purchasing agencies and live off the proceeds, not at the expense of the community."[66]

The accusation of "scrounging off the community" was a serious one: in keeping with his belief that the "productivity" of the ghetto would determine the life or death of its inhabitants, Rumkowski prioritized their capacity for work over everything. "Labour in the ghetto" would guarantee their survival; those unfit for work had to be "carried" by the workers.[67] Consequently, "illegitimate" drains on benefits and hence on the ghetto community's already scarce resources posed a threat to survival. In a bid to crack down on abuse, Rumkowski therefore deployed inspectors to search the apartments of relief aid applicants.[68]

After 1941, Rumkowski had to turn his attention to a further offence: the appropriation of food ration cards belonging to the sick.[69] Strict penalties applied not just to the card users but also to patients who – in violation of Jewish Council regulations – failed to surrender their cards before admission to hospital.[70] In 1942, another variant of this offence occurred when residents continued to use ration cards belonging to the over 15,000 people deported by the Gestapo in September of that year. Faced with this situation, Rumkowski was obliged to issue a stern reprimand:[71] residents using cards belonging to the deported would be caught and "punished most severely."[72] The fact that Rumkowski was forced to define these practices as crimes was due to the nature of the ghetto provisioning system. The small quantity of food allocated by the Germans was based on the number of inhabitants, and reduced accordingly after deportations: therefore, if some people used obsolete ration cards to claim more than they were entitled to, others would no longer receive their proper share.

The definition of crime was, in other words, based on a specific understanding of the balance between self-interest and the common good. Under the constraints of ghettoization, living at the expense of the community for "selfish" reasons meant jeopardizing the welfare – and, at worst, the life – of the whole population, and was therefore criminal in Rumkowski's eyes.

New crimes were also defined in the context of food distribution. From January 1940, a dedicated provisioning department under the supervision of Mengel Awigdor Szczęśliwy had assumed the distribution of the scant rations provided by the Germans.[73] The house committees were in turn responsible for distribution within residential blocks.[74] From the second half of 1940, Rumkowski announced that house committees were forbidden to withhold food rations in order to sell them on. Violations would be punished "with a fine, up to three months' imprisonment or both."[75] Victims were to inform him of any instances of missing rations and the persons responsible via a letter of complaint. The chairman warned: "I will deal with the leaders of the house committees so severely that such cases will never occur again."[76]

By the end of 1940, when Rumkowski dissolved the house committees and centralized food distribution, such "abuses" appear to have become rife. Under the new system, residents purchased ration cards from the Provisioning Department bank, which enabled them to buy food from public cooperatives in exchange for coupons called "talons."[77] Some items, such as vegetables, were also sold at higher prices in stores (known as *Freiverkauf*).[78] However, with the reorganization new practices emerged, with ghetto inhabitants now selling food – often from their own rations – at horrendous prices on the black market.[79] In response, Rumkowski banned the ghetto population from trading with food issued by the rationing department, whether on the street or in stores.[80] He branded the abusers "profiteers and speculators,"[81] threatening them with confiscation of the goods, closure of their stores, and imprisonment in the event of repeat offences,[82] and appealed to the community to notify the ghetto police of any cases of food being sold at "exorbitant prices."[83]

Poorer residents were allowed to sell part of their rations in order to be able to afford other foods.[84] What Rumkowski deemed "criminal," by contrast – as he spelled out in the *Geto-Tsaytung* in May 1941 – was the practice of selling for selfish reasons, in order to enrich oneself. In his view, "trafficking" was reprehensible if it operated on a "professional" basis and was purely for the purpose of profiteering: "It appears that a certain proportion of goods, some from rationing and some stolen, is being sold not by private individuals in genuine need, but by professional retailers, speculators and smugglers practised in exploiting the economic situation for criminal ends ... I therefore reiterate my intention to stamp out such a trade, that seeks to extract every last pfennig from the population in order to line the pockets of traffickers."[85]

For their part, ghetto residents railed repeatedly against the Jewish Council's food distribution policy, accusing Rumkowski and his staff of enriching themselves while the majority of the community suffered disease and hunger.[86] There was, however, no authority they could appeal to in order to assert their own moral values. According to a German decree, only the Jewish Council chairman was empowered to set binding internal rules.

Rumkowski's efforts to maintain the health of the ghetto population led to the definition of a plethora of unusual and diverse offences. On 16 July 1941, for example, he posted the following proclamation on a billboard in the Lodz ghetto: "This is my last warning against the production and sale of candy and confectionery. I will punish anyone continuing to produce confectionery with a minimum of three months' imprisonment. Their merchandise, along with the raw materials and production equipment, will be seized and confiscated. Anyone caught selling candy and confectionery will also be arrested and the merchandise confiscated ... In the case of children, the merchandise will be confiscated, the parents punished by me, and the family will lose its entitlement to relief aid. Children without family will be taken to my reformatory at the prison."[87] The announcement was signed "Chaim Rumkowski. The Eldest of the Jews in Lodz."

The ban on private food production did not apply only to candy. On 12 November 1940, the following proclamation was also posted: "It has come to my attention that, alongside my sausage factory and sales outlets, there are a number of unlegalized businesses producing and selling their own sausage without authorization. This sausage is made from unhealthy ingredients in unhygienic conditions, and is therefore harmful to the health of the population. For health reasons, I have therefore decided to prohibit clandestine sausage production."[88] The ban was to come into force five days later, on 17 November 1941, accompanied by the following sanctions: confiscation of the goods, closure of the stores, and punishment of the sellers.[89] Rumkowski justified these bans by arguing that the products could endanger the health of the ghetto population. Writing in the *Geto-Tsaytung*, he explained: "The above-mentioned irresponsible, harmful elements operate in the worst, unsanitary conditions, as well as using substances which are hazardous to health and can cause epidemic diseases, against which I am fighting a constant battle."[90]

The theft of wood "from the public realm" for heating purposes – a widespread practice in the ghetto – was censured by the Jewish Council not only on legal grounds but also for reasons of public health, as illustrated by a proclamation of 21 April 1941: "Since timber is disappearing daily from whole buildings and even newly built or repaired toilets and waste pits – often leaving nothing but open pits full of faeces – such thefts constitute an exceptionally *grave danger to the ghetto population*."[91] The fear was that sickness and disease could break out as a result.

In the *Geto-Tsaytung*, Rumkowski blamed "social wreckers," accusing them of jeopardizing the cohesion of the ghetto. They did not consider, he wrote, that their actions "exposed their neighbours to the risk of catastrophes, bringing various diseases and epidemics in their wake."[92] For this reason, wood theft and vandalism were classed as crimes and punished with three months' hard labour and confiscation of the stolen material.[93] In addition, the Jewish Council set up two committees: one on sanitary affairs, to oversee the containment of hygiene risks, and one on legal affairs, to develop a specific penal code for "wood thieves."[94] The natural desire to prevent disease was compounded by a further factor: given the Nazi image of Jews as "disease carriers," which had accompanied their social exclusion through to the point of ghettoization, there was a justified fear that, if epidemics were indeed to break out, the Germans would murder the ghetto community as a "disease control" measure.[95]

In the Warsaw ghetto, the deputy Jewish Council chairman Marek Lichtenbaum adopted a similar stance, announcing at the end of August 1942 that "all buildings in the Jewish Residential District – whether commercial premises or private dwellings – [were] to be kept suitably clean."[96] Here, too, house committees with house watchmen were established by the Jewish Council and, in addition to performing organizational and welfare tasks, played an important role in implementing the Council's directives within the residential buildings.[97] Those guilty of non-compliance with house-cleaning requirements would be "held criminally responsible,"[98] with the onus placed on house watchmen in particular. A "cleanliness week" was held in January 1943, which, although instigated by the Germans, was presented by the Jewish Council as being emphatically in the interests of the ghetto population as a whole in that it would prevent disease and save lives.[99] The threatened sanctions were to be applied internally, although their exact nature remained as yet unspecified: violators would face "coercive action"[100] or "severe punishment."[101]

Of the few surviving proclamations of the Warsaw Jewish Council, the majority relate to the maintenance of "cleanliness and hygiene" in the ghetto.[102] Although they arose from German orders, here too the responsibility was placed in the hands of the ghetto-internal administration. By this time, the Germans had already deported thousands of ghetto inhabitants, and the Jewish Council was aware of their extermination campaign. For this reason, it feared that an outbreak of sickness and disease would quickly destroy hopes of saving at least part of the ghetto community.

Another significant offence was that of "disturbance of the peace and public order." This covered a variety of activities including rumour-mongering. In 1940, Rumkowski issued several proclamations on this subject,[103] claiming for example that a rumoured suspension of the 8 p.m. curfew had caused residents to go out into the streets in spite of the ban.[104] On another occasion, rumours had led them to doubt the quality of the meat supplied in Jewish Council stores.[105] According to the Council chairman, this was the work of "irresponsible underworld provocateurs"[106] who were trying to sow unrest and so "sabotage"[107] his plans.[108] In response, he announced measures far severer than those that had gone before, and urged the ghetto population to inform him of any "persons spreading false rumours."[109] One proclamation of 15 November 1940 reads: "Anyone who becomes aware of any rumour-mongers is requested to send me their names in writing. Letters should be placed in the mailbox for Petitions and Complaints, Hanseatenstr. 27. In so doing, you will not only be helping me, but also yourselves."[110]

The stigmatization of "gossip" was, in the first instance, a result of the Jewish Council's desire to maintain "peace and order" in the ghetto in order to prevent a (brutal) intervention by the Germans and the consequent endangerment of the community at large.[111] The risks associated with rumour-mongering were far harder to assess than in the case of other offences, as it was virtually impossible to identify the "culprits," or predict either the response of the ghetto community or the resulting actions of the Germans. Rumkowski's wrath may have had a further cause, however. In the proclamation of 15 November 1941, in which he pledged to clamp down on "rumour-mongers," he insisted that only information published in his proclamations was "true" and "accurate."[112] In an earlier address of 30 August 1941, he had already stressed how important he felt the early days of the ghetto had been, with hindsight, to the stabilization of his authority and the implementation of his strategies: "Great efforts were made to maintain peace in the ghetto – a peace that serves as a safeguard against possible and unpredictable shocks."[113] This suggests that he was aware of the precariousness of his situation and feared for his authority: he had been appointed by the Germans to carry out their orders, not elected by the ghetto community as their representative, yet he was dependent at the same time on the latter's compliance.[114]

The Jewish Councils in Vilna and Warsaw also saw the rumour mill as a threat to "peace and order" within the ghetto community. Writing in the *Geto-Yedies* of 30 November 1942, Jakub Gens labelled residents who spread rumours of impending deportations "venomous snakes" and "scaremongers,"[115] and classified this activity as an "offence" punishable by the ghetto police with up to forty-eight hours' detention.[116]

In Warsaw, Czerniaków threatened similar penalties for rumour-mongering.[117] Following his death, the second Council chairman, Marek Lichtenbaum, feared a loss of support from the ghetto community and within Council ranks after guaranteeing the implementation of German "resettlements" in Czerniaków's place. In October 1942, after the Germans had deported thousands of residents, thereby boosting the popularity of the underground resistance and weakening the institutions of the ghetto's self-administration body, he called on Jewish Council staff to pledge themselves to "unconditional fulfilment of their obligations."[118] In a letter, he threatened severe punishments for non-compliance with these demands. At a time when people's first thought – Council staff included – was for their own survival and that of their closest family members, Lichtenbaum argued for the good of the community: "No one should count on evading my vigilance or eliciting my sympathy, the extension of which towards a harmful individual would, to my mind, constitute a crime against the collective."[119]

German Demands in the Context of the Deportations

On 4 August 1944, a proclamation was posted in the Lodz ghetto that differed from its predecessors and was signed not by Rumkowski but by Otto Bradfisch, the mayor of Lodz. The text read: "Since Plants I and II did *not* follow Instruction No. 417 of 2.8.1944 regarding evacuation of the ghetto, the following measures have been decreed with immediate effect: 1. Food rations for employees of tailoring plants I and II will be STOPPED WITH IMMEDIATE EFFECT. Rations will *only* be dispensed at the Radegast depot. 2. Anyone who gives shelter or food to an employee of tailoring plants I and II WILL BE PUNISHED BY DEATH."[120] This proclamation was issued during the last mass transports from the ghetto – now bound, for the first time, for Auschwitz-Birkenau. It was prompted by the failure of ghetto residents, particularly those working in the last remaining tailoring shops, to comply with the German order to report to the Radegast depot in preparation for the "evacuation of the ghetto." By now, the fate of deportees was common knowledge.

Rumkowski had been required to supply quotas for the German deportations – described at first as "labour transports" – since December 1941. Even after learning that the deportees were going to their deaths, however, the chairman persisted in publishing the German orders in his own name. His strategy of "rescue through labour" also included the practice of "self-selection" according to German criteria of "fitness" (or otherwise) for work. Following Bradfisch's proclamation of 4 August 1944, Rumkowski continued to appeal to the ghetto population, as on 13 August, for example: "In their own interest, I advise residents to report for the transports voluntarily in order to avoid coercive measures"[121] (such as being denied the right to bring luggage).

Whereas, in Lodz, the Jewish Council adopted German demands as its own even in the context of deportations, a clearer separation is evident in the case of Warsaw, as we can see from the official language used. Czerniaków had followed the German order to prepare for the "resettlements to the East" by issuing a notice on 22 July 1942 instructing all residents employed in German factories to continue going about their work or risk sanctions.[122] While signing the document in the name of "the Jewish Council in Warsaw," he nevertheless stated that the instructions were "by order of the officer in charge of resettlement."[123]

After Czerniaków's suicide, his successor, Marek Lichtenbaum, complied with all further German orders – including cooperating over the deportations. To this end, he issued a whole series of proclamations in German and Polish preparing the ground for the German-imposed "resettlements." Unlike Rumkowski in Lodz, he consistently advertised the German authorship of the orders, using wording such as "by order of the officer in charge" or "by order of the authorities," "the Jewish Council in Warsaw hereby announces the following."[124]

With the beginning of the "resettlements," the Germans inflicted rigorous demands on the Jewish Council, including the duty to guarantee obedience with their lives.[125] Proclamations were now also more strictly regulated, following a letter from the German authorities detailing exactly how they were to be framed during the "resettlements": "The Jewish Council shall post the following notice to the Jewish population on billboards ... By order of the German authorities, all Jewish persons, regardless of ... etc. from points 1 to 4."[126] The sanctions threatened in these notices usually meant the death penalty, reflecting German-imposed concepts of law and punishment.[127] In addition, extra food rations were promised – as in Lodz – as an incentive to anyone actively volunteering for the transports.[128]

Once the deportations began, the Jewish Council was forced more than ever to act in a manner contrary to the welfare (and life) of the ghetto community. Moreover, the Germans appear to have issued stricter and more strongly worded instructions in Warsaw in their attempt to ensure the enforcement of the deportations, being less confident of the Council's ready compliance than in the case of Lodz. In Vilna, most of the orders relating to the deportation of ghetto residents were announced directly by the responsible German authorities.[129] This was due not least to the fact that the ghettoization process had been dominated from the start by the extermination plans, and there was therefore no doubt surrounding their status as mandatory German demands.

The proclamations and regulations issued by the Jewish Councils demonstrate powerfully that criminality is a not a matter of static concepts, but of variable perceptions, definitions, and attributions by specific actors. Such shifts in meaning were common in the ghettos, where the prevailing conditions meant that a whole host of previously "harmless" actions were deemed "criminal" from one day to the next. In Rumkowski's case in particular, definitions of criminality and regulations were an expression of his attempt to understand the Germans according to rational criteria and harness their interests in order to develop survival strategies for the community. Prior to 1942 especially – before the Jewish Council learnt of the mass murder campaign – many of the regulations sprang purely from the assumptions he made with regard to German intentions and possible courses of action, and from the despotism, violence, torture, and murder he had witnessed since the beginning of the occupation.

These rules and regulations reflected a specific relationship between community and individual. Whether addressing the potential outbreak of disease, "enrichment at the expense of the community," or rumour-mongering, they were born of a constant fear that individual actions could pose a risk to everyone concerned. In these circumstances, the proclamations served the purpose of legal norms: under the ever-present threat to life, they set out guiding principles based on actual experience. In terms of the ghetto legal sphere, this amounted to a form of legislature on the basis of which certain activities were prosecuted and punished. As we shall see later on, this model shows a certain similarity to the methodology of Jewish law in pre-modern Jewish communities, where guiding norms were derived from real-life case studies. An important feature of this practice were the so-called *responsa*, in which rabbis would answer concrete legal questions put to them by members of the community on a case-by-case basis.[130] In some respects, a similar function was fulfilled by the responses to readers' letters published in the *Gazeta Żydowska*. In both situations, the aim was to fill case-specific "gaps in the law" in the wake of changing circumstances.

Chapter Three

The Jewish Police as an Executive Organ

We began work without adequate preparation, as we knew nothing of police organization, and, apart from the Legislative Journal, we had no other references at our disposal. It contained information regarding the Polish Police, but this was of little value to us. It took me several months to become partially acquainted with the available literature on the subject, but it had little practical application since the conditions under which the Order Service was to operate were so uncommon that no theoretical concepts or experiences could be implemented or used as a model.[1]

This is how Stanisław Adler, writing retrospectively in 1943, described the genesis of a Jewish police force in the Warsaw ghetto in 1940. He himself played a central role in the organization of the ghetto's internal executive body, and argued for the formulation of statutes and regulations for the new institutions. His account illustrates how Jewish functionaries attempted to shape these authorities, even though they were created on German orders. In so doing, however, they soon found that they were dealing with something fundamentally different from a conventional police force. Furthermore, neither professional experience nor legal statutes from the pre-war period proved to be of much use in the ghetto.

The Establishment of the Jewish Police Forces

The Jewish Councils had to set up Jewish police forces (known as "Order Services" in Warsaw and Lodz) more or less contemporaneously with ghettoization, but often based on already existing patrols established soon after Nazi occupation.[2] They were regarded by the Germans as auxiliary police units whose job was to enforce their notions of order in the ghetto, as communicated to the Jewish Council. As such, they were answerable to both the German and Polish or Lithuanian police authorities.

In Warsaw, the Jewish Council chairman Adam Czerniaków was instructed to assemble a Jewish Order Service in September 1940, before the ghetto area was finally sealed off. This requirement was fulfilled at a conference of the Jewish Council on 9 October 1940, and the new body assumed its duties on 15 November, the day of ghettoization. Before that, the service had had a forerunner in the shape of a patrol instituted by the Council in mid-1940 to guard the newly erected walls.[3] After other candidates rejected the post, the Jewish Council chairman appointed Józef Andrzej Szeryński, a Catholic convert and former Polish police chief, as head of the Order Service.[4] The leadership ranks were filled predominantly with law graduates, many of them with professional experience as lawyers or policemen in pre-war Poland. The number of police officers, who were distributed across six districts from January 1941, was increased several times with Gestapo approval during the lifetime of the ghetto, swelling from an original 1,700 to 2,500 in July 1942.[5] While the Polish "Blue Police" were tasked with enforcing German notions of order outside the "Jewish Residential District," the Order Service were responsible for the ghetto territory.[6] After the occupation of Poland, the Germans had begun by dissolving the Polish police. Then, on 30 October 1939, Friedrich Krüger, Higher SS and Police Leader in the Generalgouvernement from 4 October, ordered the dismissed officers to be recalled, to serve as auxiliaries to the German police.[7] Being in charge of ghetto border security, the Polish police had direct control over the Order Service and interacted with it on a regular basis. The Order Service had to issue a daily report to the Polish police.[8]

In Lodz, Rumkowski was ordered to establish an Order Service on 1 March 1940, and entrusted the former Austrian officer Leon Rozenblatt with the task of setting it up.[9] Despite this official division of responsibilities, Rumkowski was highly influential in shaping the institution and selecting its members, who numbered 717 by the end of 1940.[10]

In Vilna – on Murer's orders – the Jewish Council chairman Anatol Fried appointed Jakub Gens head of the police force in the first, larger ghetto shortly after its creation in September 1941. Until its liquidation in October 1940, the second, smaller ghetto also had a police force that was answerable to its Jewish Council. Because of the brief existence of this body and the relative lack of source material, the present account only deals in detail with the Jewish police in Ghetto I.[11] On 7 September 1941, notices went up in the first ghetto inviting candidates to apply for the new institution, which covered three districts and was known here as the "Jewish Police" rather than the "Order Service."[12] In contrast to the Order Services in Warsaw and Lodz, police officers in the Vilna ghetto did not wear a uniform initially, but simply white arm bands with a blue Star of David.[13] When uniforms were introduced in mid-October 1942, ghetto inhabitants interpreted this as a sign that there would be no further murder operations by the Germans.[14] In fact, the opposite was the case: literary scholar Gudrun Schroeter argues convincingly that the uniforms were connected with the deportation of ghetto residents from Oszmiana, in which the Vilna Jewish Police were forced to participate.[15]

Although formally subordinate to the Jewish Council, Gens from the outset assumed functions which, in other ghettos, were the responsibility of the Council chairman, such as the communication of German orders to the ghetto community.[16] "Power is almost completely and solely in the hands of the police," the ghetto chronicler Herman Kruk wrote as early as December 1941. [17] In mid-July 1942, District Commissar Murer finally dissolved the Jewish Council and transferred all its powers to Gens, who acted thereafter as "ghetto representative and police chief."[18] By summer 1942, over two hundred officers were employed in the ghetto police force.[19]

As for the Warsaw ghetto, the central tasks of its Order Service in the initial phase were outlined as follows in the *Gazeta Żydowska* of 3 January 1941:

Prevention of street gatherings

Regulation of pedestrian and road traffic, particularly at junctions and crossroads

Removal of obstacles

Oversight of pavement and road hygiene

Oversight of order and cleanliness in yards and building entrances and observance of blackout regulations

Prevention of minor and major offences

Maintenance of order in public buildings and offices, particularly those of the Jewish Council and affiliated institutions.[20]

In addition to these functions, which resulted from German instructions to the Jewish Council, the Order Service was tasked with the prevention of street trading. Internally, it soon assumed the further duty of dealing with unhygienic food production.[21]

In the Lodz ghetto, the Order Service also took action against "black market" activities – a German requirement that Rumkowski had made an internal responsibility. He soon concluded for himself that the ghetto provisioning system was being threatened by "speculators" and, in a statement of May 1941, he justified the deployment of eighty police officers in this area as being "due ... to the increasing profiteering of parasitic traders who cash in on people's poverty. Those who buy from them often sacrifice their own rations, selling them for a song in order to obtain other, urgently needed products at exorbitant prices."[22]

In all three ghettos, the Jewish police units were charged with "securing" the ghetto border, a task that included the prevention of smuggling. The Jewish police were responsible for the ghetto interior, while German and Polish or Lithuanian police patrolled the "non-Jewish" side.[23] The Germans issued concrete directions in this respect, such as the following to Rumkowski on 16 July 1940: "The Jewish Order Service staff must be instructed to position themselves at least ten metres behind the opened gates ... not to pass directly along the ghetto fence during their daytime patrols ... to ensure that Jews passing along the ghetto fence before curfew hours do not stop or communicate in any way with persons on the other side of the fence."[24] Border security was also a top priority for the Order Service in Warsaw after the erection of the ghetto wall.[25] In Vilna, Murer ordered the ghetto police to ensure that residents went to work in gangs, and that no food was brought into the ghetto. Chief of Police Gens made failure to comply with these demands punishable by death.[26] Other police duties included carrying out the confiscations ordered by the Germans and helping to "track down objects of value."[27]

The role of the Jewish police forces was, in short, to maintain "peace and order" in the ghetto and enforce the German agenda, if necessary by repressive means, for which purpose the Germans equipped them with rubber batons in all three ghettos.[28] In addition, officers were authorized to impose fines and detentions, although the Order Service in Warsaw was not officially granted the power to issue prison sentences until June 1942, with the establishment of an investigation department.[29] In Lodz, the Jewish police units were permitted right from the start to administer fines and detentions of up to forty-eight hours in the case of minor infractions, for example,[30] with individual punishments left to the officers' discretion.[31] Offenders were detained either in ghetto prisons or in cells attached to the Jewish police stations. Nonetheless, the Germans could still intervene in cases at any time and inflict their "own punishments," which often – particularly from late summer 1941 – meant the murder of the offending "delinquents."[32] Other punitive measures were introduced by the Jewish police forces at their own initiative, with both Gens and Rumkowski advocating the use of flogging, for example. In the Lodz ghetto, prison sentences were often accompanied – with German approval – by forced labour, while other internal punishments included sewage removal duties.

When it came to the prosecution of internal crimes, the powers of the ghetto authorities were limited. This reflected to some extent the ideological premise of the Nazis that the ghettos were already populated by criminals. Stripped of their status as legal subjects, ghetto residents – including the Jewish Councils – were not entitled to pass judgment on matters of right and wrong. For this reason, the powers of the Jewish police were confined to the realm of prevention. The Order Service in the Warsaw ghetto could, for example, take preventive measures against specific kinds of theft, as illustrated by an activity report of 9 January 1942: "In District V, special patrols shall provide protection against mugging and handbag theft in the area around the Zamenhof-strasse … during the afternoon hours."[33] The prosecution and punishment of more "serious" crimes was, on the other hand, the responsibility of the Polish police, who referred them in turn to the Germans. The job of the Jewish police was merely to initiate preparatory measures before delivering the arrested subjects to the higher authorities.[34]

A similar division of responsibilities existed in the Lodz ghetto: here, the Order Service had to provide the German Criminal Police with a seven-strong squad tasked solely with auxiliary duties in connection with prosecution. Writing in 1941, the ghetto chronicler names some examples: "producing individuals summoned by the Criminal Police, locating addresses, etc."[35] In the Vilna ghetto, matters of prosecution do not appear to have been explicitly regulated by the German occupiers. As mentioned earlier, it may be that they had ceased to attach any importance to the investigation of "classical" crimes within the ghetto by late summer 1941.[36]

Over time, the Jewish police units were able to extend their competence, thanks to the occupiers' indifference to ghetto-internal crimes. This happened either informally or formally, at the behest of the German authorities. Nevertheless, their official executive powers remained within the defined limits, and their evaluation criteria could be challenged at any time by the occupiers.

The intertwining of evolving German interests and ghetto-internal objectives was reflected at an institutional level. The establishment of specific police departments took place partly on German orders, and partly at the initiative of the Jewish Councils themselves. New institutions were added, modified, and dissolved.[37] In Lodz, for instance, the *Sonderkommando* was set up on 1 July 1940 as a department of the Order Service. In accordance with the German confiscation policy, this newly created special unit was responsible for "house searches … for the purpose of confiscating objects of value, fur coats, hidden goods and currency, including the German mark, and all items subject to compulsory sale to the community, e.g. sewing machines."[38] Although this department was officially subordinate to the Jewish Council, in practice it often received orders directly from the German Criminal Police and the Gestapo. In terms of personnel, Rumkowski deliberately chose leaders with a pre-war criminal past. The first of these, Szlomo Hercberg, was reputed to have close contacts with the criminal underworld of Lodz.[39] Presumably, Rumkowski reasoned that those who had acted contrarily to the prevailing norms before the war would have fewer scruples when it came to performing morally dubious actions such as cooperating with the Germans, which meant turning against their fellow ghetto residents. From 31 October 1942, the unit became known as the *Sonderabteilung* or "Special Department" and evolved under the leadership of Dawid Gertler into an authority much feared within the ghetto for its brutal methods. Its responsibilities were constantly being extended:[40] from 1943 in particular, it also prosecuted thefts and attempted increasingly to influence ghetto court practice.[41]

In all three ghettos, there were dedicated police departments for the "maintenance of hygiene." In Warsaw, a "disease control department" was set up at the beginning of 1941, which was headed by Manfred Talmus and worked closely with the health department. In addition to inspection, it was also responsible for disinfecting the homes of typhus victims, isolating the affected buildings, and carrying out delousing measures.[42] For example, the Order Service activity report of 22 January 1942 reads: "Disease control squad posting sentries at baths and health department offices and assisting with health-related inspections to detect concealed cases of typhus."[43]

Having identified the theft of timber from "public areas" as a particular risk to the health of the population in April 1941, Rumkowski went on to set up a sanitary commission.[44] This body reported to the Order Service and was henceforth responsible for hygiene control,[45] a task which included prosecuting those responsible for the demolition of wooden latrines. During their home inspections, the sanitary police were required to check simultaneously for compliance with the blackout regulations.[46] Later on, they were also mobilized whenever bodies were discovered in the ghetto.[47]

In the case of Vilna, the chronicler Herman Kruk writes of a sanitary police unit that had already been operational for some time by December 1942 and also worked closely with the health department.[48] As in Lodz, this unit was responsible for "hygiene" in the ghetto, clamping down on "bath deserters" and carrying out delousing operations, for instance.[49] For the month of November 1942, Kruk records 759 fines and 246 prison sentences for offences of this kind.[50] In addition, the sanitary police conducted campaigns to enforce the German-imposed ban on pregnancies.[51]

Other departments were specific to individual ghetto communities, such as the "labour police" in the Vilna ghetto, which was expressly responsible for pursuing work-related offences.[52] The lack of source material makes it impossible to identify exactly when this unit came into being, but the large number of detention orders issued – particularly in 1942 – for offences such as failing to turn up for work suggests that it was after the first mass shootings in Ponary. By then, people had clearly begun to doubt the efficacy of the Jewish Council's strategy of "rescue through labour" and therefore stayed away from work.

Despite following a similar strategy, Rumkowski did not set up a dedicated police department for this purpose. In both Lodz and Warsaw, it was the job of the regular Order Service to ensure that the workforce demanded by the Germans reported for labour transports.[53] The number of "labour offences" recorded for Lodz is not as high as for Vilna, however, which suggests that the hope of surviving through work persisted for longer in Lodz.

A few police departments were also created because the Jewish Councils perceived a particular need for regulation that was *not* directly connected to German demands. In Lodz, for example, a women's department existed from October 1942 to supervise underage children of workshop and factory employees.[54] This department, which was administered by Dr Karl Bondy and comprised a team of fifty-six women, was also entrusted from December 1942 with the campaign against "street trading."[55] The deployed policewomen were mostly sixth-formers from the Jewish high school; they wore their own specially designed uniform of green shorts and yellow-striped caps with the Order Service badge, and were equipped with batons.[56] The women's department was dissolved in March 1943 and its members transferred to other departments and ghetto workshops.[57]

In the Warsaw ghetto, the Order Service faced a new challenge in the shape of orphaned minors. Many of these organized themselves into gangs that were often involved in smuggling. The officers themselves were torn between sympathy with the starving children and their obligation to tackle smuggling, particularly at the ghetto border, where they had to serve directly alongside Polish and German police. Often, they would turn a blind eye to child smugglers – an act for which they risked being brutally beaten if noticed by the Polish guards.[58] Reflecting on this dilemma, Adler writes: "The tactful performance of this most thankless task required a considerable degree of alertness and emotional self-control, but an Order Service man with his head full of anxieties could not always maintain himself at the peak of attention to duty. In any case, he never got recognition from the community as a service-man; he was usually considered ... a sadist who tormented unfortunate children."[59]

Another arm of the Lodz Order Service – the "moral hygiene department" – was established in 1941 to combat a very different crime: that of "prostitution."[60] Similar efforts were made in Warsaw to establish a women's department with the explicit aim of tackling this practice.[61] Instances of women offering sexual services in return for payment are recorded by diarists and memoirists such as Arnold Mostowicz in Lodz, who wrote: "The true crime statistics are unknown, as is the scale of prostitution in numerical terms, for example. In its old 'monetized' form, the activity was virtually non-existent, but the emergence of a new form – born of the privileges of the 'ruling class' – meant that there were now whole areas where young women prostituted themselves."[62] A similar picture is painted by diarists from the Warsaw ghetto, who write of specific spots where "prostitutes" met with members of the ghetto elite.[63] Later, however, the crime of "prostitution" became less of an issue and was, in practice, disregarded by the Jewish police authorities. This was presumably a consequence of the new priorities of internal crime investigation: attention now switched to offences which posed a potential risk to the ghetto community as a whole. Besides, Jewish Council functionaries – as part of the "ghetto elite" – are unlikely to have pushed for prosecution, given that they themselves were among the potential clientele for such services. In this domain – as in others – the definition of criminal conduct depended essentially on who controlled the narrative within the ghetto.

Internal Organization Attempts

Although the Jewish police authorities were set up on German orders, there were no definitive instructions as to what form they should take. Consequently, the Jewish police functionaries in both Warsaw and Lodz agreed among themselves on the nature of the internal executive body. Their discussions to this effect reveal how much room for manoeuvre they enjoyed at different points in time.

Until ghettoization, the institution of a Jewish police force for the Jewish communities was an entirely new phenomenon. In the early days, it was even welcomed by some in the ghetto community, such as the Warsaw ghetto resident Mary Berg, who noted in her diary on

22 December 1940: "I am overcome by a strange and most paradoxical feeling of satisfaction when I see a Jewish policeman at a junction – such a thing was quite unknown in prewar Poland."[64] The specific features of the new bodies were generally pointed out by contrasting them with pre-war police authorities, which were already familiar to Jewish police officers – particularly the functionaries, many of whom had previous experience from serving with the Polish police, for example. Speaking at an event in the Lodz ghetto to mark the first anniversary of the Order Service's inauguration, OS chief Leon Rozenblatt commented as follows: "At this point, it is relevant to mention that the conditions we are working under are vastly different from, and disproportionately tougher than, those facing any other police force. The fight against smuggling, the escorting of food supplies, the never-ending phalanxes[65] of people queuing outside soup kitchens and shops, the dismantling of various timber structures – and all this at a time when we are struggling to feed 160,000 people."[66]

As is already evident from Adler's description, the functionaries responsible for the Warsaw ghetto in 1940 found themselves in the position of having to organize an internal police force without the necessary organizational and legal knowledge, let alone the equipment. Against these odds, they sought to establish a whole infrastructure with specific legal statutes.[67] Ever since its inception, discussions in the Warsaw ghetto had revolved around the question of what the ethos of the ghetto police apparatus should be. Opinion was split between advocates of a "citizen-oriented" service for the benefit of the community and supporters of a more military-style institution.[68] According to Adler, most Order Service officers – apart from the leadership team around Szeryński – subscribed to the former view and regarded the move towards a broadly military police squad with suspicion.[69] This development was chiefly attributed to Szeryński, who wanted to impose a strict martial discipline within the service and appointed people who were supportive of his approach.[70] It was also doubtless favoured by the absence of any internal rules and regulations, as well as the need to adapt to the constraints of the ghetto.

Following the force's establishment, an initiative arose from within its ranks campaigning for a citizen-focused approach, as expressed in a letter: "The Order Service is a socio-moral organization and an agency of the Jewish Council … The service regulations should clearly state the limits of OS jurisdiction and prohibit the use of brutal physical force. The service should act in the interests of the Jewish population and guarantee order in the Jewish quarter."[71] The authors called for a verification commission consisting of various figures of authority in order to "uphold the principle of a socially and morally led OS."[72] Coupled with this was an appeal for the service to communicate its objectives and functions to the ghetto population and invite their cooperation. That way, the "moral decay" of the organization could be halted and people's trust in it restored.[73] An example of such decay was seen in the fact that many joined the force as a means of obtaining privileged access to material goods. Bribe-taking from smugglers at the ghetto border was rife – on top of the extra food rations and better health care that came with the job.[74] As the activity reports of the Order Service reveal, it was not until early June 1942 that a set of official regulations was approved in Warsaw. According to these, the OS officer discharged his duty "for the good of the ghetto community"[75] – this just a few weeks before the Jewish police were forced to assist in preparing for the deportations.

In the Lodz ghetto, Rumkowski announced to the ghetto population in May 1940: "On the basis of the authority entrusted to me, I have established an Order Service Guard for the protection of the Jewish population and for the maintenance of calm and order."[76] In so doing, he outlined the parameters both for the founding of a Jewish police force and for its assimilation into his area of jurisdiction. Rumkowski demanded strict obedience to the Order Service on the part of the ghetto community, while police officers were expected to behave "calmly and politely" towards ghetto residents.[77] With the beginning of the deportations, the Jewish police authorities were faced with new tasks that many saw as being directed *against* the ghetto community.[78] In February 1943, on the third anniversary of the Order Service's inauguration, Rumkowski defined the force's tasks anew. Justifying his readiness to carry out "self-selection" according to German criteria, he wrote: "Only in the ghetto has life taught me what feats a policeman must accomplish … Here, we are not dealing with the mere maintenance of order, but quite literally with the fate of the ghetto." Addressing the OS officers, he declared: "You are not just the soldiers of the ghetto! You are the servants of this community. You must safeguard the few assets that remain to us, and on which our existence currently depends."[79] Once again, Rumkowski invokes the hope that his strategies will guarantee the survival of part of the ghetto community: "You are my only means of stopping people in this ghetto from literally devouring each other." One day, people will say that "you once toiled honestly and served strenuously for your brothers in Jewry's darkest hour."[80]

In the Vilna ghetto, the creation of a Jewish police force took place in very different circumstances. From the start, it was placed more explicitly in the service of German ambitions, which were characterized by despotism and violence. As a result, there was less scope for abstract discussions regarding the nature of such a body. Hopes of deploying the force for the benefit of the ghetto community were not nearly as widespread in Vilna after summer 1941 as they were at the beginning of ghettoization in occupied Poland. Nevertheless, there was a certain amount of debate among the relevant functionaries over what form the executive body should take. While the Bundists called for a citizen-oriented militia, adherents of the Betar movement – including Gens, the chairman of the ghetto police – favoured a force founded on military principles.[81] As Balberyszski relates, efforts by figures such as Herman Kruk to create a body dedicated to "serving the ghetto community" were rejected. Like Gens, the Jewish Council chairman Anatol Fried had argued that "under prevailing conditions one could not wait a single minute or start ... endless discussions. The police force had to be formed immediately and would have to rule with iron discipline."[82]

Another way in which the constitution of the police authorities could be influenced was in the selection of applicants, who – in the case of Warsaw and Lodz – had to fulfil certain requirements. In Warsaw, for example, these were: age between twenty-one and forty, six years' schooling, good health, a minimum height of 170 centimetres, a minimum weight of 60 kilograms, and evidence of completed military service.[83] Alongside these formal criteria, candidates also had to meet the necessary moral standards. In Warsaw, for instance, Order Service functionaries required them to demonstrate the absence of a criminal record. In the case of the Warsaw ghetto, Adler reports that large numbers of criminals had attempted to infiltrate the ranks of the OS, and that even more would have succeeded had the applications not been screened by a team of lawyers.[84] Criminals, such as those who had made a living from "petty criminal practices" like pickpocketing prior to ghettoization, were to be denied access to posts in the Order Service due to the suspicion that they would use their position to profit from smuggling offences.[85] In short, the Jewish functionaries assumed that anyone who had been a criminal in the past would act no differently in the ghetto.

For this reason, candidates' applications were initially subject to thorough scrutiny. Soon after the creation of the Order Service in Warsaw, functionaries were granted access to pre-war criminal registers, whereupon – as Adler writes – around ten of the newly recruited officers were dismissed. Significantly, some people *also* saw ghettoization as an opportunity for a "new beginning," hoping that the definitions of criminality that had led to their conviction before the war would become irrelevant in the ghetto.[86] In Warsaw, the Polish police could intervene in all personnel matters of the Jewish police, which provided opportunities for bribery and corruption.[87]

According to Herman Kruk, by the time new Jewish police officers came to be recruited in Vilna in December 1942, moral criteria were no longer a priority: "Everyone [sic] who thinks he is healthy, well built and fit for the work of a policeman can register in the police headquarters as a candidate for a police job."[88]

This change in moral standards was, however, also apparent in the other ghettos following new German demands and the creation of new Order Service institutions. In the case of Lodz, Poznański notes that the expansion of the Order Service *Sonderabteilung* in 1942 led to the recruitment of many police officers and supervisors "from the dregs of society."[89] They were, he writes, "old inmates of the central prison on Czarniecki Street. After just a few days, these trusted agents of Mr Gertler proved to be attempting to outdo each other in theft and embezzlement. No wonder some of them ended up back in prison."[90]

In all three ghettos, the Jewish police functionaries developed internal sanctioning mechanisms which allowed them to penalize certain actions *within* the force under the heading of "disciplinary offences" and to instil their own standards in terms of what was and was not acceptable. In Warsaw, a disciplinary section was set up within the Order Service investigation department, headed by the former Polish police commissar Seweryn Zylbersztajn and assisted by a commission, in order to adjudicate on offences and impose internal punishments ranging from warnings through fines to suspension from duty.[91] Despite their initially provisional nature, the resulting rulings were often permanently adopted.[92] Of the offences committed, collaboration with smuggling gangs and bribe-taking were the most vigorously pursued.[93]

That said, the internal punitive mechanisms of the ghetto were highly circumscribed because of the urgent necessity of preventing the offenders from falling into the hands of the Germans. On this point, Adler writes: "To report a functionary who had committed a serious offence and who deserved dismissal from the Service would cost the offender his life. The human conscience would not permit exposure of such a man to the danger of being handed over to the Germans. In practice then, only trifling transgressions were exposed to daylight to be investigated by the Inspection, passed on to the Disciplinary Section, and finally tried by a disciplinary court. The grave offences had to be covered up out of necessity."[94] Most of the disciplinary proceedings against OS officers in Warsaw pertained to border-related offences. And since the Service was obliged to report disciplinary cases to the Polish police, who would in turn notify the Germans, the majority of them were not followed up.[95]

In the Lodz ghetto, there was at first no institution within the Order Service explicitly responsible for disciplinary offences. Here, it was Rumkowski himself who sought to punish police "misconduct" such as bribe-taking at the ghetto border, instructing Rozenblat in several cases to dismiss the officers in question.[96] By the same token, he consistently "rewarded" positive conduct, directing the chief cashier's office on multiple occasions in July 1941 to pay fifty marks to the relevant officers for "exceptional service and incorruptibility."[97] Until spring 1941, disciplinary offences on the part of Order Service personnel were tried by the regular ghetto court in Lodz.[98] Following the establishment of the so-called summary court in March 1941 – set up by Rumkowski in an attempt to prevent criminality among officials of the self-administration bodies – this task then fell to the new authority. Among the summary court rulings listed in the Ghetto Chronicle on 6 April 1941, for example, we find: "Police officer Alter Zytenfeld sentenced to six months' imprisonment; offence: theft of firewood found in his keeping in Marysin."[99] After the dissolution of the summary court, it was the divisional head of the Order Service, the regular court, and – once again – increasingly Rumkowski himself who took charge of such cases.[100]

The resulting rulings emphasize the police officers' position of responsibility. Often, the description of their "reprehensible conduct" had little in common with "conventional" definitions of criminality. Particularly when the treatment of the identified offence was still unresolved, the officers' actions were simply described without assigning them to predefined categories such as theft. One OS officer named Biednak, for example, was reported to have "taken potatoes from the vegetable distribution point unweighed"; the same officer was further accused of having "unlawfully visited a bakery during the evening hours" without his armband and cap.[101] In the Lodz ghetto, there were various punishments for disciplinary offences within the Order Service, including suspension from duty as well as imprisonment. Sometimes the offending police officers would continue to receive their pay, however, in order to avoid inflicting any further damage on them.[102]

In the Vilna ghetto, transgressions of this kind were recorded by the regular Jewish Police force on conventional forms as with any other arrest warrant, and marked "disciplinary offence."[103] Offences included "impertinent behaviour on duty," "disobedient conduct," or "irregular conduct on duty," although which actions fell within these categories is rarely ascertainable.[104] In some cases, the sanctioned behaviour was specified in more detail: in January 1942, for example, two police officers were sentenced to twelve hours' imprisonment for "negligence while in charge of an arrested subject."[105] While it was still the case in early 1941 that Jewish Police officers – unlike other ghetto inhabitants – could not be detained for forty-eight hours,[106] this restriction appears to have been lifted in 1942: on 16 April, police chief Gens informed the head of Police District 1 that "Sergeant Stein must be punished with forty-eight hours' detention for his impertinent behaviour in the Jewish Council chairman's office in the presence of the latter."[107] In July 1942, Gens advised Jewish Police personnel that any conflicts or incidents occurring between members of different police departments were to be dealt with not by the relevant supervisors but by a police court.[108] A severe punishment may have been inflicted by this authority in April or May 1943 in connection with a case of espionage. Kruk writes of a young "informer" within the Jewish Police who was held in the ghetto prison for two weeks, after which he was due to be handed over to the Germans during an impending operation.[109] Why he was imprisoned cannot be determined for certain. Possibly he was a member of the FPO who had been using the Jewish Police as a means to obtain information on the German murder plans and "expose" Gestapo agents. According to Sutzkever, many of the organization's members sought to work for the Jewish Police for these reasons.[110] This explanation would be consistent with Gens's attempt in May 1943 to halt the activities of armed resistance groups within the ghetto. If the above theory is correct, it would make this case one of the few instances where the Jewish Council inflicted punishment for an offence in the context of armed resistance.

Prosecution and Investigations

"The prosecution of common offences remained all this time in the hands of the Polish police, at least in theory. In practice, the law of the jungle prevailed in the ghetto ... Notifications of theft and other crimes were received with compassion by the commissariats but no action was taken on them. I doubt that anybody took the trouble to investigate such matters."[111]

This is how Adler describes the circumstances that enabled the Order Service to undertake criminal investigations in the Warsaw ghetto despite German restrictions. Officially, it was only allowed to pursue criminal activities directed against Jewish Council members, along with the internal disciplinary offences already described.[112] As it soon became evident that the Polish police were neglecting their official responsibility in this regard, however, the Order Service also began to intervene informally in other cases such as theft. This situation was tolerated by the Jewish Council: "For an adequate fee or the promise of a percentage of the property recovered, they [the OS functionaries] would start an investigation. As a matter of fact, such proceedings were beyond the competence of the Order Service, but the officer in charge of the region, with the silent consent of the Superintendent of the Order Service and of the Jewish Council, would overlook that prohibition. Frequently the culprit was discovered, and then a reconciliation took place between the parties. The thief or swindler had to make restitution to the damaged person, and received a beating; the case was terminated 'amicably.'"[113]

From the beginning of June 1942, the Order Service was permitted to pursue ghetto-internal crimes with the aid of the investigation department, but it had to notify the Polish police accordingly, who would intervene where necessary and apply their own sanctioning mechanisms.[114] As their remit was extended, Order Service personnel were then also granted the right to arrest ghetto residents when there was a risk of them absconding.[115]

Far more comprehensive powers were granted – or tacitly conceded – to the Order Service in Lodz. This applied, for example, to an investigation department that served as the sole judicial authority within the ghetto up to September 1940.[116] When a regular ghetto court was subsequently established, the change seems to have caused problems for the German occupiers, who still attempted even in November 1940 to refer the punishment of crimes outside their sphere of interest to the Jewish Order Service and not to the court.[117]

In Lodz, a specific cooperative relationship emerged between the German Criminal Police and the Jewish Order Service. Needless to say, it was the Germans who dictated which ghetto cases were important, and what the respective punishments should be (more often than not, the murder of the offender). When it came to the prosecution process, however, they relied on the expertise and knowledge of the Jewish police and their rootedness in the ghetto community. The cooperative element lay in the German Criminal Police's delivery to the OS police stations of those residents whom they wanted to see punished according to their notions. One document from September 1940 reads, for example: "Weltman, Jsrael is to be delivered to your police station for severe punishment, having been found in the street without the Star of David during the police curfew. A report detailing the sentence imposed must be submitted to the State Criminal Police, Ghetto *Sonderkommando*."[118] In other words, the sentence itself was left to the (limited) discretion of the Order Service. In this particular case, the arrested subject was sentenced on 24 September 1940 to seven days' detention based on a plea of "extenuating circumstances": he had put on a jacket without a Star of David badge accidentally, and had not intended to go out into the street during the curfew, but only into the backyard.[119]

The district stations reported back to the Germans on accomplished punishments of ghetto residents as ordered by the German Criminal Police, or on cases in which they had expressed an interest. One report of December 1940, for instance, reads: "Weingart, Jakob, delivered to me by the local Criminal Police department for punishment, was sentenced by my authority to six months' imprisonment for food smuggling and fraud. The offender was admitted to the Central Prison ... to serve his sentence."[120]

In the early days especially, German interests appear to have been somewhat ill defined. In November 1940, for instance, the German Criminal Police instructed the Order Service of the Lodz ghetto to impose a four-month prison sentence in a case of blackmail between two ghetto residents – even though responsibility for such cases lay explicitly within the ghetto-internal legal sphere – and to notify them of the beginning and end of the sentence.[121] In autumn 1940, owing to the initial lack of clarity over German core interests, OS officers also notified the Criminal Police of cases that would later be confined to the internal jurisdiction of the ghetto, such as thefts, for example.[122]

Investigations likewise took a specific form in the Lodz ghetto, again involving regular communication between Jewish and German police authorities. From 1942, a clash of interests became increasingly apparent, with wrongdoers often convicted via the internal procedures of the Order Service Investigation Department, only to be deported from the ghetto central prison and murdered by the Gestapo. In June 1942, for example, the Investigation Department was informed of a robbery in the ghetto and sent its officers to inspect the scene of the crime and take down the details of the alleged perpetrator. After confessing to the crime, Icek Adler was taken to the central prison to be remanded in custody, and the case was referred to the ghetto court, which handed down a prison sentence of two and a half years.[123] Although the trial took place with the knowledge and consent of the German Criminal Police, who waited for the outcome and were duly informed of the court hearing and verdict, the offender never got to serve his sentence, being "resettled" from the ghetto on 7 September 1942 on the orders of the Gestapo.[124]

Murder cases within the Lodz ghetto officially fell within the remit of the German authorities, but they relied on Jewish police expertise to resolve them. On 13 September 1941, for instance, the Order Service notified the German Criminal Police of the "violent death of the

Jewess Tauba Herman,"[125] whose mentally ill daughter, Fania Herman, was accused of strangling her. The German Criminal Police brought a charge against the daughter and ordered her to be held in OS custody at their "disposal."[126] This was not the first time the Germans had made use of ghetto-internal institutions, having already carried out the selection process at the Jewish isolation hospital.[127] According to her registration card, Fania Herman was deported by the Gestapo, and may have been among the prison inmates singled out for the first transport to Kulmhof in January 1942.[128] In July 1942, the German Criminal Police investigated another case. After a fifty-five-year-old ghetto resident was found murdered in her home, it initially excluded the "ghetto security authorities" from the investigations.[129] A few days later, however, it delegated the task of obtaining details of the victim to the Order Service.[130]

From 1942 onwards, the German Criminal Police and Gestapo also intervened increasingly in cases which were officially the responsibility of the Order Service. In July 1942, the Order Service in Lodz conducted a search for a man who had previously attacked a female ghetto resident, issuing a physical description which was not untypical given conditions in the ghetto: "1.60–1.65 cm tall, blond … aged 20–30, medium-heavy build … clothes very dirty (work clothing). Suspect has an overworked appearance. This man has also been seen repeatedly … in Gas Kitchen A, Bachstrasse 14, being noticeable by his dirty saucepan."[131] On 31 July 1942, the Order Service notified the Criminal Police of the alleged offender's arrest following "confidential information" from a woman in the ghetto. The ensuing house search at the home of the suspect, Mordka Dawid Hochmitz, uncovered a china dish stolen during the attack.[132] After being confronted with the victim and subsequently arrested, Hochmitz confessed to the offence.[133] On 3 August, he was admitted to the ghetto central prison "at the disposal of the Gestapo" and subsequently deported on 7 September.[134]

In the case of the Vilna ghetto, there are no surviving sources indicating similar forms of (enforced) cooperation in matters of criminal prosecution. At the end of September 1941, the Jewish Council had set up a criminal police unit at its own initiative to supplement the existing Jewish police force, but the occupiers took very little interest in its ghetto-internal activities.[135] District Commissar Murer only stepped in when he perceived a risk to the fulfilment of his key demands, such as the prevention of smuggling. Even when, in June 1942, five residents were brought before the ghetto court, charged with the murder and robbery of the yeshiva student Józef Gerstein, the Germans declined to get involved.[136] By this time, they appeared to have lost interest in the pursuit and punishment of "classical" crimes, only intervening in ghetto-internal prosecutions where they were felt to be relevant to German core interests.

Crime Definitions As Reflected in Jewish Police Practice

The manner in which crimes previously defined in proclamations and elsewhere were reflected in the everyday practice of the ghetto police authorities varied from ghetto to ghetto. Which areas the Jewish police authorities in Lodz and Warsaw were responsible for and which crimes they could prosecute had been set out in 1940 with the establishment of their respective Order Services. In Lodz especially, the crimes defined by Rumkowski in his proclamations appeared in Order Service forms, statistics, and reports as *prosecuted* cases. The crime statistics and arrests in the daily bulletins, which were recorded in documents such as the Ghetto Chronicle, cited the crimes of "theft," "smuggling," "resistance," "entering or leaving the ghetto without authorization," and "miscellaneous," or an assortment of the above as applicable.[137] The statistics also included suicides, which were reported to the German Criminal Police.[138] Where the prosecution figures showed a proliferation of certain incidents, a brief note to this effect was entered, as in the bulletin of 27 May 1942: "other offences chiefly pertaining to negligent hygiene: 6,"[139] or again on 3 June 1942 with regard to the recorded thefts: "The most commonly stolen item was food. 'Miscellaneous other offences' refers to the violation of blackout regulations."[140] In this way, the crime statistics also reflect the priorities defined by Rumkowski in his campaign against ghetto criminality. During his periodic crusades against "wood theft," for example, the OS reports and statistics show a correspondingly high incidence of related offences.[141] Days when no one was arrested by the Order Service were described as a "rarity" by the chroniclers, with a note to indicate where this was due to recent "resettlements."[142]

One reason why the violation of what were often ghetto-internal legal norms was pursued so proactively in Lodz was the fact that most of them had been introduced in response to a spate of activities which Rumkowski deemed a danger to the ghetto community. Another was his authoritarian stance as chairman of the Jewish Council, a position which allowed him to identify certain activities as criminal and prosecute them using the Order Service as an executive organ. The actual activities leading to the arrests were multifarious, but could be assigned to the generic categories defined by Rumkowski, such as "fraud," "abuse," and "resistance."[143] The headings under which the Order Service crime figures for Lodz were logged were the same in 1944 as they were in 1940/1.[144] The existence of pre-printed forms and standard-ized statistics for recording crime rates reflects the degree to which the ghetto community in Lodz was institutionalized – not least because of the personal ambitions of chairman Rumkowski.

In the case of the Warsaw ghetto, whose Order Service was also set up in 1940, things were rather different. This was due partly to the specific delimitation of its responsibilities with regard to internal pros-ecution, and partly to the constitution of the controlling Jewish self-administration. Here, the official activity reports of the Order Service, which prior to the expansion of its powers were regularly forwarded to the German authorities, only referred to the formally approved areas of responsibility. As a result, violations of blackout regulations, illegal border crossings, or "unsanitary conditions" were penalized while criminal matters officially elicited only preventive measures.[145] Infor-mal punishments by the Order Service were not recorded in writing in order to avoid attracting the attention of the Polish and German police. Ghetto-internal crimes were still discussed in organs such as the *Gazeta Żydowska*, for example, but instead of being assigned to predefined, gen-eral categories as in Lodz, they were often described in concrete detail.[146]

Generic crime categories were similarly under-established in Vilna. The arrest warrants issued by the Jewish Police tended to state the partic-ulars of the offence, often in poor or Yiddishized German, and sometimes with one crime designation crossed out and replaced with another.[147] Nevertheless, the crimes cited in these documents fall into similar cat-egories to those in the ghetto-internal proclamations, namely:[148]

1. offences which were to be prosecuted directly on German orders;
2. activities deemed by the Jewish Council to pose a risk to the ghetto community in terms of their potential to trigger a brutal intervention by the Germans; and
3. activities directed against ghetto institutions.

A further category was that of "classical" crimes where individuals were generally the injured party, as in fights between residents or sex-ual abuse. Such cases were rarely recorded by the Jewish Police in the arrest warrants, however, even though sources show that they were a fact of ghetto life.[149] This may suggest that – given the German exter-mination plans – an action was most likely to be designated a crime in Vilna if it was felt to endanger the community as a whole. Typical instances were violations of German orders, or behaviour prompting fears of a violent German intervention, such as rumour-mongering or "disturbance of the peace."

Examples of the first category included crimes relating to the ghetto border. In Warsaw and Lodz, this meant (attempted) illegal border crossings; in Vilna, on the other hand, definitions were more detailed, as in the case of Sura Barbakow, who was imprisoned for twelve hours for "loitering at the gate."[150] The crime of "attempting to leave the ghetto without identification" was penalized with up to eighteen hours' detention.[151] Rachela Limon was sentenced to twenty-four hours' detention for actual "leaving of the ghetto without identification," and her husband to a full forty-eight hours.[152] In 1941, people were apprehended for violations of the labelling regulations, which were recorded in the arrest warrants using terms such as "walking around without a badge."[153]

As in the other ghettos, District Commissar Murer had ordered the Jewish Police to ensure that residents did not "bring any food into the ghetto."[154] The very wording of the command shows that the terms "smuggling" or "trafficking" were evidently less well established as a crime category in Vilna than they were in Warsaw and Lodz. Here again, the activities in question were described in concrete detail: in an arrest warrant issued by the Jewish Police in 1942, for example, the "reason for arrest" was given as "carrying excessive amounts of food on multiple occasions" and a sentence of twenty-four hours' detention imposed.[155]

However it was described, smuggling – despite being subject to prosecution according to German orders – rarely featured in the arrest warrants of the Jewish Police. That is not to say that it did not happen, however, as we know from specific reports of smuggler activity at the ghetto border, or of gate guards beating up smugglers and enriching themselves with the spoils.[156] The likelier explanation is that the Jewish Council and Jewish Police attempted where possible to "undermine" the German prosecution process in this regard. This highlights once again the ambivalent role of both bodies: on one hand, as part of the ghetto community, they had an interest in allowing food into the ghetto. That goes both for individual guards seeking to line their own pockets and for the Jewish Police as an institution, which took a very pragmatic approach to the food rations that residents were allowed to bring home from work. In May 1942, they allowed would-be bread smugglers to keep two kilos and sell the rest to the ghetto administration for sixty-five roubles a kilo.[157] On the other hand, the Council and police were also bound to comply with German demands: indeed, Murer complained to Gens that the ghetto guards were not being tough enough on smuggling, and threatened him with arrests.[158] On 17 June 1942, he proceeded to demand a hundred extra workers from the Jewish Council as a collective punishment for smuggling offences.[159]

The second category – that is, activities deemed by the Jewish Council to pose a risk to the ghetto community – encompassed a variety of "labour offences." Although this was, as already discussed, a key area of responsibility for the Jewish Police in Vilna, no generic crime categories were ever established. The criminal activities cited in arrest warrants, particularly from May 1942 onwards, were described variously as "failure to report for work," "refusal to work," or "refusal to take on a particular job."[160] While no such specific offences had been defined by the Germans, the Jewish Council was nevertheless obliged to ensure a steady supply of workers. The use of punitive measures was, therefore, part of Gens's strategy of keeping the ghetto "productive" for the Germans in order to secure the survival of at least part of the ghetto community.[161] Since individual misconduct could jeopardize that strategy, the resulting prison sentences were often longer than those for other offences.[162]

As already suggested, the sheer number of offences can be interpreted as a sign that the residents themselves no longer believed that labour would save them from being murdered by the Germans. As Kruk wrote in May 1943: "Jews don't want to work: it is the end anyway, who work [sic]? These are the complaints of most working people. The Jewish Labor Office is helpless here."[163] From 5 August 1943, when rumours of impending deportations began to spread through the ghetto, people refused to go to work any more, and the Jewish Police arrested large numbers on Gens's orders.[164]

Another activity criminalized by Gens based on the fear of German intervention was that of rumour-mongering, which the police chief had repeatedly warned against on pain of severe punishment.[165] The Jewish Police were authorized to sentence offenders to up to forty-eight hours' detention,[166] and although the culprits were doubtless difficult to identify, a number of arrests are documented.[167] Large numbers of residents were also arrested for "disturbance of the peace."[168] The sanctions for both offences were comparatively harsh because of the Jewish Council's concern to prevent an outbreak of panic among the ghetto community – something which could trigger unforeseen consequences from the German side.

Offences belonging to the third category – i.e., activities which challenged ghetto institutions – were described in similarly concrete terms. An example of such an offence was any kind of conduct directed against the Jewish Police. While this would be classified under the general crime of "resistance" in Lodz, the arrest warrants issued in Vilna contain expressions such as "insulting the Jewish Police,"[169] "striking a police officer,"[170] and "abuse of the police,"[171] referring only rarely to "resistance to the Jewish Police."[172] These offences attracted a penalty of up to twenty-four hours' imprisonment, as the Jewish Council depended on a functioning executive organ in order to implement its strategies. This was all the more important once Jewish Police officers began to be deployed in the service of German extermination plans, thus placing them at odds with the interests of the ghetto community.

As already noted, the system of ghetto proclamations was less professionalized in Vilna than in Lodz. In situations that were deemed a danger to the community, the Jewish Council had to react quickly, and specific offences were therefore dealt with on the spot, without reference to previously announced abstract definitions.

During the phases when Jewish Police officers were forced to assist with preparations for the German deportations, they appear to have been much less inclined to treat violations of their orders as "resistance." At such times, it was in any case impossible to preserve the illusion that the force had the interests of the ghetto community at heart, or was fulfilling even some of the "classical" police functions. Nor was there much point in recording criminal activities for purposes of internal prosecution, given that the offenders would be deported anyway.

As the above remarks demonstrate, the dilemma of having to meet German demands while wanting to act in the interests of the ghetto community was especially acute at the executive level. It is on this ambivalent role of the Jewish police that the bulk of research has focused to date, with particular emphasis on the aspect of profiteering from smuggling and the enforced participation of police officers in the German deportations, which many have deemed "morally reprehensible."[173] Such accusations have been voiced in numerous diaries, memoirs, and survivor stories, often leading researchers to make generalizations based on an imagined homogeneous ghetto community over its lifetime. This is, however, to ignore the fact that Jewish police officers were also part of that community; roles were not fixed, but could change as residents took up posts in the ghetto police force. In the early days of the Warsaw and Lodz ghettos, prior to the deportations, police officers commanded the respect of many residents; indeed, having a policeman in the family was sometimes even seen as a privilege.[174]

Another consequence of this research focus has been the lack of any methodical examination of the fact that, despite being forced from the outset to do the Germans' bidding, the Jewish police authorities were nevertheless also expected by the Jewish Council to perform "conventional" policing tasks within the ghetto community. In this sense, they were meant to act as executors of internally defined concepts of justice and criminality, and to regulate communal life in the ghetto.[175]

As such, they fulfilled an important role in terms of law enforcement. While their ability to conduct criminal prosecutions was hampered by the limited repressive powers granted by the German occupiers, the Jewish functionaries were in practice able to exploit what leeway there was, for example to dispense their own punishments.

On the issue of prosecution, the Council's dilemma was, moreover, compounded by a paradoxical development arising from the Germans' gradual loss of interest in ghetto-internal crimes in the wake of their extermination plans. On one hand, their reticence gave the Jewish Council more room for manoeuvre on this front; on the other, when the Germans did eventually intervene, it usually entailed murderous consequences for the parties concerned.

Some of the legal cases dealt with by the Jewish police led to trials before the ghetto courts, which took very different forms in Warsaw, Lodz, and Vilna. These were cases that either had been deemed particularly "serious" or were intended to serve an exemplary function by bringing home to the ghetto community the reality behind generic crime definitions.

Chapter Four

The Ghetto Courts

I maintained from the first that a new system of norms should be created, norms that were adjusted to the prevailing circumstances of life in order to deal with the needs of the moment. The canons of pre-war legal life should be cast away if they didn't answer actual needs.[1]

This remark by Stanisław Adler describes the premise adopted by the Jewish Council – and especially the Order Service functionaries – of the Warsaw ghetto in their efforts to pave the way for the adjudication of legal cases and disputes by improvised, Council-initiated courts. Internal courts were also set up in Lodz and Vilna to allow cases to be tried within the ghetto. These took very different forms, however, and were modified and institutionally augmented to some extent by the Jewish Councils or the responsible legal personnel over the lifetime of the respective ghettos.

Institutional Framework

In the case of Lodz, Rumkowski instructed the future presiding judge Szaja-Stanisław Jacobson to set up a judicial authority.[2] Following approval by the Gestapo, a panel of judges began to take cases from November 1940 onwards.[3] In a letter to the German Criminal Police in Lodz, the Jewish Council chairman outlined the structure and function of the newly created court: "The judiciary is composed of one president, one vice-president, and nine judges." Three prosecutors answerable to the president were to serve as examining magistrates, together with the Order Service Investigation Department.[4] The court comprised both a criminal and a civil department, as well as a "residential property dispute department."[5] Defendants had the right to a defence counsel and could appeal against verdicts.[6] A few months later, in July 1941, the lawyer Henryk Neftalin set up an additional juvenile court on Rumkowski's behalf.[7] Judicial proceedings in the ghetto were initiated either by the Jewish Council or by the German Criminal Police in Lodz, if they perceived German interests to be affected. The majority of such cases related to offences such as smuggling and illegal border crossings.[8]

In addition to the general court, a summary court was to commence operation from 15 March 1941 in order to assist in the "fight against criminality among community officials" and combat "corruption."[9] This new legal authority allowed judgments to be fast-tracked, whereby a panel consisting of a judge and two assessors ruled on cases without the presence of a public prosecutor or defence counsel, with the witnesses and defendants being fetched by the Order Service and brought directly to the hearing.[10] There had been substantial opposition to this arrangement: at the session of 14 March 1941, for example, one objector named Wajskopf pointed out that it was problematic for a prosecution to rely solely on the testimony of an informer due to the possibility of rivalry with the official concerned. In such cases, he suggested that the regular court be consulted. In late April 1941, the steering committee of the summary court requested a reorganization in order to make it possible to appeal against verdicts in future.[11] Soon after, Rumkowski introduced summary administrative procedures in an attempt to take even swifter action against "harmful elements." Writing in the *Geto-Tsaytung* in May 1941, he justified this measure as follows: "These dishonest people will not be handed over to the summary court as has been the case up to now, as even the fast pace of that court is too slow for them. I alone will be their judge. I will impose an administrative penalty on anyone guilty of dishonesty within a matter of hours."[12]

On 1 July 1941, Rumkowski dissolved the summary court, arguing that it had served its purpose. In the *Geto-Tsaytung*, he announced: "The number of cases that reach the summary court is extremely small, so that the maintenance of the institution as a separate body is superfluous at the present time."[13] From then on, such matters were dealt with by the regular court, while in urgent cases Rumkowski could adjudicate alone by a summary procedure, requiring only a statement by the lawyer Henryk Neftalin.[14] His reason for dissolving the institution seems rather implausible, especially given his subsequent dedication to the "fight against crime" within the Jewish Council departments.[15] The more likely explanation is that he wanted to judge critical cases by himself, in order to put his survival strategy for the ghetto community into practice "without complications."

In the Warsaw ghetto, the judicial authorities took different forms. Here, faced with the German restrictions on internal prosecutions, the Jewish Council legal department tried in vain to secure decision-making powers in matters of law.[16] On 15 August 1940 – before the final sealing of the ghetto – the Jewish Council chairman, Czerniaków, recorded in his diary that "the power to represent the Community in the courts" had been refused.[17] After ghettoization, therefore, special departments headed by so-called instructors were set up at the ghetto police stations without German approval. According to the OS functionary Zygmunt Millet, one of the main drivers of this initiative was Rafał Lederman, the head of the ghetto police training department.[18] Officially, the job of the instructors, who were mostly lawyers, was to intervene in the pursuit of offenders *before* the cases were referred to the Polish police.[19] Often, the accused would pay for their cases to be adjudicated internally rather than be passed to the Polish police or the Germans.[20] Under this arrangement, they were entitled to submit an appeal to the OS headquarters within two days.[21] In this way, as OS functionary Stanisław Adler relates, informal procedures came to be established by the Jewish Council and overarching standards formulated based on previous rulings.[22]

From 1940 to July 1942, judicial functions – particularly those relating to disciplinary offences by members of the Jewish self-administration – were also performed by the Jewish Council's so-called legal department and judicial authorities, between which there was a certain amount of personnel overlap.[23] In addition, the Council maintained an arbitration tribunal which intervened in case of conflicts such as rent disputes between tenants.[24] Presided over by "experienced legal personnel or figures of authority from the Jewish community," it was also able to impose certain limited sanctions, against which the convicted party had the right to appeal within seven days.[25] The house committees likewise assumed a mediating role in case of conflicts between tenants and married couples.[26] Their procedures were largely improvised, however, and the secretaries responsible for transcribing the "court hearings" often barely literate.[27] As mentioned earlier, after the mass deportations from the Warsaw ghetto in July 1942, almost all the Jewish Council's institutions ceased to exist – and hence also the judicial authorities, including the legal department.

In Vilna, the Jewish Council established the ghetto court at the Council's headquarters at 7 Rudnicka Street, most likely in mid-November 1941. While previous research has dated its inauguration to February 1942, Kruk gives the date as 15 November 1941, and indeed reports in an entry of 10 February 1942 on court hearings which had already taken place.[28] The Jewish Council initially served as an appeal body, until an appeal court was established, along with a civil court, in August 1942.[29] A report of December 1941 by Jewish Police chief Gens also testifies to the existence of a summary court, or at least summary procedures.[30] In Vilna too, the judicial authorities were closely linked to the Jewish Police, which had been the only other source of judicial power beside the Jewish Council chairman.[31] After the establishment of the court, power was shared by both authorities: while offences such as illegal border crossings, misconduct at the ghetto gates, and smuggling were dealt with directly by the Jewish Police, "classical" cases such as robberies and disputes between residents came under the jurisdiction of the courts.[32] Peculiar to the Vilna ghetto was an initiative founded on 8 February 1942 by a team of lawyers and law students from the ghetto community which granted residents legal advice and guaranteed them legal assistance in court.[33] The team consisted of thirty-eight people, including some with no previous professional experience.[34]

Official and Unofficial Separation from German Jurisdiction

Officially, the ghetto courts dealt with those cases which the German occupiers did not explicitly claim for themselves. These included offences relating to the ghetto border (illegal border crossings and smuggling) and "political" offences, such as the receipt of radio broadcasts and messages.[35] Which cases were of interest to the Germans and which a matter of indifference – even when part of their declared remit – only became apparent in practice, however.[36] Here too, their conduct was characteristically arbitrary, although certain areas of interest were discernible at different times.

Following the occurrence of the first murder within the Lodz ghetto in April 1941, the Germans demanded that the case be referred to their jurisdiction.[37] The Jewish police investigation department duly handed over the reins to the German Criminal Police,[38] whereupon the accused, Moszek Lajb Czosnek, was sentenced to death by the German court.[39] Over time, however, the divisions of responsibility and associated legal practices began to change. In Lodz, for example, the Jewish Council chairman Rumkowski met on 4 August 1941 with ghetto court representatives and functionaries from the German authorities in order to negotiate an expansion of the ghetto's internal jurisdiction. The German authorities granted the ghetto court new powers to rule on cases which had previously been their own responsibility: "smuggling, currency offences, the dissemination of information harmful to the German Reich, and murders both inside and outside the ghetto. The court was authorized to impose any punishment, up to and including the death penalty."[40] The fact that the Germans were prepared to augment the powers of Jewish authorities to this extent appears to be due partly to an assumption that the rulings of the ghetto court would conform more or less to the German agenda, and partly to a lack of interest in the cases described.[41] And since the measure was introduced in August 1941, after the German attack on the Soviet Union, it can already be cautiously interpreted as a reflection of the change in German core interests: from here on in, their sights were set on the wholesale murder of the Jewish population.

The separation between ghetto-internal and German jurisdiction did not only take place at an official level, however. In Warsaw especially, the members of the Jewish self-administration established practices designed to prevent the Germans from getting wind of the cases tried internally. By creating its own informal legal authorities, the Order Service thus sought to attract as little attention as possible. According to OS functionary Józef Rode, 90 per cent of all cases were kept out of the hands of the Germans, and interventions by the Polish police were also largely avoided.[42] The OS officer Stanisław Adler even suggested that no written notes be made during hearings in order to avoid any evidence of legal cases.[43]

In Vilna, the equivalent court likewise attempted to prevent the intervention of the German occupiers. This was not always successful, however – with catastrophic consequences for the defendants. In one case of 9 February 1942, for example, three residents were tried for attempted robbery.[44] After the sentences were pronounced – consisting of several months' imprisonment plus fines – the SS officer August Hering[45] entered the courtroom along with two Lithuanians and took the convicted subjects away; a few days later, their families were also taken. All were subsequently shot in Ponary.[46] The judges were horrified at this intervention, which brought home to them the limits of the court's autonomy: "The events made a strong impression and roused much bitterness in legal circles ... They think the judges weren't properly recognized and, unfortunately, they weren't independent!"[47]

When a murder case was heard before the ghetto court in Vilna in early June 1942, the court staff feared a similar intervention. In this case, however, the German authorities were content "merely" to be present at the enactment of the death penalty imposed by the court.[48] The ghetto court in Lodz was no less susceptible to German interference, despite the wide-ranging judicial powers conceded to it by the Germans. This applied particularly to thefts from workshops producing goods for the German army, such actions being classed as "sabotage."[49] In September

1943, for example, the German Criminal Police intervened when offcuts from the leather and saddlery workshop were found in the home of one of the workers, Icek Bekerman.[50] Bekerman was sent to the gallows on German orders, with all his colleagues forced to attend, along with delegates from all the workshops and his own family.[51]

Legal Traditions and Professional Experience

The staff of the ghetto courts often came with relevant experience in legal professions, with many having previously worked as lawyers or judges. In Warsaw, the establishment of the legal department was closely associated with Bolesław Rozensztat, who had been a lawyer prior to ghettoization and had tried for years to obtain a post as a legal advisor on Warsaw's city council.[52] The judge Mojżesz Prachownik, who was active in the ghetto court from its inception, had studied at the Warsaw faculty of law and humanities and gone on to work as a legal advisor.[53] Among the judges sworn in in November 1941, having arrived in the ghetto with the wave of "new resettlers" that autumn, there were likewise six lawyers from Vienna, Prague, and Frankfurt, including Dr Meyer Ber Kitz from Vienna, who was known as a "defence lawyer of European-wide renown."[54] Yisroel Kaplan, presiding judge of the regular court in the Vilna ghetto, had been a legal advisor on Vilna city council before the war and a former member of the local bar association.[55] Besides experienced lawyers, the Vilna judicial panel also comprised members who had not yet completed their law degrees or who had worked in other professions such as engineering before the war.[56]

The vast majority of the court personnel were men. Only in Lodz were a few women – with similar professional experience – to be found working at the ghetto courts. One of these, Romana Byteńska, was appointed in March 1941.[57] Another prominent employee was Regina Rumkowska, wife of the Jewish Council chairman Rumkowski, who had already worked as a lawyer prior to ghettoization.[58]

An entry in the Ghetto Chronicle indicates that "newcomers" to the Lodz ghetto were assessed on arrival for their potential as legal personnel: in December 1941, for example, the Chronicle notes that "with all the transports, especially those from Prague, at least five hundred former lawyers and judicial officers have arrived in the ghetto."[59] Over time, however, pre-war professional experience would prove to be of limited use in the ghetto. Besides a sound legal knowledge, the qualities in demand from now on were adaptability and a flexible approach to legal practice.

Needless to say, ghettoization brought a dramatic disruption to legal careers. Nevertheless, court employees – particularly in the early days of the ghettos in occupied Poland – still aspired to a professional future after the war, and this impacted in turn on the organization of the legal bodies. In the Vilna ghetto, court employees were anxious for their future prospects. In September 1942, Grisza Jaszuński declined his appointment to the judicial panel: he too harboured the desire to continue practising as a lawyer in a "free Poland" after the war, but feared that he would be forced in the ghetto to act "against the interests of the ghetto community," and that this would make it impossible for him to resume his occupation after the war. His concern suggests that people in the Vilna ghetto were already aware of the German murder campaign by this point. His response to the Jewish Council chairman's request was: "Why should only we do the dirty work while others wash their hands of it?"[60] As Kruk reports, Gens criticized Jaszuński's decision thus: "None of us think of what they will do after the ghetto. Meanwhile, we have an objective – to save ourselves."[61] With that, Jaszuński was suspended for a month without pay and deprived of his food ration.[62]

According to Adler, the recruitment of suitably qualified people for legal occupations was similarly problematic in the Warsaw ghetto.[63] Potential candidates seemed to anticipate the fact that working within the internal judicial system might force them to make morally dubious decisions. Some, on the other hand, took advantage of the career openings presented by the new situation: Adler himself records that he saw the task of formulating regulations and laws adapted to life in the ghetto as a unique judicial challenge and an opportunity.[64]

In the Lodz ghetto, the new judges sworn in in December 1941 expressed their surprise and gratitude at being allowed to continue practising in the ghetto. The Viennese lawyer Dr Kitz, for example, spoke for all the new appointees in declaring that he had "never expected even in my wildest dreams to be able to continue exercising my own profession after moving to the ghetto."[65]

When the death penalty was imposed on six defendants in relation to two murder cases tried in the Vilna ghetto in June 1942, the ghetto chronicler Kruk described this as a new professional experience for the judges: "For many years, a judge could work at his desk and live his whole life without pronouncing a death sentence. These simple Jews, the Jewish ghetto judges, were cast by destiny in the role of pronouncing six death sentences."[66] Unfortunately, the sources do not provide any reliable clues as to how the judges themselves felt about imposing the death penalties. Kruk's descriptions give the impression that they did not shy away from dispensing such harsh punishments, however; indeed, he himself appears to regard this as a "positive" opportunity for work experience.

In Lodz, it became clear that even the judiciary was subordinate to Rumkowski's "rescue through labour" strategy when, on 14 March 1944, ten members of staff were detailed to Radegast for manual work.[67] In July 1944, the Jewish Council chairman reduced the court staff dramatically in order to redistribute them to the workshops. As the chronicler notes: "Even the judges themselves were dispatched to production – Byteński and Dr Feygl to Metal Department I, for example."[68]

It was not only in matters of personnel that pre-war practices served as a model. In many ghettos, the same applied to the legal statutes employed by court officials,[69] who resorted to the legal norms familiar to them before ghettoization. The judicial panel in Vilna did introduce their own legal procedures, but only after a time. These were documented in a procedural code of July/August 1942 and a criminal law statute of 5 February 1943 running to 141 paragraphs.[70] Eventually, however, legal professionals in all the ghettos under discussion realized that pre-war laws were ill equipped to deal with the circumstances they were facing. The functionaries of the Jewish self-administration bodies therefore conceded that deviations were permissible where necessary because of ghetto conditions. As is clear from Adler's words at the top of this chapter, the extent to which the old legal norms could be applied to this novel situation was a matter of explicit debate in the Warsaw ghetto.[71] This approach was also reflected in the legal practice of the arbitration tribunal, which, according to the *Gazeta Żydowska*, was run by experienced lawyers along the lines of a Polish court, "whereby the hearing procedures [were] likewise adapted to the prevailing social conditions."[72]

In this respect, the legal practice of the Warsaw ghetto seems to have been characterized by a certain pragmatic flexibility. An anonymous member of the Jewish police writes of a form of arbitration based on rabbinic law – *Din Torah* – which was conducted by so-called instructors.[73] Since ghetto jurisdiction was officially based on the Polish legal system, the instructors are likely to have drawn on moral standards enshrined in Jewish law, appealing to people's consciences through their position of authority and imposing penalties that were often symbolic. According to Adler and Rode, different sanctions were applied in each district, with the instructors sometimes issuing mere threats.[74]

While Adler criticized the "arbitrariness" of these procedures, they can also be seen as a case-based form of jurisdiction in line with Jewish tradition. Another source points to the fact that religious influences on ghetto jurisdiction were officially suppressed by the Jewish Council. On 4 June 1942, the department for religious affairs addressed a letter to the Council's legal department proposing the creation of a court to adjudicate on violations of the Sabbath.[75] The legal department responded that there were no plans for any change with regard to the Sabbath, and hence no need for such a court.[76] Nevertheless, the evaluation criteria applied to individual cases do not appear to have been subject to any overall control by the Jewish Council. Although the legal personnel did not refer explicitly to religiously based legal principles, adapting to changing circumstances – and under exceptional conditions – was part of their mode of operation. As we shall see, this is a characteristic of Jewish law that was already observable in pre-eighteenth-century Jewish communities, for example.

In the Lodz ghetto, legal professionals had difficulty aligning themselves with pre-war Polish law from the outset. In the absence of any legal literature, the responsible commission – led by Jacobson and Neftalin – had to draw up the standards of the ghetto legal system "from memory."[77] On 19 August 1941, Rumkowski notified the German ghetto administration of the need for law books, "whether new or second-hand."[78] A modified version of pre-war Polish law was then formulated, including a statement in the ghetto-internal code of criminal procedure to the effect that any violation either of generally accepted principles of criminal law or of regulations issued by the German authorities or the Eldest of the Jews would be deemed a punishable offence.[79] At the same time, the delivery of the offender to the Germans was officially established as a punitive measure.[80]

Although Jewish law was not officially invoked in Lodz, religious matters did have a role to play. At their inauguration, the newly appointed judges swore before "the Almighty," the ghetto community, and the Jewish Council chairman to act according to the best of their knowledge and belief and, in the fulfilment of their obligations and particularly their sentencing, "to be guided neither by fear or favour, nor by any other circumstances, so help [me] God."[81] The ceremony was conducted in the presence of two rabbis.[82]

In December 1943, the Chronicle noted that the jurisdiction – and indeed the whole set-up – of the ghetto was founded on the principles of the Torah: law and justice.[83] The fact that all amnesties declared by Rumkowski took place on Jewish holidays, and that court witnesses had to swear an oath on the Torah scroll, is a further sign that traditional Jewish legal principles were still incorporated despite the official application of pre-war Polish law.[84]

The norms eventually formulated by the judicial panel in Vilna more than a year after ghettoization reflected the community's adjustment to the new reality of life in the ghetto, taking into account the intervening experiences. Here – in contrast to the situation in Warsaw and Lodz – the Jewish Council and ghetto population were already aware of the Germans' systematic murder plans. As a result, the legal practice of the ghetto was also shaped by German despotism, by the violence, hunger, and uncertainty endured, and by the need to create specific structures in response.

Excursus: Jewish Courts and Jewish Law
from a Historical Perspective

By the time Europe came to embrace the comprehensive modernization processes of the eighteenth century, its Jewish communities had evolved their own autonomous legal practices. Within this sphere, the Jewish court, *Bet Din*, and its members (the *dayanim*) enjoyed an exclusive legal status.[85] They drew their inspiration from Jewish law, or in other words the religiously based principles of *halakha*.[86] This term refers to interpretations of the written part of the Torah in the form of commandments issued by rabbis and Jewish scholars in relation to everyday conduct. In many places, lay courts (*hedyotot*) also emerged, which adjudicated on legal cases and conflicts within the community without explicit reference to *halakha*. The judges appointed by these authorities often lacked a thorough grounding in halakhic theory; consequently, their practice was often criticized by employees of the official Jewish courts and people in positions of religious authority, and the binding force of their decisions called into question. (*Hedyotot* translates roughly as "people with no expertise in Jewish law.")[87] Nevertheless, their rulings were still preferred over those pronounced by the non-Jewish courts of the "external," centralized authorities.

One reason for the emergence of these judicial institutions was the requirement by the central authorities that Jewish communities organize themselves.[88] At the same time, it was in the communities' own interest to structure their communal life independently and enforce their own legal values via suitable sanctions. A further reason was the fact that Jews were prohibited by the central powers from availing themselves of non-Jewish courts.[89] The legal practice evolved by the Jewish communities was characterized by a close relationship to everyday life and its changing nature. At the same time, certain normative lines of development served to guarantee a measure of continuity.[90]

These characteristics are reflected in a few key modes of exposition, such as interpretive method (*midrash*),[91] legislative enactments (*takkanot* and *gezeirot*),[92] and common law.[93]

The interpretative method partly consists in applying rules from the religious sphere in order to settle (legal) problems not resolved in the halakhic script. Most of these sources centre on the interplay between oral and written elements of the Torah. The "Oral Torah" encompasses all aspects of *halakha* not recorded in the ("Written") Torah, and owes its existence to the fact that it was actually forbidden to write down the various expositions of *halakha*. It was because of the failure to observe this prohibition that the Mishnah and the Jerusalem and Babylonian Talmud came into being.[94] The Mishnah is a collection of actual case studies from which abstract norms are derived.[95] Another sign of adjustment to new living conditions were the so-called *responsa* – a collection of statements in which rabbis responded to concrete, case-related legal questions put to them by members of the community.[96] This approach is typical of Jewish law more generally, where legal principles do not constitute a self-contained normative legal code, but are extrapolated from concrete situations.

Jewish law also served to fill gaps in legislation as a result of progress or changing circumstances, and to amend laws that were deemed to be out of date.[97] It was, however, rare for acts prohibited by the Torah to be transformed into lawful ones.[98] One exception in the field of criminal law was the death penalty. On this point it was decided that, although such a penalty was not specified in the Torah, it was necessary in exceptional cases "not because [the offender] deserved it, but because the circumstances of the time demanded it."[99] Prohibitions could also be justified if scholars identified a particular social need for them.[100] This approach demonstrates the preventive and exemplary theory of punishment typical of Jewish law: most of the penalties handed down were intended as a warning and deterrent to other potential wrongdoers.[101]

While matters of civil law could usually be adjudicated according to Jewish law without the imposition of restrictions by "external" state powers, jurisdiction over criminal prosecution always depended on the degree of independence granted to the Jewish communities by the relevant government. When it came to criminal law, the autonomy of the Jewish courts tended to be limited to more minor offences such as defamations or offences against property or "public morality."[102]

In terms of sanctions, many Jewish courts were allowed to issue custodial sentences to be served in their own prisons under the supervision of Jewish community officials. In rare cases, members of the court went as far as to impose death penalties.[103] One of the most common sanctions was banishment, which could range from debarment from worship in the synagogue to exclusion from the Jewish community.[104]

Another important feature was the frequent reliance on common law to decide matters such as the closure of regulatory gaps in line with changing circumstances.[105] This interweaving of religious and secular elements has given rise to a special relationship between Jewish law and morality. Although a distinction is made in *halakha* between normative rules, whose violation can be sanctioned by the courts, and plain ethical standards, Jewish courts can nevertheless deal with cases in which moral values are central by appealing to the faith and ethical conscience of the individuals concerned – without imposing penalties.[106]

A final key factor in the development of Jewish law is that of precedent. This may be a court decision, or alternatively the conduct of a halakhic scholar, if it can be developed into a legal principle.[107]

Following their legal alignment with non-Jewish majority societies from the end of the eighteenth century, the autonomy of Jewish communities was eventually restricted and Jewish law adapted to new circumstances. As Novak writes, "Whereas the traditional Jewish communities had a contracted status as a tolerated foreign enclave in premodern European nations, political emancipation gradually gave Jews rights as individual citizens in the new modern states, while simultaneously eliminating the collective privileges of the traditional communities."[108]

Tried Cases

The number of cases tried by the ghetto courts is hard to determine with any great accuracy. According to Józef Rode, the monthly total in the police districts of the Warsaw ghetto was around 150.[109] In the case of Vilna, Arad cites 115 cases involving 172 people in the first half of 1942, with a further 183 summary convictions by individual judges or Jewish police officers over the same period.[110] A table compiled by the ghetto court in Vilna shows that 93 sentences were pronounced by the court during the period from 15 November 1941 to 31 March 1942, and 45 by a police magistrate between 26 January and 31 March of that year.[111] In the Lodz ghetto, only a few cases were recorded in the first half of 1942, the Germans having deported 55,000 residents from the ghetto between mid-January and May.[112] On the other hand, the Jewish Council statistical department in Lodz recorded as many as 48 cases for the period from April to May 1944.[113] The main courtroom languages in the Lodz ghetto were Yiddish and Polish, though German was also permissible.[114] In Vilna, Yiddish dominated as the official language, while cases in the Warsaw ghetto are likely to have been conducted mainly in Polish.[115]

As illustrated below, the cases tried in the ghetto courts were based – to varying degrees – on both German and ghetto-internal definitions of criminality [116]

"German" Offences

It was only in Lodz that the German occupiers made systematic use of the ghetto-internal judicial system in order to punish the offences they had defined. This was because its internal legal sphere was the only one they recognized as such. In their view, it was "the sole genuinely enclosed residential area for Jews with its own law enforcement and penal institutions anywhere in the east." [117] In 1941 and the first half of 1942 in particular, the German Criminal Police referred numerous cases to the Jewish Council court with instructions to try them internally and report back on the sentence. Most of these – in line with the focus of German interests at the time – related to smuggling offences and illegal border crossings. [118] The judges based their verdicts on German crime definitions, and a copy of the rulings was forwarded to the German Criminal Police. On 15 April 1941, for instance, one resident named Silberstein – charged with "violation of ghetto curfew regulations and violation of Decree No. 78 of 9.VII.1940" (that is, smuggling) – was found guilty by Presiding Judge Prachownik of "conducting conversations at the border on 10.IV.1940 with people outside the ghetto in the execution of systematic smuggling activities." The offender was sentenced to four months' detention in the ghetto prison. [119]

The wording of the verdicts reflected the fact that the cases had been brought on *German* orders. They contained no explanation as to how the actions in question endangered the ghetto community, and were often very brief. Berek Nusbaum and Chaim Zeligman, for example – charged on 12 June 1941 with "violation of the police regulation concerning the Jewish Residential District" – were sentenced to four weeks' imprisonment for smuggling and made to pay fees and costs, the sole reason given being the "harmful nature of the activity." [120] No further details were provided.

Cases which saw "professional" smugglers in the dock seem to have been given more weight by the ghetto judges. On 9 April 1941, for instance, four men named Kaliński, Silberszac, Frajlich, and Strusik appeared in court accused of "violation of the ghetto curfew regulation" and were charged with the unauthorized import and sale of goods. In his verdict, Judge Merenleder drew particular attention to the men's criminal past: "Both Kaliński and Strusik enjoyed a very poor reputation before the war. Kaliński used to be a pimp and has lately associated exclusively with smugglers ... Likewise, Strusik ran a brothel before the war and has been seen constantly in the company of smugglers in the ghetto."[121] The accused were sentenced to four months' imprisonment plus court fees.[122] This verdict was clearly also influenced by ghetto-internal criteria, reflecting the Jewish Council's censure of those it regarded as profiting *individually* at the expense of the ghetto community by joining professional smuggling gangs.

Some trials involved both "German" and "internal" offences. A woman named Ester Chlebolub was accused, for example, of "violating the police regulation concerning the Jewish Residential District, aiding and abetting the escape of a prisoner and resisting Order Service officers."[123] In such cases, where internal issues also came into play, the judges appear to have imposed stricter sentences. In this instance, the accused was condemned to ten months' imprisonment, although her confession, remorse, age, and "absence of previous convictions" were taken into account as mitigating circumstances.[124]

It was German Criminal Police policy to hand over Jews – even if not previously resident in the ghetto – to the ghetto's internal jurisdiction. It had already begun using the ghetto central prison to detain non-resident Jews from August 1941, on the basis that conditions in German prisons were "too comfortable." This too was explained by the Germans with reference to the efficient law enforcement and penal institutions within the ghetto.[125] The same fate befell some non-Jews accused of offences regarded by the Germans as typically "Jewish," such as smuggling and illegal trafficking. On 13 August 1942, for example, a Polish woman named Anna Kozlowska was sent to the ghetto central prison by the German Criminal Police,[126] on the accusation of selling food she had bought up from farmers and unlawfully leaving her place of residence. Her case was likewise passed to the ghetto court, where Judge Motyl handed down a three-month prison sentence.[127]

From 1942, the number of cases transferred to the ghetto court began to dwindle.[128] Again, this is likely to have been due to changing German interests: by now, the priority was no longer "border enforcement" but the deportation and organized murder of ghetto residents. Of the few cases that continued to be referred in 1942, some were now based on new crime definitions, with food smuggling recast as a "crime against the wartime economy."[129]

Actions Prompting Fears of German Intervention

Individual actions which the Jewish Councils considered a threat to the ghetto community at large because of their potential to trigger a brutal intervention by the Germans were seldom the object of court proceedings. This was because infractions such as rumour-mongering or "hygiene offences" had to be quickly stifled,[100] and were therefore often punished directly by the Jewish police authorities. For this reason, explanations of why these actions were deemed a danger, and hence criminal, tended to be given in a preventive context, in the form of proclamations and notices in ghetto newspapers.

With the expansion of Rumkowski's "judicial" powers following the dissolution of the summary court, however, he also began increasingly to adjudicate on "hygiene offences" by means of summary administrative procedures. Thus, the "illegal candy production" condemned in his proclamations appears among the verdicts announced by the *Geto-Tsaytung* in summer 1941 under the headline *Administrative sentence for health harmers.* The offenders included "manufacturers" (one- to two-month prison sentences, in some cases with the withdrawal of two weeks' relief aid); "dealers" (prison sentences, in some cases with hard labour, withdrawal of their benefit entitlement, and, for one six-year-old, one month's detention in a reformatory); "accessories" who had allowed the production in their homes (one month's imprisonment); and those accused of concealing the goods (two weeks' strict imprisonment plus two weeks' hard labour for "provision of premises").[131] This detailed breakdown served to spell out to the ghetto community all that was encompassed by the offence of illegal candy production.

In the Vilna ghetto, the pressure to punish "harmful activities" without delay was even greater, as demonstrated by the numerous arrest warrants issued by the Jewish Police. The only case of this kind that came before the ghetto court was in December 1942, when a resident was sentenced to seven days' imprisonment for "spreading false rumours."[132]

Offences against Jewish Council Institutions and Regulations

Offences against ghetto-internal institutions and regulations were the object of numerous court proceedings, particularly in Lodz and Vilna, where the Jewish Council chairmen Rumkowski and Gens championed the strategy of "rescue through labour." Such cases were pursued energetically by the Lodz ghetto court: Rumkowski wanted a strict ban on any activities that represented a challenge to his institutions, and he brought his authority to bear on the judicial panel in order to get his way. Going by the sources, there appears to have been a sudden spike in thefts and bribery offences in Lodz in April 1941. That said, it should be borne in mind that the summary court had only been created shortly before, in March, and that there was therefore an imperative to justify the new judicial authority – hence the declaration in the *Geto-Tsaytung* that the summary court had had to work through the night on the very first day of its existence.[133] This episode shows, once again, that there was no "objective" criterion for defining criminality. It was only through the subjective classification of certain actions as criminal, and therefore prosecutable, that "offences" were created, which could then be cited in turn in order to justify the creation of new authorities.

With the establishment of the summary court, offences by members of the Jewish self-administration also came increasingly under scrutiny – especially the theft of goods and items from ghetto institutions and workshops. Given the sheer number of ghetto-internal departments, the potential for such offences was wide-ranging. In April 1941, the judicial panel issued eight tailors with prison sentences ranging from one to three months for stealing yarn and tailoring accessories from the workshops.[134] The caretaker of a cooperative, Bram Berenfeld, was sentenced to a month in prison for stealing regularly from a store, while the carter Icchok Zameczowski was charged with the theft of a cart and sentenced to a month's detention.[135] The longest sentence was six months, and was applied for instance in April 1941, in the case of Mordcha Gdalewicz, who had been accused of stealing fabric from a workshop.[136] In June 1941, the summary court also sentenced a clerk named Fajn from the purchasing department to six months' imprisonment for the embezzlement of nine hundred marks' worth of lunch tickets.[137] After the dissolution of the summary court, thefts were dealt with by summary administrative proceedings; in the case of thefts from bakeries, for example, activities such as "complicity to theft" or "keeping flour for the purpose of resale" became further criminal offences.[138] In addition, a whole range of activities on the part of community officials were defined under the headings of "bribery" and "abuse of office," and the individuals concerned accused of exploiting their position within the Jewish Council institutions for selfish motives. In April 1941, for example, a prison guard named Szeps was sentenced to six months' imprisonment after the court found him guilty of accepting bribes from inmates' relatives in return for allowing them to smuggle in food parcels, which he then also kept for himself.[139]

Another, more unusual legal case concerned an "offence" with which the head of the sewage disposal department, Lajzer Dąbrowski, was charged in April 1941. He had allegedly taken bribes from employees in return for assigning them shorter routes. By this means, the employees were able to boost their wages, which were paid according to the number of transported barrels, not the distance walked. Dąbrowski was sentenced to five months' imprisonment, half of which was to be spent transporting sewage himself.[140] In a further "fraud case" in April 1943, an overseer was sentenced to two months' imprisonment and a hundred-mark fine for giving priority to paying individuals in the bread rationing queue and procuring them jobs in return for money.[141]

On 16 January 1941, a dairy store manager named Bravermann was given a hefty jail sentence by the ghetto court for falsifying ration cards and accounts.[142] The verdict was reprinted three months later in the *Geto-Tsaytung* "to ensure the continued disgrace of the convict's name."[143] This case is a further example of the key importance attached to the public announcement of verdicts as a means of hammering home ghetto-internal definitions of criminality and deterring others from committing similar offences.

One case that provoked uproar within the ghetto community was the trial in May 1943 of Jakub Ratner, the head of the so-called criminal section of the ration card department, the central dispensing point for food coupons. Ratner was accused of appropriating bread and food coupons belonging to deportees and selling the food thus obtained, "as it would have been impossible for him and his family to consume such quantities between them."[144] Such conduct was deemed particularly scandalous on the part of someone who was himself officially responsible for pursuing "ration card malversations" (i.e., fraud cases), and who already enjoyed an extra food allowance in that capacity.[145] Rumkowski, who acted as judge, examining magistrate, and moderator under the "administrative procedure," seriously considered the death penalty in this case, reasoning that "I took on a heavy task when I assumed the duties of a court of law. But the circumstances of the time demanded it. Action had to be taken in order to render harmless one of the most dangerous individuals in the ghetto. This took the form not of an elaborate court procedure, but of a conference that resulted in a verdict. The man, who was supposed to work for the good of the ghetto, only inflicted harm on it ... I have no sympathy for this kind of person, and if I didn't fear for the consequences and the possibility of setting a precedent, my hand would not falter in signing his death warrant."[146] Instead, the judicial panel imposed a three-year prison sentence, a fast day every fortnight, and fifty cane strokes on commencement of the sentence.[147]

It is unclear why Rumkowski stopped short of enforcing the death penalty. As discussed earlier, precedent was a key factor in Jewish law, helping to adapt the dispensation of justice to changing circumstances.[148] Although Rumkowski did not defer officially to *halakha*, it may nevertheless have been part of the reason for his hesitation in applying the ultimate sanction. Two motives may have played a role here: first, Rumkowski himself belonged to the circle of officials who were constantly being accused of corruption and self-enrichment from community property. As such, he may have feared that the imposition of the death penalty on a Jewish Council member could set a precedent and rebound on him personally at some point. Second, he may have been loath to create new judicial standards at the time of the trial in May 1943, on the basis that the "external" circumstances of the ghetto were changing too fast to allow much adaptation. Faced with this situation, he may have preferred to adopt a flexible approach to legal matters that avoided creating precedents.

The Lodz ghetto court remained in operation until the beginning of summer 1944, when the ghetto was liquidated. The last cases to be tried mostly concerned the offence of "lunch fraud." In January 1944, the head of the carpet workshop, Gustaw Garfinkel, was accused, among other things, of issuing soup passes for employees who had long since ceased to work there and, furthermore, trading in them.[149] On 26 January 1944, he was sentenced by the court to two years' imprisonment, only to be "resettled" from the central prison the very same day.[150] Even at this late stage, when Rumkowski knew about the German murder campaign, he still attempted to assert his own legal objectives at the judicial level. The resulting verdicts reflected his survival strategy for the ghetto community, which involved ensuring the efficient working of his complex administrative apparatus and the prevention of "personal enrichment at the expense of the ghetto community." His efforts to achieve this continued even after thousands of residents had already been deported and the prompt arrival of the Red Army remained the only hope.

The ghetto courts ruled not only on the conduct of members of the Jewish self-administration but also on violations of ghetto regulations by ordinary residents. These differed from offences such as conventional thefts in that they affected the entire ghetto community as opposed to merely harming private individuals.

As threatened by Rumkowski in his proclamations, it was the policy of the Lodz ghetto court to sanction residents "for unauthorized receipt of relief aid." In July 1941, for instance, a resident named Jacob Freniel was sentenced to thirty days' detention and made to repay the amount claimed plus a fine.[151] Cases where the recipients were already profiting from "community property" in the context of their activities were highlighted accordingly in the court reports of the *Geto-Tsaytung*: one such offender was Aleksander Majer, who was censured for using more than his fair share of gas in order to cook lunches for paying customers.

That he should claim benefits in these circumstances was regarded as particularly reprehensible.[152]

Besides offences against "ghetto community property," other moral criteria were brought to bear in court. Special condemnation was reserved, for example, for those who concealed dead family members – often children – in order to appropriate their ration cards. On 25 March 1941, a resident named Szlama was to have stood trial for hiding the body of his seven-year-old son for that very purpose; in the event, however, the "unnatural father" – as the ghetto chronicler described him – died the day before the trial.[153]

In July 1941, the court sentenced several residents to fines and imprisonment for a specific kind of theft at the ghetto administration's expense: the "theft of electricity" or "complicity to the theft of electricity."[154] This included activities such as "removing seals from electricity meters or current limiters ... and bypassing the latter," or diverting current to earth via a lead cable.[155] While the penalties for bypassing current limiters and tapping into the main meter ranged from five to thirty marks and four weeks' detention, sometimes with six months' probation, the "use of a special wiring arrangement damaging to the electricity plant" was punished somewhat more severely, with a fifty-mark fine and one month's imprisonment.[156] In his proclamations from spring 1941 onwards, Rumkowski had begun by simply appealing to residents to save electricity. It was not until the above practices had been "field-tested" that the offence of "electricity theft" became an established category.

The judicial staff in Vilna were similarly occupied with violations of ghetto regulations. In late 1941 and early 1942, the court ruled on several cases in which the passes of skilled workers had been stolen and used by other residents.[157] The sentences imposed were harsher than those for conventional thefts, indicating that here, as in Lodz, such activities were seen as a challenge to ghetto institutions. On 5 March 1942, the court heard two cases involving the use of stolen bread ration cards,[158] and again censured the offenders for undermining the ghetto provisioning system: "By this act, the accused [Fania Pulkin] has harmed others who were entitled to ration cards, and is therefore guilty of an offence."[159] Pulkin was sentenced to seven days' detention and fined seventy-five reichsmarks for the possession of stolen bread ration cards during the period from December 1941 to January 1942, while her fellow accused, a man named Spokoini, was acquitted.[160]

Not all prosecuted offences related to the ghetto food supply, however: in one case of April 1943, for example, eight residents who had failed to return books to the public library were given suspended one-day prison sentences and made to pay the cost of the books and court proceedings.[161] The term "theft" was not used in this case, however, which – along with the largely symbolic nature of the prison sentence – suggests that the judicial panel was more concerned with the challenge to the ghetto library as an institution than with the "appropriation of another's property." This shows just how central cultural activity in the ghetto was to the Jewish Council's survival strategies: public access to books in the ghetto was designed to help residents create meaning and distraction for themselves, in the hope that this would strengthen their individual will to survive.[162]

Offences involving acts of resistance against the Jewish police authorities were generally handled by the authorities themselves. In July 1943, however, the ghetto court took the unusual step of prosecuting two cases of this kind – a measure that the chronicler Kruk also describes as exceptional. The trial resulted in the two defendants being sentenced respectively to fourteen and seventeen nights' detention in the ghetto prison.[163] This course of action may have been prompted by the fact that, by July 1943, Gens was more reliant than ever on the ability of the Jewish Police, as the executive organ, to drive home German demands in the ghetto community. By this time, the Germans had already murdered thousands of Jews in surrounding ghettos, and the armed resistance groups in Vilna had been gaining support since spring 1943.

"Classical" Legal Cases

The ghetto courts also tried "classical" cases of criminal law: that is, criminal activities already defined as such prior to ghettoization, such as robberies or murders perpetrated on individuals. These, too, assumed specific forms in the ghettos, however – and the courts applied their own standards when judging them.

Cases involving conflicts between private individuals are normally tried under civil law. Because the Jewish Councils in Lodz and Vilna stepped into the role of "prosecutor," however – on the grounds that the actions in question posed a danger to the community – such cases took on a criminal character. In the Warsaw ghetto, the court dealt predominantly with matters that would traditionally be subject to civil law. These related to disputes between individuals without the intervention of a third-party "prosecutor" such as the Jewish Council. Adler writes, for example, of cases involving altercations between tenants which were handled by the instructors at the district police stations: "The most typical conflicts were between the principal tenant and his sub-tenants, the latter being arbitrarily deprived of electricity, gas and other conveniences, in order to force them to accept a rent increase or leave the premises."[164] According to Adler, criminal offences were also tried, but tended to be of a relatively "harmless" nature. Here too, the jurisdiction was constrained by the desire to avoid escalation to the German courts.[165]

The small number of "classical" criminal cases prosecuted in the Warsaw ghetto was partly due to the informal nature of its judicial authorities. Another factor was that its Jewish Council – in contrast to those led by Gens and Rumkowski – did not place the courts in the service of an overarching survival strategy in which "classical" legal cases were also increasingly classed as a danger to the community at large.

In Lodz, the ghetto court also tried cases of theft in which the focus was on the individual as the injured party. Usually, these involved actions that were considered particularly morally reprehensible. In March 1941, for instance, two women named Blutsztajn and Owsiana went before the court charged with "robbery of the late Mrs Kronzylber and in particular the theft of her gold teeth." The court sentenced the former to six weeks' detention, and the latter to four weeks with six months' probation.[166]

On 4 August 1941, the ghetto chronicler in Lodz reported on what was in his view a "fairly typical trial" in a case of theft:[167] charged with stealing the flesh of a dead horse which had lain unburied on the waste dump overnight, the accused parties stated that "they had been driven by their extreme poverty to seek meat in order to quell their hunger."[168] In view of the motive, the judicial panel issued a relatively lenient verdict, recommending a prison sentence of four weeks each.[169]

Property offences were also tried on a regular basis in the Vilna ghetto. In January 1942, for instance, Chaim Leib Kriszański and Schmuel Kriszański were sentenced respectively to four weeks' detention plus a thousand-rouble fine and three weeks' detention plus a thousand-rouble fine for "theft of another person's property."[170] Even cases involving relatively small quantities of "stolen goods" went before the court: one example in October 1942 concerned a woman who had stolen her neighbour's *cholent* – a traditional Sabbath stew – for which the victim demanded generous compensation. Similarly, in January 1943, a defendant named Levit was sentenced to three weeks' detention for the theft of a fellow resident's coat.[171] The court's remit extended to conflicts between residents which had occurred *outside* the ghetto. In one case in September 1942, it found a resident guilty of stealing a watch and a small sum of money while working at a forest camp.[172]

In addition, the courts in Lodz and Vilna dealt with violent robberies within the ghetto communities. In Vilna, one such case was tried in February 1942 in which the defendant, Chaim Rajman, was accused of attacking the gold dealer Herman Feigenbaum with the aid of his accomplices, Holts and Glezer. He had managed to get away with 1,600 reichsmarks, five pounds of silver, and a watch, which he planned to use in order to obtain a work certificate in advance of an impending German operation.[173] As mentioned earlier, these documents served to identify the bearer as having a job in the ghetto, thus protecting him from murder by the Germans. Rajman was sentenced to six months' imprisonment and a two-hundred-mark fine for this offence, and his accomplices to three months' imprisonment each.[174]

In the Lodz ghetto, few of the violent robberies tried focused on the harm done to individuals. Here, too, the emphasis was invariably on the potential harm to the ghetto community. This is illustrated by a robbery of August 1942, in which Icek Adler was accused of obtaining a sack of flour from a food depot by force, "knocking down the guard on duty, Bornstein Boruch, with three punches to the head, then binding his hands and gagging him."[175] What exercised the court most was the fact that Adler had stolen a sack of flour "to the detriment of the Eldest of the Jews."[176] The verdict was reported to the ghetto criminal investigation department, which suggests that the German Criminal Police had expressed an unusual interest in the case.[177] On 7 September 1942, the offender was deported from the ghetto by the Gestapo.[178]

The cases handled by the judicial authorities reflect how the characterization of "violent crimes" changed under the conditions of ghettoization. As mentioned earlier, one case tried in the Warsaw ghetto concerned an old beggar woman who took in vulnerable residents for many months under the pretext of caring for them, only to wait for them to die so that she could sell their clothes.[179]

Another issue that sometimes came before the ghetto courts was that of blackmail – an activity that took specific forms in the ghetto. On 3 March 1943, for example, three youths named Kucharski, Neuhaus, and Koprowski went on trial for sending a malicious letter to a woman in the ghetto threatening to report her husband for criminal activities unless she paid them two hundred dollars in gold.[180] The victim took the case to the *Sonderkommando*, whereupon the perpetrators claimed to have acted "out of youthful exuberance," insisting that they had intended to spend the money on essential clothing. The defence pointed to the boys' good family background, reminded the court that the "detrimental social conditions were chiefly to blame for the youthful prank,"[181] and recommended that they be acquitted. The judicial panel stood firm, however, and sentenced Kucharski to three months' imprisonment, Neuhaus to two months, and Koprowski to six weeks, arguing that the youths were sufficiently mentally mature to be "aware of the consequences of their prank."[182] This case shows that the young-sters' social background cut relatively little ice with the judges in 1943. In the ghetto, former social class distinctions became less significant. All residents faced similar hardships and, in their attempt to get by and secure their own survival, they resorted to whatever means they could – including those defined as criminal – regardless of whether or not they were "from a good family."

In the Vilna ghetto, a case of blackmail was tried in March 1943 which drew a large audience.[183] One resident had written an anonymous letter to a woman in the ghetto demanding that she send him a sum of money placed inside a book; otherwise, he would kill her husband. While the defence pleaded for a lenient punishment, emphasizing the naivety of the accused, the judicial panel debated whether or not he should be treated like a "professional" blackmailer. A sentence of six weeks' detention was eventually imposed.[184]

Cases of sexual abuse and rape were handled extremely rarely by the ghetto courts, although we know from the sources that such offences were committed.[185] Here again, however, it was the crime-defining agents – that is, the Jewish Councils – who called the tune, and their crit-ical scrutiny (particularly in the case of Vilna and Lodz) was reserved for those activities that represented a danger to the community. This is illustrated by the only case of abuse for which records exist. It was tried by the Lodz court on 5 September 1943 and saw a man named Ordynans convicted of "defiling" a fifteen-year-old orphan girl, Cyrla Goldsztejn, who had been entrusted to his care. In the verdict, the ele-ments of this offence were defined as follows: "The crime of indecent assault consists inter alia in touching the sexual organs or other covered parts of another person's body if done with lewd intentions."[186] The defence in this case was assumed by Regina Rumkowska.[187] Sentencing the accused, the judge emphasized that the punishment was intended to reflect the fact "that the defendant has committed a criminal act against a child entrusted to his care by the Welfare Committee for Juve-niles, and that he has abused the trust not only of this committee, but of the whole community."[188] Reference was made to the fact not just that Ordynans had exploited the child's predicament and inflicted "moral harm" on her, but that a crime had been committed against the ghetto community.

The ghetto court judges adjudicated in some murder cases. Two examples, from the Lodz and Vilna ghettos respectively, illustrate the changing evaluation criteria applied by the judges over time. After the first ghetto-internal murder case in Lodz had been tried by a German Special Court in April 1941, a resident named Szlomo Bernstein was summoned on 24 December[189] to appear before the ghetto court, charged with killing his brother-in-law, Szmul Jankiel Litwak, in a brawl in October.[190] In the ruling, the facts were set out as follows: "In addition to various pre-war offences, the victim had already been convicted twice by the ghetto court, for the crimes of wood theft and fraud. The murderer, who had been a pedlar before the war, was sentenced to one and a half years in prison for the purchase of stolen goods."[191]

As this verdict demonstrates, offences committed prior to ghettoization were deemed relevant to the trial. Both the accused and the victim were referred to by the judge as belonging to the "criminal milieu of Bałuty."[192] The judicial panel complained that the parties' social background made it difficult to clarify the circumstances of the crime, and that the witnesses – also from the criminal underworld – persisted in making untrue and contradictory statements.[193] In that sense, they were emphasizing the point that the crime was a "conventional" one, and not primarily a "ghetto-specific offence" associated with the catastrophic living conditions and new prohibitions under German occupation.

The duty counsel, on the other hand, drew the attention of the judicial panel to the accused's social background, describing him in her own words as "crude" and "simple." She also pointed out that the thirty marks at issue were a large sum to him, and that he had four children to feed. She argued that Bernstein had asked Litwak for the money amicably on several occasions. Moreover, the brother-in-law had been the first to resort to violence, and Bernstein had been more or less forced to defend himself.[194] Nevertheless, Judge Alexander Bienstock concluded that Bernstein had murdered his brother-in-law deliberately, although he insisted that "the sentence [must] be adjusted to the prevailing circumstances in the ghetto and the times we are living in."[195]

Bienstock rejected the death penalty in this case, even though Rumkowski had repeatedly called for its use in the ghetto. At the same time, he chose harsh words when delivering the verdict, stressing the need to "clear the atmosphere in the ghetto of filth and root out such dangerous elements with the greatest rigour, so as not to feel ashamed in future of having tolerated such elements in times as hard as these."[196] In so doing, the judge was looking beyond December 1940, considering how the treatment of criminal behaviour in the ghetto would be judged after the war, and worrying that the sentences might be seen as too lenient. The eventual sentence in the Bernstein case consisted of two years' imprisonment with hard labour.[197]

A murder case was also tried by the ghetto court in Vilna. Unlike the Lodz case, the trial took place at a time when the Jewish Council was already aware of mass shootings in Ponary. In his Chronicle entry of 4 June 1942, Herman Kruk chose the heading "Murder in the ghetto – a Sherlock Holmes story" to describe the sensational decision by the Jewish judges to impose the first death penalty on ghetto residents. Their ruling was approved by the Jewish Council – without obtaining German consent.[198] The judges found five defendants guilty of murdering the yeshiva student Józef Gerstein on 3 June 1942 and burying his body. In court, the accused also confessed to the murder and robbery of Hertsl Lides.[199]

Another resident, Yankl Avidon, was sentenced to death for murdering the Jewish Police officer Yankl Greenfeld. Avidon had already been detained in the Vilna ghetto prison since March 1942.[200] Arad writes that the Jewish Council and court used the murder of the policeman merely as a pretext for executing Avidon. Their real motives, he argues, were far more serious: the Jewish Council was afraid that the accused might become a danger to itself and hence to the ghetto community as a whole.[201] The reason for this fear of Avidon was the allegation that he had already put the Jewish Council in great danger in the Lida ghetto. Kruk relates the background as follows: in March 1942, a Russian Orthodox priest had been murdered and robbed in Lida, a town close to Vilna. During the incident, one of the perpetrators had dropped a jacket bearing a Star of David. The Germans reacted by ordering the Jewish Council in Lida to hand over "the Jewish criminals" within ten hours; otherwise they would murder a thousand ghetto residents. The Council duly delivered six suspects to the German occupiers.[202] The suspects were resourceful, however, and denounced the Jewish Council, telling the Germans that it had issued fake passports for escapees from the Vilna ghetto. This accusation led the Germans to arrest seven members of the Jewish Council in Lida. Now, the Jewish Council in Vilna feared that Avidon could have been one of the denunciators, the suspicion being that he had been released as a reward before coming to the Vilna ghetto.[203] These reasons were not mentioned by the judges before the ghetto court, however, and the official subject of the trial on June 1942 was exclusively the murder of the Jewish Police officer. "The ghetto court sentenced the murderers to death by hanging. The sentence was carried out by Jewish policemen in the presence of Commandant Gens."[204]

In his account, Kruk quotes the speech made by Gens prior to the execution in the ghetto. "Police, *Judenrat*: Of seventy-five thousand Vilna Jews, only sixteen (thousand) remain. These sixteen (thousand) must be good, honest and hardworking people. Anyone who isn't will end the same way as those who were sentenced today. We will punish every such case and will even kill with our own hands. Today we carry out an execution of six Jewish murderers who killed Jews. The sentence will be carried out by the Jewish Police, who protect the ghetto and will go on protecting it."[205]

The death sentences pronounced by the Vilna ghetto judges in the above case stand in contrast to the more lenient treatment of the murder case in Lodz. The difference between the two had to do with awareness of German intentions. In December 1941, at the time of the trial in the Lodz ghetto, the Jewish Council was still ignorant of the German murder plans, and the case against Bernstein therefore focused primarily on the subjective motives of the accused. At that stage, offences committed by individual residents were not yet deemed a danger to the Jewish Council or the ghetto community at large. For this reason, the judge argued against the death penalty. Besides, he was looking to the future and considering how his conduct in the ghetto would be judged after the war. In this respect, the judges still enjoyed a certain amount of independence from the Jewish Council chairman. The ghetto court in Vilna, by contrast, operated under quite different circumstances: ever since the creation of the ghetto in September 1941, the Jewish Council had known about the German mass shootings in Ponary. In June 1942, Gens effectively had more power than the Council chairman himself and sought to prohibit individual actions he thought might endanger the Jewish Council or ghetto community. The court was likewise placed in the service of his goals. Also at stake was the ability to judge the case *autonomously* within the ghetto. This is evident, too, from Kruk's accounts in the Chronicle: "Everyone was relieved at the announcement that the accused would not be turned over to the 'outside world', that their sentence would be carried out by the ghetto and that ... [the ghetto had made its own judgment]."[206]

In December 1941, legal professionals in the Lodz ghetto still distinguished indirectly between "conventional murder," according to pre-war criteria, and new ghetto offences. This distinction no longer applied in the Vilna ghetto, where a crime meant any action that might jeopardize the ghetto community. Here, "classical" pre-war offences affecting only private individuals were now rarely prosecuted.

The situation was different again in the Warsaw ghetto, where neither internal murders nor serious robberies were tried. Whether no such cases occurred, as Adler claims, is unclear.[207] The diary of one Order Service officer certainly attests to a murder in the community in September 1942.[208] And in a report from the Warsaw ghetto, a case of 7 December 1941 is described in which a sixteen-year-old boy had strangled his sick younger sister, an act to which he had apparently been driven by severe material hardship resulting from the death of their parents.[209] There were, in short, sufficient reasons to initiate court proceedings. The fact that this did not happen was due, as mentioned earlier, to the informal character of the judicial authorities in the Warsaw ghetto, which lacked the necessary clout. Besides – unlike its counterparts in Vilna and Lodz – the Jewish Council in Warsaw did not seek to make such proceedings part of an overarching survival strategy.

"Extenuating Circumstances" and Amnesties

Despite their limited scope for action, the legal personnel conducting the trials argued where possible for "extenuating circumstances," in an attempt to exercise their own evaluation criteria. In Lodz, this was true regardless of whether the trial took place on German orders or at the initiative of the Jewish Council. One court ruling of August 1942 in a smuggling case against Szmul Dimantsztajn stated, for example, that "The accused's youth and poverty, hunger and lack of proper housing were accepted as extenuating circumstances."[210] The difficult material situation facing ghetto residents could, therefore, have a mitigating effect, especially if the accused had sick family members to care for.[211] In Lodz, this was a common occurrence. In Vilna, too, the "difficult material situation of the accused" was taken into account in the ruling of 5 March 1942 against Fania Pulkin, charged with the appropriation of stolen food ration cards. She was sentenced to seven days' detention and a fine of seventy-five reichsmarks.[212]

Confessions of guilt also worked in the defendants' favour,[213] and were usually accompanied by a pledge to refrain from any future wrongdoing.[214] In the Lodz ghetto, the possession of a clean record both before and after ghettoization was likewise an advantage.[215] For this purpose, the court could require the Order Service to produce supporting character references for individual residents. These were based on the statements of fellow residents who had known the person concerned prior to ghettoization.[216] The problem with this system was that it carried the inevitable risk of recriminations arising from personal disputes and revenge fantasies, and it was virtually impossible to verify past criminal conduct via official documents. In other words, even though definitions of criminality and law had changed under ghettoization conditions, pre-war evaluation criteria were still considered relevant.

A further notable mitigating factor was the youth of the accused.[217] In Lodz, the judiciary worked with the schools department – probably from June 1941 onwards – to devise an educational concept for dealing with adolescent offenders. Their conduct, unlike that of adults, was attributed directly to the "catastrophic material conditions" in the ghetto.[218] Another consideration was that families often pressurized youngsters into committing criminal acts.[219] The prisons where they would have to serve their sentences were described as nothing short of "schools of crime,"[220] and it was therefore argued that adolescents should be punished differently in order to help them get back on the "straight and narrow."[221] These efforts gave rise to the establishment in July 1941 of a juvenile court.[222] In addition, an initiative on the part of court representatives and the schools department – most likely in August 1941 – led to the foundation of a group of trustees with the aim of combating juvenile delinquency in the ghetto.[223] With regard to punishments, the juvenile magistrate was to consult with the group of trustees, which included teachers and educationalists. Key consideration was to be given to the circumstances of the offence, the "mental and moral state"[224] of the minors, their past, and the moral and material circumstances of their families.[225]

How to deal with minors within the criminal justice system was a matter of similar debate in Vilna. One reason for this was the detention in March 1942 of thirteen children thought to belong to a criminal gang of forty youngsters. On this occasion, court representatives, Jewish Police functionaries, and the education specialists Miriam Gutgestalt, Rokhl Brojdo, and Mojsze Olicki from the Jewish Council's education and schools department came together to discuss what measures to take.[226] Kruk reports on a case of October 1942 in which a minor named Wiesenberg went before the court for stealing wood from the police kitchen, and was subsequently referred to the juvenile magistrate Dimitrowski.[227] Possibly, the magistrate in question was appointed to the regular court as a result of the deliberations of that spring.

In summary, social and material hardship was given special emphasis in cases involving offences committed by children and adolescents. Instead of harsh prison sentences, other measures for deterring criminal activities had to be found. To this end, a certain responsibility was placed on the ghetto community in both Lodz and Vilna.[228] Young offenders were not sent to the ghetto prison, for example, but to a specially created reformatory where the concept of custodial care was given rather more weight.[229] Another idea propagated by the judiciary in the Lodz ghetto was the creation of guardianships for orphans.[230]

A further way in which the Jewish Council chairmen could exercise a degree of autonomy was through the internal amnesties in their gift. The choice of beneficiaries fell in some instances to the court personnel, and in the Lodz ghetto to the court chairman. In the case of "repeat offenders" and "professional criminals," he was obliged to consult the public prosecutor or investigation department. If a verdict had already been pronounced, the decision to declare an amnesty had to be taken at a public hearing.[231] Such amnesties marked a turning point in that they rendered previously punishable activities lawful again. The reasons for their proclamation, and the people who stood to benefit from them, were many and various. In Lodz, Jewish Council chairman Rumkowski issued numerous amnesties on Jewish holidays. In 1941, for example, prisoners were pardoned at Passover, at Jewish New Year in September, and at Hanukkah;[232] in 1943, the same thing happened at Passover and Yom Kippur.[233] In 1942, when the Germans deported over 70,000 people from the ghetto to Kulmhof, the chairman refrained from issuing a general pardon, so that he could draw on the inmates of the ghetto prison to help make up the required deportation quota.

The large number of amnesties in the Lodz ghetto appears at odds with Rumkowski's threat to deal severely with criminals regardless of whether they had simply stolen a potato or were guilty of a more serious crime.[234] The fact that he, in concert with the judicial panel, granted some offenders exemption from punishment while continuing to punish others suggests that the Jewish Council – in contrast to its rhetoric – did indeed operate some kind of classificatory system.

In the case of so-called general amnesties, such as that of September 1941 or Passover 1943, certain sentences were either rescinded or curtailed. During the New Year amnesty of September 1941, for example, Rumkowski cancelled all sentences of up to one month and half of sentences from one to three months. Prison sentences of *more than* three months remained unchanged, however. In other words, the existing evaluation criteria continued to be applied, but the overall effect was one of mitigation.[235] In addition, certain offences could be explicitly ruled in or out of an amnesty. In September 1941, for instance, all prison sentences for "candy offences" were revoked alongside those described above.[236] At Yom Kippur 1943, punishments were waived for a variety of offences: "thefts of a trifling nature, mainly involving potatoes and smaller quantities of food, along with minor vegetable and wood thefts. A few garden trespasses, three cases of fraud, one of defamation, one of criminal negligence in office, one incautious purchase and two cases of street trading."[237] The September 1941 amnesty, on the other hand, did not include wood theft, flour theft from bakeries and in transit, or passive and active bribery.[238] In 1943, only food thefts from private homes were excluded.[239]

In the case of the remissions granted in October 1943, the Jewish Council paid special attention to the circumstances of the "delinquents." Stealing offences were now often classed as "hand to mouth thefts." Poverty, the "exceptional predicament" of an entire sick family, and "hunger oedema" were taken into consideration as "mitigating circumstances."[240] Despite this policy of clemency, however, the crime-fighting priorities set by Rumkowski at various times were still maintained. In 1941, the theft of wood or flour from Jewish Council bakeries remained a punishable offence, for example, while sentences for infractions such as "candy offences," which endangered the health of the population but did not challenge the ghetto's internal administration system, were remitted. Sources show that the evaluation criteria for amnesties in the Lodz ghetto were altogether less stringent in 1943. The fact that the hunger and sickness of relatives were deemed "mitigating circumstances" meant that greater allowances were made for the hardships suffered by ghetto residents.

In the Vilna ghetto, Jakub Gens proclaimed a broad amnesty on 15 July 1942 on the occasion of his appointment as Jewish Council chairman,[241] in order to offer even "genuine criminals" the chance to pledge themselves to a "life of honesty."[242] In this case, all imprisoned residents were to be released. At the same time, however, Gens threatened to act with the utmost severity "in the fight against criminal elements" should they reoffend.[243] Under the pardon, ongoing criminal investigations and court proceedings were also suspended, and residents were given the opportunity to surrender any "illegally" obtained bread ration cards to the Jewish Council by 19 July 1942 without fear of sanctions.[244]

The commitment to an "honest life" promoted by Gens in summer 1942 was based on the hope that the survival of the ghetto community could be secured through labour until the arrival of the Red Army. Following the amnesty, former crime definitions were subordinated to new priorities in response to the German extermination campaign, with the emphasis on *"labour, discipline, and order."*[245] By this stage, supplying a workforce was evidently more important than dealing with the challenge posed to ghetto institutions by the use of illegal bread ration cards.

The Jewish Council in Warsaw did not grant any amnesties. Once again, however, we must remember that its judicial bodies were of a more improvised nature than those of Vilna and Lodz. Court proceedings and arbitration processes operated on an altogether more informal basis, and legal staff were keen to avoid attracting German attention. It is possible, therefore, that extenuating circumstances were claimed in specific, individual cases without being part of any overall strategy.

Specific Legal Problems

The living conditions of the ghetto and its subjugation to the German agenda posed specific problems for the court personnel. Writing on the Warsaw ghetto, Adler describes, for instance, how difficult it was to obtain witnesses for the trials. Often, residents were afraid that the accused might be in cahoots with the Germans and thus in a position to "make use of their connections."[246] The judicial staff also complained that witnesses tended to be unreliable: in many cases, they had to be summoned several times, sometimes to the point of being forcibly escorted to the police station by Order Service officers. Nor was it uncommon for them to withdraw their testimonies after the trial in order to exonerate the defendant.[247]

The house committees also suffered from a lack of acceptance among ghetto residents. According to Opoczyński, many found it arrogant of committee members to think they had the right to summon people to court. Some residents dismissed them as "peasants," since many of them had enjoyed a lower status before the war, and some could not even write.[248] Another difficulty for the judicial bodies in Warsaw was their inability to prosecute witnesses for false testimony: "Since the witnesses were not under oath, when they or the claimants came from the public they were not liable to a penalty for giving false evidence."[249] In the Vilna ghetto, by contrast, the Jewish Police were able to punish witnesses for "non-appearance."[250]

Similarly problematic was the effect exerted by the fear of German intervention on the administration of justice: indeed, some judges in Warsaw imposed universally lenient sentences out of fear that the accused might be in contact with the Gestapo. According to Adler, this applied not only to Judge Goldfarb, of the internal disciplinary court, but also to Judge Maślanko: "His conscious tendency to pass mild sentences was to a large extent motivated by his fear of denunciation. At that time, one could never know in advance whether the villain under judgment would turn out to be someone with such connections with the German police circles that he might cause the dissolution of the whole disciplinary court of the Jewish Council."[251]

The work of the courts was also hampered by the deportations. According to one judge in the Lodz ghetto, it was hard to reconstruct the circumstances of the crime at the first internal murder trial in December 1941 because some of the defendant's witnesses and neighbours had already been deported.[252] In a letter of 8 January 1943 to the German Criminal Police office in the Lodz ghetto regarding a case delegated to the ghetto court on German orders, the Jewish Council announced "that a verdict was not reached in the case of the above as they had been dispatched from the central prison ... to work outside the ghetto on 4.1.1943. Because of this ... the prosecution was temporarily suspended."[253] A further factor preventing defendants or witnesses from attending court was the prevalence of death and sickness.[254] In a case against two brothers for negligent arson, the ghetto public prosecutor informed the German Criminal Police in November 1942 that the proceedings had been closed because one had died in custody and the other had been resettled.[255]

It was presumably for the above reasons that the following paragraph was included in the Vilna ghetto code of criminal procedure of February 1943, with specific reference to the ghetto court: "The court shall not initiate proceedings, and shall cancel any ongoing proceedings, in the event of the defendant's death or other reasons rendering such proceedings impossible."[256] Statistics from the ghetto court in Vilna show that some trials had to be postponed because the accused could not be tracked down.[257] For one thing, hardships such as hunger, disease, and the constant fear of death are likely to have outweighed the obligation to attend court. Secondly, we must bear in mind that many ghetto residents – as already mentioned – would have gone into hiding or joined the partisans in the surrounding forests.

Institutional changes in the ghetto-internal administration also had an impact on legal practice, sometimes with devastating consequences for the accused. From the end of 1942, the Lodz ghetto *Sonderabteilung* ("Special Department") extended its influence to court proceedings.[258] As a consequence, residents began to complain increasingly in the courtroom that their confessions had been extorted from them beforehand by the *Sonderabteilung* using violent means. In October 1942, twelve bakers and Order Service officers who stood accused of stealing bread stated that their confessions had been "extracted by beatings."[259] On 5 July 1943, the defendants in an appeal hearing concerning a case of theft from a cooperative store withdrew their statements to the *Sonderabteilung* on the basis that they had been beaten and threatened with "resettlement."[260] According to the Lodz chronicle, a "parallel system"[261] appeared to be operating in legal matters after spring 1943 in that a representative of the *Sonderabteilung* would now often be present during proceedings, especially in cases which it had referred to the court. Although these officers seldom intervened in the early stages, the chronicler suspected that they were there to make sure the sentence was sufficiently severe.[262] In April 1943, the court staff began to have cases taken away from them by the *Sonderabteilung*, to be handled administratively without any court involvement. Most of these concerned minor food thefts, while thefts from workshops and cooperatives remained within the jurisdiction of the court.[263] Although those convicted by this route could lodge a subsequent appeal with Rumkowski, it was speculated in the Chronicle that the chairman preferred the harsh jurisdiction of the *Sonderabteilung* to the previous arrangement.[264]

Historian Dina Porat has argued with respect to the ghetto courts in Vilna, Kaunas, and Šiauliai that their intended purpose was to maintain at least a modicum of pre-war morality in the face of the Germans' arbitrary brutality.[265] This must have impacted in turn on the motivation of the legal personnel. In the case of Warsaw, Lodz, and Vilna, we have seen that people often had very personal motives for wanting to work in the courts. In the early days of the ghettos, future career prospects were a consideration. Some also saw the development of a legal practice capable of responding to the specific circumstances of the ghetto as a professional challenge. Consequently, the judges' agenda in the cases that came before them was not to maintain abstract pre-war standards but to align themselves with the survival strategies of the respective Jewish Councils. Often, the ghetto trials served to provide a concrete illustration of abstract crime definitions. At the same time, the sentences in particular served a "deterrent" and hence preventive purpose, since many residents followed the court cases attentively, and the verdicts were announced in the ghetto newspapers.

Although the judicial authorities of the ghettos were not explicitly founded on religious law, they do show certain similarities with pre-eighteenth-century Jewish courts. Both are examples of improvised bodies which attempted to claim legal powers as distinct from an external authority in order to define their own evaluation criteria. The ghetto system also had an equivalent to the lay courts in the form of the Warsaw house committees, whose personnel rarely possessed any detailed legal knowledge, and whose decisions were less accepted among the residents. As with the *hedyotot*, their purpose was to prevent legal cases from being transferred to the "external" power at all costs. In the ghettos, as in pre-eighteenth-century Jewish society, the external powers conceded only limited authority to the courts in matters of prosecution.

On the whole, the ghetto courts appear to have been slightly more successful than other institutions such as the German-instigated Jewish police at exploiting certain liberties in the interests of the ghetto community. The judges often attempted, for example, to clarify how far the criminal actions of ghetto residents were attributable to the catastrophic living conditions created by the Germans. These liberties existed because the Germans' attention was not primarily focused on the ghetto courts and ghetto-internal disputes. Moreover, the court staff seem to have been able initially to maintain a certain degree of independence – however limited – from the Jewish Council chairman.

It is notable that the Jewish Councils created extremely complex structures, and were bent on adhering wherever possible to established procedures. Had their aim been merely to clamp down on "dangerous activities," they could have found easier methods of prosecution. It is therefore reasonable to assume that the court authorities and their legal practice were also and especially intended to preserve an appearance of "normality." To that extent, they performed a stabilizing function at a time of mortal fear and insecurity.

Chapter Five

The Ghetto Penal System

When, at the end of December 1941, the Germans ordered Rumkowski to hand over first 20,000 then 10,000 people for deportation from Lodz, some of the first to be selected by the Jewish Council chairman were those "who were regarded as an undesirable element vis-à-vis the good of the ghetto community – namely, those 'under sentence' and their families."[1] These people were inmates of the ghetto prison founded at the initiative of the Jewish Council, where they were serving sentences imposed by the ghetto courts for violations of internal ghetto regulations as well as German orders. In a speech of 20 December 1941, Rumkowski defended his decision to deliver up prisoners first with the words: "Only then will we be able to eradicate the evil at its roots."[2]

This decision serves to illustrate some of the central premises of the ghetto penal system, which encapsulated the specific features of the ghetto-internal legal sphere to a unique degree. On one hand, the Jewish Councils and the legal authorities answerable to them sought constantly to impose their *own* sanctions on offenders and prevent any intervention by the German occupiers, on the basis that punishment by the latter usually meant death (and had done since 1940 in the case of occupied Poland). On the other hand, the penal system was also predicated on the need for vigorous repression of individual actions deemed a danger to the ghetto community. With this in mind, Rumkowski – and, to a certain extent, Gens in Vilna – effectively integrated the surrender of prisoners to the Germans into the penal system as a punitive measure, thereby allowing "dangerous" elements to be "banished" from the ghetto community.[3] Even the threat of surrender became a powerful lever.[4]

The key issue here is what Rumkowski knew at what stage about the German plans. In his speech, he referred to "deportations," which had been understood up to then as labour transports. At this point, he was not aware that the "surrendered" subjects were being murdered at the Kulmhof extermination camp. Even when he did find out, probably by May 1942, however, the chairman stuck to his strategy, making "self-selection" likewise part of the ghetto-internal penal system.

Spectrum of Punishments

What punishments can be imposed in a coerced community where people's first concern is to feed themselves and ensure their own and their relatives' survival? This was the question faced by the Jewish functionaries, who adapted the penalties over time to the radically altered "life-world" of the ghetto population. In the early days, prison sentences and fines were the most commonly imposed sanctions. The latter option soon became obsolete, however, as people ran out of money. Moreover, other punishments promised greater efficacy in view of the changing value system in the ghetto.[5] Fines were still imposed, but were supplemented with further sanctions. In case of "non-payment," they could also be converted to days of detention, although the "conversion formula" was highly variable: in the Vilna ghetto at the beginning of 1942, for instance, one day's detention corresponded to an unpaid fine of between 2.50 and 5 reichsmarks.[6]

The purpose of these punishments was to prevent any future recurrence of "harmful activities." This applied particularly in the case of penalties which were geared to the individual offender: thus, "*any cart driver* caught stealing even the smallest item" would, according to Rumkowski, be immediately deprived of his cart and horse, arrested, and sentenced to hard labour.[7] Ghetto residents practising "usury" with foodstuffs from the distribution points would have the produce confiscated – and in the case of "vegetable traders," the entire crop, sometimes with a prison sentence on top.[8] Illegitimate recipients of "relief aid" were threatened with withdrawal of the payments, a penalty also imposed on residents guilty of other offences.[9] In some cases the loss of relief aid, and of the "right to relief aid," was threatened – and duly implemented – with respect to the whole family.[10] In July 1941, for example, the *Geto-Tsaytung* announced: "Should any of the specified workers [factory workers, day labourers, sewage and waste disposal workers] attempt to sabotage operations, not only they themselves, but their whole family shall forfeit the right to relief aid."[11]

This punitive regime was recognized as having its problems, however: as early as March 1941, it was argued at a meeting regarding the planned establishment of the summary court in Lodz that family members might not always be aware of each other's criminal activities (particularly in the case of husbands and wives), and that it would therefore be unfair to make them suffer the same punishment.[12] Rumkowski evidently took this on board and, in August 1941, instructed the Relief Department as follows: "If the offender is known to have spent the payments without implicating his family, the Relief Department shall be justified in special cases in proposing that Neftalin [the lawyer] refrain from punishing the family."[13] Parents were, on the other hand, liable for the actions of their children, as Rumkowski had already signalled in his proclamations regarding illegal candy production. And in the Chronicle, an entry of July 1941 reads: "The ban on fruit picking in Marysin is being strictly enforced ... one schoolgirl was expelled for picking a few strawberries, and her family's benefits withdrawn."[14] The fact that exclusion from school was used as a punishment shows how much importance the Jewish Council attached to education within the ghetto community.

Another sanction deployed in the Lodz ghetto was the suspension of offenders from their jobs – particularly in the case of employees of the Jewish self-administration; here too, the punishment could be extended to family members. One instance of this was a "bribery case" within the Central Purchasing Agency, in which two residents named Warszawski and Markowiszin were found guilty of extorting money from suppliers. Not only were they both given prison sentences but their sons were also fired from the carpentry department where they worked.[15] This penalty was not very common, however, and only a few instances are recorded after 1942. While it gave Rumkowski a powerful tool against delinquents, the dismissal of experienced workers also disrupted work procedures, potentially leading to a loss of ghetto productivity which conflicted with his interests.

A feature of the penal system in Lodz was the integration of unpopular tasks such as sewage removal into the punishment regime.[16] "Sewage duty" was a sanction imposed increasingly by Rumkowski following the establishment of the summary court in spring 1941, and from summer 1941 onwards.

These punishments hit ghetto residents hard. Losing their benefits as well as their jobs exacerbated the already severe hardships people had to face, and could mean starvation. By the beginning of 1942, being rendered jobless already effectively meant losing the right to exist. When the Germans demanded quotas for deportation, the unemployed came straight after criminals on Rumkowski's list of those to be "sacrificed" according to his "rescue through labour strategy."[17] From spring 1941, the Jewish Council chairman also introduced forced labour as a general punishment, often in combination with prison sentences.

It was announced in the *Geto-Tsaytung* of 1 August 1941, for example, that some traders had been sentenced to imprisonment with "hard labour" for illegal candy production. The owner of the premises used for production was likewise given two weeks' "hard labour."[18] In an announcement of 21 April, also published in the *Geto-Tsaytung*, Rumkowski defined the status of those sentenced. They would be "treated as prisoners, but without being incarcerated."[19] They had to present themselves regularly, but were allowed to sleep at home, provided they carried out their unpaid forced labour satisfactorily. "In this way, anyone acting in a manner detrimental to the ghetto will be forced to work for the benefit of the community. The discipline of forced labour will teach them that it is better to be a decent and useful worker than to go down the route of immoral and harmful conduct."[20]

Here again, the Jewish Council chairman contrasted "damaging egoism" with the need to ensure the common good of the ghetto community. The same was true of other punishments. The Germans threatened collective penalties for certain individual criminal acts, and Rumkowski transferred this procedure to the internal penal system, particularly in the case of offences which gave him cause to fear German intervention. In June 1941, the Germans announced severe punishments for the entire community following the alleged shooting of two German guards from within the ghetto. In response, Rumkowski sanctioned all residents with a general curfew and the withdrawal of food rations, and was thus able to avert punitive measures by the Germans.[21]

When the chairman made "rescue through labour" his top priority, in a later phase of the ghetto's existence, those hardest hit by the collective punishments were the factory workers supplying orders for the German army. In one incident at the end of September 1943 involving the theft of some wood by a sawmill worker, the entire workforce was punished with the withdrawal of their extra soup ration for a day – a punishment far less harsh, as the chairman was at pains to point out, than those threatened by the Germans for material thefts, bearing in mind the importance of the order to the army.[22] The workers responded by refusing their regular soup ration in protest against the collective punishment. As they saw it, only the guilty party should be accountable for violations of the rules.[23]

In Lodz and Warsaw, collective punishment mechanisms were also applied at the level of residential buildings. If an individual tenant shirked his cleaning duties, for example, the entire building faced the threat of punishment. Similar measures had already been announced by Rumkowski on the establishment of the house committees, in order to ensure that this was done according to the correct procedures.[24]

In March 1941, as part of his war on "wood thieves," he announced that the tenants of an apartment building would have to bear the costs of any damage incurred, on the assumption that they would know about any criminal activities perpetrated by their neighbours. In addition, the house watchman would lose his "right to relief aid" and his job. "Therefore pull together one and all to root out the vermin," Rumkowski appealed, "then you will have done your duty by the whole ghetto community."[25]

Rumkowski granted the chairmen of the house committees a key role in the prevention of criminal activities in the ghetto: "To you [house administrators and house watchmen] I have entrusted the roof over every head in the ghetto and you must guard it jealously. I will not allow such damage [e.g., to buildings] to be inflicted because of self-seeking individuals. You had better think twice, and help me with my difficult task, otherwise you will pay for it with your livelihood. Each and every one of you must place yourselves at the service of the community and help to keep the peace in the ghetto."[26] Rumkowski had already appealed to the house administrators' sense of responsibility in June 1941, after identifying "coal diggers" as a new criminal type. This term referred to ghetto residents who, while digging in the ground in search of coal, sometimes undermined residential walls, which he saw as a danger to public safety. Henceforward, house administrators were to assume "full responsibility" for the prevention of such activities.[27]

In the Warsaw ghetto, the Jewish Council chairman Marek Lichtenbaum imposed similar responsibilities on the chairmen of the house committees, who were obliged to enforce "hygiene measures," for example. Collective punishment mechanisms such as those applied in the Lodz ghetto were not part of his plan, however.[28]

The ghetto community, too, was deployed as a moral authority. In Lodz, offenders faced the threat – and indeed the reality – of being publicly named, the idea being that the social exclusion of those deemed by the Jewish Council to be a danger to the community at large would act as a deterrent against criminal activities in the ghetto.[29]

In the Warsaw and Vilna ghettos, very specific, case-related sanctions were sometimes applied in order to settle disputes between residents. In the previously cited case of the Vilna woman who stole her neighbour's *cholent* (a traditional Jewish stew), the thief was ordered to give the victim three kilos of potatoes.[30] In hearings at the Warsaw police stations, punishments were sometimes merely threatened, as the OS functionaries Adler and Rode testify. "Creative punishments" were also invented, "such as forcing the guilty party to clean the bathrooms in the camps."[31] Their main purpose seems to have been to mitigate the severity of the accused's sentence, however – provided that person's actions were not judged an existential threat to the community. At any rate, they were not part of a coherently designed, ghetto-internal penal system as in Rumkowski's case.

Corporal punishment was discussed in the Lodz and Vilna ghettos, and indeed deployed in Vilna especially, on the basis that it served to suppress "dangerous behaviour." In a speech to the ghetto population in August 1941, Rumkowski advocated the use of "physical chastisement" as a tool in the "fight against crime"; in future, offenders were to be "introduced to the cane."[32] At the "reformatory" attached to the central prison, the cane had already been used on young offenders since spring 1941.[33]

There are only a few records of corporal punishments being officially imposed by ghetto-internal institutions. One example is the punishment of a coal-yard supervisor for "coal theft" in November 1941: in this case, the offender was "publicly chastised" in the square in Marysin.[34] Presumably, this method failed to become officially established in spite of Rumkowski's wishes. For the year 1943, however, there is increasing evidence – as in the Chronicle – that those in supervisory roles were using beatings as a punishment. In February 1943, residents working outside the ghetto reported that their Jewish foremen "bullied" them with physical abuse and blows.[35] The same year also saw an increased use of punitive beatings by workshop managers and Order Service officers. In the ghetto chronicler's view, a box on the ear by the Jewish Council chairman may have been justified by the "patriarchal style of the constitution," but the fact that "every boss or OS officer ... has now taken to striking their staff" was not acceptable.[36] Comparing this with other punishments in the ghetto, the Chronicle comments in September 1943: "It may be that hitting someone with a stick is still a milder punishment than taking away their soup ration ... nevertheless, it has to be said that both punishments are improper. One violates the last vestige of human dignity, while the other is an attack on life itself."[37] With the Jewish Council officially approving the use of punitive beatings, those in a supervisory capacity are likely to have found it that much easier to overcome their own scruples regarding corporal punishment – and all the more so given the increasing "external" threat posed by the Germans.

"Beatings. We have to have beatings, otherwise they won't listen to us,"[38] Jewish Police chief Gens had insisted back in September 1941, immediately after the creation of the Vilna ghetto. This attitude was consistent with his later efforts, notably after 1943, to introduce caning and flogging, especially for those who refused to work.[39] As early

as July 1942, Kruk records an incident in the Chronicle in which Gens
had brutally beaten a doctor named Steinman for refusing to attend a
case outside the ghetto.[40] Even children were sometimes given punitive beatings at the Jewish police station in Vilna. According to a report
by Yaakov Shvartsberg regarding a bread theft, the children concerned
were ordered to thrash each other with a wooden stick before being
released.[41]

With regard to the use of corporal punishment in Vilna, a distinction
must doubtless be made between one-off incidents and officially established policy. The latter is likely to have come into force at the beginning of 1943. On 18 February of that year, Kruk reports on a speech in
which the Jewish Council chairman referred to the recently introduced
"official sanction" of flogging: "He [Gens] announces that he personally
will whip everyone who commits something filthy against the ghetto,
and he will whip them so that he will be remembered. He also says
that he considers it better for him to whip them than the Gestapo."[42]
This technique of contrasting ghetto-internal sanctions with the worse
punishments threatened by the German occupiers can be consistently
observed.

According to Rode, the Warsaw ghetto police stations also used caning as a punitive measure.[43] Unlike in Vilna, however, it was not applied
systematically in the interests of the Jewish Council's survival strategy.
The fact that Gens was able to get these measures past the rest of the
Council was probably due to the German arbitrariness and brutality
that had characterized everyday life in the Vilna ghetto from day one.
In these circumstances, ghetto residents and the other Council members
are likely to have agreed that internal punishments were the "lesser evil"
when compared with the prospect of German intervention, as the debate
over the death penalty within the ghetto would later demonstrate.

In the Lodz ghetto, at the meeting of 4 August 1941 in which the powers of the ghetto-internal judiciary were extended, the Germans also
granted the Jewish Council the authority to impose death penalties at
its own initiative.[44] While Rumkowski favoured the introduction of the
death penalty in the ghetto, four ghetto court judges who were in atten-
dance argued vehemently against it, and were promptly dismissed from
office.[45] To protest their dismissal, a total of eleven court officials then
resigned (four of whom asked to return to their posts in October 1941 and
were duly reinstated by Rumkowski).[46] The chairman did not venture to
assert his will against the opposition of the judicial panel, however, and
no death penalties were imposed during the lifetime of the court.[47]

In Vilna, the picture was very different. As mentioned previously,
the ghetto court imposed death penalties on six ghetto residents in

a murder case of June 1942. The members of the court accepted this with relatively little opposition, probably because of their awareness of the German extermination plans. Besides, Gens's position as Jewish Council chairman and chief of police allowed him to act as an autocratic ruler. Even members of the Jewish self-administration who were otherwise extremely critical of Gens's actions, such as Kruk and Balberyszski, seem to have supported the imposition of the death penalty. Advocates argued that it was a necessary measure for the protection of the community, given the "exceptional circumstances." And, as noted earlier, there was even a measure of pride surrounding the fact that it was a *ghetto-internal* measure.

In the Warsaw ghetto, the Jewish Council neither used the death penalty nor talked of introducing it. This was due to the fact that its legal sphere was not fully institutionalized; moreover, the Council's strategies differed from those of Gens and Rumkowski. After the mass German deportations of summer 1942, it was the armed resistance groups who called for the execution of Jewish functionaries, particularly those accused of collaboration with the German occupiers. In so doing, they were expressing an ethos radically at odds with that of the Jewish Council.

The positions adopted by the Jewish Councils regarding the ghetto-internal death penalty were, in other words, dictated by their survival strategies and their knowledge of German intentions. It was because the Council in Lodz was not yet aware of the extermination campaign at the time of the debate in August 1941 that the judicial panel was able to overrule Rumkowski. At this point, his power over ghetto-internal affairs came up against its limits – even if he did find another way to assert his belief in the need to "eliminate" "dangerous elements" from the community: namely, by surrendering criminals to the Germans.

In some cases where the Jewish Councils were ordered to impose "German" punishments on ghetto residents, they sought to negotiate with the occupiers. The tension between the threatened German intervention and the Councils' attempts to apply their own sanctions manifested itself in specific ways.

Rumkowski was particularly inclined to push for leniency when innocent residents were threatened with collective punishments by the Germans. This was the case in June 1941, for example, when the Gestapo ordered the Jewish Council to publicly flog twenty-five residents after a shot had allegedly been fired at German guards from inside the ghetto.[48] On 2 June 1941, Rumkowski wrote to the Gestapo proposing a general curfew on the whole community instead of the flogging. The curfew was to be imposed from 9:00 p.m. on Friday to

8:00 p.m. on Saturday, accompanied by the closure of public kitchens.[49] "The implementation [of the flogging] is very difficult for me, and it won't work as a punishment for the whole ghetto population, as only a small part of it will be affected. I want the entire population to be punished for this regrettable incident, however, and I therefore propose to carry out the penalty as follows."[50] In response, the Germans "allowed" Rumkowski to impose a one-day universal curfew order for 7 June 1941.[51] In other cases, the Jewish Council chairman pursued specific ghetto-internal interests: in June 1940, for example, he approached the senior medical officer in Lodz in order to procure the release of an internist who had previously lived and worked in the ghetto. The doctor in question had been arrested on suspicion of having concealed a case of typhus in the ghetto and subsequently convicted by a German Special Court. Rumkowski justified his request as follows: "I should stress that Dr Rożowski is a specialist in internal medicine, who is urgently needed due to the exceptional increase in infectious diseases."[52]

In the Vilna ghetto, Gens also negotiated with the Germans in his capacity as Jewish Council chairman and chief of police. When, on 25 July 1942, the Gestapo demanded the surrender of three hundred residents – two hundred by way of punishment for a suspected prisoner substitution by the Jewish Council in advance of a German "operation," and one hundred as a penalty for the increase in food smuggling[53] – he attempted to bargain with Franz Murer, and managed to beat the quota down to eighty elderly residents who were no longer "fit for work." Being unable to prevent the handover altogether by this point, he thus opted for a course of action in line with the ghetto-internal priority at the time: namely, "rescue through labour." In another case in late October 1942, Gens failed to procure any form of "mitigation." The Gestapo demanded the surrender of ten named women accused of smuggling food into the ghetto: "For two days, negotiations went on between the ghetto leadership and the Gestapo about whether the ghetto itself would punish the ten women. Nothing helped, and the ghetto had to turn over all ten."[54]

The unpredictability of the Germans in negotiations of this kind is demonstrated by an incident of January 1943. In a tailoring workshop that made field clothing for the German Luftwaffe, two residents had left work half an hour before the official clocking-off time. Someone reported the offence to the German police, who arrested the people concerned and sentenced them to death. The deputy chief of the Jewish Police, Dessler, then attempted to obtain a "concession" from the Germans, whereupon both workers were allowed to go and the death penalty was remitted.[55]

In the Warsaw ghetto, the Jewish Council made similar efforts to head off the threat of German punishments, although far less frequently than in the case of Lodz and Vilna, and without attempting to "offer" the Germans alternative ghetto-internal punishments.[56] In June 1942, for example, Heinz Auerswald, commissar for the Jewish Residential District, announced that a hundred Jews and ten Order Service officers were to be shot for "violent resistance to German police orders." Czerniaków recorded in his diary: "Later in the afternoon I telephoned Auerswald that the ten patrolmen – not to mention the others – were guilty of no crime. Some of them were seized in the street."[57] When the Germans declared an amnesty in March 1942, Czerniaków tried to get them to increase the number of those pardoned. And he had been trying, without success, since January of that year to negotiate a fine instead of the death penalty for already imprisoned smugglers.[58]

Other members of the Jewish Council were also confronted directly with German punitive regimes which they attempted to oppose. The OS chairman Szeryński, for instance, had been ordered by the Germans in November 1941 to carry out the execution of eight ghetto residents convicted of illegal border crossing by the German Special Court. Szeryński threatened to commit suicide rather than implement the order, whereupon the Germans instructed the Polish police to perform the execution instead.[59] While the OS made preparations for the execution on 12 November 1941, it was the Polish police who carried it out – the first time they had been called on to do so for the crime of leaving the ghetto.[60] Once again, although the chairman sought to avoid becoming the executor of German punishments, he did not engage in any strategic negotiations as part of an overall "survival strategy" for the ghetto community.

The Ghetto Central Prisons

All three ghettos were equipped with prisons that had been set up on German orders. In these microcosms of the coerced ghetto community, where people's freedom of movement was already restricted, the tension between external power and internal autonomy was amplified, for although the prisoners had been sentenced by ghetto-internal authorities, they were also accessible to the Germans at any time. Some prison cells were attached to the Jewish police stations and were mainly used for brief detentions of a few hours.[61] In addition, however, the German occupiers had ordered the Jewish Councils in Warsaw, Lodz, and Vilna to establish ghetto-internal central prisons, to be run by the Jewish police authorities. This was where those convicted of German-defined offences such as smuggling and illegal border crossing were to serve their sentences, while remaining at the Germans' disposal at all times.[62] These facilities were also used by the Jewish Councils for imprisoning "internal" offenders and for remanding suspects in custody.[63]

The Germans' motives for installing central prisons within the ghetto stemmed from their notion of the "criminal Jew." In their view, putting Jews in German prisons was not an adequate punishment: because the conditions there were better than in the Jewish ghetto, the likelihood was – given the "criminal mentality of the Jews" – that they would try anything to get into a German penitentiary.[64] Added to this was the fear of "Jewish diseases" already discussed. In April 1942, the higher state prosecutor in Lodz argued against the Frankfurt district court regarding the punishment of a ghetto resident named Hans-Israel Rosenbaum: "Given the prevailing conditions in the local ghetto … transferring the Jew [Rosenbaum] to the German penal system – whether in the form of prison or penal camp – would scarcely be a punishment for him. The Lodz ghetto is a closed Jewish ghetto. Apart from anything else, the step of sealing it off completely was necessary on public health grounds, and from this perspective alone there are compelling reasons against introducing a Jew from the ghetto into the penal system."[65]

In October 1940, on German orders, Rumkowski set up a central prison in the Lodz ghetto as a subdivision of the ghetto court, to be administered by the Jewish Order Service with Szlomo Hercberg as prison governor[66] – a man notorious for his exceptionally brutal methods. The ghetto chronicler suspected Rumkowski of deliberately selecting a native of the Bałuty district, an "energetic person … who speaks the criminals' language." The prison was also frequently used to house "new arrivals" before they were assigned "regular" accommodation.[67] Furthermore, at the initiative of the ghetto administration, a reformatory for young offenders[68] was attached to the facility where juveniles up to the age of sixteen were held separately from the other inmates. Here, specific assessment criteria and punishments were to be applied according to plans devised by Jewish functionaries and educationalists, and which sometimes went as far as to include punitive beatings.[69]

The affiliation of the central prison to the ghetto court was suspended by Rumkowski in April 1943. Thereafter, court chairman Jacobson no longer had any influence on the management of the prison and only had access to prisoners whose cases were still pending in court.[70] This administrative change meant that, when the Germans demanded quotas for deportation, Rumkowski was able to decide quickly and single-handedly on the selection of inmates.

In Warsaw, too, the Jewish Council was ordered in summer 1941 to establish a central prison. In this case, the fear of "Jewish diseases" also seems to have played a role. The deputy chief of the Polish police, Major Przymusiński, passed on a German order to Czerniaków to install a central detention centre for the ghetto in June 1941. According to a note in Czerniaków's diary dated 6 June 1941, this followed the infection of ten Polish policemen with typhus, the implication being that Jewish prisoners had transmitted the disease.[71] The new facility was located on Gęsia Street and was run by the Jewish Order Service under the direct control of the Polish police.[72] In its activity report of June 1942, the Council stated that "The Order Service is also responsible for the special detention facility for Jews, to which individuals apprehended by the Polish police or sentenced to imprisonment for violating the regulations are brought."[73]

In Vilna, in addition to the German Lukiszki prison[74] outside the ghetto, there was an internal prison in the Lidzker Alley which appears to have existed from the end of 1941. It was administered by the Jewish Police and was the place where those convicted of ghetto-internal offences served their sentences.[75]

The occupancy of the ghetto prison fluctuated considerably, not least because of changing crime definitions and punitive mechanisms. Systematic records are only available for the Lodz ghetto, whose prisoner count was regularly noted in the Chronicle. The number of inmates – leaving aside major variations during the deportation periods – was around 50 to 200, the majority of whom (according to the statistics) were male.[76] According to one ghetto resident, the Warsaw prison consisted of cells which were designed to hold 8 to 25 people, but which were sometimes occupied by 100 to 120.[77] In Vilna, by contrast, the prison appears to have been largely empty for long periods because custodial sentences were altogether much shorter there than in Warsaw and Lodz. It was only prior to deportations that the cells were used, for example to detain elderly ghetto residents pending their delivery to the Germans.

In effect, the Germans integrated the prisons into their penal system, using them to detain offenders for deployment at their convenience. A wealth of correspondence between the German Criminal Police or the Gestapo, the Jewish Council chairman, and the governor of the central prison in the Lodz ghetto reveals how "Jewish delinquents" were committed by the Germans to the ghetto-internal penal system, to be detained in the ghetto prison "at the disposal" of the Criminal Police or Gestapo.[78] According to "availability," the Germans could also decide which inmates to release for "labour deployment."[79] The Jewish

Council prosecutor would then report the release and the closure of the relevant proceedings.[80] One letter from the German Criminal Police to the governor of the central prison reads: "You are hereby instructed to place the Jew Jsrael Brysz ... arrested for the murder and robbery of the thirteen-year-old Jewess Etla Sznal, at the disposal of the Secret State Police. Your signature is requested as confirmation of receipt of the prisoner."[81]

In addition to detention, the German Criminal Police in Lodz sometimes ordered "their" prisoners to be given hard labour: "You are hereby instructed to detain the Jewesses Bela Glinowiecka ... Stefania Graw ... in your prison and deploy them continuously for hard labour. You will be held personally responsible for the proper execution of the sentence."[82] The relevant sentences, which were still passed by German Special Courts, particularly in the early days of the ghetto, were communicated to the prison governor and thence to the Jewish Council chairman.[83] Conversely, any movements – such as the transfer of "German" prisoners to hospital on suspicion of typhus – were reported by the prison governor to the German Criminal Police.[84] Recoveries were similarly reported, with a view to returning the inmates to the German penal system where possible. On 31 October 1940, for example, the ghetto hospital advised the Jewish Council that a fourteen-year-old inmate named Rosenberg was now "rehabilitated," and that this was to be communicated to the police prison in Radogoszcz, from where he had presumably been "delivered" to the Lodz ghetto.[85]

With the onset of the deportations, the prison governor sent lists of inmates to the Lodz Criminal Police[86] or the Gestapo.[87] These lists were the result of the "self-selection" process into which Rumkowski had been forced by the Germans in preparation for the deportations beginning in December 1941 and January 1942. The fact that prisoners were his first resort stemmed from his conviction that those whose actions posed a danger to the ghetto community should be excluded from it. Indeed, after January 1942 he went on to issue an official threat of "resettlement" for anyone jeopardizing the "order" he had established in the ghetto.[88] At this point, he was unaware that such a "banishment" meant the death of the people concerned, and even after probably learning the truth by May 1942, he accepted this in view of the "exceptional circumstances," in order to save at least part of the population.

In Vilna, too, the Germans took inmates from the ghetto prison during their periodic "operations." The first time this occurred was in December 1941. Writing retrospectively on these events in May 1942, Kruk noted: "On December 3, people were taken out of the so-called ghetto underworld: sixty-seven Jews. On December 4, more were taken out of the so-called underworld: ninety Jews. On the night of December 15, all the residents of the 'Gestapo' block were taken. Not returned: three hundred Jews."[89] As far as can be concluded from Kruk's accounts – which are cryptic by the standards of the time – it seems that the prisoners were seized directly by Gestapo representatives with the aid of Lithuanian auxiliaries rather than being surrendered by the Jewish Council. Although the chronicler deemed it noteworthy that the people concerned were offenders, they were probably regarded by the Germans merely as part of the general mass of deportees. The fact that there were criminals among their number is not surprising, given the ease of access to prisoners.[90]

By comparison with Rumkowski, the Jewish Council in Vilna – or at least its chairman, Anatol Fried – appeared to take a more differentiated approach to imprisoned offenders. When Murer ordered the surrender of a hundred residents in June 1942 as punishment for the Council's failure to prevent smuggling, it temporarily released a few prisoners: "Hence the head of the prison immediately released twenty of those who were arrested for minor offences, and only when the danger was past did he summon them back again."[91]

In May 1943, ten residents of the Vilna ghetto were apprehended by the Jewish Police and taken to the ghetto prison. These were earmarked by the Jewish Council chairman to be "made available" in the event of a German "operation."[92] They were not offenders, however, but mostly old people who were no longer fit for work.[93] In other words, he too complied with the German quotas, but without associating them systematically with the ghetto penal regime as in Rumkowski's case – although he did warn "malingerers" in January 1943 that "repeat offenders" would be sent to the German-controlled prison outside the ghetto: "The first time, twenty-five [lashes] and Lidzki [prison ghetto]; and the second time, Lukiszki."[94]

As for the Warsaw ghetto, its Jewish Council was likewise expected to provide the Germans with regular updates on the occupancy of the ghetto prison,[95] and occasionally had to surrender some of its inmates.[96] During the mass deportations in July 1942, the prisoners were taken from the central prison to Treblinka,[97] a move with which the Jewish Council refused to cooperate.

Conditions in the ghetto prisons were extreme, particularly in terms of hygiene and food supplies. One inmate of the Warsaw ghetto reported that many prisoners were sick, since hygiene was even worse than in the ghetto itself, and that the nutritional value of their food rations was as low as four to five hundred calories.[98] Despite this, entertainment evenings were staged featuring comic turns.[99] It is worth noting in this context that perceptions of prison conditions could vary according to previous experience. Chana Gorodecka, a former inmate of the German-administered prisons of Pawiak and Daniłowiczowska, reports in her diary that, to her, conditions in Gęsia Street in summer 1942 seemed comparatively "luxurious": "The cell was open all day. All the prisoners sat on the grass in the garden sunning themselves."[100] What she did not know was that the inmates would be deported to Treblinka the next day, 18 August 1942, in order to be murdered.

As in the courts, the Jewish Council chairmen sometimes introduced mitigating measures within the ghetto penal system. Prison conditions were relaxed on some Jewish holidays, for example. At Passover and New Year 1941, Rumkowski granted almost all prisoners "holiday leave."[101] Given the enclosed nature of the ghetto, it was unlikely that they would abscond; indeed, the chronicler notes in April 1941 that all 120 inmates returned to prison when their leave was up.[102]

Things changed, however, after Rumkowski began to make prisoners available for German "labour transports" from January 1942.[103] For the subsequent period from spring 1942 onwards, numerous reports by the Criminal Police in the Lodz ghetto testify to "sudden deaths" of ghetto residents held in the central prison. One report of March 1942 records, for example: "Death of a Jewish prisoner (Cham Cytrin), died in cell on 28.3.1942."[104] In such cases – as with deaths occurring in criminal contexts – Jewish doctors from the ghetto were consulted to certify the death and release the body for burial.[105] It is noticeable that the recorded causes of death, such as "heart failure," were often similar, particularly in the early deportation phase. Whether this is a consequence of the source material available for this period, or whether there genuinely was an accumulation of deaths, is a moot point. There are good reasons to assume the latter, however, since the communication between the German Criminal Police and the central prison staff is well documented. One possible cause is that prisoners were exposed to even more threats and insecurity than other ghetto residents. Word must have got round that they would be the first to be "resettled," even though the news that deportation meant death did not begin to circulate until after summer 1942. Although it is unclear how prisoners gained access to information, the fact that – in Lodz, at least – they were given holiday leave and were taken out of the prison for hard labour during the day suggests that news circulating among ghetto residents would have reached them too.

The variety of offences dealt with by the Germans and the Jewish Councils was such that all walks of life were represented in the ghetto prison, with the exception of juveniles, who, at least in Lodz and

Vilna, were detained separately.[106] In this sense, the prison was also a place where different value systems collided, and where new criminal plans were sometimes forged. In July 1941, prison governor Hercberg reported that some inmates detained at the disposal of the Gestapo in Lodz had hatched a blackmail plot and were planning to force another prisoner to join them: "Their plan was to extort money from various members of the ghetto community, including senior officials, on the basis of certain communications that were alleged to have been sent, with the justification that their families were starving and they had no other way of helping them while in prison."[107]

In the Vilna ghetto, legal aid was of particular importance to prisoners, as lawyers were granted access to the jail for the purposes of their defence.[108] These were probably the same lawyers who had launched a public initiative in February 1942 to grant legal assistance to ghetto residents. In some cases, "social criteria" were also taken into account within the penal system. In Vilna, prisoners were released in order to care for their sick children, for example.[109] Records show that a female inmate in Lodz spent a temporary period in hospital after giving birth.[110] And on payment of bail, prisoners in the Vilna ghetto could be released from custody pending a court ruling.[111] That such liberties were possible in Vilna seems to be partly due to the Germans' lack of interference in the running of the ghetto prison.

The perception of time in the ghetto was subject to constant change, depending – among other factors – on the level of awareness of the German extermination campaign. This was reflected, for example, in the length of prison sentences, which invariably provide a clue to the Jewish Councils' visions of their communities' future. Thus, the sentences imposed in the Lodz ghetto were significantly longer in the early days than in the period after 1942. In Vilna, where the Jewish Council knew about the German murder plans from the outset, and the shooting of thousands of ghetto residents in Ponary was a cruel reality, both the detention orders issued by the Jewish Police and the sentences imposed by the courts were much shorter than in the other ghettos. Most prison sentences did not exceed forty-eight hours, while detention orders often lasted just one or two hours. One reason for this was the Jewish Council's prioritization of labour above all things: as long as they were in prison, residents could not work.[112] Where the accused's actions posed a grave danger to the ghetto community in the eyes of the Jewish Council, they were not given long prison sentences but, as described, could expect to face death or "delivery" to the Germans.

The Germans' approach to the ghetto penal system was, as in other spheres, arbitrary, and sometimes even contrary to the expectations of the ghetto community. A case in point was an amnesty declared by the occupiers in the Warsaw ghetto, resulting in the release of inmates from the ghetto prison in March 1942. The prisoners' "reintegration" into the ghetto community was not easy: on 11 March 1942, the governor of the central prison notified the Jewish Council that, of the 151 released inmates, 31 were homeless, of whom 24 were women and 7 men. The majority were also underage, and 7 of the inmates had had to be taken straight to hospital, where 5 had died.[113] Released prisoners were hit especially hard by the constantly changing circumstances in the ghetto, often finding relatives who might otherwise have been able to give them shelter already dead or deported. The social welfare network was very limited, and the fact that many of those released ended up dying in hospital was probably owing to poor health induced by the catastrophic conditions in the central prison.

As we have seen, the ghetto penal system provided a particularly vivid illustration of the conflict between external German power and internal autonomy. On one hand, the Jewish Councils sought to prevent German intervention and exercise their own evaluation criteria. On the other, they set themselves the task of stamping out individual criminal activities that posed a potential risk to the ghetto community at large. In Lodz in particular, this objective took precedence, in case of doubt, over internal sanctions. Hence, Rumkowski "banished" "dangerous" members of the ghetto community by turning them over to the Germans, in the knowledge that this meant condemning them to brutal punishment or even murder. In Vilna, Gens was similarly vehement in his mission to prevent "dangerous" activities by individuals, the difference being that punishments were enacted within the ghetto, with death sentences imposed by the ghetto court and implemented by the Jewish Police.

From a historical perspective, a parallel can be drawn here with Jewish courts in the eighteenth century. There too, social exclusion in the form of banishment was a common punishment for individuals whose actions endangered the community. And in extreme cases, such conduct was even used to justify the use of the death penalty.

As for the function of ghetto-internal punishments, it can be described as essentially preventive, the aim being to contain the feared dangers to the community posed by the Germans. The penalties were partly directed at the "offenders" themselves, but were also designed to have a deterrent effect on the rest of the ghetto population. Their primary purpose, therefore, was one of "general prevention" – hence the fact that sentences were publicly announced in newspapers or proclamations, and that the few death penalties imposed by the Jewish Council in Vilna were executed in public.

That said, ghetto residents were not simply passive objects of German caprice and Jewish Council-defined concepts of criminality and law: as we shall see, they also behaved as active subjects within the ghetto's internal legal sphere.

Chapter Six

Ordinary Ghetto Residents and Their Relationship with Internal and External Authorities

On 27 August 1941, Jankiel Landau reported the following incident to the Jewish police station in the Lodz ghetto: "For some time, various food items had consistently gone missing from my cellar compartment. How this theft was accomplished was a mystery to me. Finally, at 6.00 a.m. on 26.8, the house watchman, Gotlieb Szulum, came to tell me that he had seen a tenant named Moszkowicz outside my cellar compartment. I went down to the cellar with the house watchman to look for Moszkowicz; instead, after a thorough search, we discovered a hole hewn out of the wall, and found that it led to Moszkowicz's apartment. At last, the mystery of my persistent robber was solved."[1]

Jankiel Landau turned to the Jewish police in the hope that they would call the perpetrator to account. He was by no means alone in seeking to report the criminal activities of others to ghetto authorities such as the Order Service. In January 1941, for example, an anonymous letter was addressed to the Jewish Council chairman personally, informing him that a certain Sról Gliksman was keeping a stash of wood stolen from a workshop: "Please carry out an official search, I notice that he [Gliksman] has stolen wood at home. This person has earned several thousand marks in the meantime ... while other people are dying of cold and hunger. Please investigate this whole matter. What has happened to human justice?"[2]

Large numbers of similar reports were addressed to ghetto-internal institutions, notably in Lodz, but also in Warsaw and Vilna. In this way, residents attempted to pursue individual objectives in the expectation that the legal authorities would assume "conventional" law enforcement functions within the ghetto. Sometimes – as in the second example – they would bring to bear their own notions of justice. The concepts of criminal activity, morality, and justice they expressed were not formulated in a "vacuum," however, but in relation – whether positive or negative – to the definitions pronounced by the holders of (interpretive) power.

Interaction with Ghetto-Internal Legal Authorities

What was the attitude of ghetto residents towards the criminal activities they were accused of by the Jewish Councils? As a trial before the Lodz ghetto court in April 1941 illustrates, particularizing and contextualizing one's own actions was sometimes used as a strategy to obtain a mitigated sentence. The ghetto resident Ester Chlebolub, accused of "aiding and abetting the escape of a prisoner" and "resisting the OS," described her motives for the "offence" as follows: she had tried to stop her own son from smuggling because she preferred to earn her living "by the sweat of her brow," but he would not be dissuaded. When he was arrested by an OS officer, her "maternal instincts" had kicked in, hence her attempt to help him escape.[3]

This case had been referred to the ghetto court by the German Criminal Police, which meant that the imposed sentence would have to be reported back to the Germans. In her statement, the accused confirmed that her conduct had been criminal, but added – in awareness of the Jewish Council's priorities at the time – that she was willing to perform "hard labour" in the ghetto. In this sense, she was indirectly setting her own "productive" labour against the selfish act of smuggling at the expense of the community. The attempt to free her son was, she claimed, the "act of a desperate mother," and not – as described by the Order Service – an act of "planned" resistance to assist the escape of a prisoner. Her appeal to the legal understanding of the Jewish Council was "successful": both her repentance and age were taken into account as mitigating factors, and she was sentenced to ten months' imprisonment.[4] Ghetto residents often employed arguments that were accepted by the institutions of the Jewish Council. The success or failure of such justifications often meant the difference between life and death for the person concerned.

Even in more serious cases, offenders attempted to claim "mitigating circumstances" by placing their actions in the context of ghetto conditions. In July 1942, the Order Service of the Lodz ghetto referred a robbery committed by a ghetto resident to the German Criminal Police. Confronted with his crime, the accused made the following statement: "An old woman was lying in bed. Directly next to the bed was a stool with a tray on it. On this was a piece of bread and next to it some butter in a china dish. I had a sudden urge to take the butter, remembering I had some bread to spread it on at home. The woman tried to stop me ... so I gave her a few slaps around the face, took the dish of butter and left the apartment. I only took the butter in order to put it on my bread at home. And that's exactly what I did. I didn't take the bread, because I already had some at home."[5] Although the "robber" did not deny the act itself, he nevertheless put it to the Order Service that he had acted out of hunger, not greed, and had only stolen what he didn't have. In light of the increasing hardship and hunger of the ghetto community in 1942, the offender hoped to be able to claim these as mitigating circumstances vis-à-vis the Jewish police.[6]

After some initial hesitation, Hersz Arachier Badchan, who had hidden his child's body in his apartment for two weeks in February 1941, confessed to the Order Service that he had done it in order to use his son's bread and food ration cards.[7] Given the living conditions in the ghetto, the man's motives cannot be doubted. What is significant, however, is that he hoped to have his sentence lessened by naming the reasons for his crime, which was considered especially "heinous" within the ghetto. The distinction drawn by the Jewish Councils between "professional smugglers" and those bringing food into the ghetto purely for private consumption was likewise reflected in the testimonies of residents eager to clear themselves of any suggestion of habitual or prospective "dealing." Indeed, such statements were often made beforehand, to the Ghetto Special Commissariat of the German Criminal Police in Lodz, which made the same distinction; moreover, the residents knew that most cases would be referred to the jurisdiction of the ghetto. "I had no intention of trading with the purchased food,"[8] one resident named Abram Gecelew typically insisted at his hearing on 6 July 1940.

As demonstrated by the example of Jankiel Landau at the beginning of this chapter, people also turned to the Jewish Order Services expecting them to perform "conventional" police duties, such as law enforcement tasks. The idea that the Jewish police authorities were predominantly hated within the ghetto communities is, therefore, not the whole story, at least during the early phase of ghettoization in occupied Poland. In the period up to 1941, people in the Lodz ghetto reported numerous "criminal activities" by fellow residents to the Jewish police. Even though this was doubtless done in the hope of asserting their *own* interests, it nevertheless shows that the Order Service was more or less accepted as a police authority whose task was to combat crime in the ghetto.

People complained to the Order Service of offences by others which either affected them personally or which they had observed as bystanders. On 26 September 1941, for example, Chana Brandwajman notified the Jewish police that her child's shoes had been stolen.[9] It was not uncommon for residents of the Lodz ghetto to find other people wearing items of clothing that had been stolen from them, whereupon they would ask the Order Service to intervene.[10] On 27 July 1941, the Order Service in Lodz documented the following: "Szajnberg, Fela ... reports that the residents Hersz Epstajn, Blech Ester, and Langer Franin destroyed a cherry tree, tore down the cherries and trod the foliage into the garden."[11] The widespread ghetto offence of stealing wood from the "public realm" also prompted similar reports. Instead of the term "wood theft" used by the Jewish Council, residents would describe the specific actions involved, such as "ripping out boards."[12] The same applied to other ghetto-specific offences: in April 1941, for example, a house watchman reported that a tenant named Marjam Rosenberg was claiming food rations for her son who – contrary to her claims – was *not* in hospital,[13] but he did not use the official crime designation of "ration card fraud." By contrast, criminal activities that were common *before* ghettoization were referred to by name: one altercation between ghetto residents on a stairway was reported to the Order Service in Lodz as a "brawl";[14] likewise with a rape that Szmul Halle claimed had been perpetrated on his "mentally ill" daughter.[15] In other words, the new crime definitions were not yet established in the everyday language of the ghetto in 1941, and were only referred to if this was felt to be of direct assistance in obtaining a more lenient sentence.

Ghetto residents sometimes also complained about the behaviour of the Jewish police. In Lodz, for example, following a scuffle between two women on the staircase of an apartment block, one of the parties, Miriam Gojchbarg, complained in a letter to the Order Service police station about the conduct of an OS officer who was present during the fight and knew the other woman: "I shouted for help, whereupon the 'OS officer' came up the stairs towards me and smacked me in the face ... I demanded that he come with me to the 'OS department,' but he kept shouting at me."[16] As this letter demonstrates, the writer was still under the impression in June 1941 that the Jewish police had a duty to act in the interests of ghetto residents and, where necessary, as arbitrators, and that their supervisors would punish the kind of behaviour encountered here. After January 1942, when the OS officers in Lodz were made to assist with preparations for the German deportations,[17] the letters of complaint come to a noticeable halt.[18] Presumably, it was clear by this time that the ghetto police had become an instrument of the German campaign, and that its actions were therefore necessarily contrary to residents' interests.

In the Vilna ghetto, which was not established until September 1941, residents rarely appealed to the Jewish Police to fulfil "conventional" police functions. When they did contact them, it was usually to report the theft or loss of work permits and other official documents vital for survival in the ghetto.[19] This difference suggests that the Jewish Council in Vilna, and hence also its police force, had less room for manoeuvre from the start, and that people were aware of this.

In March 1942, the Jewish Police received a letter of complaint from a woman in the Vilna ghetto requesting that charges be brought against a police officer on duty on 22 March 1942 for "compromising behaviour." She complained that he had refused to tell her where she could obtain a pass after 8.00 p.m. and described his conduct as "arrogant." The "gentleman in question," she claimed, had taken out "his own inferiority complex" on her.[20] There are no records of whether the report had any consequences for the police officer. Since disciplinary proceedings against the Jewish Police in Vilna were more concerned with work procedures than with cultivating good relations with ghetto residents, however, he is unlikely to have been penalized for his conduct. This assumption is further supported by the existence of so few other complaints of this kind – perhaps partly because residents had come to realize since ghettoization that their concerns would no longer be listened to.

The attitude of residents towards the ghetto courts is hard to judge with any accuracy, given the relative lack of comments on the subject in diaries and survivors' accounts. This in itself is evidence that they did not play a central role in the everyday lives of ordinary residents.[21] In December 1941 – shortly before the beginning of the first deportations from the Lodz ghetto – the Viennese lawyer Dr Kitz, who had just been appointed a judge of the general ghetto court, reported that the court system enjoyed a "high level of recognition and respect" among the ghetto population.[22] In May 1941, the *Gazeta Żydowska* gave an equally positive assessment of the informal mediation services provided by the OS, commenting that they were widely recognized and trusted by the Jewish population.[23] This contrasts with statements by ghetto survivors from the immediate post-war period, which are dominated by criticisms of the ghetto judiciary echoing those already expressed with regard to the Jewish Councils in general. Judges are accused of applying "double standards," to the detriment of ordinary residents. One survivor, Yankl Nirenberg, writes of the court system in Lodz: "The big thieves were never brought to justice but petty thieves who had stolen a piece of bread or a few potatoes filled the court."[24] Writing in 1950, Bendet Hershkovitch levels a similar criticism at the judicial authorities in Lodz. According to him, offenders with good connections to the Jewish Council were able to escape sentencing, while those imprisoned for minor transgressions were the first to be deported: "The court sessions were generally more of a mockery than solemn proceedings."[25]

A certain amount of criticism was also voiced by members of the Jewish Council institutions, even if they recognized the necessity of internal judicial authorities in principle. The Chronicle author and ghetto archivist Józef Zełkowicz, for instance, argued that Rumkowski's summary court was justified by the need to suppress "dangerous activities" on the part of individuals. Nevertheless, he too complained that ordinary residents and their families were being subjected to harsh punishments while the "ghetto elite" was spared.[26] This attitude is reflected in the satisfaction with which – according to the Chronicle – the severe sentence imposed on Jakub Ratner was greeted by the ghetto community in May 1943. As previously mentioned, Ratner, an employee in the criminal section of the ration card department, had been found guilty of appropriating the bread and food ration cards of "resettled" residents and sentenced to three years' imprisonment, a biweekly day of fasting, and fifty cane strokes.[27] The Chronicle records the reaction of the ghetto community as follows: "It appeased the outrage which had erupted in all sections of the ghetto population following the discovery of the corruption scandal."[28] The criticism directed at Jewish Council members in general was also partly aimed at court officials, who were classed as part of the hated "ghetto elite." Thus, the chairman of the court, Szaja-Stanisław Jacobson, was described by the chronicler in 1943 as a "fat cat" because of his summer home in Marysin and the special privileges he enjoyed.[29]

Court cases aroused interest among residents in both the Lodz and Vilna ghettos. In March 1941, the Geto-Tsaytung in Lodz reported on Rumkowski's summary court: "The trials have provoked widespread interest among the population, to the point where – even though the proceedings are often held late at night – the courtroom is nevertheless full to overflowing."[30] Admittedly, this account needs to be read in light of the fact that the court had only recently been established. The resulting circumvention of normal jurisdiction, which effectively allowed the chairman to sentence offenders singlehandedly, had to be justified vis-à-vis the ghetto community, and he may therefore have got the Geto-Tsaytung to promote a positive image of the new authority. Even so, a report by an unknown resident also states that the trials attracted so many people that there were not enough seats to accommodate them all.[31]

Why were residents interested in the trials? For one thing, such occasions must have had a certain entertainment value. In times of fear, insecurity, hunger, and misery, they doubtless provided an element of diversion. Beyond that, the ghetto rulings may have served as an indicator of the Jewish Council's strategies and hence indirectly – at a time when information was in short supply – a clue to German plans.

Particular interest was aroused by the (few) internally tried murder cases. The Lodz ghetto chronicler reports that the first trial of this kind, in December 1941, involving a man named Litwak who was accused of murdering his brother-in-law over an old dispute, made a "big impression" on the community.[32] And in Vilna, residents followed the murder cases of June 1942 with similar interest. According to the chronicler, the harsh death sentences imposed on five residents for the robbery and murder of a yeshiva scholar, and on another resident for the murder of a Jewish Police officer, were met with approval: "No one in the ghetto resented this act of justice. No one doubted the just verdict or the guilt of the accused."[33]

Whether the majority of residents really did agree with the verdicts remains open to question. What is certain, however, is that death sentences could be imposed in Vilna – unlike in Lodz – without any appreciable resistance from Jewish functionaries or the ghetto community. The attitude of residents is likely to have been ambivalent: on one hand, the verdicts must have provoked fears of suffering a similar fate one day, particularly among those who had joined the armed resistance movement despite Jewish Council opposition. On the other hand, people in Vilna had already seen at first hand how criminal behaviour on the part of individuals could pose an existential threat to the community.

In Warsaw, the court authorities were not entirely accepted by the ghetto community. Reporting on the hearings held at Jewish police stations, the OS functionary Adler writes: "Often, when the witnesses and the claimant came from the general public, the problem of establishing the facts presented insurmountable difficulties: many times, the injured party withdrew his accusation or considerably blunted its edge. When an additional examination was necessary, witnesses had to be brought by force to the Order Service, even though they had given evidence gladly at the preliminary hearing. When brought back to court, either they could recollect nothing of the charges that had gone before, or they would try to help the accused with their evidence."[34]

It was not only the Jewish Council institutions that faced such problems, however. The house committees, which were a kind of tenants' association designed to facilitate greater resident participation, also suffered from a lack of public credibility as legal authorities. Reasons for this included a widespread shortage of qualifications, insufficient legal knowledge on the part of committee members, and the lack of opportunities to back up committee rulings – which were often little more than conciliation measures – with appropriate sanctions. In his diary, Perec Opoczyński refers to a case in which the house committee came up against a witness who refused to recognize the court's authority. Despite warnings, she could not be silenced and would not obey the instructions of the "court members."[35]

In Warsaw, this lack of acceptance was also due in part to the German restrictions imposed on the ghetto's judicial authorities at their inception, as a result of which they remained highly improvised in nature, leaving the Jewish Council with only limited powers to adjudicate in legal cases. This is likely to have been compounded by their short lifetime, and by the general opposition to the Jewish Council among the ghetto community. However critical they were of the legal authorities, some residents nevertheless found a way of using them for their own ends or "factoring in" weaknesses in the legal system. In the case of the Warsaw ghetto, Adler reports that some people committed offences in full knowledge that they would not be publicly pursued by the Jewish Council – and especially the judicial authorities of the Order Service – for fear of attracting the attention of the Germans.[36]

In Lodz, too, there were similar instances of residents capitalizing on their knowledge of internal evaluation criteria and potential "mitigating circumstances." In June 1941, for example, the Order Service handed over a case of wood theft to the public prosecutor with the warning: "We note that Pilater shifts the blame for all his offences onto his wife, calculating that she will be spared because of her three young children."[37] Pilater's "calculation" paid off: on 22 June 1941, the Order Service advised the ghetto prosecutor that the "main culprit," Mrs Pilater, could not be brought before the court, on the grounds of "having three small children and her husband being held in the central prison for wood theft."[38]

Appeal Procedures

The availability of institutional appeal procedures varied from ghetto to ghetto according to Jewish Council policy. In Lodz, Rumkowski set up a dedicated Secretariat for Complaints and Requests as early as October 1940, which was responsible for dealing with written petitions from ghetto residents.[39] Szmul Rozenstajn, the editor of the *Geto-Tsaytung*, characterized this office as follows: "It is a kind of direct mediator between the ghetto population and the governor, who does not have the opportunity of direct contact with the mass of people seeking a word in his ear."[40] As well as submitting their individual concerns to it, Rumkowski envisaged that people would also inform the institution explicitly of the criminal activities of others: "Anyone who discovers a dishonest or abusive practice detrimental to the ghetto, or learns of any kind of harmful activity in relation to the ghetto, must report it without fail to the lawyer Henryk Neftalin, who will investigate the matter and submit a detailed report to me."[41] The first task was to impress the purpose of the newly created office on the ghetto community. In the *Geto-Tsaytung*, Rumkowski repeatedly exhorted residents to make use of it and not to accost him personally in the street: "I must insist quite categorically that I will not accept any further petitions in person from this day forward ... I therefore request that you let me work in peace, as any disturbance will be of no help to you, and only a hindrance to me."[42]

According to a report in the *Geto-Tsaytung* of 2 May 1941, 20,000 proposals and 6,700 different requests had been received in the previous six months. As Rozenstajn notes, four permanent clerks and four supervisors were employed to deal with the workload.[43] Rumkowski announced that correspondents could expect to receive a reply within three weeks, and that the absence of a reply should be interpreted as a rejection.[44] The petitions and complaints addressed to him covered a multitude of subjects. Many consisted of appeals for work or financial assistance owing to hunger or the need to feed sick family members.[45] The letters were written in German, Yiddish, and Polish, mostly by hand, or in rare cases on a typewriter.[46]

In August 1942, Rumkowski set up additional complaints offices in all departments and workshops,[47] perhaps because the volume of correspondence had increased by this time to the point that the Secretariat was no longer able to process it alone. There were certainly reasons enough for complaint in 1942: thousands had been deported, and people were suffering the effects of hunger, disease, and forced labour. The supreme prioritization of physical labour even affected the Secretariat itself: on 11 May 1944 the ghetto chronicler noted that the Secretariat for Complaints and Requests had been dissolved by Rumkowski and the staff placed at the disposal of the labour office.[48]

A complaints office was likewise established in the Warsaw ghetto in January 1941.[49] Headed by Bernard Zundelewicz, its job was to deal with residents' grievances concerning the Jewish Council departments. A committee adjudicated on the complaints and necessary measures and forwarded its decisions to the relevant departments, and in some cases to chairman Czerniaków. In June 1941, the *Gazeta Żydowska* recorded the receipt of 286 complaints within the space of six months.[50]

In the Vilna ghetto, there was no authority with explicit responsibility for complaints and petitions from the ghetto community. The Jewish

Council had been set up in September 1941, when it was already becoming clear that there was little scope for action in view of the German murder plans. By this stage, it was no longer possible to give much weight to residents' individual concerns. Gens did, however, appeal to the population in 1942 and 1943, in his capacity as chief of police and Jewish Council chairman, to notify him of any activities harmful to the community, such as the concealment of furs or armed resistance.[51]

Particularly illuminating are petitions in which residents refer to the Jewish Councils' concepts of criminality and law. From these, we can see which requests they thought most likely to succeed. As such, the petitions also tell us something about how the ghetto community viewed the Jewish Council and its potential for influence. Residents of the Lodz ghetto, for example, wrote letters complaining of the injustice of sentences imposed by the ghetto judiciary and asking the Jewish Council for clemency. One such petitioner, Mordka Wajngot, wrote to the chairman on 18 July 1941 claiming that he had been wrongly sentenced to two months' imprisonment because a co-defendant had put the blame on him in order to save his own skin.[52] In December 1942, Israel Scher wrote to Rumkowski stating that he had completed his two-month sentence on sewage removal duty – imposed because of a few potatoes that had been found in his room – and now wanted to be posted to a "normal" workshop again.[53] Another resident, F. Urbach, also sentenced to sewage disposal duty after being convicted of "potato theft," insisted, "I would never be capable of stealing potatoes; such a suspicion is unfounded."[54]

In their letters, the petitioners tended to invoke known ghetto-internal evaluation criteria, citing reasons they hoped would be recognized by the Jewish Council as "mitigating circumstances." These were often accompanied by promises never to commit any further offences in future. Chaim Welzmann, sentenced for the alleged theft of four potatoes, wrote in October 1942: "Unfortunately, my defence was not heard out, and I have been sentenced to two months on sewage removal, I would like to take this opportunity to state that I don't feel I have committed an offence and am completely innocent, and I would also point out that I have never done anything wrong in my life. As I am in poor health, and not capable of doing such work, may I ask you most kindly to take my predicament into account and be so good as to refrain from enforcing the sentence, I am a tailor by profession, I hope my request will not be refused."[55]

While most letters received in Lodz related to "minor" offences such as wood theft, in Vilna even the previously mentioned Yankl Avidon – accused of murdering a Jewish Police officer – wrote to Gens as follows:

"I have been held at the ghetto detention centre since 7.III.1942. I urge you to bring me to trial or to come to some kind of decision ... If I am released soon, I pledge ... to work as a carpenter and be a good citizen of the ghetto."[56] Thus, even Avidon referred to the values promoted by Gens – as Jewish Council chairman and chief of police – as part of his strategy of "rescue through labour," in the hope that these would be more important to the Jewish Council than the offences of which he stood accused.

In their letters, residents of the Lodz ghetto sought clemency not only for themselves but in many cases also for family members. A large proportion of the petitioners were women seeking the release of their sons or husbands from the ghetto prisons and asserting their innocence.[57] That the majority were female was probably because women in the ghetto were heavily dependent on the earnings of their husbands, who were employed by the Jewish Council to carry out the necessary manual work. It was also mostly women who wrote expressing concerns for their children.[58] That said, the desperate conditions of the ghetto forced a change in traditional roles over time, an aspect which has not yet been systematically explored in relation to the ghetto communities. In the name of productivity, women too were forced to work, for example in the numerous tailoring shops and sewing factories of the Lodz ghetto. Even so, when it came to letter writing, the traditional roles seem to have persisted. In one typical letter to Rumkowski on 28 March 1941, a mother protests her son's innocence of the crime of stealing swedes. Besides her fears for her "sick and ailing" child, who would not survive four weeks in prison, she expresses concern over the loss of financial support facing the family, having read about it in the *Geto-Tsaytung*.[59] After 1942 in particular, following Rumkowski's reiteration of the importance of labour for the survival of the ghetto community, correspondents frequently drew attention to the "fitness for work" of their imprisoned relatives. On 10 May 1943, one resident named Nacha Okladek wrote to Rumkowski: "I am writing to your good self, as the only sister of Getzel Abram, who returned from working in Poznań three weeks ago and is currently being detained in the central prison, to politely request his release. He is a tailor by trade, so he would be very useful to the ghetto and not a burden on anyone."[60] Sickness and pregnancy were also commonly cited cases of need, as illustrated by a letter of 12 May 1943 from Rachela Rachol, requesting the release of her husband from prison on the grounds that she was ill and seven months pregnant.[61]

Only rarely did the letter writers allude to the activities for which they or their relatives had been arrested or sentenced. One mother complained in a letter to Rumkowski in February 1941: "My daughter was taken into custody from her sick bed along with my son-in-law for no reason, my children and I don't know why and are not aware of any criminal activity. I assume that my two innocent children have fallen victim to a case of professional envy."[62] The petitioners were evidently not always aware of the reasons for their relatives' imprisonment. This was because there were no reliable institutional structures in the ghetto to help them ascertain the whereabouts of family members and the grounds for their arrest. What's more, the offences in question were, as discussed, often newly defined ones which had not yet become embedded in the public consciousness as criminal acts and were therefore not perceived as such. Promises to refrain from any wrongdoing in future proved almost impossible to keep in practice, since – in light of the Germans' changing intentions and the arbitrariness of their behaviour thus far – the Jewish Council was continually defining and prosecuting new crimes which the promiser could not foresee.

A far larger collection of appeal correspondence exists for Lodz than for either Warsaw or Vilna. In the case of Warsaw, this seems to be due to the poor survival of source material. As a report from the *Gazeta Żydowska* of July 1941 shows, people clearly did send letters to the Jewish Council complaints department. Only a few of these are still extant, however, such as Szmul Winter's complaint to Council chairman Czerniaków regarding the arrest of the "old and ailing" house committee chairman by the Order Service for failing to collect money from the tenants.[63] Another anonymous letter of complaint was received by Czerniaków – probably before the sealing of the ghetto territory – calling on the chairman to put a stop to the random arrest of Jewish people.[64] In June and July 1941, two workers from Shop No. 12 wrote to Czerniaków objecting to their long working hours without breaks and lack of remuneration. Above all, they complained that they were unable to feed their families. The letter goes on to say that "many of our colleagues have already considered approaching the German powers," but that they wanted to take their complaint to the Jewish Council first.[65] Although the letter was not sent, workers from the same factory on Prosta Street subsequently informed the chairman on 6 July 1941 that they had downed tools in a gesture of protest.[66] The letter and the threat it contained can be seen as a helpless attempt to obtain improvements from the Jewish Council even though the writers cannot have had much faith in its powers to influence such matters. At the same time, the fact that the letter was addressed directly to the Council shows that the complaints department, which had existed since January 1941, was not sufficiently established within the ghetto community for correspondents to recognize it as the relevant authority, if indeed they knew about it at all.

The creation of complaints departments is a further reflection of Jewish Council strategies. Thanks to his compliance with German demands, Rumkowski calculated that he had enough internal room for manoeuvre – particularly before 1942 – to go some way towards granting residents' requests. The fact that people took up this "offer" suggests that they still believed in his ability to act, or that it was at least their only hope.

Information as to which requests had received a positive response is likely to have been shared among the community: had all appeals been refused, people would have stopped writing. It is significant in this respect that most of the letters date from 1940 and 1941. With the beginning of deportations in the Lodz ghetto, the volume of correspondence declined[67] – partly because of the removal of large numbers of potential correspondents, and partly because people's faith in the Jewish Council's freedom to act was presumably dwindling by this time. From then on – in accordance with the increased focus on "rescue through labour" – most of the letters received by the Council were requests for jobs. Given the limited scope for action in Vilna, it is not hard to see why the Jewish Council there did not have a complaints department, or why it received so little correspondence of this kind from ghetto residents.

In some cases, people sent letters to the Jewish Council, and sometimes even to the Germans, accusing fellow residents of criminal acts. Such allegations were also made in witness statements.

In January 1941, the Lodz ghetto chronicler wrote: "The decline of moral standards among the broad mass of the ghetto population is illustrated by the increasingly rampant practice of denunciation. Complaints of all kinds are being lodged with the community authorities on a daily basis."[68] These complaints, also in the form of letters, were the means by which ghetto residents notified the Jewish Council or the Order Service of criminal activities, as they had been repeatedly called on by Rumkowski to do.[69] The motives behind this practice were various, and resulted from the catastrophic living conditions in the ghetto and the limited opportunities for people to assert their own interests. The denunciations usually related to "activities" which the correspondents knew would be of interest to the Jewish Council in a criminal context. In Lodz, for instance, a "confidential message" was sent to the director of the meat distribution centre stating that an employee was selling salted meat which could only have come from that source, and that a case of theft was therefore suspected.[70] Often, denunciations were triggered by a sense of outrage at the fact that some residents were faring better than the majority as a result of their criminal activities. A case in point is the letter quoted at the beginning of this chapter regarding Sról Gliksman, in which the writer condemns the "crime" of concealing stolen wood as particularly reprehensible when others were suffering from hunger and cold, and appeals to the authorities' sense of "human justice."[71]

It was not only people's sense of justice that prompted such denunciations, however, but often private disputes between residents, or the sheer struggle for survival. An extreme example of the growing dog-eat-dog mentality is that of an eight-year-old boy in the Lodz ghetto who turned up at a police station in January 1941 to report his own parents for depriving him of his rightful bread ration.[72]

Sometimes, denunciations would lead to arrests and court proceedings. Much of the information turned out to be false, however, and it was not uncommon for the accused to reject the allegations as pure retribution. While this is virtually impossible to verify, the existence of such a motive in the ghetto is noteworthy in itself. In a trial before the ghetto court on 9 April 1941 for "violation of the ghetto curfew regulation," the defendant, a man named Strusik, insisted that the accusation was an "act of revenge," explaining "that he [had] borrowed two hundred marks in instalments from an acquaintance. Since Strusik was not in a position to return the money, his creditor [had] duly reported him."[73] The majority of revenge-driven denunciations seem to have occurred in the Lodz ghetto, where the existence of a dedicated infrastructure for complaints is quite likely to have been exploited in order to settle "old scores."

Residents also disclosed information about each other in the capacity of witnesses and "informants" before the ghetto-internal judiciary. Such information could be instrumental to the decision-making process in internal trials. This was true, for example, of the character references provided by the Order Service in Lodz for the ghetto courts and other purposes. These were based on statements by residents who had known the individuals in question before the war. The veracity of such statements was often questionable, however – a fact which could have serious repercussions, particularly when personal animosities were in play. One smuggling case of March 1941 tried by the ghetto court in Lodz illustrates the point: while the defendant, Moszek Hecht, confessed to "professional" goods smuggling, his co-defendant, Kaweblum, denied any involvement and dismissed Hecht's allegation as a "lie."[74] In the end, Kaweblum was convicted based on a character reference supplied by a neighbour that revealed his involvement in "professional" smuggling activities prior to the war.[75] A character reference proved similarly fateful for another ghetto resident, Gitla Ehrlich. The statement read: "Gitla Ehrlich ... was convicted of theft by the Polish courts several times before the war. On the last occasion, she was sentenced to two years' imprisonment. The above information was obtained from her neighbours David Nisarowajg, Marji Ruszccki, and Szcel Rosengarten."[76] The reference was duly forwarded by the Order Service to the ghetto public prosecutor.

The role that witnesses' own interests – and sometimes their personal quarrels and antipathies – could play is reflected in an account by Perec Opoczński of a hearing before a house committee in the Warsaw ghetto. The witness summoned to testify in relation to a rent dispute between two female tenants – a bagel seller and a carpenter's wife – regaled members of the house committee with information entirely superfluous to the case. Her statement ran: "I heard the milliner's daughter saying: 'Who are these committee people to summon me to court? Why can't the chairman work it out for himself, he's being paid good money, after all; why, he's practically rolling in it, just for sitting in his committee chair.' ... What do I know? All I know is that the bagel seller shouted at the carpenter's wife, saying she was a bad woman and that she would never forgive her for charging such a steep rent ... And besides, that she turned a blind eye to the fact that another woman is entertaining men in her apartment."[77] As this case demonstrates, a witness statement could also serve as a vehicle for furthering personal interests and expressing moral values and frustrations for which there was virtually no other outlet. Ghetto-wide sentiments such as resentment of functionaries with special privileges were, by default, taken out on fellow residents. Often, testimonies were coloured by personal conflicts between residents, such as the above witness's indignation at a fellow tenant's "indecent behaviour."

In the case of Vilna, we find far fewer records of denunciations or favourable testimonies. This is surprising, since its Jewish Council made similar appeals to the population for assistance in combating "harmful" individual activities. While this may be partly due to a lack of surviving source material, there are some indications that the practice was not at all common. Sometime after the German order to confiscate furs had been announced to the ghetto community in December 1941, with instructions to report any furs being hidden by fellow residents, the Jewish Police noted that no reports had been received in the intervening period.[78] A further indication comes from Kruk himself. After Gens introduced even tighter measures in the internal labour sphere from spring 1943, warning that Jews in supervisory roles would be held responsible for the offences of their staff, the supervisor Marek

Kozik – an acquaintance of Kruk's – was arrested. In the Chronicle entry of 4 April 1943, Kruk writes: "He was beaten twice in order to [make him] denounce employees involved in so-called speculation. Needless to say, he said nothing."[79]

In Vilna, it had become clear at an early stage that even "fitness for work" was no guarantee of survival. This evidently led to a different level of solidarity, or at least to a sense of disillusionment with regard to any such hopes. As a result, the population may have had less faith in the Jewish Council's strategy of "rescue through labour," and was therefore less inclined to follow its exhortations to betray criminal individuals for the sake of the community's survival.

In a few cases, residents even pleaded their causes to the German authorities. One mother, in her anxiety for her son, Chaim Jankiel Reichman, wrote to the Lodz division of the German Criminal Police: "Dear Commissar, May I humbly crave a great favour. My sixteen-year-old son was imprisoned six months ago for smuggling a packet of saccharine into the ghetto. It is the first time my son has ever broken the law, and he asks … for forgiveness and promises to keep on the straight and narrow in future. I am appealing for his release as a mother, for I am a sick woman and am suffering terribly under my child's imprisonment."[80]

In the case of Lodz, most of the surviving petitions of this kind date from the period shortly after ghettoization or from 1941.[81] In going over the Jewish Council's head to the Germans, the petitioners were breaching established institutional boundaries whereby internal matters were the affair of the Council. For them, all means were justified if they furthered their individual cause. The letters were often accompanied by an explanation for the offence and a pledge to refrain from any further criminal acts.[82] In 1941, there seems to have been a certain amount of flexibility on the part of the German Criminal Police, and a will to take such pledges into account as mitigating factors. Thus, two adolescent brothers accused of smuggling were recognized as having "diminished criminal responsibility," which the Germans justified by arguing that "[t]he guilty parties did not act out of avarice … therefore no sentence will be imposed."[83]

The fact that the bulk of these petitions date from 1940 and 1941, in the early days of ghettoization in Lodz, demonstrates that people still hoped to elicit a response from the German authorities at that stage, and that the Jewish Council's areas of jurisdiction were not yet anchored in the public consciousness. At the same time, the interests and powers of the German authorities were also still fluid, so that those writing before 1942 sometimes even had their requests granted.

Ghetto residents also wrote to the German police authorities seeking to "enlighten" them with regard to alleged criminal activities in the ghetto. The German Criminal Police in Lodz was informed, for example, of "objects of value" supposedly hidden by other residents. One of their reports of June 1940 reads: "Confidential information was received from the Jew Icek Zygmuntowicz ... stating that various valuables were buried under the floor in the apartment of the Jewess Frajdla Wygodna."[84] Some letters make no secret of the writer's motivation. In July 1941, for instance, the German Criminal Police received a letter in Yiddish-German accusing a family named Ast living in the ghetto of dealing in "dollars, diamonds and rings":[85] "The Asts are a very bad lot; they won't spare a crumb for a poor Jew ... I urge you not to reveal my name, and will send a couple more reports so as to get my own back on the Ast gang."[86] The Criminal Police staff found that such denunciations never led to anything, and speculated with regard to the writers' motives that "Jews are ... unlikely to betray their fellow citizens out of any kind of sympathy with the German authorities. If they do so, then it is purely for their own gain ... Their purpose is either to mislead the authorities, or they should be interpreted as an act of revenge against specific individuals."[87]

Reports were also received from residents claiming to have observed smuggling activities. A police report of May 1940 by the German Special Commissariat in Lodz reads: "A Jew called in to this office and, without giving his name, reported that the carters bringing horsemeat to the ghetto were also smuggling in food ... According to him, the buyers of the smuggled wares were to be found among the Jewish butchers."[88] And in an anonymous letter to the Criminal Police, the carter Kazimierz Nowacki was alleged to be stealing and smuggling milk – an insinuation that subsequently turned out to be groundless and was deemed an "act of revenge."[89] Many other similar tip-offs regarding smuggling offences within the community came to nothing.[90]

The reports received by the Lodz Criminal Police were not confined to issues which the writers knew would be seen as relevant by the Germans, however. Residents also denounced each other for the theft of a watch or a wallet – matters which, being of no interest to the Germans, were duly forwarded to the Jewish Order Service.[91] Appealing to the Germans as a higher, more powerful authority was thus seen as a way of escalating individual concerns. In this sense, the Jewish Councils' premise of dealing with legal issues internally was effectively "undermined" by individual residents.

In the case of the Warsaw ghetto, the majority of denunciation letters to German authorities date from 1940/1.[92] A common theme during this period was the failure of certain Jews to relocate to the "Jewish Residential District." One such missive reads: "As the writer of this anonymous letter, I would like to stress that I too am Jewish and am not ashamed of it. I have complied with the order and moved to the Jewish Residential District, but cannot stand by while another Jew makes a mockery of the German authorities by continuing to live in the Polish residential area when he has no right to do so."[93]

Ghetto residents would sometimes accuse each other of certain activities deemed criminal according to German definitions when called as witnesses before German Special Courts. Trials involving Polish-Jewish "smuggling gangs" often degenerated into mutual recriminations: one witness named Mojsze Smoliński, for instance, accused fellow residents before the German district court of Lodz of establishing contact with the Polish smugglers. In a hearing at the State Police premises in Lodz involving an alleged people smuggler named Bittermann, Artur Berkowitsch testified: "I observed him smuggling people out of the ghetto and into the city."[94] One motive for such statements was the witnesses' fear of arbitrary brutality on the part of the German occupiers. At an individual level, however, the sources show that residents were also motivated by internal, personal disputes. In one case tried before the German Special Court in Lodz, a resident named Goldberg, who stood accused of smuggling, suspected that he had been betrayed by his neighbour Breitmann for having failed – because of illness – to sweep the yard in front of their apartment block in accordance with Jewish Council orders. For his part, Breitmann denied having reported the smuggling activities out of revenge, arguing: "It is true that I quarrelled with Goldberg about sweeping the road. I also threatened to report him to the Jewish police station – which I didn't do. That doesn't mean that I reported the smuggling out of revenge. Everything I said, I have either seen or been told by Goldberg."[95]

Statements before the German court displayed the same rationale as in ghetto-internal trials, and sprang from the same emotions of envy and perceived social injustices. In the above smuggling case, for instance, Breitmann stated in his testimony: "My reason for reporting Goldberg ... today is that I can no longer stand by and watch one person living a life of luxury while another goes hungry."[96]

Criminality as Resistance?

In the research, criminal acts by ghetto residents under the conditions of German occupation are often classed as "resistance," particularly in the case of the prominent offence of smuggling.[97] Such acts are deemed to be essentially driven by the sheer will to survive that led the Jewish people to resist the German murder campaign. Writing on the background to criminality in the ghetto, Grabowski and Engelking remark: "In order to survive, [German legal norms] had to be breached."[98] Underlying this notion is a definition of resistance based on the concept of *amidah* (Hebrew for "withstanding" or "standing upright"), as formulated by scholars such as Yehuda Bauer. This includes the whole spectrum of individual solidarity behaviour, from cultural activities designed to strengthen the will to survive through to armed resistance.[99]

This concept of resistance and the corresponding classifications of criminality in the ghetto were formulated from a post-war perspective – in awareness of the systematic extermination of the Jewish population by the Germans during the Second World War.[100] However justified such a definition may be, it can easily mask the fact that Jewish people living through ghettoization had all kinds of reasons for committing acts classified by the Germans and/or Jewish Councils as criminal, as some of the examples in this chapter have shown. It matters whether an action is classified as "resistance" with hindsight, or in the contemporary context of the situation itself. If we are to consider the people in the ghetto as active subjects, we also need to factor in their different motives. To do this, we need – as argued here – to at least recognize that individual reasons for defying particular rules and norms were many and various, and that the sense of performing an act of "resistance" against the German plans was seldom uppermost in people's minds at the time.

Given the catastrophic conditions under German ghettoization, the will to survive was doubtless the primary motive for criminal activity among the majority of the population. Others, however – such as professional, organized smugglers – did not bring food into the ghetto simply to ensure their own survival or that of the ghetto community, but often sold the goods at horrendous prices to maximize their profits. These people surrounded themselves with "luxury goods" out of the reach of ordinary residents, and cultivated a lifestyle of drinking and revelry, often in the company of Polish policemen.[101]

In the case of children and adolescents, a further motive for criminal behaviour needs to be considered. There is no question that many were forced to steal provisions or smuggle food in order to avoid starvation or to help feed their family. At the same time, however, they may also have been driven by a spirit of adventure, or dared by their peers. One survivor, Yaakov Shvartsberg, recalling how he joined a gang of orphans in the Vilna ghetto as a child because his parents were too busy working, describes the desire to be accepted by the others as a key impulse.[102] Similarly, in the previously mentioned blackmail case tried by the Lodz ghetto court in March 1943, the offenders' "youthful exuberance" was cited as a motivation alongside their need for clothing.[103]

It is not possible – nor indeed is it my intention – to make a judgment here regarding the true motives behind criminal acts in the ghetto. Rather, my purpose is to show that an agenda of "resistance" to the German occupiers' plans and/or the Jewish Council strategies was seldom explicitly articulated by ghetto residents at the time. People judged the criminal activities of others in very different ways – partly influenced by the fear that individual actions might endanger the ghetto community at large – and perceptions varied according to both social criteria and the point at which they were formed.

Ghetto residents formulated moral standards in response to the social inequalities of their environment. For example, they would intervene out of solidarity in certain situations to protect victims whom they regarded as ordinary citizens, such as women who were liable to be mugged in the street when returning with food rations from the distribution points. In relation to the Warsaw ghetto, Adler writes: "In some cases, blows would be inflicted on the starveling [by the thief], but the crowd in the street would then usually defend the victim against the offender and criminal proceedings were invoked."[104] Residents also intervened in attacks of this kind in Lodz, in one case beating up a "robber" who had snatched two *striezel* (plaited buns) from a woman's hand and devoured them on the spot.[105]

Attitudes to smuggling were similarly discriminating. Unlike the Germans, who did not distinguish explicitly between private and professionally organized smugglers when it came to sentencing and prosecution, ghetto residents saw this as a significant difference. While they tended to be sympathetic towards people who smuggled for their own needs, professional smugglers were viewed with suspicion,[106] and motives of personal enrichment were regarded as morally reprehensible.[107] Here again, however, it should be borne in mind that judgments were based less on objective criteria than on the perceptions of individuals, some of whom believed that even ordinary people smuggled out of pure greed, as demonstrated by the letters of denunciation. That said, the internal judgment of smuggling seems to have become less of an issue once residents learned of the German murder plans. In Warsaw, professional smuggling was no longer considered as offensive after the mass deportations of July 1942. This change in perception is noted by Adler, for example: "The 'players' were in every way the most active members, if not the leaders, of the smuggling gangs. The official attitude toward them also underwent a gradual change. In the beginning they were reviled, later on tolerated, and in time, glorified. From their numbers came the heroes of the loading point because they were able to smuggle out hundreds of those who were caught and destined for transport."[108]

In some ways, awareness of the German murder plans had a "levelling" effect within the coerced community. The knowledge that the Germans would carry them out indiscriminately – "Jewishness" being the only criterion that counted – led to a softening of attitudes towards the smugglers' activities. Indeed, attention actually switched to their contribution to the preservation and provisioning of the ghetto community.

A similar tendency can be observed in the Vilna ghetto from its very inception in September 1941. By this stage, the residents already suspected that they might have to rely on the food brought into the ghetto by professional smugglers. This resulted in an ambivalent attitude towards the ghetto guards deployed by the Jewish Police, who were themselves involved in smuggling plots. On one hand, they disapproved of the guards' self-enrichment and the according brutality they often showed towards residents. On the other hand, their very corruptibility was seen as helping to feed the ghetto community. In January 1943, the chronicler Herman Kruk wrote of the feared ghetto guard commander Levas: "We must say that in spite of everything we have written about him, he is a bold and daring fellow. If not for him, that contraband would never have gotten into the ghetto. In fact we must admit that Levas is personally responsible to the [German] authorities for it."[109]

One group of offenders in the Lodz ghetto who were viewed comparatively favourably by fellow residents after summer 1942 were the "illegal radio listeners." In defiance of the German ban, they had hidden radio sets in order to keep up with the news, and often relayed information on the course of the war to the Zionist groups and parties. According to a report by Mojsze Białkower on the "unsung heroes of the ghetto,"[110] one resident named Mojsze Tofel continued to listen in to political broadcasts despite the criminalization of the practice by Rumkowski, who turned offenders over to the Germans: "He was, in effect, the master of radio listeners in the Lodz ghetto. He was not afraid to receive programs on his radio by day or night, and spent the whole night searching for stations from all over the world."[111] In this case, however, it was a crime that gave an informational advantage to the whole ghetto population, particularly since hopes of survival were no longer pinned to the strategy of "rescue through labour" but to the speedy arrival of the Red Army.[112] By this time, ghetto residents had lost faith in the idea that refraining from criminal activities would save their skin.

The lack of any systematic study of the various perceptions of criminal behaviour continues to represent a gap in the research which cannot be completely filled here. Which social strata were associated with particular views, for example, and how attitudes may have changed over the lifetime of the ghetto are aspects that have yet to be explored. My intention here is merely to note the absence of any static, generalizable perceptions of criminal activity in the ghetto.

It was not until after the end of the Second World War that changing definitions of resistance and criminality eventually emerged in the accounts of ghetto survivors, who were now in a position to speak freely. In this context, criminal acts earned a new respect.[113] Under ghettoization, there would have been little interest in discussing such matters, or the fear of criminal prosecution or social sanctioning would have prevented it. Now, however, actions which had been regarded with ambivalence *during* the ghetto's existence were presented as "resistance," in keeping with accepted narratives of the post-war period. Judgments of this kind are often adopted uncritically in the secondary literature, rather than being interpreted as the point of view of a specific individual at a specific time.

Studying survivor stories in detail and reading between the lines can provide more nuanced insights into the actors' motives. This can be demonstrated via the example of the previously mentioned account by Yaakov Shvartsberg, who, as a child in the Vilna ghetto, stole bread along with a group of other youngsters. After the war, he recalled: "I wanted to be one of the lads. I was a skinny little boy ... I climbed through the bars [of a bread storeroom] and started to throw bread down to them. We went around like a gang in the ghetto, stealing bread. To us, it wasn't stealing. It was survival. Bread belonged to the ghetto."[114] This last statement is a narrative articulated after the war. The childish motives discernible in his account – his sense of abandonment, his aversion to being left alone by his parents, and the struggle for peer recognition – appear to have been just as significant as the desire to avoid starvation. Whatever his motives were at the time, the rationale he formulated after the war would have been almost impossible to voice during the ghetto's existence for fear of prosecution by the Jewish Council or the Germans, and the resulting punishment and potential outrage of fellow residents.

A further example of how reports of criminal activities in the ghetto attracted a new interest after the end of the war can be found in the accounts by the Warsaw ghetto survivor Symcha Binem Motyl. Writing retrospectively, he relates how he and fellow residents were given passes in order to obtain necessary materials from outside the ghetto.

Instead of following their instructions, however, he and his colleagues took advantage of the temporary release chiefly in order to sell raw materials and clothing from the ghetto on the "Aryan side." Reflecting on his motives, he writes: "You could earn a great deal at this ... This trade was of course illegal, for our formal occupation was – or rather should have been – buying up old iron in the villages, but in practice we never did this."[115] Such activities could be described differently in retrospect, since there was no longer any threat of prosecution or social exclusion.

Another question requiring investigation in the context of survivor stories is the degree to which the survival strategies pursued by the Jewish Councils in the ghettos impacted on the forms and limits of expression for Holocaust survivors. Did survivors from the Vilna and Lodz ghettos – where the Jewish Councils subscribed to the notion of "rescue through labour" and associated definitions of criminality – express a different post-war view of criminal acts committed there from those who had lived in ghettos where there were no comparable internal norms? Even after the event, those whose individual activities were regarded by the Jewish Councils as a grave danger to the community are likely to have remained under considerable pressure to justify themselves. As such, the practice of classing past actions as "resistance," as in the above examples from the Vilna ghetto, may have been to some extent a way of dealing with possible (self-)accusations of guilt.

The idea still persists that ordinary ghetto residents not employed in the Jewish self-administration were deeply opposed to the Jewish Councils. It is certainly true that the Councils enforced German demands that were often contrary to the interests and well-being of the ghetto population. While the Councils enjoyed certain – albeit limited – internal powers to define which actions were criminal and which were just, ghetto residents had no institutional means of asserting their moral values, which varied from person to person and were situation- and time-specific.

As discussed in greater detail at the beginning of this study, legal orders usually arise from the social morality of a community. In the coerced communities of the ghettos, however, the legal norms did *not* arise from the moral values of the majority. Instead, the Jewish Councils had to bow to the (legal) notions of the German occupiers and comply with demands that ran counter to the welfare of the ghetto community. Moreover, the acts deemed criminal by the Jewish Councils were often committed out of the sheer necessity of survival – and this did indeed make people generally critical of, if not hostile to, the Councils. As we have seen, however, ghetto residents persisted in referring to Council rules and norms in their letters, or in the dock as defendants or witnesses. They developed strategies for making pragmatic use of ghetto-internal legal authorities and regulations in order to further their own ends. In some cases, they even turned to the German authorities. That they resorted to such measures was due not least to their lack of access to any other means of influence within the coerced community of the ghetto.

Criminality and Law between the Poles of External Power and Internal Autonomy

This study has reevaluated everyday life within the coerced ghetto communities in Nazi-occupied Europe with a focus on concepts of crime and law as formulated by the Jewish Councils. In so doing, it has broken with two main assumptions that still prevail in Holocaust scholarship and public discourse. The first is that the Jewish Councils had no scope for action in the face of German brutality, arbitrariness, and ultimately systematic mass murder, not to mention that they must have had other priorities than to decide on questions of "criminal behaviour" and legal judgment within the ghetto community. The second is that – despite the terrible circumstances in the ghettos – a "heightened Jewish morality" prevented "criminal behaviour" within these communities. This latter notion led Samuel Gringauz to invent the following formula: "V/A = L, where V equals the social and moral value of the members of the community, A the animal instinct of self-preservation, and L the level of communal social and moral values. Since the enormous pressures of external conditions made for an immeasurable increase of A, it was necessary for V to increase tremendously to retain L at a high level. The increase of V was possible only through the fact of Jewish national community, through the fact of heightened Jewish morality that had its roots in the community of fate and destiny."[1]

Contrary to this, we have seen that, in the ghettos forcibly created by the Germans in the Second World War, there were in fact plenty of actions that were classed as criminal and prosecuted via internal legal authorities, and plenty of voices complaining of a "moral decay" within the ghetto communities. Our analysis has centred on the Jewish Councils that, in accordance with German orders, had already been established in many places shortly after the occupation of Eastern Europe. These institutions were forced to comply with ever-changing German demands, which – whatever form they took – ran counter to the welfare of the ghetto population. For them, the only means of dealing with this dilemma lay in a desperate attempt to interpret the Germans' actions according to rational criteria and second-guess their plans in order to play to their interests, such as the need for labour power, for example. By this means, they hoped to be able to ensure the survival of the ghetto community, or at least – once the Germans' systematic exterminations had begun – a proportion of it.

It was in the internal legal sphere of the ghetto that the Jewish Councils' dilemma was at its most acute: here, they were expected to rule on legal matters in an environment whose involuntary occupants had already been wholly disenfranchised and, as such, effectively had no choice but to act in a criminal manner in order to survive. The balancing act performed by the Councils consisted in having to suppress such activities in accordance with German orders, while at the same time attempting to regulate communal life under exceptional and life-threatening conditions in order to ensure as far as possible the well-being and survival of the community. To that end, they established their own definitions of criminality and law. As we have seen, the Jewish Councils enjoyed a certain amount of leeway when it came to defining which actions should be deemed criminal and how they should be punished. Crucial to this were the demands imposed on the Councils by the Germans, the point at which they became aware of the German murder plans, and the survival strategies they devised for the ghetto communities on that basis.

This study has shown that, despite the differences between the ghetto communities discussed here, all three exhibited similar generic categories of criminal behaviour:

1. Crimes that were to be prosecuted directly on German orders, such as illegal border crossing or smuggling.
2. Behaviour that was deemed by the Jewish Council to pose a danger to the ghetto in that it might trigger a brutal intervention by the Germans. This covered a wide variety of activities such as unhygienic candy production, rumour-mongering, and labour offences.
3. Actions directed against ghetto institutions, whose efficient operation was regarded as essential to the survival of the ghetto community.
4. "Classical" crimes in which private individuals were the injured party, such as brawls, sexual abuse, or murders.

As we have seen, however, the content of these categories and their relative importance in the ghetto-internal legal sphere varied according to the changing German plans, the extent to which the Jewish

Councils were aware of them, and the conclusions they drew from that knowledge. Criminal offences belonging to categories (2) and (3) were especially relevant in the ghettos of Lodz and Vilna, where the Jewish Councils pursued a strategy of "rescue through survival." Here, these categories became part of comprehensive definitions of potentially "harmful behaviour" that could not only trigger German intervention but also prevent the Councils' institutions from enforcing their survival strategy and corresponding agendas. In Warsaw, by contrast, where Czerniaków was more reluctant to fulfil German demands, it was especially crimes of category (1) that were officially prosecuted, accompanied by the emergence of parallel, informal ways of settling internal disputes that sought to uphold evaluation criteria from the pre-war period. From the second half of 1942 onwards, armed resistance groups also gained in authority here and began to challenge the evaluation criteria and survival strategy of the Jewish Council.

"Classical" crimes of category (4) diminished in importance in all three ghettos, especially once the Jewish Councils knew of the Germans' systematic murder plans. From now on, their main emphasis lay on preventing individual acts that could endanger the whole ghetto community, while the prosecution of "harmful acts" directed against individuals, which had been punishable in pre-war times, became less relevant. It was here that the changing relationship between individual and community under the enforced conditions of German rule became most apparent.

Based on the new crime definitions, the Jewish Councils created a ghetto-internal legal sphere. The definitions were proclaimed as de facto legal norms via announcements and ghetto newspapers. Jewish police authorities set up on German orders to ensure "peace and order" in the ghetto also served as a vehicle for implementing internal concepts of criminality and law. And at the Jewish Councils' initiative, courts were established in order to try disputes and legal cases. The sentences reflected the new evaluation criteria and were often served in ghetto prisons, which, although administered by the Jewish Councils, were accessible to the Germans.

The organization of the internal legal sphere as a whole was characterized by the attempt to exploit the evolving scope for action, and hence by a high level of improvisation. Underpinning it throughout were the Jewish Councils' efforts to assert their *own* evaluation criteria and sanctions in order to avert the threat of worse punishments by the Germans. The liberties conceded to the Councils were arbitrary, unpredictable, and constantly changing. This resulted in a paradoxical development: in some ways, the German authorities' decision to embark on the wholesale murder of the ghetto population actually gave the Councils more room for manoeuvre. This was particularly evident in matters of criminal prosecution, in which the Germans increasingly lost interest. When they did intervene, however, the consequences were all the more devastating: after the end of 1941 in particular, the delivery of offenders to the occupiers no longer led to sentencing by German courts but, in most cases, straight to murder.

In formulating definitions of criminality and law, the Jewish Councils were forced to take German demands into account. As such, instead of being guided by the values and needs of the ghetto population, as is usual in democratic societies, they often acted in direct opposition to them. Despite this – or rather precisely because of it – ghetto residents sought outlets through which to assert their own notions of criminal behaviour and justice, as well as their individual interests. These included petitions or letters of denunciation to the Jewish Councils (and occasionally even to the Germans). Wherever it paid them to do so – that is, if they thought it offered a chance of survival – they would attempt to use the ghetto-internal legal authorities to advance their own cause.

As these reflections have shown, definitions of criminality and law often involved value judgments about modes of human behaviour and, as such, were influenced not least by moral issues. Under National Socialism, the actions of the Germans ran counter to all hitherto prevailing notions of morality and rendered legal principles invalid. It was not only in their actions that they exhibited arbitrary brutality, however: their very definitions of criminality and law were an expression of the power structure they had established.

The whole concept of morality is something that cannot be ignored in Holocaust research, especially in the context of the Jewish Councils. On one hand, as mentioned in the Introduction, Hannah Arendt condemned the Councils' cooperation with the German perpetrators as "morally reprehensible." On the other, Samuel Gringauz, for one, credited the ghetto population with a "heightened Jewish morality." These judgments, too, require explanation. Commentators who observed a low level of criminality in the ghettos can be assumed to have been thinking primarily of the "classical" offences defined under category (4), which were anchored in the public consciousness as criminal both before and after the war and were regarded as objective. Offences of this kind were doubtless rarely recorded during the lifetime of the ghetto, not least because the Jewish Councils did not see them as a priority compared with other activities which might jeopardize the survival of the whole community. The claim that violent crime was scarce in the ghettos may be true according to "classical" evaluation criteria, but it ignores the fact that the new criminal acts defined within the ghetto could have grave consequences for those concerned. Under the catastrophic living conditions of the ghetto, "minor" food thefts could mean the death of the victim and possibly other members of their family.

Contrary to Gringauz's assessment, ghetto residents frequently complained in diaries and memoirs of a "moral decline." In most cases, they were referring to their perception of the Jewish Council functionaries and Jewish police authorities, who often profited from smuggling and were made to assist with deportations. These actions, though considered "morally reprehensible" by ordinary ghetto residents, were not officially – that is, from the Jewish Council's perspective – classed as criminal. Only concepts devised by the Germans and the Jewish Councils could attain the status of binding crime definitions and legal norms. In light of this, the idea of an inherently strong "Jewish morality" should be treated with caution.

It is clear from the above that morality, like criminality and law, is a relative concept – a construct that changes according to circumstances. And yet this notion of the constructedness of concepts, now well established among history scholars, seems to cause a problem for Holocaust researchers, especially when it comes to moral values. That said, scholars have slowly begun to consider concepts of morality and law and the resulting legal organs in Nazi-occupied Eastern Europe.[2] Such research looks first at the concepts of the Germans themselves, in order to understand the role of an emerging German jurisdiction in light of their violent and arbitrary actions, and the extent to which it was rooted in specific moral considerations and ideological premises.[3] Second, and importantly, scholars have started to shed light on the role of Polish courts under Nazi rule, as well as that of the Polish police, which continued to exist and operate alongside German bodies.[4] Although research premised on the constructedness of concepts of morality and law is still in its infancy, these studies give us a glimpse into the complex web of legal procedures resulting from the combination of new ideological premises, coercion, and a reality characterized by the need for professional experience and personnel. They are crucial if we are to understand the context of coercion within which the Jewish Councils operated, and future research will hopefully allow us to explore the topic in further thematic and geographical depth.

Looking at this internal legal sphere confronts us with highly sensitive issues regarding the scope for action, patterns of behaviour, and choices between collective and individual survival of those classified as "Jewish" by the Germans. It ultimately touches upon the delicate question of who could and did exert power over others, which behaviours were deemed likely to guarantee survival for whom and at what cost. In Lodz, the private production of candy could lead to sentences in the ghetto prison, from where Rumkowski then drew the quotas he was forced to provide for the German deportations; Jewish judges in the Vilna ghetto pronounced death sentences; ghetto inhabitants stole food from their neighbours and were willing to report on the "criminal acts" of others before the Jewish Council institutions.

However, to morally judge or condemn these actions would be highly problematic in two regards. First, it would prevent us from understanding the dilemma of the Jewish Councils, which found its most prominent expression in the legal sphere. It is precisely by looking at such sensitive issues that we are able to grasp the complexity of the dynamics between the Germans' actions and demands and the Jewish Councils' attempts to exploit the perceived scope for action. Second, it would be to ignore the coerced nature of the ghetto communities. It was not the inhabitants' choice but the Germans' racial segregation policies that had forced individuals from heterogeneous backgrounds to live in confined spaces, deprived of food and appropriate accommodation and facing the constant danger of disease and death. It is no surprise that, under these circumstances, people displayed not only empathy and solidarity but the whole range of human behaviour, including acts motivated by envy, anger, and revenge. Accordingly, we should be open to moving away from expectations of clear-cut "good" and "bad" patterns of behaviour, often associated with the opposite poles of "resistance" and "collaboration." This study has instead sought to integrate ambivalence and paint a more nuanced picture. It has broken with simplifying narratives of dictatorial Jewish Council leaders and ghettos as "legal vacuums." It has questioned accounts of smugglers as heroic resistance fighters, Jewish policemen who only enriched themselves and assisted the deportations, and a strong "Jewish morality" that prevented crime in the ghetto. Furthermore, it has overhauled the assumption of an exclusively hostile relationship between Jewish Councils and ghetto inhabitants.

In short, we have seen that people in these coerced communities behaved in different ways and from various motives. This undoubtedly complicates the picture. Nevertheless, with more recent studies contributing significantly to a shift away from the depiction of "passive Jewish victims," emphasizing the variety of behaviour exhibited in the struggle for survival, the next step must be to acknowledge that not all actions were "morally good." The aim of this study has not been to produce a moral verdict on any kind of behaviour but to understand behavioural patterns, to classify them, both within the historical context and retrospectively, and to reevaluate them against the background of existing scholarship. In so doing, it has sought to actively encourage an examination of those sensitive issues which are often distorted by expectations and wishful thinking. Only then can attention be drawn to aspects hitherto disregarded by the research community.

The question remains why the Jewish Councils created such complex legal authorities, and why they accorded so much importance to legal practice – even in the Vilna ghetto, where the German extermination campaign was known about from its inception in September 1941. References to a "heightened Jewish morality" and the endeavour to uphold pre-war moral standards at a time of German tyranny and brutality do not provide a satisfactory answer. There are no statements by Jewish Council chairmen or the responsible judicial staff from the days of the ghettos explicitly citing the preservation of pre-war morality as a rationale. What they did state emphatically, however, was – as we have seen – their intention to secure the survival of as many ghetto residents as possible. Consequently, they gave priority to the definition, prosecution, judgment, and punishment of individual actions which, for various reasons, they deemed a danger to the community. It was natural that Jewish Council members should begin by resorting to familiar, learned practices, drawing on legal knowledge and traditions from before the war. As demonstrated, however, it soon became clear that this knowledge needed to be adapted to the exceptional circumstances of the ghetto.

That the Jewish Council functionaries maintained their legal institutions and procedures almost to the last is unlikely to have been motivated by an overriding desire to preserve moral standards for their own sake. More probably, their intention was to achieve a modicum of social stability in order to guarantee some kind of "normality." An example of this was their effort to prevent an outbreak of panic among the ghetto community, which would have threatened its survival. In the case of Rumkowski's rule in the Lodz ghetto, there is another dimension to consider. The Lodz ghetto was the only ghetto where there was no armed resistance, a phenomenon that Isaiah Trunk addressed in an important essay of 1981.[5] He suggested a number of convincing explanations, such as the invisibility of the Polish anti-Nazi underground in the city of Lodz, the relative isolation of the ghetto, and the fact that 1943, the year in which attempts at armed resistance took place in other ghettos, was a period of relative calm in the Lodz ghetto. At the same time, we have seen that it was Rumkowski who established and enforced the most comprehensive legal institutions and procedures, such as a petitions department, and that ghetto inhabitants did make some use of these. This suggests that such procedures not only helped to enforce the chairman's authoritarian rule but may also have served to channel anger and despair within the ghetto community, providing the population with a means of expressing their needs and sorrows.

The moral evaluation criteria applied by the Jewish Councils also depended on what they knew about the German plans at any one time, and to what extent they feared having to act against the interests of the ghetto population. Other significant factors were their hopes of survival, and hence their visions of the post-war period, which were influenced both by professional considerations and the fear of being judged by posterity on their actions in the ghetto. As already noted, one judge in the Lodz ghetto justified his severe punishment of a defendant by arguing that he did not want to be criticized after the war for his failure to uphold moral principles and take a sufficiently tough line on offenders.[6] In the Vilna ghetto, one candidate refused to accept his appointment as judge because he was concerned that "morally dubious" verdicts passed in the ghetto might disqualify him from office in any post-war Polish court.[7] Such considerations doubtless also depended on the individual moral standards of the people concerned. Above all, however, they indicate that the organization of the legal sphere and the associated practice were underpinned right to the end by (individual) hopes of survival and escape from murder by the Germans.

To help explain the motives behind the organization of the ghetto-internal legal sphere, let us consider once again the previously discussed continuities with regard to Jewish law. Although the Jewish Councils did not draw explicitly on the religiously derived legal principles of *halakha*, some parallels could be discerned between pre-eighteenth-century Jewish case law and the institutions within the ghetto, including its legal practice. Such similarities were not primarily to do with the "Jewish identity" of the ghetto residents, however, but rather with the fact that both systems are examples of legal communities which were largely unconnected with the state, and which attempted to assert their own legal principles in contradistinction to an external power.

For one thing, the degree of internal autonomy in both instances invariably depended on the legal competence granted by the external power. Both in pre-modern Jewish communities and in the ghetto, most of the freedoms thus conceded related to civil law, while the external authorities sought to retain their control over criminal matters. In these circumstances, a specific set of norms arose which were formulated, communicated, and concretized via internal judicial authorities based on actual case studies. A further parallel lay in the attempt by both eighteenth-century Jewish communities and the ghettos to try cases internally where possible. If the behaviour of an individual was deemed particularly dangerous to the community, however, they would be excluded by default from its ranks. Punishments in general were supposed to have a preventive effect, in order to deter threats to the group. In pre-modern Jewish communities and ghettos alike, such a threat was used to justify the banishment of the offender – or indeed, in the latter case, their surrender to the Germans and consequent death. In both instances, periods of crisis, exceptional circumstances, and impending dangers to the community as a whole could lead to the imposition of individual death sentences.

After the harmonization of legal relations between Jewish and non-Jewish communities in the nineteenth century in the wake of widespread modernization movements, the return to a "Jewish" legal practice in the ghettos represented something of a backward step from a legal-historical perspective. It is important to stress, however, that this was primarily a result of the Germans' exclusion of Jews from state legal institutions. Moreover, the situation in the Nazi ghettos was unprecedented: never before had the external power envisaged a complete extermination of the Jewish community or created such catastrophic conditions through ghettoization, inflicting hunger, disease, poverty, and often death, on the residents.

As it happened, the ghettos were not the last instance in which "Jewish" judicial authorities were created as distinct from an external power. After liberation, survivors in Jewish Displaced Persons Camps inside the British- and American-occupied zones of Germany and Italy set up Jewish honour courts. After 1946, the Jewish Central Committee in Poland followed suit with a civic court (*sąd społeczny*). For these authorities, which again existed alongside national courts, the issue of cooperation between Jewish Council members and the German occupiers became central.[8] Actions which were not considered criminal during ghettoization were now prosecuted. In a series of trials, former Jewish Council members and Jewish police officers were accused of "betrayal of the Jewish people" and punished with "banishment" from the Jewish community. Now, the primary function of the courts was no longer, as in the days of the ghetto, to act *preventively* in order to suppress behaviour that might endanger the entire ghetto community. This time, sentences were imposed *retrospectively* for actions consistent with the morality professed by the majority of ordinary residents during the lifetime of the ghetto. At the same time, however, the rulings also had implications for the future: by introducing definitions of criminality according to which individual actions could now be classed as a "betrayal of the Jewish people," it became possible to establish a "national Jewish identity" that was regarded as essential for the foundation of a Jewish state in Israel.

The strong "national Jewish community" that Gringauz transposes in the opening quotation to the time of the ghetto essentially came to the fore in the immediate post-war period. The relationship of the individual to the "Jewish" community was, without question, of central importance both in the ghettos and after the end of the Second World War, and manifested itself specifically in definitions of criminal behaviour. Nevertheless, it was based on very different premises in either case: the ghettos were coerced communities whose composition was dictated by the Germans according to their definition of the "Jewish race." Which individual actions the Jewish Councils deemed a danger to the community was determined partly by the German extermination plans, and partly by the brutal collective punishments imposed by the Germans for individual "misconduct" from the beginning of the occupation onwards. Consequently, the Councils' definitions of criminality related to concrete – if highly diverse – actions by individuals. What mattered was the potential danger to the community, which could only be assessed on the basis of speculation and (violent) experience.

The constitution of a "national Jewish community" after the Second World War – along with the aspiration towards a national state – was, by contrast, a *consequence* of traumatic Jewish experiences during the Holocaust. It was because of the Germans' classification and systematic extermination of the Jewish population according to their "racist criteria" under National Socialism that it was felt important to create a future state that would constitute a place of refuge for Jewish people from around the world. A national, unifying "Jewish identity" aimed at bringing together people from different countries and social strata, with different levels of socialization and life experiences, was something that first had to be created. "Jewish law," which now attained the status of national law for the first time, once again played a salient role in this process, being characterized – as in the past – by flexibility and adaptability to changing external circumstances.

The relationship between the individual and the community and their conflicting interests always lies at the heart of law and associated questions of morality and justice. Legal norms, in any context, are socially constructed, relative, and subject to change, embedded as they are in moral principles and broader theories of human nature. However, they also invariably depend on external circumstances. Historically, these characteristics found very specific expression in the emergence of "Jewish law," or legal norms within communities classified as "Jewish." Here, the external circumstances imposed by the non-Jewish environment were marked by restrictions and systematic exclusion, culminating in the withdrawal of all legal rights. The emergence of a ghetto-internal legal sphere should thus be read not least as a highly interesting case study of legal history, which has shed light on local forms of law and governance in coerced communities existing on the edge of survival.

Notes

Introduction

1 This book will refer to the city of Łódź as Lodz without diacritical marks, as this is the convention in English scholarly writings on the topic. On 11 April 1940, Gauleiter Arthur Greiser had renamed the city "Litzmannstadt" after the German general Karl Litzmann, whose unit had defeated Russian troops in the vicinity in November 1941. See Feuchert, *Chronik. Supplemente*, p. 148. The term Litzmannstadt will only be used when referring to names of institutions, in bibliographical references, and in direct quotes. On the Germanization of the city following Nazi occupation, see Horwitz, *Ghettostadt*.

2 APŁ, PSŻ, 278/1076, *Geto-Tsaytung* no. 8, 25.4.1941, orig. p. 2. Quotations from the *Geto-Tsaytung* are derived from the German translations, which were prepared by the Jewish Council for the occupiers and have been subsequently aligned with the original Yiddish.

3 Kruk, *The Last Days*, 13.12.1942, p. 425.

4 Adler, *In the Warsaw Ghetto*, p. 258.

5 Feuchert, *Chronik* 1941, 24.12.1941, p. 324f.

6 Feuchert, *Chronik* 1943, 11.4.1943, p. 91.

7 Kruk, *The Last Days*, p. 598, unknown date between 1941 and 1943, probably before summer 1942.

8 The term "ordinary ghetto inhabitant" is used here when referring to those who were not part of the Jewish Council's administration. This does not imply an assumption of two homogeneous, clearly differentiated groups. Affiliations could change, for example, if an ordinary ghetto inhabitant was appointed to the Jewish Council; also, biographical information cannot always be reliably ascertained.

9 Arendt, *Eichmann in Jerusalem*, p. 117. On this claim, see ibid, p. 153ff.

10 See Keckeisen, *Die gesellschaftliche Definition*, p. 110. Keckeisen refers (p. 94) to the concept of power and dominance propagated by Max Weber, who defines power as "the probability that one actor within a social relationship will be in a position to carry out his own will despite resistance, regardless of the basis on which this probability rests" (Weber, *Economy and Society*, p. 53. Turk identifies a reciprocal relationship whereby power constellations affect enforceability, while the establishment of legal norms stabilizes power relationships ("Prospects for Theories").

11 Diner, *Beyond the Conceivable*, pp. 130–7.

12 Ibid., p. 128f.

13 See ibid., p. 130.

14 In Vilna, two ghettos had coexisted for a few weeks, but the inhabitants of the smaller one were murdered early on, between mid-September and the end of October 1941.

15 The term "legal authorities" is used in this study to refer collectively to the institutions authorized on German orders or at the Jewish Council's behest to impose – to a variable extent – their own binding regulations and sanctions within the ghetto community.

16 One of the main thrusts of this study is the subjective, variable – and hence relative – nature of concepts such as criminality, law, morality, justice, offence, misconduct, or violation. For the sake of readability, these terms are not placed in quotation marks in the text, but they are nonetheless implied throughout, especially in the context of Nazi definitions.

17 Gringauz's comment was based on the Kovno ghetto, but he also applied it to other ghetto communities. See Gringauz, "The Ghetto as an Experiment," p. 6f.

18 ŻIH, RG 302, (Pamiętniki) 129, Józef Rode.

19 Adler, *In the Warsaw Ghetto*, e.g., pp. 48, 257, 259.

20 Rosenfeld, *In the Beginning*, p. 20.

21 This book is the English translation of the German edition that was published by Hamburger Edition in 2015. Given the rapid development of Holocaust scholarship, studies published after 2015 could only be integrated to a limited extent. I apologize in advance to my colleagues whose works I have not taken into account.

22 For a relevant summary, see Cole, *Holocaust City*, pp. 25–34.

23 See, e.g., the studies by the Lemberg ghetto survivor Philip Friedman, "American Jewish Research," especially p. 235f., and "Research and Literature."

24 On this tendency see also Cole, *Holocaust City*, pp. 26–48; Cole, "Ghettoization," pp. 67–77.

25 See Gringauz, "Some Methodological Problems," p. 67.

26 See Gringauz, "The Ghetto as an Experiment," p. 6f; Adler, *In the Warsaw Ghetto*, pp. 48, 257, 259; Rosenfeld, *In the Beginning*, p. 20; and Judge

Bienstock at the first internal murder trial in the Lodz ghetto. Feuchert, *Chronik 1941*, 24.12.1941, p. 325.

27 See, e.g., Arendt, *Eichmann in Jerusalem*, pp. 117, 153ff; Hilberg, *Destruction*, p. 1037; on Rumkowski: Bloom, "Towards the Ghetto Dictator"; Huppert, "King of the Ghetto"; and Friedman, "Pseudo-Saviors"; on Jakub Gens, see Friedman, "Jacob Gens." For a summary, see Michman, "Kontroversen über die Judenräte."

28 See Unger, *Reassessment*, pp. 7–9; Robinson, *Discontinuity*, p. 35. On Rumkowski: Bloom, "Towards the Ghetto Dictator" and "Dictator"; Huppert, "King of the Ghetto"; and Friedman, "Pseudo-Saviors." On Jakub Gens, see Friedman, "Jacob Gens."

29 Arendt, *Eichmann in Jerusalem*; Hilberg, *Destruction*, p. 1037; on the debates, see Marrus, "Jewish Resistance."

30 See in particular Trunk's monumental work *Judenrat*; Trunk, *Łódź Ghetto*; specifically on the attitude of ghetto residents: Trunk, "The Opposition to the Jewish Councils"; Trunk, "The Judenrat and Jewish Responses"; as well as Robinson, "And the Crooked" and "Introduction," p. xxvi. On the Jewish police, see Weiss, "Ha'mishtara hayehudit"; Weiss, "Jüdischer Ordnungsdienst"; Weiss, "The Relations." On the relationship between ghetto residents and Jewish Councils, see Weiss, "Jewish Leadership" and, for the Warsaw ghetto, Gutman, *Jews of Warsaw*. Studies of everyday life, with particular reference to its Jewish Council, were also produced for the Vilna ghetto. See Arad, *Ghetto in Flames*. Similarly commendable studies were produced by Dworzecki, *Yerushaleyim de Lite*, and Balberyszski, *Stronger Than Iron*.

31 See Cole, *Holocaust City*, pp. 1–48, esp. p. 29. For a summary of the discussion with reference to the intentionalist versus the functionalist approach, see Browning, "Nazi Ghettoization Policy." As an earlier example of the intentionalist approach, Philip Friedman described ghettoization as part of the overall destruction process in an essay of 1954. See Friedman, "The Jewish Ghettos," and similarly Hilberg, *Destruction*, pp. 152–3. A focus on ghettos as Holocaust spaces prevailed in both comprehensive studies on the Holocaust and monographs on ghettos. See, e.g., Corni, *Hitler's Ghettos*.

32 For a relevant summary with a broader focus on the Holocaust, see, e.g., Bergen, Hájková, and Löw, "Warum eine Alltagsgeschichte des Holocaust?"; see also Bergen, Hájková, and Löw, *Alltag*.

33 Friedländer, "Eine integrierte Geschichte"; Friedländer, "An Integrated History." On this aspect, see also Löw, *Juden im Getto*, p. 9.

34 See, e.g., Sakowska, "Komitety domowe," on house committees in the Warsaw ghetto. On the Lodz ghetto, see Dąbrowska, "Administracja żydowska"; Dąbrowska, "Struktura i funkcje," part 1; Dąbrowska,

"Struktura i funkcje," part 2; Galiński, "Policja w getcie"; and Rubin, *Żydzi w Łodzi*, whose uncritical championing of Rumkowski is, however, somewhat problematic. After 1991, see, for Warsaw, Sakowska, *Menschen im Ghetto*; Engelking, Leociak, and Libionka, *Prowincja noc*; Engelking and Leociak, *Warsaw Ghetto*; and Roth and Löw, *Das Warschauer Ghetto*; for Lodz, see Baranowski, *The Łódź Ghetto*, "Utworzenie," and *Zigeunerlager*, and especially Löw, *Juden im Getto*; on the Vilna ghetto, see Schroeter, *Worte*. Since 2003, crucial impulses have also come from the Polish Centre for Holocaust Research with its journal *Zagłada Żydów: studia i materiały*, incorporating interdisciplinary and international expertise to complement prevailing narratives on the Holocaust and the Jewish experience. See, e.g., Skibińska, "Życie codzienne"; Gregorowicz, "Komunikacja telefoniczna"; Majewska, "Czym wytłumaczy."

35 See Bauer, "Forms," pp. 26–40; on the evolution, see Cohen, *Israeli Holocaust Research*, pp. 213–18.

36 See, e.g., Battrick, "Smuggling," in relation to the Warsaw ghetto. For a critique of this categorization, see Bauer, *Rethinking*, pp. 119–66.

37 See Engelking and Grabowski, *Żydów łamiących*, p. 8; see also Jan Grabowski, "Jewish Criminality."

38 See, e.g., the remark that it is difficult "to obtain concrete information on criminality in the ghetto" from activity reports submitted by the Jewish police to the German police, in Engelking and Grabowski, *Żydów łamiących*, p. 32, echoed on pp. 33 and 34; on the other hand, the authors assume that reports by the Polish police could provide "verified information on Jewish criminality in occupied Warsaw" (p. 36).

39 Initial research findings have already been published in the form of essays: Bethke, "Regeln und Sanktionen"; Bethke, "Crime and Punishment."

40 See Michman, "Reevaluating"; Diner, *Beyond the Conceivable*, pp. 130–7. Specifically for the Lodz ghetto see, e.g., Sitarek, "W obliczu."

41 See, e.g., Trunk, *Judenrat*, pp. 172–5, 475–527; Löw, *Juden im Getto*, pp. 105–16; Engelking and Leociak, *Warsaw Ghetto*, pp. 190–217; Arad, *Ghetto in Flames*, pp. 124–8. Exceptionally, an essay by Dina Porat deals explicitly with the establishment of the courts in the ghettos of Vilna, Kovno, and Šiauliai, interpreting them as an expression of the attempt to uphold pre-war moral standards in the ghetto. See Porat, "The Justice System," p. 49f.; Furthermore, Antoni Galiński turns his attention to the institutional framework of the central prison of the Lodz ghetto. See Galiński, "Centralne więzienie."

42 See Trunk, *Judenrat*, p. 498ff.; Weiss, "Ha'mishtara hayehudit"; for Warsaw, see, e.g., Engelking and Leociak, *Warsaw Ghetto*, p. 207ff. For Warsaw and Lodz, see Fox, "The Jewish Ghetto Police" (which also

mentions acts of solidarity, however), and Löw, "Ordnungsdienst im Getto Litzmannstadt."

43 An exception is Katarzyna Person's monograph on the Jewish policemen in the Warsaw Ghetto that illuminates their range of motivations and behaviours in the face of changing tasks. See Person, *Policjanci*. See also – in relation to the Kovno ghetto – Levin, "How the Jewish Police." Engelking and Leociak, *Warsaw Ghetto*, likewise draw on the diaries of Jewish police officers. Another exemplary instance is the first monograph on the Jewish police in Warsaw by Aldona Podolska, only here the tone is more descriptive, with a focus on historical events. See Podolska, *Służba Porządkowa*. Importantly, researchers have also started to shed light on the complex interactions between the Jewish police and the Polish police, to which the former was subordinate. See, e.g., Szymańska-Smolkin, "Fateful Decisions."

44 While scholars such as Dan Diner and Dan Michman have importantly built upon the earlier studies on the Jewish Councils, research at the micro-level of the ghetto communities, exploring their dilemma in greater depth based on actual case studies, is still scant. See, e.g., Michman, "Reevaluating"; Michman, "Why Did Heydrich Write the Schnellbrief?"; Diner, *Beyond the Conceivable*. For more on this, see also my reflections in Bethke, "Attempts." An exception is Adam Sitarek's monograph on the Jewish administration in the Lodz ghetto, *Wire-Bound State*.

45 One exception is the biographical-style monograph by Monika Polit, which applies this approach to the actions of Council chairman Rumkowski. See Polit, *"Moja żydowska dusza"*. For a more concise summary of the research findings to date, see Unger, *Reassessment*, and Polit, "Mordechaj." A similar approach to the dilemmas facing Jewish functionaries and their room for manoeuvre under National Socialism is adopted by Rabinovoci in relation to the Jewish Council in Vienna (*Eichman's Jews*), and by Meyer in relation to the Reich Association of Jews in Germany (*Tödliche Gratwanderung*).

46 In terms of the concentration camps, it was Primo Levi who most prominently located such actions in the "gray zone," stressing the frequent blurring of the distinction between victim and perpetrator (*The Drowned and the Saved*, p. 48). See also Petropoulos and Roth, *Gray Zones*.

47 See, e.g., Wachsmann, *KL*, ch. 10; Pingel, "Social Life"; Suderland, *Inside Concentration Camps*. For the ghettos, a number of innovative studies have started to reveal in a non-judgmental way a variety of behaviour amid old and new social dynamics and hierarchies. See Hájková, *The Last Ghetto*, and "Sexual Barter." See also Ostrowska, "Prostytucja w Polsce"; Person, "Sexual Violence."

48 See, e.g., Engel, "Who Is"; Finder, "Jewish Collaborators"; Finder, "The Trial"; Finder, "Sweep Out"; and, for a comparative European perspective, Finder and Jockusch, *Jewish Honor Courts*. See also Dehnel, "Wszystkie procesy."

49 See, e.g., Gringauz, "Ghetto as an Experiment," pp. 6–7. On the debate, see Goldberg, "History," p. 85, referring to Friedländer, *Nazi Germany and the Jews, Vol. 2,* pp 458, 528, 623.

50 This was labelled an "absurdity" by the German mayor of Lodz, Franz Schiffer, for example: USHMM, RG 05.008 M 3/126, copy of situation report by Mayor Schiffer to the Lodz District Governor, 9.4.1940, fol. 30; on this phenomenon, see also Dreifuss, "Warsaw," p. 902.

51 APŁ, 278/1076, *Geto-Tsaytung* no. 13, 20.6.1941, p. 1.

52 Term derived from Schütz and Luckmann, *Structures*, p. 108ff.

53 Adler, *In the Warsaw Ghetto*, p. 124.

54 Schütz and Luckmann, *Structures*. This term, and the so-called interpretative paradigm, were derived from the phenomenological approach of Edmund Husserl in *The Crisis*. On the theory behind this approach, see Ofer, "Everyday Life"; with regard to ghettos, Bethke and Schmidt Holländer, "Lebenswelt Ghetto"; Hansen, Steffen, and Tauber, *Lebenswelt Ghetto*; and Bethke, *Tanz*, 28–40. The idea of applying Schütz and Luckmann's approach to research on ghetto communities arose from the project "Lebenswelt Ghetto" initiated by Professor Frank Golczewski at the University of Hamburg in 2009. For more detail, see the conference "Lebenswelt Ghetto" held at the North-East Institute in Lüneburg, Germany, 9–11 October 2009, and Florin, "Tagungsbericht." Important research trends on this subject were prompted by the 2002 Act referred to as "German Pensions for Work in Ghettos" (ZRBG), which drew on historical expert witness reports whose effect was to lend ghetto-internal sources a new relevance in terms of the labour sphere. See Zarusky, *Ghettorenten*; Lehnstaedt, *Geschichte und Gesetzesauslegung*.

55 For a more detailed study on how to apply this approach with a focus on "criminal behaviours" and education in ghettos, see Bethke and Schmidt Holländer, "Lebenswelt Ghetto."

56 Durkheim, "Kriminalität," pp. 4, 7.

57 Sack, *Probleme der Kriminalsoziologie*, p. 268.

58 See ibid, pp. 282, 319.

59 Howard Becker, *Outsiders*, p. 14, quoted in Keckeisen, *Die gesellschaftliche Definition*, p. 36.

60 See, e.g., Kunz, *Die wissenschaftliche Zugänglichkeit*.

61 Adler, *In the Warsaw Ghetto*, p. 140.

62 See Zippelius, *Rechtsphilosophie*, pp. 15, 26f. Jurisprudential definitions can be divided into two groups. Exponents of what is known as legal positivism define law exclusively as the body of state-imposed norms (Kelsen), whereas suprapositive law also subsumes non-statutory norms under this concept – hence the claim, for example, that laws which run counter to basic justice criteria have no validity. Zippelius provides an

excellent overview of key jurisprudential theories, and the following
section is accordingly based largely on his arguments. On the different
definitions, see, e.g., ibid., p. 156; Kant, *The Metaphysical Elements of Justice*,
p. 337; and Kaufmann, "Gustav Radbruch."

63 See Zippelius, *Rechtsphilosophie*, p. 35.

64 The term "hegemony," coined by Antonio Gramsci, is substituted by its
exponents for "ideology" in order to emphasize the notion of a living social
practice designed to secure the (capitalist) social order. See Buckel and
Fischer-Lescano, "Gramsci Reconsidered" (quotation p. 442); Kennedy, *A
Critique*; Benney, "Gramsci on Law."

65 Among these was Abraham Gepner, for example, who worked in the
Jewish Council provisioning department. There were also Councils whose
members collectively supported armed underground activities, as in the
Piotrków Trybunalski ghetto, for instance. See Trunk, *Judenrat*, p. 463f.;
Trunk, "The Attitude." According to Diner, those Councils that subscribed
to the "rescue through labour" strategy and the associated policy of "self-
selection" were the most vehement in their rejection of armed resistance.
See Diner, *Beyond the Conceivable*, pp. 117–29.

66 Jakub Gens's address to the foremen of the forced labour gangs, 15 May
1943, reproduced in Arad and Gutman, *Documents on the Holocaust*,
pp. 451ff., D.1.355.

67 See, e.g., Geiger, *Vorstudien*, pp. 19ff., and Luhmann, *A Sociological Theory of
Law*. This approach is also associated with Max Weber, who sees the social
order as being guaranteed by the probability that coercion will be applied
(*Economy and Society*, p. 34).

68 See Zippelius, *Rechtsphilosophie*, p. 58.

69 See Gehlen, *Moral und Hypermoral*, pp. 69ff., and Zippelius, who argues
that violence is more common in periods of change, where there is no
certainty of orientation (*Rechtsphilosophie*, p. 131).

70 Zippelius points out that the law often lags behind the evolution of social
morality, a fact which is, nevertheless, perceived as a stabilizing force
(ibid., p. 58f).

71 According to this view, certainty of orientation is guaranteed by the
clarity and transparency of the law, i.e., the relevant individuals and
circumstances must be clearly identified. See ibid., p. 133. Geiger named
certainty of orientation "certitudo." This required rules of conduct
to be formulated clearly, unambiguously, and consistently. Certainty
of implementation, which he termed "securitas," required the law-
finding process to be conducted efficiently and speedily, leading to the
enforcement of the relevant norms. See Geiger, *Vorstudien*, p. 63ff.

72 On the concept of "social normality" in general, see Diner, "Rupture in
Civilization."

73 It was on the basis of this assumption that Thomas Hobbes formulated the duty of the state to guarantee the rule of law. See Hobbes, *De cive*, Preface, quoted in Zippelius, *Rechtsphilosophie*, p. 132.

74 Zippelius, *Rechtsphilosophie*, p. 58.

75 Kant described this approach as follows: "Even if a civil society were to be dissolved by the consent of all its members (e.g. if a people inhabiting an island decided to separate and disperse throughout the world), the last murderer remaining in the prison would first have to be executed, so that each has done to him what his deeds deserve and blood guilt does not cling to the people for not having insisted upon this punishment; for otherwise the people can be regarded as collaborators in this public violation of justice" (*Metaphysical Elements of Justice*, p. 333).

76 See Zippelius, *Rechtsphilosophie*, pp. 167, 199.

77 The open ghettos were not hermetically sealed, and were often located on the outskirts of small towns. Here, the German occupiers often made use of existing walls or buildings for demarcation purposes and sometimes left the area open. See Pohl, "Ghettos im Holocaust," p. 40.

78 This was often the case even before ghettoization in the occupied Soviet territories, judging by documents such as the arrest warrants issued by the public order office of the Jewish Council in Pinsk (in the Reichskommissariat Ukraine), where a ghetto existed from May to November 1942. YVA, Archives of Belarus (M-41), 949.

79 That said, civil cases are undoubtedly also relevant in terms of shedding light on everyday life in the ghettos. Rulings on divorce cases, for example, can provide insights into changing family structures under ghettoization, which created new dependency structures on one hand, but on the other burdened many women and even children with responsibilities that led to a redistribution of roles.

80 For the Lodz ghetto: YVA, JM-1440, JM-1454, JM-1455, JM-1496 (Kriminalkommissariat w Łodzi); USHMM, RG 05.008 (Akta Miasta Łodzi, Lodz City Council); for the Vilna ghetto (partly): YIVO, RG 223 (Abraham Sutzkever-Szmerke Kaczerginski Collection, 1806–1945), YIVO, RG 225 (Hersch Wasser Collection, 1939–46); for the Warsaw ghetto: ŻIH, AR I/II (RING I//II), ŻIH, RG 205 (Getto Łódź), ŻIH, RG 241 (Obwieszczenia).

81 YVA, JM-834, JM-836, JM-839, JM-845 (Lodz Special Court). The correspondence is contained in the above collections.

82 See Kassow, "Vilna and Warsaw"; for the Vilna ghetto, Schroeter, *Worte*, p. 38ff.; for the Lodz ghetto, Löw, *Juden im Getto*, pp. 43–50; Feuchert, "Die Getto-Chronik."

83 See Kassow, *Who Will Write*.

84 Filed under the Ringelblum Collection in ŻIH, RING I, II; reports on criminal activity in the ghetto are also contained in ŻIH, Bernard Mark Collection, and ŻIH, RG 221 (Judenraty), as well as in YIVO, RG 225.

85 USHMM, RG 15.083 (PSŻ).

86 On the genesis of this document, see Feuchert, "Die Getto-Chronik."

87 Kruk belonged to the Bund (Algemeyner Yidisher Arbeyterbund in Poyln, Lite un Rusland), an association which had been founded in tsarist Russia as a Jewish socialist workers' party and promoted Yiddish as the Jewish national language. The chronicle was published in Yiddish in 1961 (Kruk, *Togbuch*). It has been available in an edited English version since 2002 (Kruk, *The Last Days*). Documents of the Vilna Jewish Council are preserved in USHMM, 1999.A.0105 (Vilnius Ghetto Records, 1941–4) and YIVO, RG 223.

88 In the Lodz ghetto, these were buried in separate sections and partly saved by Nachman Zonabend, who escaped from the ghetto. See Feuchert, *Chronik 1944*, pp. 24–5. In the Warsaw ghetto, the sources were buried in metal boxes and milk cans, in 1942 at the height of the Great Deportation and in 1943 before the ghetto uprising. See Kassow, *Who Will Write*, pp. 1–16, 215, 219, 333. Herman Kruk hid his diary in the concentration camp Lagedi in Estonia. See Harshav, "Introduction."

89 ŻIH, RING I/702. The *Gazeta Żydowska*, the Polish-language newspaper officially approved by the Germans for the ghettos in the Generalgouvernement, was published between 23 July 1940 and 30 August 1942, initially appearing twice a week, then three times a week from July 1941.

90 APŁ, 278/1075, APŁ 278/1076. The Yiddish-language *Geto-Tsaytung* was published from March to September 1941 and was discontinued after eighteen editions due to a paper shortage.

91 GFH, Collections Section, 554, *Geto-Yedies*. Only fragments of the Yiddish-language *Geto-Yedies* are preserved at the GFH.

92 Preserved in APŁ, 278; YIVO, RG 241 (Nachman Zonabend Collection), YVA, O-34 (Nachman Zonabend Collection), and ŻIH, RG 205. For the Warsaw ghetto, they can be found in ŻIH, Bernard Mark Collection, and ŻIH, RING II, and for the Vilna ghetto, in YIVO, RG 223, with some reprinted in Kruk, *The Last Days*.

93 Contained in the ghetto collections and chronicles. Activity reports from the Warsaw ghetto can be found in IPN, 165/367 (Commander of the Security Police and Security Service for the Warsaw district, Raporty dzienne KSP dla niemieckiego komisarza o planowanych czynnościach służbowych i stwierdzonych uchybieniach porządkowych w getcie). Arrest warrants from the Vilna ghetto are contained in YIVO, RG 223, USHMM, 1999.A.0105, and GFH; 1575/Registry Holdings 1215.

94 Adler, *In the Warsaw Ghetto*. Further sources include Czerniaków, *Warsaw Diary*; Gombiński, *Wspomnienia*; the diary of Józef Rode (ŻIH, RG 302/129); Zygmunt Millet, Order Service District Commander (ŻIH, 435. RING I/100, March 1941); 7. AR I/PH/23–3–2, Contents of a Conversation with a Member of the Order Police, in Kermish, *To Live with Honor*, p. 310 (corresponding to ŻIH, RING I/435). Also referenced are statements by a former Order Service

(Jewish police) functionary before a civic court (Polish: *sąd społeczny*) of the Jewish Central Committee in Warsaw after the end of the war. ŻIH, Ekspertyzy Korespondencja ŻIH (sąd społeczny), testimony of Henryk (Hersz) Wasser, 1948 (also YIVO, RG 225/422, report by Hersch Wasser).

95 Contained in the above-mentioned ghetto collections. Rulings from the Lodz ghetto can also be found in the GFH Collections Section and, as a copy for the German Criminal Police, in USHMM, RG 05.008 and in YVA, JM-1440

96 ŻIH, RG 205/349 (Getto-Enzyklopädie – Zbiór Materiałów do dziejów ludności Żydowskiej w Łodzi 1939–44)/1–99. Further entries can be found in YIVO, RG 241.

97 Besides Adler, *Warsaw Ghetto*, the proceedings of the district police stations were also reported on by Józef Rode (ŻIH, RG 302/129) and an anonymous police officer (ŻIH, RING I/435; reprinted in 7. AR I/PH/23–3–2, Contents of a Conversation with a Member of the Order Police, in Kermish, *To Live with Honor*, pp. 310–17); accounts of the proceedings of the house committees in Warsaw can be found in Opoczyński, *Reportaże*, p. 87ff.

98 The majority of these relate to the Lodz ghetto and are contained in USHMM, RG 15.083, USHMM, RG 05.008, and YVA, JM-836, JM-839, JM-845, JM-1483, YVA, JM-1496; a few relating to the Warsaw ghetto can be found in ŻIH, RING I, and at the IPN, 165/367.

99 Viewed in YVA, O-3 (Testimonies) and ŻIH, RG 301 (*Relacje*).

100 Through this strategy, which was also adopted by Gens in Vilna, Rumkowski hoped to secure the survival of the ghetto population by increasing "ghetto productivity." From 1942 onwards, it also included the policy of "self-selection," i.e., the surrender of those unfit for work to the German occupiers. As Dan Diner points out, it can be seen as exemplifying the Jewish Councils' dilemma. See Diner, *Beyond the Conceivable*, pp. 117–29.

101 See ibid.; Browning, *Origins*, p. 115.

1 Nazi Jewish Policy in Eastern Europe and the Perspective of the Jewish Councils

1 ŻIH, RG 205/155, re: ghetto-based *Sonderkommando* (special unit) of the Criminal Police, 19.5.1940, fol. 3ff.: justification for setting up a branch of the German Criminal Police inside the ghetto (in this case with particular reference to smuggling).

2 For more on the German Criminal Police, see Chu, "'Wir sind keine Deutschen.'"

3 USHMM, RG 05.008, 26/63, performance report of the Lodz Ghetto Commissariat for the period from 1.9.1941 to 15.9.1942, 16.9.1942, fol. 14.

4 See, e.g., Bergmann, *Geschichte des Antisemitismus*, p. 102ff.; Holz, *Nationaler Antisemitismus*, pp. 248–358.
5 Bogeyman images of the "criminal Jew" were part of a long anti-Semitic tradition. See Klier, "Crime and Criminals."
6 Berkowitz, *The Crime*, pp. xiv, xv. According to Berkowitz, it was not, however, a defining element of Nazi ideology like racial anti-Semitism.
7 From the nineteenth century onwards in particular, biologistic narratives have been associated with notions of a "criminal character." See, e.g., Wetzell, *Inventing the Criminal*; Liang, *Criminal-Biological Theory*. On "Jewish criminality" specifically, see Vyleta, "Jewish Crimes"; more generally, see Katz, *From Prejudice to Destruction*, p. 245ff; Gilman, *Jewish Self-Hatred*.
8 The special edition of *Der Stürmer* was published to coincide with the NSDAP Nuremberg Rally. The poster can be viewed at: https://www.dhm.de/lemo/Bestand/objekt/xp991312 [22 04 2015] (emphasis orig.)
9 See Longerich, *Holocaust*, p. 60.
10 On the exclusion of Jews from the economy from 1936, see ibid., p. 65; on anti-Jewish legislation from 1938, see ibid, pp. 117, 134f. In occupied Poland, the Germans ordered the Jewish population to wear armbands or yellow badges sewn onto their sleeves bearing the word "Jew" (announced for the Generalgouvernement in November 1941, with effect from 1 December 1939, and for the Reichgau Wartheland on 14 November, with effect from 2 December 1939). Imposed on the Reichskommissariat Ostland (occupied eastern territories) on 13 August 1941. In Germany, compulsory identification was not introduced until September 1941. See Gutman, *Encyclopaedia*, "Badge, Jewish," vol. 2, pp. 138–43, and Pohl, *Von der "Judenpolitik"*, p. 63f.
11 See Berkowitz, *The Crime*, p. 30.
12 From 500,000 in 1933, the Jewish population of the German Reich within the 1937 borders had dwindled to just 190,000 by the end of 1939. See Benz, *Dimension des Völkermords*, pp. 23, 32, 34.
13 See Michman, *The Emergence*, pp. 45–60; Steffen, "Connotations of Exclusion."
14 See Hilberg, *Destruction*, p. 225f.; Pohl; *Von der "Judenpolitik"*, p. 71ff.
15 Document of 21.9.1939, dispatch from the chief of the Reich Main Security Office, R. Heydrich, to the heads of the Security Police *Einsatzgruppen*, Document 1, in Berenstein and Eisenbach, *Faschismus – Getto – Massenmord*, pp. 37–41.
16 See Browning, *Origins*, p. 111.
17 The plan was to integrate the western part of Poland into the Reich and "Germanize" it by populating it with "ethnic Germans" from the Soviet Union. Central Poland was to serve as a "reservoir of cheap Polish labour." See ibid., p. 106
18 See ibid, p. 57f.; Musiał, *Aktion Reinhardt*; Michman, *The Emergence*, p. 64f.; Pohl, *Von der "Judenpolitik"*, p. 60f.; Libionka, *Zagłada*, p. 53f.

19 See Hilberg, *Destruction*, p. 193; Browning, "Nazi Ghettoization Policy," pp. 344–5. On freedom of action, see Michman, *The Emergence*, p. 62; Musiał, *Aktion Reinhardt*, p. 60ff.; Wildt, *An Uncompromising Generation*.
20 See Hilberg, *Destruction*, p. 217. The Germans had already established the first ghetto in Piotrków Trybunalski/Petrikau in October 1939, and further ghettoizations of the Jewish population occurred in Puławy and Radomsko. See Engelking and Leociak, *Warsaw Ghetto*, p. 64.
21 See Browning, "Nazi Ghettoization Policy," p. 364f.
22 See Musiał, *Aktion Reinhardt*, pp. 113–53; Browning, *Origins*, pp. 295, 302.
23 The consensus view today is that this was a gradual process driven both by the decision-makers of the Nazi regime and by the actions of the German *Einsatzgruppen* and *Wehrmacht* soldiers in occupied Eastern Europe. The decision in favour of systematic extermination is dated (depending on the relevant author), to July/August 1941 in the case of Soviet Jews, and to September/October 1941 in that of the Jewish population of occupied Poland. On this aspect, see, e.g., Musiał, *Aktion Reinhardt*; Browning, *Origins*; Aly, *Final Solution*; Gerlach, "The Wannsee Conference," pp. 763–5; and Pohl, *Von der "Judenpolitik"*, p. 101; on the consequences for the ghettos, see Browning, "Nazi Ghettoization Policy," pp. 365–6.
24 See Pohl, "Ghettos im Holocaust," p. 47; Longerich, *Holocaust*, p. 212; Michman, *The Emergence*, p. 120.
25 See Berkowitz, *The Crime*, p. 49ff.; Michman, *The Emergence*, p. 114.
26 ŻIH, RG 241/265, Proclamation, Governor Dr Fischer, 13.5.1943.
27 Beside "Jewish Council," terms such as Council of Elders, Elder of the Jews, Head Jew, or Association of Jews were used, according to time and place. On the multiplicity of terms, see Trunk, *Judenrat*, p. 10f., and Michman, "Reevaluating," p. 72.
28 On 28 November 1939, a Generalgouvernement decree was then issued instructing all Jewish communities with up to 10,000 members to elect a council of 12, and all communities with more than 10,000 members, a council of 24. See Hilberg, *Destruction*, p. 218. On Heydrich's dispatch, see Trunk, *Judenrat*, pp. 1–13.
29 See Trunk, *Judenrat*, p. 2f.; Browning, *Origins*, p. 111. On the debate concerning the legal status of the *Schnellbrief*, see Trunk, *Judenrat*, pp. 4–6 – which construes it as the legal basis for ghettoization – versus Michman, "Reevaluating," p. 75ff., and Michman, "Why Did Heydrich Write the *Schnellbrief*?" – which interpret it as a retrospective adjustment of the already ongoing ghettoization process.
30 "Verordnung über die Einsetzung von Judenräten. Vom 28. November 1939, gez. Frank," in Weh, *Das Recht des Generalgouvernements*, p. 489f.
31 *Schnellbrief*, quoted in Trunk, *Judenrat*, p. 2.

32 In the Generalgouvernement, they were answerable to the city governors in urban areas and to the district governors in rural areas; in the annexed territories, they were answerable to the mayor or district administrators. See Hilberg, *Destruction*, p. 220. On the decree, see Trunk, *Judenrat*, p. 3f.
33 General von Schenckendorff, rear echelon commander of Army Group Centre, Official Order no. 2, 13.7.1941, YVA, DN-7–2, quoted (in German) in Michman, *The Emergence*, p. 108f.
34 Ibid.
35 See ibid., p. 114.
36 General von Schenckendorff, rear echelon commander of Army Group Centre, Official Order no. 2, 13.7.1941, YVA, DN-7–2, quoted (in German) in Michman, *The Emergence*, p. 108f. Names of candidates were to be submitted to the local command post by 31 July 1941. Following inspection, basic instructions would be issued in writing by the German authority. These were to be obeyed by all Jews; see ibid.
37 See ibid.
38 See Stanisławski, "Kahal (kehillah)."
39 ŻIH, 46. RING II/127, after 26.3.1940, Czerniaków: Memorial "Die neuen Aufgaben der Jüdischen Gemeinde in Warschau und die Lage der jüdischen Bevölkerung," fol. 1.
40 Trunk distinguishes between "tasks imposed by the Germans," "routine tasks," which – in the case of welfare and culture – he classifies as a continuation of pre-war activities, and new tasks resulting from social exclusion, such as the organization of provisions or the establishment of legal authorities. See Trunk, *Judenrat*, p. 44.
41 An aptly chosen term used by Löw (*Juden im Getto*, p. 97).
42 Trunk, *Judenrat*, p. 44.
43 On this assessment re Warsaw, see, e.g., the diary of Henryk Bryskier, *Żydzi pod swastyką*, p. 209.
44 See Trunk, *Judenrat*, p. 44. Trunk is inaccurate here, ignoring the fact that the organization of the self-administration bodies – particularly in the large ghettos in occupied Poland – took place before the "Final Solution" had been decided.
45 Ibid., p. 44. This applies in particular to the large, closed ghettos in occupied Poland.
46 ŻIH, Judenraty, RG 221/File 1 or 2 (archive discrepancy), Bericht über die Tätigkeit des Judenrates in Warschau im Zeitraum vom 7. Oktober 1939 bis 31. Dezember 1940, fol. 20 (emphasis orig.).
47 See Trunk, *Judenrat*, pp. 8–10, 28–35.
48 See ibid., p. 14. In other parts of the occupied Soviet Union, where the Jewish authorities had already been dissolved by the Soviets twenty years earlier, the Germans were working from a different basis when it came to

setting up the Jewish Councils. See Diner, *Beyond the Conceivable*, pp. 117–29; Robinson, "Introduction," p. xxvi.

49 See Gutman, *Jews of Warsaw*, Introduction, p. xiii; Dreifuss, "Warsaw," p. 899. On the history of the Jewish community prior to 1939, see the overview in Engelking and Leociak, *Warsaw Ghetto*, pp. 2–26.

50 See Musiał, *Aktion Reinhardt*, pp. 113–53.

51 At the same time, the SS – headquartered in Warsaw – acted partially independently of the civil administration, imposing its own demands on the Jewish Council. See Dreifuss, "Warsaw," p. 899.

52 According to Engelking and Leociak, this was the department responsible for planning the ghettoization process for Warsaw. See *Warsaw Ghetto*, p. 57.

53 See ibid., p. 79.

54 See ibid., p. 138f.; Dreifuss, "Warsaw," p. 899.

55 See Kermish, *To Live with Honor*, p. 132f.; Dreifuss, "Warsaw," p. 899. On Czerniaków, see Engelking and Leociak, *Warsaw Ghetto*, p. 159ff.

56 For further reference, see the remarks by Warsaw Jewish Council member Apolinary Hartglas, "How Did Czerniakow Become Head?" p. 6. In contrast to the Zionists, the Bundists were against emigration to Palestine. The Aguda was an Orthodox anti-Zionist party. Among the new Jewish Council members were Apolinary Hartglas and Mojżesz Koerner (Zionists), Szmul Zygielbojm (Bundist), and Icchak Meir Lewin (Aguda). See Engelking and Leociak, *Warsaw Ghetto*, p. 139.

57 See Hilberg, *Destruction*, p. 227; Engelking and Leociak, *Warsaw Ghetto*, p. 52.

58 The text of the decree signed by Fischer was reprinted in the *Nowy Kurier Warszawski* on 14 October 1940. See Engelking and Leociak, *Warsaw Ghetto*, p. 65ff.

59 After this time only holders of special passes – such as those working outside the ghetto – were allowed to leave, while Poles were allowed to cross the ghetto border freely until 26 November 1940. See ibid., p. 72.

60 In other words, 30 per cent of Warsaw's population were crammed into 2.4 per cent of the city's surface area. See Dreifuss, "Warsaw," p. 902.

61 See ibid. On new social stratification criteria that evolved over time, for instance based on occupation, see Engelking and Leociak, *Warsaw Ghetto*, p. 158.

62 ŻIH, RG 221/File 1 or 2 (archive discrepancy), Bericht über die Tätigkeit des Judenrates in Warschau im Zeitraum vom 7. Oktober 1939 bis 31. Dezember 1940. fol. 15.

63 In May 1941, there were departments covering areas such as production, trade and industry, labour, social welfare, health, vocational training, schools, postal services, civil records, and street cleaning. See Sakowska, *Menschen im Ghetto*, p. 177; for a detailed list of individual institutions between 1940 and 1942, see Engelking and Leociak, *Warsaw Ghetto*, pp. 174–89.

64 Kaplan, quoted in Engelking and Leociak, *Warsaw Ghetto*, p. 153 (emphasis orig.).

65 On the difficulty of reconstructing the changing architecture of the Jewish Council, see Engelking and Leociak, *Warsaw Ghetto*, p. 147f.

66 See Sakowska, *Menschen im Ghetto*, p. 183; Sakowska, "Komitety domowe"; see also Adler, *In the Warsaw Ghetto*, p. 54ff. See ŻIH, 177. RING II/62, rights and obligations of the house committees, Jewish Council legal department, 30.4.1942.

67 These activities are described, for instance, by the diarist Opoczyński, *Reportaże*, p. 87ff.

68 See Dreifuss, "Warsaw," p. 902. Falling back on the financial reserves of the ghetto population was hardly an option; because the Germans had confiscated their property and removed their means of existence, 70,000 to 80,000 people had been left without an income even before ghettoization. See Engelking and Leociak, *Warsaw Ghetto*, p. 382f. On the financial demands, see also ibid., p. 149ff.

69 These had been set up in the Generalgouvernement from summer 1940 onwards under the supervision of the German civil administration or by the SS and police.

70 See Engelking and Leociak, *Warsaw Ghetto*, p. 145f.

71 See ibid., p. 146; Gutman, *Jews of Warsaw*, p. 24.

72 See Dreifuss, "Warsaw," p. 906. The Transfer Office had been set up in December 1940 but did not assume a prominent role until after May 1941, when Heinz Auerswald became commissar for the Jewish Residential District. Its purpose was to coordinate trade between the ghetto and the "Aryan" side, drawing heavily on the exploitation of ghetto labour power, and especially skilled labour. See Engelking and Leociak, *Warsaw Ghetto*, p. 391. After February 1941, a production department was created under the auspices of the Jewish Council and placed in charge of the shops. See ibid., p. 394.

73 Examples include Walter Többens's textile firm and Fritz Schulz's fur production firm. See ibid., p. 396ff.

74 See ibid., p. 400; Dreifuss, "Warsaw," p. 906. The problem with this was that the unemployed were in the majority: while the number of people "fit for work" in September 1941 was theoretically 173,000 out of a population of 400,000, the number of actual workers registered by the German Transfer Office at the time was between 50,000 and 60,000. An unknown number were involved in activities classed as illegal by the Germans, such as smuggling. See Engelking and Leociak, *Warsaw Ghetto*, p. 409.

75 The choice was very limited and quantities were small. See ibid., p. 412ff.

76 See ibid., p. 153.

77 Rumours of impending resettlements began to spread from mid-July 1941. One report from the Warsaw ghetto, for instance, expresses the fear

harboured from this point onwards that 150,000 to 300,000 people would be "sent away" because of the proliferation of diseases. YIVO, RG 225, Folder 31.8, July–September 1941, fol. 1

78 See Sakowska, *Menschen im Ghetto*, p. 216. Szlamek had been forced to work in the Jewish *Sonderkommando* in Kulmhof and was given refuge after his escape by Hersz Wasser, the secretary of the underground archive in Warsaw. Wasser then wrote up the report and passed it to the underground press for publication. See Löw, *Juden im Getto*, p. 282f. The report can be found in ŻIH, RING I/412 and is reprinted in German translation in Sakowska, *Menschen im Ghetto*, pp. 159–85.

79 See Edelman, *The Ghetto Fights*, p. 43.

80 See Sakowska, *Menschen im Ghetto*, pp. 220, 222.

81 An account of this can be found in Goldstein, *The Stars Bear Witness*, p. 104.

82 Czerniaków, *Warsaw Diary*, 19.1.1942, p. 317. Auerswald's visit was probably in connection with the Wannsee conference of 20 January 1942, where the "Final Solution to the Jewish question" was discussed, even though he did not take part in the conference himself (ibid., p. 317, n. 13).

83 Engelking and Leociak, *Warsaw Ghetto*, p. 164.

84 See ibid., p. 703ff.; Gutman, *Jews of Warsaw*, p. 197ff. At that time, many residents still assumed that the transports were bound for labour camps; from August onwards, their diaries increasingly express the fear that death was the real end point. Abraham Lewin, for one, after clinging until the end of July 1942 to the hope that these were just rumours, wrote on 9 August 1942: "It is clear to us that 99 percent of those transported are being taken to their deaths" (*A Cup of Tears*, p. 150). From August 1942, escapees from Treblinka began to bring word of the murders perpetrated there. See Gutman, *Jews of Warsaw*, p. 223.

85 See Engelking and Leociak, *Warsaw Ghetto*, p. 164; Libionka, *Zagłada*, pp. 137–8.

86 From Czerniaków's farewell letter to his wife; quoted in Engelking and Leociak, *Warsaw Ghetto*, p. 164;

87 On Czerniaków's strategy vis-à-vis the German demands, see ibid., p. 162.

88 This brought the Jewish Council chairman further criticism from the ghetto community and commentators of the immediate post-war period, who viewed his suicide as "egoistic." See ibid., p. 160. Other diary entries such as those of Kaplan, for example, show some sympathy (cited in Engelking and Leociak, *Warsaw Ghetto*, p. 165). On this point, see also Gombiński, *Wspomnienia*, p. 81.

89 See Dreifuss, "Warsaw," p. 912.

90 See Engelking and Leociak, *Warsaw Ghetto*, p. 405.

91 See Gutman, *Jews of Warsaw*, p. 236ff.

92 "Aktion Reinhardt," named after Security Police chief Reinhardt Heydrich, was the code name for the systematic extermination of Jews in the

Generalgouvernement and in Białystok. The relevant order was issued by Himmler in autumn 1941 to Odilo Globocnik, the SS and police chief of the Lublin district. By summer 1942, three extermination camps had been built: Belzec, Sobibor, and Treblinka. For more detail, see, e.g., Libionka, *Zagłada*, p. 95ff.

93 A further 11,000 residents were sent to labour camps, 10,000 died in the ghetto, and approximately 8,000 managed to escape. See Dreifuss, "Warsaw," p. 913f.

94 See Gutman, *Jews of Warsaw*, p. 268; on the collapse of ghetto-internal structures, e.g. with regard to provisioning, see ibid., p. 273.

95 See ibid., p. 275, and Engelking and Leociak, *Warsaw Ghetto*, p. 165f. Even the internal food distribution system no longer functioned as before, however; instead of having to register their ration entitlements at a fixed distribution point, residents could now redeem them in any store. See ibid., p. 416.

96 See Dreifuss, "Warsaw," p. 915; Libionka, *Zagłada*, pp. 146–9.

97 Some of these were laid out in a letter published on 30 October 1942, in which the ŻOB claimed responsibility for the execution of the Jewish police functionary Jakub Lejkin. ŻIH, Bernard Mark Collection/526, ŻOB announcement re the death penalty for Jakub Lejkin, 30.10.1942

98 On this aspect, see also Bauer, *Rethinking the Holocaust*, pp. 119–66.

99 All fighters except the commander, Mordechaj Anielewicz, were shot. See Dreifuss, "Warsaw," p. 915f.

100 Ibid., p. 916; on this assessment, see also Gutman, *Jews of Warsaw*, p. 276. By this time, the Jewish Councils' remit had been reduced to limited, supply-related activities. See Engelking and Leociak, *Warsaw Ghetto*, p. 166.

101 See Dreifuss, "Warsaw," p. 917.

102 See ibid., p. 918ff.

103 See Löw, *Juden im Getto*, p. 72ff.

104 Rumkowski, born in 1877 in Iliono in tsarist Russia, had come to the industrial city of Lodz at around the turn of the century. After establishing a silk factory, which he later had to abandon, he worked for an insurance company and also founded an orphanage. Rumkowski had been a member of the Jewish municipal council, where he represented the General Zionists. See Löw, *Juden im Getto*, p. 72f. Polit sees a close link between the Jewish Council chairman's Zionist outlook and his aspiration to power in the ghetto. For a detailed pre-war biography of Rumkowski, see Polit, *"Moja żydowska dusza"*, pp. 9–43.

105 See Löw, *Juden im Getto*, p. 76f.

106 See Hilberg, *Destruction*, p. 224; Löw, *Juden im Getto*, p. 92; Freund, Perz, and Stuhlpfarrer, "Das Getto in Litzmannstadt," p. 19; Baranowski, "Utworzenie." For a broader focus on the Germanization of the city of Lodz, see Horwitz, *Ghettostadt*, and on the spatial dimension, also van Pelt, *Łódź*.

107 By October 1941, this area had been reduced from 4.13 to 3.18 square kilometres. See Alberti, *Die Anfänge*, p. 161.
108 Politically, they fell into Zionist and non-Zionist groupings, the latter belonging to socialist, non-socialist, and religious currents. See Löw, *Juden im Getto*, p. 56ff.
109 See ibid., p. 224, Baranowski, *The Łódź Ghetto*, p. 120; Baranowski, *Zigeunerlager*.
110 See Löw, *Juden im Getto*, p. 251.
111 Hilberg, *Destruction*, p. 219; Bender, "Judenräte and Other Representative Bodies."
112 See Löw, *Juden im Getto*, p. 107.
113 See Feuchert, *Chronik 1941*, p. 349, n. 85.
114 See Dąbrowska, "Struktura i funkcje," part 2, p. 40; Löw, *Juden im Getto*, p. 118.
115 See ibid., p. 117; Klein, *Gettoverwaltung Litzmannstadt*, p. 266ff.
116 See Löw, *Juden im Getto*, p. 120f.; Alberti, *Die Anfänge*, p. 219. As of 8 July 1940, the reichsmark had been replaced 1:1 in the ghetto by mark tokens issued by the Jewish Elder. Outside the ghetto, these were worth nothing. This measure by the Germans was intended to extract all supposed value from the ghetto and allay fears of outside trading. See Hans-Ludwig Grabowski, *Das Geld*, p. 362.
117 See Dąbrowska, "Struktura i funkcje," part 1, pp. 51–4; Feuchert, *Chronik 1941*, 13.1.1941, p. 24f.; Löw, *Juden im Getto*, pp. 142, 145.
118 See Alberti, *Die Anfänge*, pp. 366–70; Rubin, *Żydzi w Łodzi*, p. 337f.
119 See Löw, *Juden im Getto*, p. 265.
120 See Unger, "Łódź," p. 409.
121 See ibid.
122 In January 1942, Rumkowski initially persuaded the Germans to halve the required number – but only for a short time. The resettlement commission set up on 5 January 1942 consisted of members of the Jewish Council and was at first divided over who to select, since the destination of the transports was unknown.
123 Address by Rumkowski on 4 January 1942, APŁ, 278/1192, fol. 273f. From February 1942 onwards, the committee began increasingly to target "unproductive" residents – the elderly, sick, and unemployed – in addition to offenders. See Löw, *Juden im Getto*, table 4, p. 265ff.
124 See Alberti, *Die Anfänge*, p. 405f.; Löw, "Ordnungsdienst," p. 163f. Patients had already been deported from the hospital on 1 and 2 September. The "general curfew" lasted from 5 to 12 September 1942. See Löw, *Juden im Getto*, p. 292.
125 See ibid., table 4, p. 265.
126 The postal ban had been imposed by the Germans in July 1940, when the first cases of dysentery appeared in the ghetto and fears arose that

it could be transmitted to "non-epidemic zones" by this route. See ibid., p. 283; Baranowski, *The Łódź Ghetto*, p. 33.

127 Feuchert, *Chronik 1942*, 30/31.5.1942, p. 248ff. What worried people most was seeing the deportees' luggage returned to the ghetto. See Löw, *Juden im Getto*, p. 284, n. 12; Joanna Podolska, "Nie w naszej mocy przebaczać," p. 218, n. 11.

128 E.g., Rosenfeld, *In the Beginning*, Notebook E, undated (but attributable chronologically to around this time, according to Löw), p. 112. In his diary, the teenager Dawid Sierakowiak reports rumours of the Germans' intention to "finish off the Jews in Europe." Sierakowiak, *Diary*, 17.8.1942, p. 208.

129 See Friedman, "Pseudo-Saviors"; Huppert, "King of the Ghetto"; Unger, *Reassessment*, specifically pp. 7–11; Joanna Podolska, "Nie w naszej mocy przebaczać," p. 205ff.; Polit, *"Moja żydowska dusza"*, p. 6ff.

130 See Löw, *Juden im Getto*, p. 116ff.

131 See Diner, *Beyond the Conceivable*, pp. 117–29.

132 See Arad, *Ghetto in Flames*, p. 9f.

133 See ibid., p. 21.

134 See Schroeter, *Worte*, p. 65; Gutman, *Encyclopaedia*, vol. 3, "Lithuania," pp. 895–9.

135 These were carried out by *Einsatzkommando* 9 and the Wehrmacht, supported by Lithuanian units. See Arad, *Ghetto in Flames*, p. 53f.

136 See Schroeter, *Worte*, pp. 94–7; Kruk, *Togbuch*, 1.7.1941, p. 53.

137 See Arad, *Ghetto in Flames*, p. 58ff.; Kruk, *The Last Days*, pp. 8–9; Schroeter, *Worte*, p. 95.

138 On 17 July 1941, Hitler issued the order to create civil administrations in the new eastern territories, while responsibility for police security was assigned to Heinrich Himmler and the SS. See Arad, *Ghetto in Flames*, p. 81f.; Dieckmann, "Die Zivilverwaltung," p. 101.

139 See Arad, *Ghetto in Flames*, p. 84ff.

140 The official in charge of "Jewish affairs" on the part of the local Lithuanian authorities was Petras Buragas. See ibid., p. 89.

141 Browning, *Origins*, p. 296; Schroeter, *Worte*, p. 104f.; Arad, *Ghetto in Flames*, p. 101.

142 As expressed in a letter to the civil administration entitled "Provisional Directives for the Treatment of Jews in Reichskommissariat Ostland," reprinted in Arad, *Ghetto in Flames*, pp. 471–7. See ibid., p. 91.

143 See ibid., p. 66. Before the deportations to the mass extermination camps from the beginning of 1942 onwards, Germans and their collaborators shot two-thirds of Lithuanian Jews in places such as Ponary or the surrounding forests. See Atamuk, *Juden in Litauen*, p. 172.

144 Certificates identifying Jews as workers employed by the German army or Lithuanian factories were meant to give them "protection," but could not be relied on in practice. See Arad, *Ghetto in Flames*, pp. 69, 72.

145 See ibid., pp. 102, 107. For greater context, see also Kruk, *The Last Days*, pp. 42, 44, 53; Sutzkever, *Wilner Getto*, p. 33ff.

146 Proclamation, District Commissar Hingst, 1.9.1941, reprinted in ibid., p. 34.

147 Schroeter, *Worte*, p. 104; Arad, *Ghetto in Flames*, p. 104f. The few members who had managed to escape arrest by the Germans turned to the Lithuanian authorities for help. See Arad, *Ghetto in Flames*, p. 106f., and Sutzkever, *Wilner Ghetto*, p. 40ff.

148 See Schroeter, *Worte*, p. 116f.; Arad, *Ghetto in Flames*, p. 175.

149 Kruk, *The Last Days*, 4.9.1941, p. 92.

150 See Arad, *Ghetto in Flames*, pp. 108, 113, 116; Kruk, *The Last Days*, pp. 71, 259; Sutzkever, *Wilner Ghetto*, p. 46ff.

151 According to a report by the *Einsatzkommando*, 3,334 Jewish men, women, and children were murdered on 12 September 1941. Jäger Report, p. 6, cited in Arad, *Ghetto in Flames*, p. 116; see Schroeter, *Worte*, p. 120; on the Lukiszki prison, see Arad, *Ghetto in Flames*, p. 74f.

152 Also on the Council alongside Anatol Fried was G. Jaszuński, a lawyer and one of the leaders of the Bund. J. Fishman, a Bund member, S. Milkonovicki, a lawyer and Zionist, and the engineer G. Guchman had already been active in the Jewish community before the war. See Arad, *Ghetto in Flames*, p. 123; Schroeter, *Worte*, p. 122f.

153 See Arad, *Ghetto in Flames*, p. 124.

154 See Schroeter, *Worte*, p. 124f.; Arad, *Ghetto in Flames*, p. 133f.

155 See ibid., p. 136f.; Schroeter, *Worte*, p. 128. In Vilna the official name was "Jewish Police" rather than "Order Service."

156 See Arad, *Ghetto in Flames*, p. 176f. Sutzkever, too, writes that Gens knew about the German murder campaign from September 1941 (*Wilner Getto*, p. 55).

157 See Arad, *Ghetto in Flames*, p. 179f.

158 See ibid., p. 182.

159 According to Sutzkever, the Germans used this system of colours, certificates, documents, and numbers to sow confusion. See Sutzkever, *Wilner Ghetto*, p. 60.

160 On the different certificates, see ibid., p. 58ff.; Schroeter, *Worte*, p. 130f.

161 See Arad, *Ghetto in Flames*, p. 164.

162 Kruk, *The Last Days*, 2.1.1942, p. 153. Similar information was published on 1 January 1942 in a manifesto launched by a youth organization in the ghetto (see Arad, *Ghetto in Flames*, p. 182).

163 While the civil administration and army had an interest in continuing the exploitation of Jewish labour, the SS functionaries called for the murder of Lithuania's entire Jewish population. See Arad, *Ghetto in Flames*, p. 164ff.

164 See Balberyszski, *Stronger Than Iron*, p. 216; Schroeter, *Worte*, p. 137.

165 Murer justified this on the grounds of Fried's alleged inefficiency. See
    Schroeter, *Worte*, p. 136ff.; Arad, *Ghetto in Flames*, p. 333ff.

166 This movement exerted a special attraction on the Jewish population of
    Eastern Europe in the 1930s, and encouraged emigration to Palestine.

167 See, e.g., the "Address by Gens after His Appointment as Ghetto Leader,"
    15.7.1942, Announcement, reprinted in Arad and Gutman, *Documents on
    the Holocaust*, p. 438ff.

168 See Dieckmann, *Deutsche Besatzungspolitik*, vol. 2, p. 1134ff.

169 The average wage was officially 30 to 50 pfennigs per hour according to
    skill level, but amounted in real terms to just 15 pfennigs. See Sutzkever,
    Wilner Getto, p. 102; Schroeter, *Worte*, p. 139.

170 See ibid. The Vilna ghetto did not experience the major famines of
    Warsaw and Lodz, which claimed thousands of lives. Nevertheless,
    strict controls were periodically applied at the ghetto border, inflicting
    severe hunger on the ghetto community. See ibid., p. 183, and Kruk, *The
    Last Days*, 30.4.1942, p. 275.

171 The working wage was subject to a 10 per cent tax. Further payments
    were due for housing and hot water, and small businesses such as
    bakeries and laundries also had to pay a trade tax. See Schroeter, *Worte*,
    p. 140; Dworzecki, *Yerushaleyim de Lite*, p. 170f.

172 The anti-Semitic Lithuanian, Polish, and German newspapers available
    in the ghetto did not report explicitly on defeats, but residents learned
    to "read between the lines." See Balberyszski, *Stronger Than Iron*, p. 213;
    Schroeter, *Worte*, p. 200ff. It was already evident by July 1941 that the
    "Blitzkrieg" was not going to plan for the Germans. See Browning,
    Origins, p. 427ff.

173 See Schroeter, *Worte*, p. 142f.

174 See ibid., pp. 144–7.

175 Kruk, *The Last Days*, 30.10.1942, report by the Warsaw underground
    press regarding mass murders, p. 396; ibid., 18.11.1942, report from
    Kovno: murder of twenty Jews, p. 416; ibid., 26.11.1942, reports from the
    underground press re public execution and murder of ghetto residents in
    Warsaw, p. 420; ibid., 26.12.1942, news of murders in other ghettos such
    as Grodno, p. 439.

176 See Arad, *Ghetto in Flames*, p. 192f.; Schroeter, *Worte*, p. 90ff.; Sutzkever,
    Wilner Getto, p. 19ff.

177 Kruk, *The Last Days*, 26.11.1942, p. 420.

178 Ibid., 19.4.1943, pp. 519ff., 523f.

179 The FPO propagated its strategy as a "social and national struggle."
    Dworzecki, reprinted in Arad and Gutman, *Documents on the Holocaust*, p. 437.

180 See Schroeter, *Worte*, p. 375ff. The groups Hashomer Hatzair and Hanoar
    Hatzioni were Zionist youth organizations. While the former championed

socialist ideals, the latter focused on emigration to Israel and the importance of Jewish culture and religion. Within the Bund, there was at first no uniform strategy for political activity in the ghetto; moreover, some in the FPO had reservations with regard to the "Revisionists," i.e., members of Betar. The first FPO command consisted of Yitzak Witenberg (Communist), Abba Kovner (Hashomer Hatzair), and Yozef Glazman (Betar). See ibid.

181 See ibid., p. 375; Arad, *Ghetto in Flames*, p. 235.

182 The FPO command even included the deputy chief of the ghetto police, Yozef Glazman. See Schroeter, *Worte*, p. 376.

183 See ibid., p. 385ff.

184 The Yechiel Group – named after its leader – included numerous members of the youth organization Dror. An initial stronghold was established in the Rudnicka Forests at the end of April 1943. See ibid., p. 179; Arad, *Ghetto in Flames*, p. 266.

185 The smaller ghettos in Sventsian and Oshemene had been liquidated, and Jewish Police officers from Vilna forced to bury the bodies. According to Schroeter, this "operation" signalled a turning point in the history of the Vilna ghetto: for the first time, the German occupiers had made no effort to conceal their murder plans from the Jewish Council and ghetto population. See Schroeter, *Worte*, p. 152ff. In early summer 1943, the FPO numbered approximately 300 members in the ghetto and a further 300 in the surrounding area. See ibid., p. 395.

186 See ibid., p. 381; Arad, *Ghetto in Flames*, p. 381ff.

187 See Schroeter, *Worte*, p. 395; Arad, *Ghetto in Flames*, p. 377ff.; also GFH 1646/ Registry Holdings 4471, "Rede fun dem getofarshteyer Gens," 24.6.1943.

188 Address to the foremen of the forced labour gangs, 15.5.1943, reprinted in Arad and Gutman, *Documents on the Holocaust*, p. 454ff. (orig. Moreshet Archives, D. 1.355).

189 See Schroeter, *Worte*, p. 154f.

190 See Arad, *Ghetto in Flames*, p. 420ff.; Schroeter, *Worte*, p. 155ff.

191 See ibid., p. 399f.

192 See ibid., p. 157; Arad, *Ghetto in Flames*, p. 429ff.; Shneidman, *The Three Tragic Heroes*, p. 130.

193 See Hilberg, *Destruction*, p. 243; Browning, *Origins*, p. 139f.; Trunk, *Judenrat*, pp. 62–8.

194 Re the pre-ghettoization period in Warsaw, see Engelking and Leociak, *Warsaw Ghetto*, p. 139f.

195 See Hilberg, *Destruction*, pp. 245, 249.

196 On 6 August 1941, for example, Murer demanded 2,000,000 roubles or the equivalent in property, plus a further 3,000,000 the following day; otherwise all Jewish Council members would be murdered. On 9 August

1941, 170 Jews were taken hostage and a ransom of 564,000 roubles was demanded. See Dieckmann, *Deutsche Besatzungspolitik*, vol. 2, p. 972.
197 See ibid., pp. 1004–8.
198 Many Jewish Councils supplied the Germans with "Jewish labour" prior to ghettoization in order to pre-empt such arbitrary actions. See Diner, *Beyond the Conceivable*, pp. 117–29; Hilberg, *Destruction*, p. 252; re Warsaw: Dreifuss, *Warsaw*, p. 906ff. On 26 October 1939, the Germans issued a decree introducing compulsory labour for Jewish men between the ages of fourteen and sixty; random capture had already occurred before this point. See Trunk, *Judenrat*, p. 72; Engelking and Leociak, *Warsaw Ghetto*, p. 143; re the situation in Vilna, Kruk, *The Last Days*, 10.7.1941, p. 61.
199 See Trunk, *Judenrat*, p. 73ff.; Browning, "Nazi Ghettoization Policy," pp. 348, 345; Löw, *Juden im Getto*, p. 117.
200 Re Lodz, see ibid.; re Warsaw, see Gutman, *Jews of Warsaw*, p. 23.
201 See Hilberg, *Destruction*, p. 256.
202 See Engelking and Leociak, *Warsaw Ghetto*, p. 394; for more on the debate between the so-called productionist and attritionist policies, see Browning, "Nazi Ghettoization Policy."
203 See Michman, *The Emergence*, p. 116; Dieckmann and Quinkert, "Einleitung," p. 13f.
204 The first instance of this occurred in December 1941 in the Lodz ghetto.
205 This applies not only in a moral sense, as Engelking and Leociak remark: "The extermination of the Jews was contrary to the economic and military interests of the Third Reich ... Ideology won not only over the dictates of religion and the traditions of European civilization and culture but also over common sense and economic calculations" (*Warsaw Ghetto*, p. 411).
206 Special Courts had been established in the German Reich by a decree of 21 March 1933. On the Special Courts in the occupied territories, see Heuer, *Geheime Staatspolizei*, p. 121ff.; on Lodz, see Schlüter, "*... für die Menschlichkeit*"; on Warsaw, see Jan Grabowski, "Żydzi przed obliczem"; Engelking and Grabowski, *Żydów łamiących*, p. 40; Jan Grabowski, "Jewish Criminality," p. 118ff.; Maximilian Becker, *Mitstreiter im Volkstumskampf*.
207 With specific reference to the spatial segregation created by ghettoization in Budapest, see the pioneering study by Cole, *Holocaust City*; on the contribution of spatial theory to research into ghetto communities, see also Bethke and Schmidt Holländer, "Lebenswelt Ghetto."
208 Re Warsaw, see Engelking and Leociak, *Warsaw Ghetto*, pp. 52–107, esp. p. 71ff.; re Lodz, see Löw, *Juden im Getto*, p. 86ff.; re Vilna, see Arad, *Ghetto in Flames*, p. 108ff.
209 ŻIH, RG 205/155, SS Brigadier Schäfer, "Sonderanweisung für den Verkehr mit dem Ghetto an die deutsche Kriminalpolizei," 10.5.1940, fol. 1, 2.

210 At this stage, offenders could be fined, imprisoned, or sent to a labour camp. Ludwig Leist, Decree of 14.1.1941, quoted in Engelking and Leociak, *Warsaw Ghetto*, p. 76.

211 A corresponding decree had already been issued for the entire Generalgouvernement by Hans Frank on 15 October 1941. This came into force on 10 November 1941, following a proclamation by Ludwig Fischer, governor of the Warsaw ghetto. See Engelking and Leociak, *Warsaw Ghetto*, pp. 84, 86.

212 ŻIH, RG 205/155, SS Brigadier Schäfer, "Sonderanweisung für den Verkehr mit dem Ghetto an die deutsche Kriminalpolizei," 10.5.1940, fol. 1.

213 On the introduction of compulsory labelling, see the report by Kruk, *The Last Days*, 8.7.1941, p. 60.

214 See, e.g., Battrick, "Smuggling," p. 200. While Trunk, *Judenrat*, p. 61, likewise assumes that starvation was part of the German plan, Browning, *Origins*, p. 166, rightly contradicts him with respect to this early phase. On the relevance of smuggling from the German perspective in comparison with other "ghetto-internal offences," see the report re Warsaw by the contemporary witness Bryskier, *Żydzi pod swastyką*, p. 209.

215 The primary reason for enforcing the border is clear from a special instruction issued by SS Brigadier Schäfer spelling out the border demarcation and associated criminal acts, together with the offence of smuggling. See ŻIH, RG 205/155, "Schäfer Sp. Brigadeführer, Sonderanweisung für den Verkehr mit dem Ghetto," 10.5.1940, fol. 1, 2. See also ŻIH, RG 205/155, "Bericht betr. die Veränderung der Ghettogrenze, 4.10.1940, gez. Sp. Hauptscharführer u. Krim. Oberass," fols. 12, 13. This letter also blames smuggling on the border situation and lack of security, highlighting the issue of infiltration by Polish smugglers.

216 On this aspect, see also Browning, *Origins*, p. 162.

217 By this stage – in contrast to the situation in Warsaw and Lodz – District Commissar Murer's warnings no longer alluded to the necessary enforcement of the ghetto border. For more detail, see Kruk, *The Last Days*, 5.2.1942, p. 193.

218 Official order by District Commissar Franz Murer, reprinted in ibid.; definition of the duties of Police Chief Gens, reprinted in ibid., 29.4.1942, p. 274.

219 See Trunk, *Judenrat*, p. 183f.; Adler, *In the Warsaw Ghetto*, p. 77ff. In the case of the Lodz ghetto, this can be inferred partly from relevant changes made by the Germans to the powers of the ghetto court from August 1942. See Feuchert, *Chronik 1941*, 4.8.1941, p. 210. It is also evident from individual instructions of the German Criminal Police to the Jewish Council.

220 Evident from reports by the German Criminal Police: USHMM, RG 05.008, 26/63, Ghetto Commissariat performance report, 16.9.1942, especially cases processed during the period September 1941–September 1942, fol. 15 (including, in this instance, suicides and suicide attempts), as well as

numerous notifications showing that suicides were reported in accordance with German orders. See, e.g., Feuchert, *Chronik* 1942, 31.3.1942.

221 For the Lodz ghetto, see, e.g., ŻIH, RG 205/155, SS Brigadier Schäfer, 10.5.1940, fol. 1, 2; fol. 1: curfew; ŻIH, RG 205/66, 14.11.1940: German police regulation for the ghetto: blackout instructions; for the Warsaw ghetto, e.g., ŻIH, RING I/208 (Lb. 1452), ŻIH, 779, W 10, News Gazette for the Jewish Residential District in Warsaw, no. 1, 1.2.1942. Curfews and blackout measures were sometimes declared as an air raid precaution in the general context of the war, and were therefore not always specific to the ghettos.

222 Announced in Lodz by the Jewish Council: see ŻIH, RG 241/556, Proclamation no. 410, 16.2.1944 ("by order of the authority"); for Vilna, see YIVO, RG 223/32, Notice no. 87, 3.12.1942, issued by Council chairman Gens; for Warsaw, see report on the proclamation regarding compulsory greeting of German officers in the ghetto: Kaplan, *Scroll of Agony*, 6.11.1940, p. 222.

223 On this subject with regard to the Generalgouvernement, see Chapoutot, "Eradiquer le typhus."

224 See Engelking and Leociak, *Warsaw Ghetto*, p. 52; Sutzkever, *Wilner Ghetto*, p. 56.

225 See Berkowitz, *The Crime*, p. 54.

226 For Warsaw, see, e.g., Czerniaków, *Warsaw Diary*, 3.2.1940, p. 114: delousing order and subsequent sanctioning of Jewish Council for non-appearance of summoned individuals; ŻIH, RING I/208 (Lb. 1452); ŻIH, 779, W 10, News Gazette for the Jewish Residential District in Warsaw, no. 1, 1.2.1942, fol. 1: introduction of compulsory vaccination against dysentery; for Lodz, see, e.g., YVA, O-34/222, Proclamation no. 213, 7.2.1941: horse vaccinations; YVA, O-34/119, Proclamation no. 112, 27.8.1940: cull of all dogs due to risk of rabies.

227 The risk of spreading typhus was also used to justify the introduction of the death penalty for illegal border crossing in November 1941 (ŻIH, RG 241/262, Governor General Hans Frank, 10.11.1941). In Lodz, the Germans had already imposed a postal ban in July 1940, citing the risk of dysentery infection. See Löw, *Juden im Getto*, p. 283; Baranowski, *The Łódź Ghetto*, p. 33.

228 Remark by Himmler, as recorded by an army officer in his memoirs and quoted by Pohl, *Von der "Judenpolitik"*, p. 49 [translation by Dan Michman in *The Emergence*, p. 75].

229 See also Michman, *The Emergence*, on Heydrich's efforts to prevent epidemics in the ghetto (p. 31), and Engelking and Leociak, *Warsaw Ghetto*, p. 233, on similar measures in the Warsaw ghetto.

230 See Dieckmann, *Deutsche Besatzungspolitik*, vol. 2, p. 970f.

231 References to sanitary inspections by the German occupiers can be found in Kruk, *The Last Days*, 27.9.1941, p. 119. Again, these are likely to have been prompted chiefly by the fear of contagion. A sanitary police unit was

also set up within the ghetto police, however, which was responsible for taking the necessary precautions.

232 Sutzkever, *Wilner Getto*, p. 116.
233 The Jewish Council – particularly in the early days of the ghetto – had to surrender objects of value to the German ghetto administration and was allotted small amounts of food for the ghetto community in return.
234 ŻIH, RG 205/155, matter for the administrative meeting of 28.8.1940 at the District Governor's office, fol. 9, 10. For the Lodz ghetto, it was decreed in October 1940 that all confiscated items should be delivered to the German ghetto administration for the purpose of provisioning the ghetto, except for "exhibits from criminal trials." ŻIH, RG 205/158, minutes of a meeting of 23.10.1940 between the ghetto administration and Criminal Police, fol. 1.
235 USHMM, RG 05.008, 9/23, mayor of Lodz (Department of Food and Economy) to the Gestapo, re the sale in the ghetto of newspapers brought into the Jewish residential district by illegal means, 18.5.1940, fol. 287.
236 Statement by Goldberg as forwarded to the German Criminal Police by the Gestapo. USHMM RG 05.008, 9/23, Gestapo to the State Criminal Police, 26.5.1940, fol. 288, 289.
237 A note of 27 June 1940 stated that the publisher and the Jewish Council had since been notified and agreement had been reached on the need to take "all conceivable measures to prevent the smuggling of newspapers." USHMM, RG 05.008, 9/23, Ghetto *Sonderkommando* ("Special Unit"), note of 27.6.1940. See also USHMM, RG 05.008, 9/23, Ghetto *Sonderkommando*, re an arrest for the "illegal sale of newspapers" on 18.6.1940, fol. 372, 373.
238 ŻIH, RING I/208 (Lb. 1452), ŻIH, 779, W 10, News Gazette for the Jewish Residential District in Warsaw, no. 1, 1.2.1942, fol. 1.
239 See Heuer, *Geheime Staatspolizei*, p. 122.
240 See (re Warsaw) Engelking and Grabowski, *Żydów łamiących*, p. 40.
241 On smuggling cases tried in 1940 and 1941, see, e.g., YVA, JM-839, Abbe/Walfisz, verdict of 15.10.1940, fol. 182f.; YVA, JM-836, Bittermann/Bialek, ruling of 2.8.1941; YVA, JM-845, Goldmann, criminal charge of 6.3.1941, fol. 2; on cases dropped owing to "insufficient public interest," see YVA, JM-836, July 1942, fol. 28; USHMM, RG 05.008, 27/64, German Criminal Police, register of ghetto prisoners convicted under German law, fol. 165, 206, USHMM, RG 05.008, 29/75, register 1941–2, fols. 60, 87, 141.
242 USHMM, RG 05.008, 9/23, Lodz Criminal Police department reports 1940, e.g., fol. 46 (annotated "purpose of smuggling to feed sick mother; food returned").
243 USHMM, RG 05.008, 9/23, Lodz Criminal Police department reports 1940, e.g., fol. 131 (annotated "food returned to Jewess due to small quantities involved"); similarly, fol. 157 and fols. 431, 302f., 386.

244 In the case of Lodz, for example, see the Health Department reports for 1940 concerning "persons shot at the perimeter fence." USHMM, RG 05.008 6/43, fol. 139. Re shootings of smugglers in the Warsaw ghetto, see, e.g., Adler, *In the Warsaw Ghetto*, p. 116f. In Vilna, smugglers were rarely shot directly at the ghetto border, but faced subsequent execution instead. On this, see Kruk, *The Last Days*, 18.11.1942, p. 417.

245 See Dreifuss, "Warsaw," p. 907f. See also the reports YIVO, RG 225/32.2, Ghetto Diary (Abraham Levin), 14–15.5.1942: murder of a smuggler; YIVO, RG 225/32.5, 29.6–10.7.1942: shooting of smugglers.

246 See Engelking and Leociak, *Warsaw Ghetto*, p. 86f.; see also the report of June 1942 concerning further executions of seventeen smugglers in the Warsaw ghetto. YIVO, RG 225/31.14, author unknown, 20.6.1942.

247 ŻIH, 44. RING II/140, Auerswald to the Jewish Council chairman, 10.3.1942, re pardoning of Jews, fol. 7; also ŻIH, 62. RING II/151, telegram from the head of the central prison and commander of the central prison patrol to the Jewish Council, 11.3.1942, re discharge from prison. The release followed a pardon, which, according to the correspondence, had already been announced on 9 January 1942. See also Czerniaków, *Warsaw Diary*, 11.3.1942, p. 334.

248 Ringelblum, *Notes*, p. 372.

249 See Engelking and Leociak, *Warsaw Ghetto*, p. 679.

250 See ibid.

251 See Dreifuss, "Warsaw," p. 911.

252 YIVO, RG 225, 29.6–10.7.1942, report, author unknown.

253 See Schroeter, *Worte*, p. 397ff.

254 A resident named Moszek Lajb Czosnek was accused of murdering his wife and son. Feuchert, *Chronik* 1941, 22.4.1941, p. 131. The Germans imposed the death penalty, which was carried out on 5 August 1941 at Posen prison. Cited in ibid., p. 438, n. 96.

255 Robinson, "Introduction," p. 1. On this aspect in general, see also Fraenkel, *The Dual State*, p. 46; Wildt, "Die Transformation."

256 Berkowitz, *The Crime*, p. 73.

2 Jewish Council Proclamations: Definitions of Criminal Activity

1 ŻIH, RING I/428, Stanisław Różycki, "To jest getto," Reportaż z inferna XX wieku, XII 1941 r. This was one of four reports Różycki wrote for the Ringelblum Archive. Kassow assumes the writer to have been a secondary school teacher. See Kassow, *Who Will Write*, p. 253.

2 Proclamations similar in form and function to those of the Lodz ghetto were issued by the Jewish Council chairman Efraim Barasz in the Białystok ghetto. See Furła-Buszek, "Charakteristika."

3 During the early war years, the objective was to regulate communal life under the new and exceptional conditions. With the beginning of deportations to Kulmhof in 1942, the "pseudo-autonomy" of the ghetto was curtailed by the Germans, particularly from September 1942 onwards, and this was duly reflected in the quantity and content of the proclamations. See Löw, "Das Getto Litzmannstadt," p. 159ff.

4 On the printing and posting of proclamations on ghetto walls, see APŁ, 278/1076, *Geto-Tsaytung* no. 10, 11.5.1941, p. 1.

5 From February 1941, the content of these was also frequently raised in the Council chairman's public addresses. On the purpose of these addresses, see Polit, *"Moja żydowska dusza"*, p. 44ff.

6 APŁ, 278/1076, *Geto-Tsaytung* no. 1, 7.3.1941, p. 1.

7 YVA, O-34/330, 7.11.1941.

8 This applied, for example, to the German ban on wearing furs, which had been in force since 1 January 1941, and the order to deliver them without delay to the ghetto sales outlets. ŻIH, RG 241/577, 27.11.1941 (first announced on 2.11.1941), fol. 458.

9 This was, indeed, their official purpose, according to the editors of *Gazeta Żydowska*. ŻIH, RING I/702, *Gazeta Żydowska* no. 47, 13.6.1941, p. 8.

10 ŻIH, RING I/702, *Gazeta Żydowska* no. 45, 6.6.1941, p. 6, call no. 2261.

11 In the *Gazeta Żydowska*, these usually appeared in the "Daily bulletin" column. See, e.g., ŻIH, RING I/702, *Gazeta Żydowska* no. 42, 13.7.1940: report on a shoplifting case; *Gazeta Żydowska* no. 12, 11.2.1941: report on a case of pickpocketing in the street; *Gazeta Żydowska* no. 93, 3.10.1941: warning against con men in the context of resettlements due to the redrawing of the ghetto border; *Gazeta Żydowska* no. 70, 11.8.1941: warning against fraudsters employing "magic tricks" to steal money.

12 These featured particularly prominently in the Lodz *Geto-Tsaytung*. See, e.g., the verdicts of the summary court including details of offences and sentences: APŁ PSŻ, 278/1076, *Geto-Tsaytung* no. 3, 21.3.1941, orig. p. 4, *Geto-Tsaytung* no. 5, 4.4.1941, p. 10.

13 GFH, Collections Section, 554, *Geto-Yedies* no. 30, 14.3.1943, fol. 6.

14 Conclusions based on the surviving proclamations should be treated with caution. Given the relative dearth of material for Vilna and Warsaw in particular, it is often impossible to say for certain whether the thematic priorities are truly representative, or merely a reflection of the available sources. Because of this, the following discussion centres mainly on the proclamations by Rumkowski, using a few examples from the Warsaw and Vilna ghettos to highlight distinctive features.

15 ŻIH, RG 205/219, Proclamation, 8.5.1940, fol. 92.

16 YVA, O-34/84, Proclamation no. 78, 9.7.1940 (emphasis orig.).

17 The ghetto resident Jakub Poznański, for example, notes in his diary that large quantities of goods found their way into the ghetto during the first few months in particular. Poznański, *Tagebuch*, p. 52.

18 See, e.g., the entry of 26.3.1941 in Feuchert, *Chronik* 1941: "Chana Lewkowicz shot. Alleged reason: smuggling" (p. 99); a further report appears on 1.4.1941 (p. 110).

19 APŁ, 278/1076, *Geto-Tsaytung* no. 7, 17.4.1941, p. 2. This follows a similar warning in APŁ, 278/1076, *Geto-Tsaytung* no. 2, 14.3.1941, p. 3.

20 For more detail, see chapter 3, "The Jewish Police as an Executive Organ," below.

21 Ghetto Police Regulation no. 22 of 6.12.1941, reprinted in Kruk, *The Last Days*, 22.12.1941, p. 13

22 YVA, O-34/141, Proclamation no. 133, 4.10.1940.

23 The general curfews were mostly imposed in connection with planned deportations, in order to locate people destined for "dispatch." For this reason, the deportations which took place in the week from 5 to 12 September 1942 were also referred to as "operation curfew." YVA, O-34/402, 5.9.1942, ŻIH, RG 241/541, Proclamation no. 382, 12.9.1942, suspension of general curfew imposed on 5.9.1942; ŻIH, RG 241/557, Proclamation no. 411, 18.2.1944, re blanket curfew in connection with the dispatch of 1,600 workers to work outside the ghetto.

24 ŻIH, RG 241/437, Proclamation no. 244, 4.4.1941 (emphasis orig.); ŻIH, RG 241/464, Proclamation no. 287, 1.7.1941. In addition to requiring the blacking out of windows, this also prohibited "smoking cigarettes on the streets and in yards" during curfew hours and described the correct use of flashlights.

25 It was merely stated, for example, that "the punishment for violations … will be most severe." ŻIH, RG 241/437, Proclamation no. 244, 4.4.1941 (emphasis orig.). See also APŁ, 278/1076, *Geto-Tsaytung* no. 7, 17.4.1941, p. 2.

26 "Violations will be severely punished and their electric current will be cut off." ŻIH, RG 241/497, Proclamation no. 330, 8.11.1941.

27 ŻIH, RG 241/561, 2.5.1944. The liability of house committee chairmen and house managers is specified from 1942 onwards: YVA, O-34/401, Proclamation, 31.8.1942.

28 YIVO 223/16, Order no. 26, Jakub Gens, Chief of Jewish Police, 24.3.1942. See also Kruk, *The Last Days*, 24.3.1942, p. 248.

29 Precise instructions on how to salute were also issued. Feuchert, *Chronik* 1942, 24.5.1942, p. 230.

30 YVA, O-34/396, Proclamation no. 387, 27.6.1942. Further reminders followed in 1944: see ŻIH, RG 241/552, Proclamation no. 406, 6.1.1944 and

ŻIH, RG 241/556, Proclamation no. 410, 16.2.1944 – here again with the wording "by order of the authorities."

31 YIVO, RG 223/32, Notification no. 87, 3.12.1942, issued by ghetto governor Jakub Gens.

32 GFH, Collections Section, 554, *Geto-Yedies* no. 15, 30.11.1942, fol. 1.

33 YIVO, RG 223/29, Proclamation issued by ghetto governor and Chief of Police Jakub Gens, 3.10.1942.

34 Cited in Kruk, *The Last Days*, 10.11.1942, p. 408. Pregnancies had been banned in the Vilna ghetto from February 1942, on pain of death for both mother and baby. Women hid new-born babies in secret locations with the aid of the health department. Leah Preiss also writes of cases where pregnant women were pressurized into abortion ("Women's Health"). For further context, see also Sutzkever, *Wilner Getto*, p. 57f, and Ben-Sefer, "Forced Sterilization and Abortion," p. 168.

35 Proclaimed by Gens on Murer's orders. See also Kruk, *The Last Days*, 5.3.1943, p. 471.

36 YVA, O-34/146, Proclamation no. 138, 11.10.1940; YVA, O-34/231, Proclamation no. 222, 27.2.1941; ŻIH, 241/490, Proclamation no. 322, 2.11.1941; YVA, O-34/398, Proclamation no. 389, 8.7.1942.

37 YVA, O-34/146, Proclamation no. 138, 11.10.1940 (emphasis orig.); YVA, O-34/231, Proclamation no. 222, 27.2.1941; ŻIH, RG 241/490, Proclamation no. 322, 2.11.1941; YVA, O-34/398, Proclamation no. 389, 8.7.1942.

38 A different approach was adopted by the *Sonderkommando* (subsequently *Sonderabteilung*), which was responsible for "tracking down" objects of value in the ghetto from June 1940 onwards, and which – particularly under the leadership of Dawid Gertler – employed brutal methods extending to torture. See Löw, *Juden im Getto*, p. 108.

39 ŻIH, 241/311, Proclamation no. 385, 10.6.1942.

40 ŻIH, 24. RING II/144, 25.12.1941.

41 Mentioned in Kruk, *The Last Days*, 28.12.1941, p. 144; on the reiteration of the order by the ghetto police, see Order no. 28, 31.12.1941, reprinted in Kruk, *The Last Days*, 31.12.1941, p. 148. The German order of November/December 1941 was also connected with the invasion of the Soviet Union, the furs being intended for the German troops there.

42 ŻIH, 241/357, Proclamation no. 148, 26.10.1941 (emphasis orig.).

43 YVA, O-34/285, Proclamation no. 285, 29.6.1941: men to register with the labour department; ŻIH, 241/462, Proclamation no. 285: all men in receipt of relief aid to register with the labour deployment department or face punishment and withdrawal of benefits; ŻIH, 241/469, Proclamation no. 294, 27.6.1941: all men in receipt of relief aid to register with the labour deployment department or face punishment and withdrawal of benefits.

44 YVA, O-34/362, Proclamation no. 355, 14.1.1942 (emphasis orig.); YVA, O-34/379, Proclamation no. 371, 22.3.1942.
45 Ibid.
46 ŻIH, Bernard Mark Collection/478, letter of 29.1.1940 by Czerniaków, call to the Jewish population of Warsaw.
47 ŻIH, 52. RING II/186, 22.7.1942, fol. 2.
48 Ibid.
49 YIVO, RG 223/34, Notification no. 108 of 31.1.1942 from the Jewish Council labour department to all workers.
50 GFH, 7361, Franz Murer, District Commissar of the city of Vilna, 7.4.1942.
51 According to Kruk, *The Last Days*, 21.1.1943, p. 453.
52 ŻIH, 205/219, Proclamation no. 56, 6.6.1940, fol. 158 (emphasis orig.).
53 YVA, O-34/10, Proclamation no. 4, undated, execution of police regulation of 8.2.1940. This stipulated that the transfer of the Jews to the "residential district" could only be effected by the Jewish Council or resettlement department. Moving and renting an apartment without the Council's permission carried a severe penalty, and anyone guilty of this would be "ruthlessly expelled and punished by the police." See also YVA, O-34/19, Proclamation no. 13, 8.4.1940, and O-34/32, Proclamation no. 27, reminder of previous proclamations.
54 The German authorities' initial plan to separate off part of the ghetto territory did not come to fruition because of the numerous workshops and factories in this area, although some non-working residents had to move regardless. Feuchert, *Chronik* 1941, 31.1.1941, p. 357, n. 177.
55 ŻIH, RG 241/407, Proclamation no. 208, 1.2.1941 (emphasis orig.). See also YVA O-34/323, 31.10.1941, concerning the practice of renting to "new resettlers" lodgings which may only be allocated by the housing department. Here again, Rumkowski declared that non-compliant landlords would be punished by expulsion from their premises.
56 Order no. 26, Chief of Ghetto Police, 18.12.1941, reprinted in Kruk, *The Last Days*, 21.12.1941, p. 136.
57 ŻIH, RG 205/219, Decree no. 35, 9.5.1940, fol. 96: registration with the Jewish Council on pain of severe punishment; YVA, O-34/124, Proclamation no. 117, 2.9.1940: obligation to register births within seven days, on pain of withdrawal of food ration cards for offspring; ŻIH, RG 241/397, Proclamation no. 192, 15.1.1941: requirement that the identity of deceased residents be confirmed by two witnesses at burials, on pain of severe punishment.
58 ŻIH, RG 205/219, Injunction no. 7, 26.3.1940, fol. 20.
59 ŻIH, definition of tasks with regard to cleaning: ŻIH, RG 205/219, Injunction no. 8, 27.3.1940, fol. 22; ŻIH, RG 241/401, Decree no. 198, 18.1.1941.
60 ŻIH, RG 241/424, Proclamation no. 235, 3.3.1941. See also ŻIH, RG 205/237, circular to heads of the bread and milk distribution centres,

10.3.1941, fol. 27; ŻIH, RG 205/234, circular to all departments, workshops and factories, 21.1.1943, fol. 10.

61 On the German ghetto administration's electricity charging policy, see Alberti, *Die Anfänge*, p. 219. On the increase in electricity prices, see, e.g., Feuchert, *Chronik 1942*, 19.5.1942, p. 210. In 1942, the German occupiers also warned the municipal authority to "keep fuel, electricity and gas consumption as low as humanly possible." USHMM, RG 05.008, administrative report for the months October to December 1942, 14.1.1943, p. 3, fol. 103.

62 In September 1940, 60,000 adults received a monthly payment of 9 marks each, while 15,000 children up to the age of fourteen and 7,000 adults above the age of sixty received 10 marks. See Löw, *Juden im Getto*, p. 185.

63 YVA, O-34/144, Proclamation no. 136, 11.10.1940 (emphasis orig.).

64 ŻIH, 241/338, Proclamation no. 125, 20.9.1940

65 APŁ, 278/1076, *Geto-Tsaytung* no. 14, 15.7.1941, p. 1. Such cases were tried before the ghetto court and the verdicts subsequently published in the *Geto-Tsaytung*. APŁ, 278/1076, *Geto-Tsaytung* no. 13, 20.6.1941, p. 3.

66 APŁ, 278/1076, *Geto-Tsaytung* no. 14, 15.7.1941, p. 1.

67 See Löw, *Juden im Getto*, p. 120f.

68 See ibid., p. 185. The writer Józef Zełkowicz left to posterity several reports on his work as an inspector in the ghetto. See Zełkowicz, *In Those Terrible Days*, especially "A Bruise and a Welt in Every Dwelling," pp. 31–178.

69 ŻIH, 241/398, Proclamation no. 193, 15.1.1941.

70 Ibid. Potential violators were threatened with detention and removal of the cards by the ghetto police.

71 YVA, O-34/405, Proclamation no. 393, 13.9.1942; YVA O-34/406, Proclamation no. 394, 17.9.1942.

72 YVA O-34/406, Proclamation no. 394, 17.9.1942.

73 See Löw, *Juden im Getto*, p. 124ff.; Baranowski, "Utworzenie," p. 123; Rubin, *Żydzi w Łodzi*, pp. 276–85. Rumkowski published proclamations detailing the calculated rations per resident for items such as meat, e.g., ŻIH, 241/409, Proclamation no. 208, 3.2.1941.

74 See Feuchert, *Chronik 1941*, p. 349, n. 85.

75 YVA, O-34/159, Proclamation no. 151, 30.10.1941; YVA, O-34/182, Proclamation no. 173, 4.12.1940.

76 YVA, O-34/175, Proclamation no. 167, 20.11.1940.

77 See Löw, *Juden im Getto*, p. 126.

78 This concept is defined by Oskar Rosenfeld in ŻIH, Getto-Enzyklopädie, fol. 127f.

79 See Löw, *Juden im Getto*, p. 126.

80 YVA, O-34/185, Proclamation no. 176, 8.12.1940; YVA, O-34/274, Proclamation no. 273, 25.5.1941.

81 YVA, O-34/274, Proclamation no. 273, 25.5.1941; see also Feuchert, *Chronik 1941*, 21–26.5.1941, p. 152, and 12.1.1941, p. 20f.

82 YVA, O-34/185, Proclamation no. 176, 8.12.1940; YVA, O-34/274, Proclamation no. 273, 25.5.1941.

83 YVA, O-34/143, Proclamation no. 135, 11.10.1940.

84 APŁ, 278/1076, *Geto-Tsaytung* no. 11–12, 30.5.1941, p. 2.

85 Ibid.; Rumkowski announced in the *Geto-Tsaytung* that he would be deploying 80 ghetto police officers to crack down on these crimes.

86 See Löw, *Juden im Getto*, p. 128f.; see, e.g., Sierakowiak, *Diary*, 7.7.1941, pp. 109–10; Poznański, *Tagebuch*, 3.10.1943, p. 158f.

87 YVA, O-34/292, Proclamation no. 292, 18.7.1941. Similarly, YVA, O-34/292, Proclamation no. 292, 18.7.1941.

88 YVA, O-34/168, Proclamation no. 160, 12.11.1940.

89 Ibid.

90 Explanation given in APŁ, 278/1076, *Geto-Tsaytung* no. 15, 1.8.1941, p. 1: "regarding the forbidden trade in confectionery products."

91 YVA, O-34/257, Proclamation no. 252, 21.4.1941 (emphasis orig.).

92 APŁ, 278/1076, *Geto-Tsaytung* no. 4, 28.3.1941, p. 50. The poor living conditions led to a huge rise in disease and mortality in the ghetto. Disease and hunger claimed the lives of 43,500 people – nearly 22 per cent of the population. Feuchert, *Chronik* 1942, p. 336.

93 YVA, O-34/257, Proclamation no. 252, 21.4.1941. Similar rebuke and reminder in APŁ, 278/1076, *Geto-Tsaytung* no. 4, 28.3.1941, p. 50.

94 APŁ, 278/1076, *Geto-Tsaytung* no. 8, 25.4.1941, p. 2.

95 For this reason, Rumkowski also introduced compulsory vaccinations, both for ghetto inhabitants and their pets. See, e.g., ŻIH, RG 241/484, Proclamation no. 313, 16.10.1941: smallpox vaccinations for children on pain of withdrawal of milk and food ration cards. Similarly, compulsory muzzling of dogs because of the risk of rabies: ŻIH, RG 241/291, Proclamation no. 76, 2.7.1940.

96 ŻIH, 52. RING II/186, the Jewish Council in Warsaw, proclamation 22.7.1942, fol. 2.

97 See Sakowska, *Menschen im Ghetto*, p. 183; Sakowska, "Komitety domowe"; see also Adler, *In the Warsaw Ghetto*, p. 54ff. ŻIH, 177. RING II/62, rights and obligations of the house committees, Jewish Council legal department, 30.4.1942.

98 Ibid.

99 ŻIH, 56. RING II/262, to the Inhabitants of the Jewish Residential District, 3.1.1943 (Polish and Yiddish), announcement of Cleanliness Week from 3–9.1.1943.

100 ŻIH, 56. RING II/262, the chairman of the Jewish Council in Warsaw, proclamation (German and Polish), 23.12.1942, announcement of "Cleanliness Week" from 3–9.1.1943.

101 ŻIH, 57. RING II/263 Jewish Council in Warsaw, instructions for the implementation of "Cleanliness Week," 29.12.1942.

102 Strict regulations were also issued in connection with typhus cases, but have not survived in the original. Engelking and Leociak write – based on the testimony of ghetto residents – that private treatment of such cases was prohibited by the Germans on pain of death prior to autumn 1941; thereafter, with the establishment of ghetto medical commissions, the regulations were partially relaxed. See *Warsaw Ghetto*, p. 288.
103 YVA, O-34/80, Proclamation no. 74, 2.7.1940; YVA, O-34/70, Proclamation no. 64, 18.6.1940, YVA; O-34/129, Proclamation no. 123, 20.9.1940; YVA, O-34/172, Proclamation no. 164, 15.11.1940; YVA, O-34/110, Proclamation no. 104, 12.8.1940.
104 YVA, O-34/80, Proclamation no. 74, 2.7.1940. By way of punishment, Rumkowski imposed a curfew from 6 p.m. on 3.7.1940.
105 YVA, O-34/70, Proclamation no. 64, 18.7.1940.
106 YVA, O-34/80, Proclamation no. 74, 2.7.1940.
107 YVA, O-34/110, Proclamation no. 104, 12.8.1940.
108 Ibid.; similarly, YVA, O-34/172, Proclamation no. 164, 15.11.1940. See also Rumkowski's outrage over alleged "agitation" against him in his absence. APŁ, 278/1076, *Geto-Tsaytung* no. 11–12, 30.5.1941.
109 YVA, O-34/129, Proclamation no. 123, 20.9.1940, fol. 2. Address by Rumkowski on 30.8.1941, in Feuchert, *Chronik* 1941, p. 216
110 YVA, O-34/172, Proclamation no. 164, 15.11.1940.
111 Rumkowski repeatedly declared the assurance of "peace and order in the ghetto" to be his aim: see, e.g., the solutions he announced in the first *Geto-Tsaytung*. APŁ, 278/1076, *Geto-Tsaytung* no. 1, 7.3.1941, p. 1, and APŁ, 278/1076, *Geto-Tsaytung* no. 11–12, 30.5.1941.
112 YVA, O-34/172, Proclamation no. 164, 15.11.1940.
113 Address by Rumkowski, 30.8.1941, reprinted in Feuchert, *Chronik* 1941, p. 217.
114 YVA, O-34/129, Proclamation no. 123, 20.9.1940, fol. 2.
115 GFH, Collections Section, 554, *Geto-Yedies* no. 15, 30.11.1942, fol. 1.
116 USHMM, 1999.A. 0105, 3/63. fol. 347: "Spread of fake news is a punishable offence; 48h and referral to court in serious cases."
117 These are described by the Jewish police functionary Gombiński, *Wspomnienia*, p. 69.
118 ŻIH, 55. RING II/266, circular of 2.10.1942 from the Jewish Council (Lichtenbaum) to Council staff.
119 Ibid.
120 Proclamation no. 418, 4.8.1944, in Eisenbach, *Dokumenty i Materiały*, p. 269 (emphasis orig.). On the different tone of this proclamation, see also Löw, *Juden im Getto*, p. 472.
121 ŻIH, RG 241/592, 13.8.1944; similarly, YVA, O-34/435, proclamation, 19.8.1944.

122 ŻIH, 52. RING II/186, 22.7.1942, the Jewish Council in Warsaw, fol. 2.

123 Ibid.

124 ŻIH, 54. RING II/187, Jewish Council in Warsaw, proclamation, 5.9.1942, announcement of preparatory measures for resettlement; ŻIH, 52. RING II/186, proclamation, 25.8.1942.

125 ŻIH, 25. RING II/190, after 22.7.1942, notification and requirements to be met by the Jewish Council with regard to resettlements, fol. 1.

126 Ibid., fol. 2

127 E.g., ŻIH, 52. RING II/186, announcements by the Jewish Council to ghetto residents regarding resettlement, 22.7.1942; ŻIH, 52. RING II/186, proclamation by the Jewish Council in Warsaw, 16.8.1942, ŻIH, 54. RING II/187, proclamation by the Jewish Council in Warsaw, 5.9.1942.

128 ŻIH, 68. RING II/188 proclamation of 26.7.1942 by the chief of the Jewish police regarding resettlements: specifically, food rewards for voluntary participation.

129 This impression is also supported by Kruk, *The Last Days*, 31.2.1943, p. 492, where he writes that orders from Murer and Hingst were awaited in fear and suspense by the ghetto community.

130 See Ta-Shma, Tal, and Slae, "Responsa"; on the significance of this practice for Polish Jewry, see Guesnet, *Polnische Juden*, p. 203.

3 The Jewish Police as an Executive Organ

1 Adler, *In the Warsaw Ghetto*, p. 29.

2 "Jewish Order Service" has become the accepted term in the literature. This reflects the persistent tendency among researchers to focus on the large ghettos in occupied Poland and extrapolate (sometimes unthinkingly) to the ghettos in the occupied Soviet Union, for example.

3 This institution was based on the Security Guard set up by the Jewish Council's Labour Battalion, a paramilitary organization that had been in existence since the end of 1939. See Person, *Policjanci*, p. 11ff. On the creation of the Order Service, see ibid.; Engelking and Leociak, *Warsaw Ghetto*, p. 190ff.; the diary of the Order Service functionary Stanisław Adler, *In the Warsaw Ghetto*, p. 38; and ŻIH, Ekspertyzy Korespondencja ŻIH, sąd społeczny, Testimony of Henryk (Hersz) Wasser, 1948.

4 Szeryński is said to have harboured considerable doubts as to his ability to take on such a central function in the Jewish ghetto community. See Engelking and Leociak, *Warsaw Ghetto*, p. 190.

5 See Trunk, *Judenrat*, p. 493; Engelking and Leociak, *Warsaw Ghetto*, p. 195f., 198; Adler, *In the Warsaw Ghetto*, p. 73f.

6 On the "Blue Police" during the Holocaust in general, see, e.g., Jan Grabowski, *Hunt*. For more details on the Jewish police's dependency on

the Polish police and the complex entanglement of the two police forces in the Warsaw ghetto, see Szymańska-Smolkin, "Fateful Decisions," pp. 70–113.

7 The term "Blue Police" referred to the colour of the officers' uniforms. See Trunk, *Judenrat*, p. 475; Engelking and Leociak, *Warsaw Ghetto*, p. 190.

8 Szymańska-Smolkin, "Fateful Decisions," p. 79; Passenstein, "Szmugiel," p. 57.

9 Rozenblat's appointed deputy was Zymunt Reingold. See Löw, *Juden im Getto*, p. 105f.; Löw, "Ordnungsdienst im Getto Litzmannstadt," pp. 155–67; Dąbrowska, "Administracja żydowska," p. 134; Galiński, "Policja w getcie."

10 See Löw, *Juden im Getto*, p. 108f.

11 Balberyszski gives a comparatively positive assessment of the relationship between residents and the Jewish Police in Ghetto II (*Stronger Than Iron*, p. 202).

12 See Arad, *Ghetto in Flames*, p. 124f.; on the establishment of the police service, see also Balberyszski, *Stronger Than Iron*, p. 195ff.; Schroeter, *Worte*, p. 123.

13 See Arad, *Ghetto in Flames*, p. 128, and Sutzkever, *Wilner Getto*, p. 54f.

14 Kruk, *The Last Days*, 18.10.1942, p. 381.

15 See Schroeter, *Worte*, p. 144.

16 E.g., Order no. 22, 6.12.1941, Police Chief Gens, concerning compulsory labelling, the prohibition of gatherings, and the ban on leaving the ghetto without permission or attempting to approach the ghetto gates, reprinted in Kruk, *The Last Days*, 22.12.1941, p. 136; Order no. 26, 18.12.1941, Police Chief Gens, order to move into allocated housing, reprinted in Kruk, *The Last Days*, 12.12.1941, p. 136.

17 Kruk, *The Last Days*, 22.12.1941, p. 135.

18 Trunk, *Judenrat*, p. 12; Kruk, *The Last Days*, 11 and 12.7.1942, pp. 326–8.

19 Balberyszski, *Stronger Than Iron*, p. 201.

20 ŻIH, RING I/702, *Gazeta Żydowska* no. 1, 3.1.1941. "Hygiene" maintenance soon morphed into "disease control." See, e.g., ŻIH, Judenraty, RG 221/1 or 2 (archive discrepancy), "Der Jüdische Wohnbezirk in Warschau (Zahlen und Tatsachen)," June 1942, fol. 7.

21 See, e.g., ŻIH, 252. RING I/14, *Rozkaz* no. 43, 24.2.1940, communication of instructions for the Order Service with regard to road traffic and street trading, signed Szeryński, fol. 26; e.g., IPN, BU 165, 367/A, OS activity report, 9.1.1942, fol. 205; ibid., 16.1.1942, fol. 194. On the concerns regarding hygiene, see Adler, *In the Warsaw Ghetto*, p. 123.

22 Feuchert, *Chronik* 1941, 27–31.5.1941, p. 154.

23 For Warsaw, see Adler, *In the Warsaw Ghetto*, p. 78. For Lodz, see Feuchert, *Chronik* 1941, 7.4.1941, p. 116; also Löw, *Juden im Getto*, p. 107. For Vilna, see duties of Police Chief Gens as defined by District Commissar Murer, reprinted in Kruk, *The Last Days*, 29.4.1942, p. 274.

24 USHMM, RG 05.008, 6/73, orders issued to the Eldest of the Jews, author unknown, 16.7.1940, fol. 109. These referred specifically to the

immediate closure of the gates on the Hohensteiner Street between the Deutschlandplatz and the Baluter Ring, which were henceforth to be opened only to allow the passage of vehicles (ibid.).

25 IPN, BU 165/367/A, Getto w Warszawie, Kopie raportów Kierownika Służby Porządkowej, 1942, fol. 207, Report on scheduled OS activities for 8.1.1942.

26 Duties of Police Chief Gens as defined by District Commissar Murer, reprinted in Kruk, *The Last Days*, 29.4.1942, p. 274.

27 For Lodz, see Feuchert, *Chronik* 1941, 7.4.1941, "Organisation des Ordnungsdienstes," p. 115f. and Löw, *Juden im Getto*, p. 108; for Vilna, see, e.g., Kruk, *The Last Days*, 28.12.1941, p. 144.

28 See Löw, *Juden im Getto*, p. 107. For Warsaw, see the rules for the use of rubber batons by OS staff: ZIH, 251. RING I/227.

29 ŻIH, RING I/702, *Gazeta Żydowska* no. 65, 3.6.1942.

30 Feuchert, *Chronik* 1941, 7.4.1941, "Organisation des Ordnungsdienstes," p. 115f. Serious cases were to be referred to the Order Service investigation department and ruled on in consultation with the ghetto public prosecutor.

31 For Warsaw, see Engelking and Leociak, *Warsaw Ghetto*, p. 200. In the case of Lodz and Vilna, this is also apparent from arrest warrants detailing punishments of varying severity for similar offences.

32 As we shall see, the German occupiers often secured access to prisoners where the offence affected German core interests. This practice varied from case to case, however.

33 IPN, BU 165/367/A, report on OS activity scheduled for 9.1.1942, fol. 205a. OS staff were often dispatched to the Zamenhof Street intersection with Miła Street on special operations, in particular for the prevention of robberies after dark. IPN, BU 165, 367/A, report of 13.1.1942, fol. 200; 10.1.1942, fol. 204a.

34 For a detailed account of the procedure in Warsaw, see Adler, *In the Warsaw Ghetto*, p. 77ff., ŻIH, RING I/702, *Gazeta Żydowska* no. 65, 3.6.1942.

35 Feuchert, *Chronik* 1941, 7.4.1941, "Organisation des Ordnungsdienstes," p. 115. See Löw, *Juden im Getto*, p. 107.

36 This was exemplified by a murder case tried before the ghetto court in June 1942. Although the occupiers monitored the proceedings and the execution of the internally imposed death penalty, they did not intervene.

37 My purpose here is not to provide an exhaustive list, but rather to highlight examples of institutions which were either typical or fulfilled a key function in the ghetto's internal legal sphere.

38 Feuchert, *Chronik* 1941, 7.4.1941, "Organisation des Ordnungsdienstes," p. 116; ŻIH, RG 05/303, 26.6.1941, proclamation re establishment of *Sonderkommando*, fols. 1 & 2.

39 See Löw, *Juden im Getto*, p. 108.

40 See Löw,"Ordnungsdienst," p. 165f., Rubin, *Żydzi w Łodzi*, p. 233.

41 For an example, see Feuchert, *Chronik* 1943, April 1943, p. 154: conviction by the *Sonderabteilung* for the theft of a sack of sago (a thickening agent); Feuchert, *Chronik* 1943, "Festnahmen durch die Untersuchungskanzlei der Sonderabteilung," 11–20.4.1943, p. 172. On the department's increasing influence on court proceedings, see Feuchert, *Chronik* 1943, 14.3.1943, p. 98.

42 Engelking and Leociak, *Warsaw Ghetto*, pp. 201f., 216.

43 IPN, OS activity report, 18.1.1942, fol. 190. See also Report of 22.1.1942, fol. 184: execution of household bathroom inspections in cooperation with the health department; blockading of buildings with suspected cases of typhus.

44 For more detail, see the report in the *Geto-Tsaytung* regarding the creation of a sanitary commission to contain hygiene risks. APŁ, 278/1076, *Geto-Tsaytung* no. 8, 25.4.1941, p. 2.

45 Feuchert, *Chronik* 1941, 24.4.1941, p. 132; ibid., 7.4.1941, p. 116.

46 Ibid., 24.4.1941, p. 132.

47 See, e.g., Feuchert, *Chronik* 1943, 27.7.1941, p. 199.

48 Kruk, *The Last Days*, 5.12.1942, p. 423; ibid., 14.12.1942, p. 427.

49 Ibid.

50 Ibid., 5.12.1942, p. 423.

51 Ibid., 20.12.1942, p. 437.

52 YIVO, RG 223/318.9, fol. 322, 1, report by the labour police to the chief of police.

53 See Trunk, *Judenrat*, p. 501.

54 Feuchert, *Chronik* 1942, 7.10.1942, p. 494 and 7.11.1942, p. 540. In larger apartment buildings, a room was made available for this purpose. Feuchert, *Chronik* 1942, p. 494. In the case of the Warsaw ghetto, Adler writes of plans for a women's department within the Order Service to help combat prostitution (*In the Warsaw Ghetto*, p. 68).

55 Feuchert, *Chronik* 1942, 7.11.1942, p. 540; ibid., 5.12.1942, p. 588f.

56 Ibid., 23.11.1942, p. 568f.; ibid., 26.11.1942, p. 577.

57 Feuchert, *Chronik* 1943, 3.3.1943, p. 75. An entry in the Chronicle records an increase in street trading following the department's dissolution (15–21.3.1943, p. 118). On the redistribution to other departments, see ibid., 4.4.1943, p. 134.

58 Adler, *In the Warsaw Ghetto*, p. 116f.; Passenstein, "Szmugiel," pp. 63–4.

59 Adler, *In the Warsaw Ghetto*, p. 116f.; see also Gombiński, *Wspomnienia*, p. 57f.

60 See Trunk, *Łódź Ghetto*, p. 357, n. 343.

61 Adler, *In the Warsaw Ghetto*, p. 68.

62 Mostowicz, "Alltagsleben im Getto," p. 44.

63 YIVO, RG 225/32.3, 21–9.5.1942. See also the entry by Ringelblum: Kronika getta warszawskiego, wrzesień 1939–styczeń 1943, Warszawa 1983, p. 230, February 1941, quoted in Engelking and Grabowski, *Żydów łamiących*,

p. 115. Mary Berg cites the Café Hirschfeld as a meeting place (*Warsaw Ghetto*, p. 89). Tadeusz Szymel writes in his memoirs that prostitutes from the whole Warsaw district were concentrated in the ghetto. YVA, E/258, Tadeusz Szymel, *Pamiętnik*, k. 87.

64 Berg, *Warsaw Ghetto*, entry of 22.12.1940, p. 42. The unknown author of an activity report from the Lodz ghetto writes: "As inhabitants of Eastern Europe, such an administrative institution was new to us." ŻIH, RG 205/304, author and date unknown, fol. 1.

65 Here in the sense of "formations." See Feuchert, *Chronik* 1941, p. 367, n. 29.

66 Annex to Daily Chronicle entry no. 49, 28.2.1941, in Feuchert, *Chronik* 1941, p. 72.

67 Adler was formally responsible for all legal matters within the OS; most of these related to administrative law, and a few to civil law. The statutes were approved at a meeting attended by other high-level OS functionaries, following the submission of various drafts. In special cases, approval by the Jewish Council chairman and consultation with other Council departments were required. Adler, *In the Warsaw Ghetto*, pp. 70, 199f.

68 Ibid., pp. 144, 174.

69 Ibid., p. 144.

70 See Engelking and Leociak, *Warsaw Ghetto*, p. 191.

71 ŻIH, 645. RING I/233. The date of writing cannot be ascertained, but was probably after the foundation of the OS in October 1940.

72 This was to consist of: "1. The head of the supervisory board as a delegate of the Jewish Council, 2. The head of the Order Service, 3. A person unconnected with either the OS or the Jewish Council who commands ethical and moral authority, 4. An OS discipline spokesperson, 5. A district functionary or sub-district functionary appointed by the head of the OS." ŻIH, 645. RING I/233.

73 ŻIH, 645. RING I/233, after October 1940.

74 See Engelking and Leociak, *Warsaw Ghetto*, p. 197.

75 ŻIH, 251. RING I/227, official regulations of the OS in Warsaw, 1.6.1942.

76 ŻIH, RG 205/219, 1.5.1940, Rumkowski's decree regarding the establishment of the Order Service, fol. 80. [English translation in Trunk, *Łódź Ghetto*, p. 70.]

77 ŻIH, RG 205/219, 1.5.1940.

78 Rumkowski argued, conversely, that their actions continued to serve the interests of the ghetto community, on the assumption that the entire community would be murdered by the Germans if he refused to surrender those "unfit for work."

79 Feuchert, *Chronik* 1943, 28.2.1943, special report on the occasion of the Order Service's third anniversary celebration, p. 66f.

80 Ibid., p. 67.

81 See Arad, *Ghetto in Flames*, p. 127.
82 Balberyszski, *Stronger Than Iron*, p. 199.
83 See Engelking and Leociak, *Warsaw Ghetto*, p. 193.
84 Adler, *In the Warsaw Ghetto*, p. 12. Before an appointment could be approved, references had to be obtained from two individuals from the relevant district. See Engelking and Leociak, *Warsaw Ghetto*, p. 193.
85 Adler, *In the Warsaw Ghetto*, p. 12. In Warsaw, even functionaries with former positions of responsibility were not immune from accusations of a "criminal past," but often used their influence and connections to prevent such suspicions from being investigated (ibid., p. 51).
86 Ibid., p. 13.
87 Gombiński, *Wspomnenia*, pp. 191, 208. See Szymańska-Smolkin, "Fateful Decisions," 78f.
88 Kruk, *The Last Days*, 14.12.1942, p. 428
89 Poznański, *Tagebuch*, 2.6.1943, p. 107.
90 Ibid.
91 Mentioned briefly by Engelking and Leociak, *Warsaw Ghetto*, p. 216; for more detail, see Adler, *In the Warsaw Ghetto*, p. 45f.
92 Ibid., p. 70.
93 One instance, which resulted in the suspension of an OS officer, is described by Adler (ibid., p. 46).
94 Ibid., p. 87.
95 Ibid., p. 95. On the effort to conceal disciplinary cases from the Germans, see also ibid., p. 45.
96 See Löw, *Juden im Getto*, p. 111f.
97 USHMM, RG 15.083, 38/118, Rumkowski to the chief cashier's office, 25.7.1941, fol. 132. Similarly, ibid., fols. 135, 136, 137, 138 (100 marks), 139 (50 marks), 140 (all in July 1941). See also USHMM, RG 15.083, 38/118, Rumkowski to the investigation department, 23.7.1941, fol. 483.
98 See, e.g., Feuchert, *Chronik* 1941, 20.1.1941, p. 33f.: sentencing of a policeman to four months' hard labour for the theft of some wood which he had been tasked with guarding.
99 Feuchert, *Chronik* 1941, 6.4.1941, p. 110.
100 See, e.g., Feuchert, *Chronik* 1943, 8–14.3.1943, inspection of police officers by head of department and subsequent custodial sentences on grounds of "neglect of duty" (p. 106ff.); USHMM RG 15.083, 38/119, Rumkowski to the chairman of the court, 19.8.1941, fol. 26: suspension of OS officer Awid Gender by Rumkowski for theft of timber from demolition site.
101 ŻIH, RG 205/306, *Sonderabteilung* chief Grossbart to OS Guard of German Criminal Police, 13.11.1942, fols. 4 and 5. See also the imprecise wording of the first report on the case: ŻIH, RG 205/306, report by senior OS functionary Lewin, 12.11.1942, fol. 3.

102 This was true of the Biednak case: ŻIH, RG 205/306, *Sonderabteilung* chief
   Grossbart to OS Guard of German Criminal Police, 13.11.1942, fol. 5. How
   common this practice was is hard to determine from the available source
   material. For other suspensions from duty, see ŻIH, RG 205/307, OS
   personnel departments: suspension following court ruling, 6.12.1942,
   fols. 2 and 3; ŻIH, RG 205/302, OS Orders of the Day, 15.1.1943, Order of
   the Day no. 77, fol. 12.

103 YIVO, RG 223/318.8, 3.2.1942, fols. 448, 449, 450: "Police officers Sacker,
   Dawidowski, and Chajet have been sentenced to a forty-eight-hour
   disciplinary penalty, and are required to report to the detention centre
   immediately in order to serve their sentence."

104 YIVO, RG 223/318.6, note of 7.1.1942, fol. 338: police officers sentenced
   to twelve hours' imprisonment for "disobedient conduct"; YIVO,
   RG 223/318, police chief representative to head of detention centre,
   23.11.1941: "police officer Binimowitsch, Morduch has been sentenced to
   a disciplinary penalty of seven days' imprisonment for 'irregular conduct
   on duty'. He begins his sentence with immediate effect."

105 YIVO, RG 223/318.7, 14.1.1942, fol. 368; YIVO, RG 223/318.7, 15.1.1942,
   fol. 376.

106 YIVO, RG 223/318.6, note of 9.1.1942, fol. 342.

107 USHMM, 1999.A.0105, 4/64, head of police department to commander
   of Police Station I, 16.4.1942, fol. 48; see also USHMM, 1999.A.0105, 4/63
   (64), 24.4.1942, fol. 167: "severe reprimand for impertinent conduct at a
   concert."

108 USHMM,1999.A.0105, 4/64, chief of police to police station commanders,
   criminal department; gate guard, registration office, 19.7.1942. The police
   court is also mentioned by Balberyszski, without further details of its
   organization (*Stronger Than Iron*, p. 200). Presumably it was another
   disciplinary department within the Jewish Police, possibly a "judicial
   administration section," as already mentioned in February 1942. YIVO RG
   223/318.8, fol. 422 ghetto police judicial administration section, 7.II.1942.

109 Kruk, *The Last Days*, 12.5.1943, p. 538.

110 Sutzkever, *Wilner Ghetto*, p. 191.

111 Adler, *In the Warsaw Ghetto*, p. 93.

112 Ibid., p. 77

113 Ibid., p. 259. The ensuing dispute settlement procedures were
   professionalized over time with the introduction of so-called instructors
   at OS police stations. For more detail, see ibid., pp. 110 and 7; AR I/
   PH/23–3–2: "Contents of a Conversation with a Member of the Order
   Police," 2.5.1942, p. 316, in Kermish, *To Live with Honor*; Gombiński,
   Wspomnienia, p. 51. Since the instructors' role was effectively a judicial
   one, they are discussed in more detail in chapter 4, "The Ghetto Courts."

114 Adler, *In the Warsaw Ghetto*, pp. 77, 259.

115 ŻIH, RING I/702, *Gazeta Żydowska* no. 65, 3.6.1942.

116 See Löw, *Juden im Getto*, p. 108; Trunk, *Judenrat*, p. 181f.

117 See, e.g., the blackmail case USHMM, RG 05.008, 27/64, Criminal Police to the Eldest of the Jews, Order Service Police, 18.11.1940, fol. 322. Later on, such cases were referred directly to the ghetto court.

118 These were the instructions issued by two officers of the German Criminal Police on handing over the arrested subject to a member of the OS. USHMM, RG 05.008, 27/64, extract from the night shift report of 23/24.9.1940 for OS Police Station I, fol. 337.

119 Ibid.

120 USHMM, RG 05.008, 25/59, Order Service chief to State Criminal Police, Ghetto *Sonderkommando*, 17.12.1940, fol. 64, 65. For a similar instance, see, e.g., USHMM, RG 05.008, 25/59, Eldest of the Jews, Order Service chief to State Criminal Police, Ghetto *Sonderkommando*, 14.12.1940, fol. 64: "In accordance with your letter of 13.12.1940, I have sentenced the subjects (Jakubowicz and Windel) held at my detention premises at your department's disposal to three months' imprisonment ... They will be transferred from the detention facilities of Stations I and II to the Central Prison ... to begin their sentences with immediate effect."

121 USHMM, RG 05.008, 27/64, 18.11.1940, Criminal Police to the Eldest of the Jews, Order Service Police, fol. 322.

122 USHMM, RG 05.008, 25/59, Order Service chief to State Criminal Police, Ghetto *Sonderkommando*, 10.12.1940, fol. 66: Wolf Seherer punished for theft; transferred from detention premises of OS Police Station I to central prison.

123 USHMM, RG 05.008, 27/64, Order Service Investigation Department report, 24.6.1942, fol. 53f.; USHMM, RG 05.008, 27/64, verdict of the court of the Eldest of the Jews re Adler, Lubliński, Tułob, Szuf, 18.8.1942, fol. 47ff.

124 USHMM, RG 05.008, 27/64, chairman of the court to ghetto criminal investigation department, 12.8.1942, fol. 51; USHMM, RG 05.008, 27/64, notification of Ghetto Commissariat 16.9.1942, fol. 52. An endorsement on the OS report indicates that the Gestapo had been notified of the case on 30.7.1942. USHMM, RG 05.008, 27/64, Order Service investigation department report, 24.6.1942, fol. 54.

125 According to a report forwarded by the German Criminal Police to the district governor in Lodz. USHMM, RG 05.008, 25/59, ghetto criminal police department to the district governor in Lodz, 22.9.1941, fol. 94.

126 USHMM, RG 05.008, 25/59, superintendent of OS Police Station III to Criminal Police *Sonderkommando*, notification subject in OS detention at the disposal of the Criminal Police, 3.9.1941, fol. 103.

127 USHMM, RG 05.008, 25/59, fol. 68ff., specifically fols. 74, 75.

128 APŁ, 278/1011, registration card, undated. See Feuchert, *Chronik* 1941, September 1941, pp. 221, 407.
129 Feuchert, *Chronik* 1942, July 1942, p. 374. Here, too, the victim had been robbed of her food and money.
130 Feuchert, *Chronik* 1942, 22.7.1942, p. 380. The victim's daughter initially suspected a twenty-two-year-old female worker who had helped her mother tidy the apartment; she was later released as innocent, however (ibid.).
131 USHMM, RG. 05.008, 27/64, OS chief to ghetto public prosecutor regarding robbery of 25.7.1942, 29.7.1942, fol. 65. "Gas kitchens" were private kitchens in homes with a gas supply whose owners rented them out to other ghetto residents. After a while, Rumkowski introduced formal "hire" charges and taxed the owners, until the kitchens were eventually incorporated into the ghetto administration. For more detail, see Feuchert, *Chronik* 1941, p. 384, n. 21.
132 USHMM, RG. 05.008, 27/64, OS chief to State Criminal Police, Ghetto *Sonderkommando*, 31.7.1942, fol. 66.
133 Ibid.
134 According to a handwritten note: USHMM, RG. 05.008, 27/64, 7.9.1942, Ghetto Commissariat, decision of 3.8.1942, fol. 67.
135 Kruk, *The Last Days*, 25.9.1941, p. 118; Balberyszski, *Stronger Than Iron*, p. 200.
136 On this case, see Arad, *Ghetto in Flames*, p. 292, and Kruk, *The Last Days*, 3.6.1942, p. 300.
137 E.g., Feuchert, *Chronik* 1941, 12.1.1941, p. 20: "Crime statistics. Today's bulletin from the Order Service precincts recorded twelve thefts and six miscellaneous other offences."
138 Feuchert, *Chronik* 1942, 8.5.1942, p. 163: OS suicide reports.
139 Ibid., OS bulletin, 27.5.1942, p. 235.
140 Ibid., OS bulletin, 1.6.1942, p. 257; ibid., OS bulletin, 3.6.1942, p. 265.
141 E.g., Feuchert, *Chronik* 1941, 13.1.1941, p. 24: "Criminal statistics. Today's police reports recorded eighteen thefts. The most commonly stolen item is wood"; Feuchert, *Chronik* 1942, arrests 2.11.1942, p. 533; also in the recorded court rulings: Feuchert, *Chronik* 1943, judicial system: 10.5.1943, p. 199; courtroom: proceedings of 29.6.1943, p. 292.
142 Feuchert, *Chronik* 1942, 5.5.1942, p. 148: "Arrests: 0," "an exceptional day." "The lull in the crime figures observed by the security authorities in March was concurrent with the resettlements" (ibid., p. 76).
143 See, e.g., apprehension of community officials for playing cards while under house arrest on Rumkowski's orders: Feuchert, *Chronik* 1941, 7–9.6.1941, p. 161.
144 Categories in 1944 included theft, smuggling, resistance, and miscellaneous. USHMM, RG 05.008, 27/65, bulletin for 26–7.4.1944, signed OS chief Rozenblatt, fol. 167; additionally, under Arrests: "Entering or leaving the

ghetto without authorization." USHMM, RG 05.008, 27/66, OS chief to
Criminal Police; summary of criminal offences from 1–31.3.1944, fol. 4.

145 IPN, BU 165/367/A, OS activity reports.

146 See, e.g., the reports on a series of robberies in the *Gazeta Żydowska*: ŻIH,
RING I/702, *Gazeta Żydowska* no. 45, 6.6.1941, p. 6.

147 It should be noted in this connection that German and Yiddish courses
were organized within the ghetto for Jewish Police officers. USHMM,
1999. A. 0105, 4/64, date unknown, fol. 82.

148 The offences listed here do not cover the whole spectrum of activities
punished under the arrest warrants. Rather, I have concentrated on those
that afford particular insights into the varying definitions, or that differ
from the crime definitions in the other ghettos, and/or that reflect the
specific conditions of the Vilna ghetto.

149 YIVO, RG 223/318.7, 15.1.1942, fol. 374: "maltreatment of a woman";
twenty-four hours' detention; YIVO, RG 223/318.7, 22.1.1942, fol. 397:
brawl; eight hours' detention.

150 YIVO, RG 223/318, gate guard commander to head of prison, 22.11.1941,
fol. 19. Similarly YIVO, RG 223/318.1, 28.11.1941, fol. 96; YIVO, RG
223/318.2, 1.12.1941, fol. 110; YIVO, RG 223/318.3, 9.12.1941, fol. 168.

151 YIVO, RG 223/318.3, 11.12.1941, fol. 181; YIVO, RG 223/318.4, 14.12.1941,
fol. 222; YIVO, RG 223/318.5, gate guard to head of detention facility,
18.12.1941, fol. 257.

152 YIVO, RG 223/318.3, 11.12.1941, fol. 189, 190. Similarly YIVO, RG
223/318.3, 5.12.1941, fol. 153; YIVO, RG 223/318.3, 6.12.1941, fol. 159;
GFH, 1571, Registry Holdings 01622, fol. 4320, 17.8.1942; GFH, 1571,
Registry Holdings 01622, 1.8.1942, fol. 4232.

153 USHMM, 1999.A.0105, 2/33, fol. 685, YIVO, RG 223/318.9, 10.2.1942, fol. 487.

154 Duties of Chief of Police Gens as defined by District Commissar Murer,
reprinted in Kruk, *The Last Days*, 29.4.1942, p. 274.

155 GFH, 1575/Registry Holdings 1215, arrest warrant no. 4319.

156 E.g., Kruk, *The Last Days*, 4.7.1942, p. 318.

157 Ibid., 8.5.1942, p. 287.

158 Ibid., 5.2.1942, p. 193.

159 Ibid., 15.6.1942, p. 307; ibid., 25.7.1942, p. 337.

160 USHMM, 1999.A.0105, 4/63 (64), 29. 4. 1942, fol. 133; USHMM,
1999.A.0105, 4/63 (64), chief of police to police department, 26.3.1942,
fol. 265; GFH, Collections Section, 03960/2369, 28.11.1942.

161 USHMM, 1999.A.0105, 4/64, 6.5.1942, fol. 102: order issued by Gens to the
Jewish Police to arrest "fit for work" men who resisted the call to labour.

162 USHMM, 1999.A.0105, 4/63 (64), chief of police to police department,
26.3.1942, fol. 265: "failure to report for work" incurred five days'
detention or a fine of 10 reichsmarks.

163 Kruk, *The Last Days*, 24.5.1943, p. 549.

164 The arrested subjects were subsequently released following pressure from relatives who threatened to storm the ghetto prison. See Arad, *Ghetto in Flames*, p. 404f.

165 Collections Section, 554, *Geto-Yedies* no. 15, 30.11.1942, fol. 1.

166 USHMM, 1999.A.0105, 3/63, fol. 347: circulation of untrue information is a punishable offence (48 hours' detention); serious cases to be tried in court.

167 Proclamation no. 30, Vilna chief of police, 5.1.1942, reprinted in Kruk, *The Last Days*, 7.1.1942, p. 163f.; ibid., 18.11.1942, p. 416.

168 USHMM, 1999.A.0105, 2/33, fol. 472; USHMM, 1999.A.0105, 3/62, fol. 6.; USHMM, 1999.A.0105, 4/63, fol. 398; GFH, 3960, Collection Section, 03960, 9.11.1942.

169 YIVO, RG 223/318.2, 2.11.1941, fol. 124.

170 USHMM, 1999.A.0105, 7/89, fol. 718.

171 YIVO, RG 223/318.1, 24.11.1941, fol. 61; RG 223/318.2, 2. 12. 1941, fol. 138 (6 hours' detention), RG 223/318.2, 7.12.1941, fol. 162 (forty-eight hours' detention).

172 USHMM, 1999.A.0105, 4/64, fol. 378 (two days' detention and two-reichsmark fine.).

173 See, e.g., Trunk, *Judenrat*, p. 498ff.; for Warsaw, see Engelking and Leociak, *Warsaw Ghetto*, p. 207ff.

174 For the Lodz ghetto, see, e.g., Eichenbaum, "A Memorial for Bronia," and the Chronicle entry for November 1941, which testifies to the "friendliness" and "helpfulness" of OS personnel towards new arrivals. See Feuchert, *Chronik* 1941, 17.11.1941, p. 266f; for the Warsaw ghetto, see Engelking and Leociak, *Warsaw Ghetto*, p. 206.

175 For a categorization of these activities, see, e.g., Weiss, "The Relations," p. 211; Trunk, *Judenrat*, p. 478ff.

4 The Ghetto Courts

1 Adler, *In the Warsaw Ghetto*, p. 135 [translation of original adjusted by Sharon Howe].

2 See Löw, *Juden im Getto*, p. 112. Trunk dates the establishment of the court to June 1940. See Trunk, *Judenrat*, p. 182, and Trunk, *Łódź Ghetto*, p. 44f. As Löw rightly points out, however, this does not tally with the sources. See Löw, *Juden im Getto*, p. 112, n. 57.

3 See ibid., p. 112. Mention of Gestapo approval: USHMM, RG 15.083, 5/24, Rumkowski to the Lodz Criminal Police office, 21.11.1940, fol. 108.

4 Ibid., fol. 107. It is notable that the term *Staatsanwalt* (public or state prosecutor) came to be used in the ghetto even though the Jewish Council was not a state institution. The prosecutor did have the authority to initiate criminal investigations within the ghetto domain, however.

5 Ibid. For more detail, see also Trunk, *Judenrat*, p. 182, and Löw, *Juden im Getto*, p. 113.

6 See Trunk, *Judenrat*, p. 182; Löw, *Juden im Getto*, p. 112f., and Feuchert, *Chronik* 1941, 24.12.1941, p. 326.

7 USHMM, RG 15.083, 38/118, Rumkowski to Neftalin, 22.7.1941, fol. 33. See also Löw, *Juden im Getto*, p. 113.

8 Ascertainable from, e.g., USHMM, RG 05.008, 27/64, 20.11.1940, fol. 323: central prison governor's list of names and offences of prisoners convicted by the Jewish Council court at the instigation of the Criminal Police.

9 Feuchert, *Chronik* 1941, 9.3.1941, p. 87. On the composition of the court and the sentences imposed, see GFH, Collections Section, 271, report on session of 14.3.1941.

10 Feuchert, *Chronik* 1941, p. 87; GFH, Collections Section, 271, report on session of 14.3.1941, fol. 1.

11 Feuchert, *Chronik* 1941, 29.4.1941, p. 137.

12 APŁ, 278/1076, *Geto-Tsaytung* no. 11–12, 30.5.1941, p. 5.

13 APŁ, 278/1076, *Geto-Tsaytung* no. 14, 15.7.1941, p. 1. Also Feuchert, *Chronik* 1941, 1–5.7.1941, p. 170.

14 Ibid.

15 See, e.g., the convictions of 4 September 1941 listed in the Chronicle. Examples include a warehouse worker sentenced to six months' imprisonment for unlawfully issuing ten kilograms of potatoes to the warehouse manager, and a factory caretaker sentenced to three months' imprisonment for forging tokens and fraudulently claiming twenty lunches. Feuchert, *Chronik* 1941, 4.9.1941, p. 233f.

16 Adler, *In the Warsaw Ghetto*, p. 140f.

17 Czerniaków, *Warsaw Diary*, 15.8.1940, p. 185. There are no references in the secondary literature to this early German rejection of Jewish judicial authorities, but it is quite likely that Czerniaków endeavoured to establish them. One entry in his diary dated 8 July 1940 may refer to cases within the community that he hoped to be able to settle by this means: "Besides, all these Jewish complaints. They do not want to make payments to the Community, yet they keep demanding that I intervene on their behalf, be it in trivial private matters or in serious predicaments. And when my efforts fail, or result in delay, they blame me without end as if the outcome depended on me" (ibid., p. 172).

18 The instructors were controversial within the OS, being rejected by Szeryński, for example. They played a particularly important role in the development phase of the service, but became increasingly irrelevant thereafter. ŻIH, 435. RING I/100, Zygmunt Millet, dated after April 1941.

19 Adler, *In the Warsaw Ghetto*, pp. 110 and 7. AR I/PH/23–3–2: Contents of a Conversation with a Member of the Order Police, 2.5.1942, in Kermish, *To Live with Honor*, p. 316.

20 Kermish, *To Live with Honor*, 7. AR I/PH/23–3–2: Contents of a
Conversation with a Member of the Order Police, 2.5.1942, in Kermish, *To
Live with Honor*, p. 316. On the creation of the office of instructor, see also
ŻIH, 435. RING I/100, Zygmunt Millet, dated after April 1941.

21 Adler, *In the Warsaw Ghetto*, p. 141.

22 Ibid., p. 140.

23 The exact inauguration date of the legal department cannot be ascertained.
A key figure in its development was Bołeslaw Rozensztat, who was
also president of the appeal court for disciplinary matters. The legal
department deputed two employees to the courts, with Rozensztat
reserving the right to appoint court members. Ibid., p. 156ff.

24 These occurred frequently, owing to the system whereby a main tenant
rented the building from the Jewish Council and sublet the individual
apartments or rooms in turn to the often numerous subtentants. ŻIH,
RING I/702, *Gazeta Żydowska* no. 47, 13.6.1941, p. 8.

25 The exact inauguration date of the arbitration tribunal is unclear. The fact
that the *Gazeta Żydowska* outlined its powers on 13 June 1941, advising
ghetto residents which cases they could bring before it, indicates that it
cannot have been much earlier than June 1941. ŻIH, RING I/702, *Gazeta
Żydowska* no. 47, 13.6.1941, p. 8.

26 See Sakowska, *Menschen im Ghetto*, p. 183. An account of this role is given,
e.g., by the diarist Perec Opoczyński, *Reportaże*, p. 87ff.

27 Ibid., p. 96f.

28 Early February 1942: Arad, *Ghetto in Flames*, p. 291; 28.2.1942: Trunk,
Judenrat, p. 181; 15.11.1941: Kruk, *The Last Days*, 6.5.1942, p. 282; on
the trials, ibid., 10.2.1942, p. 197; also YIVO, RG 223/318.5, verdict of
14.12.1941, fol. 286, 287; YIVO, RG 223/318.6, court ruling of 15.1.1942, fol.
312. Arad and Trunk may have conflated the court's establishment with
the additional foundation of a public initiative by lawyers in the ghetto. It
is also conceivable that a court already existed prior to German approval
that was not officially recognized until February 1942. Kruk, *The Last Days*,
10.2.1942, p. 197.

29 On the appeal court, see Arad, *Ghetto in Flames*, p. 291. On the appointment
of the judges, see Kruk, *The Last Days*, 10.8.1942, p. 342; YIVO, RG
223/325a (proclamation of 6.8.1942). The civil court personnel consisted of
the chairman, Yisrael Kaplan, and judicial officers Solomon Deul, Avrom
Notes, Shimen Markus, Nosn Gavenda, and Abrasha Chwojnik; the appeal
court was composed of the chairman, Shabse Milkanowicki, along with
Binyomin Srolowicz, Grisza Jaszuński, and Daniel Katzenelson, plus
secretaries Efromczyk and Ovsey Bobrovski.

30 YIVO, RG 223/318.5, fol. 249–52. In the report, dated 18.12.1941, the chief
of police ordered six arrested subjects to be held in custody pending the
decision of the Jewish Council summary court.

31 See Porat, "The Justice System," p. 61; Arad, *Ghetto in Flames*, p. 291.
32 See ibid.
33 See ibid., p. 291; Kruk, *The Last Days*, pp. 162, 165, 343f., 358, 367f. Porat sees the founding of this initiative as an expression of the ghetto residents' lack of trust in Vilna's Jewish Council and Jewish Police ("The Justice System," p. 60).
34 See Trunk, *Judenrat*, p. 181; YIVO, RG 223/331.
35 See Trunk, *Judenrat*, p. 183f.
36 A case of smuggling was forwarded by the German authorities to the ghetto court for investigation for the first time in January 1941, for example, even though smuggling offences fell squarely within their remit. Feuchert, *Chronik* 1941, 23.1.1941, p. 39.
37 In April 1941, a resident named Moszek Lajb Czosnek had murdered his wife and son. Feuchert, *Chronik* 1941, 22.4.1941, p. 131.
38 Ibid.
39 The death certificate issued by Poznań registry office on 23 October 1941 testifies to the fact that Czosnek's death sentence was carried out at Poznań prison on Młynarska Street on 5 August 1941. APŁ, 278/1011, Feuchert, *Chronik* 1941, p. 438, n. 96.
40 Ibid., 4.8.1941, p. 210. In the case of murder and harm to the German Reich, German-imposed death sentences were, however, incontestable (ibid., p. 210). For more detail, see also Löw, *Juden im Getto*, p. 113.
41 The latter assumption is supported by the absence of any German investigation into why the ghetto court failed to impose a single death sentence at any point during its existence. Feuchert, *Chronik* 1941, p. 405, n. 7.
42 ŻIH, RG 302/129, Pamiętnik Józefa Rode.
43 Adler failed to get his suggestion past the other OS functionaries, however. On this discussion, see Adler, *In the Warsaw Ghetto*, p. 179f.
44 The ghetto residents Rajman, Holts, and Glezer had attempted to assault and rob the gold dealer Feigenbaum. Rajman planned to use the stolen money to obtain a pass in order to escape an impending German operation. Kruk, *The Last Days*, 11.2.1942, p. 200f.
45 From January to June 1942, Hering acted as a liaison officer, coordinating the cooperation between the Gestapo and a Lithuanian special unit. Arad, *Ghetto in Flames*, p. 90.
46 Kruk, *The Last Days*, 11.2.1942, p. 200f. Arad, by contrast, states that the Germans took the convicts from the ghetto prison, but without specifying a source. Since his remarks regarding the court are based on Kruk, however, the latter's version of events seems more plausible.
47 Kruk, *The Last Days*, 11.2.1942, p. 200f.
48 Ibid., 4.6.1942, p. 300, and Kruk, "Sechs Galgen im Wilner Ghetto: Eine literarische Kriminalchronik des Wilner Ghettos," in *The Last Days*, p. 618f.

49 Feuchert, *Chronik* 1943, 9.9.1943, p. 428.
50 The case concerned scraps of leather which the accused had intended to use for shoelaces. Feuchert, *Chronik* 1943, 13.9.1943, p. 435.
51 Ibid.
52 Adler, *In the Warsaw Ghetto*, p. 151. This was a fate common to many Jewish lawyers, who were denied access to such positions in pre-war Poland.
53 YIVO, RG 241/881, fol. 829 (Mojżesz Prachownik, born 1910). In 1942, he was transferred to the newly founded juvenile court.
54 Feuchert, *Chronik* 1941, November 1941, p. 263, and under "Kitz M.B. Dr." in the *Getto-Enzyklopädie*, 1939–44, ŻIH, RG 205, 349, fol. 204.
55 Kruk, *The Last Days*, 29.10.1942, p. 394.
56 Ibid., p. 618.
57 Romana (Romea) Byteńska had studied law at the University of Warsaw and worked within the judiciary in Lodz. Poznański, *Tagebuch*, p. 98, n. 44; see also ŻIH, *Getto-Enzyklopädie*, entry no. 2836, Byteńska, Romea.
58 Regina Rumkowska, born 2 May 1907 in Lodz, had long been among the defence lawyers listed at the ghetto court. In September 1943, Rumkowski asked the chairman of the court, Szaja-Stanisław Jacobson, whether there were any concerns regarding his wife's assumption of the defence. Jacobson replied that there were none, and Rumkowska duly served as defence counsel in a rape case against the labourer Ordynans. Feuchert, *Chronik* 1943, 24.9.1943, p. 458. See also the entry of 19.11.1943, ibid., p. 570 (divorce cases) and report of 24.9.1943.
59 Feuchert, *Chronik* 1941, 2.12.1941, p. 280.
60 Kruk, *The Last Days*, 9.9.1942, p. 353.
61 Ibid.
62 Ibid.
63 Adler, *In the Warsaw Ghetto*, p. 153.
64 Ibid., p. 14
65 Feuchert, *Chronik* 1941, 2.12.1941, p. 281.
66 Kruk, *The Last Days*, p. 618.
67 Feuchert, *Chronik* 1944, 14.3.1944, p. 208.
68 Ibid., 11.7.1944, p. 416.
69 For Lodz, see Trunk, *Judenrat*, p. 183; also USHMM, RG 15.083, 5/24, Rumkowski to the Criminal Police, 21.11.1940, fol. 107f.
70 See Trunk, *Judenrat*, p. 183; YIVO, RG 223/323 and 324.
71 Adler, *In the Warsaw Ghetto*, p. 135.
72 ŻIH, RING I/702, *Gazeta Żydowska* no. 47, 13.6.1941, p. 8.
73 7. AR I/PH/23–3–2: Contents of a Conversation with a Member of the Order Police, 2.5.1942, Kermish, *To Live with Honor*, p. 316. Engelking and Leociak, *The Warsaw Ghetto*, p. 204, refer to these secret hearings as *ditojra*,

this being the expression used in the original Polish source. They do not discuss the similarity between *ditojra* and *Din Torah*, however, nor do they refer to the rabbinic character of the arbitration process.

74 Adler, *In the Warsaw Ghetto*, p. 111, and ŻIH, RG 302/129, Pamiętnik Józefa Rode.

75 ŻIH, 264. RING I/244, fol. 1–2. Specifically, this would involve detailing staff to monitor the observance of the Sabbath. Violations would be judged by a five-strong court including a rabbi, a member of the legal department, an OS official, and two other people. See Dreifuss, "Warsaw," p. 910.

76 ŻIH, 264. RING I/244. The Jewish Council had, nevertheless – under pressure from Orthodox believers – agreed to the creation of a committee to oversee the observance of the Sabbath, with authority to punish violations. According to Adler, this was under the control of the Jewish police for a brief period; in all, such violations were only pursued for a few weeks. See Adler, *In the Warsaw Ghetto*, p. 257.

77 The principles thus formulated were subsequently approved at an assembly of lawyers and representatives of the Order Service. See Löw, *Juden im Getto*, p. 112.

78 ŻIH, RG 205/276, 19.8.1941, fol. 22

79 See Trunk, *Judenrat*, p. 183, and Source no. 45. YI-862A, Criminal law procedure in the ghetto (1940), reprinted in Trunk, *Łódź Ghetto*, p. 74.

80 No. 45. YI-862A, Criminal law procedure in the ghetto (1940), reprinted in Trunk, *Łódź Ghetto*, p. 74.

81 Feuchert, *Chronik* 1941, 2.12.1941, p. 281.

82 Ibid.

83 Feuchert, *Chronik* 1943, December 1943, p. 637.

84 Re the oath on the Torah scroll, see Löw, *Juden im Getto*, p. 112.

85 See Cohn and Levitats, "Bet Din and Judges," pp. 512–24.

86 The concept of *halakha* is multifaceted. It refers on one hand to the parts of the collective literature of the Talmud and Midrash, which contain all the legal norms and relevant interpretations and traditions, and on the other to a single legal order, a resolved judicial problem or the prevailing opinion. See Elon, *Jewish Law*, vol. 1, p. 93f.; Jacobs, "Halakhah." One ghetto where Jewish law was explicitly applied was the Šiauliai ghetto on former Lithuanian territory, which existed from July 1941 to July 1944. See Trunk, *Judenrat*, p. 183.

87 On the different judicial bodies and resulting rivalries, see Broyde and Ausubel, "Legal Institutions," p. 1007f.

88 This made it easier to collect taxes, for example.

89 For a basic introduction to this issue, see Goldfine, *Einführung*, p. 15f., and Elon, *Jewish Law*, vol. 1, pp. 6f., 13–18; Broyde and Ausubel, "Legal Institutions."

90 Gotzmann also identifies a dynamic between "norm" and "variance" in the development of Jewish law among German Jews in the nineteenth century. See Gotzmann, *Jüdisches Recht im kulturellen Prozess*, p. 4.

91 In case of ambiguities resulting from the judge's interpretation of a law, a new *halakha* can arise concerning the same law. On the Midrash, see Elon, *Jewish Law*, vol. 1, p. 275ff., and Goldfine, *Einführung*, p. 41ff.

92 This method is chosen if no answer to a particular question can be found in the law. See ibid., p. 47ff.

93 See ibid., p. 64ff.

94 See Elon, *Jewish Law*, vol. 1, p. 190ff.

95 See Goldfine, *Einführung*, p. 34. Edited in the second century by Rabbi Jehuda ha-Nassi, this work represented the most important legal source of the time. See ibid., p. 31ff.

96 See Ta-Shma, Tal, and Slae, "Responsa"; on the importance of these for Polish Jewry, see Guesnet, *Polnische Juden*, p. 203.

97 See Elon, *Jewish Law*, vol. 2, p. 495; Goldfine, *Einführung*, p. 50.

98 See Elon, *Jewish Law*, vol. 2, p. 505ff.; Goldfine, *Einführung*, p. 51.

99 Synhedrin 46a, quoted in Goldfine, *Einführung*, p. 51. For example, the death penalty was imposed on a man for riding a horse on the Sabbath. Although this was not an act for which the death penalty was prescribed in the Torah, scholars chose this punishment because there was a widespread lack of compliance with rules and restrictions at the time. See ibid., p. 52; Elon, *Jewish Law*, vol. 2, p. 515f.

100 See Goldfine, *Einführung*, p. 52. In addition to scholars, the community could also issue decrees – *takkanot ha-kahal* – that were based on a democratic process. See ibid., p. 61f.

101 See ibid., p. 52.

102 See ibid., p. 63.

103 Broyde and Ausubel, "Legal Institutions," p. 1008f. The death penalty was applied in Poland in the sixteenth century, for example; there were Jewish prisons in places such as Babylonia, Poland, Germany, and Italy. See Goldfine, *Einführung*, p. 63.

104 This sometimes also extended to family members: for example, the son of a banished offender could be denied circumcision. See Broyde and Ausubel, "Legal Institutions," p. 1009; on imposed sanctions, see Elon, *Jewish Law*, vol. 1, p. 10f.; for a historical perspective on the "Jewish ban," see Wiesner, *Der Bann*; Gotzmann, "Die Grenzen der Autonomie."

105 See Elon, *Jewish Law*, vol. 2, p. 880ff. Unlike *halakha*, the invocation of common law was only permissible in the field of business law and in order to regulate interpersonal relationships where necessary owing to changing forms of employment. See Goldfine, *Einführung*, p. 64f.

106 See Elon, *Jewish Law*, vol. 1, pp. 144, 147. Elon refers to a "heavenly obligation" (ibid., p. 147).

107 See Goldfine, *Einführung*, p. 66.

108 Novak, "Modern Responsa," p. 379. The modernization processes of the late eighteenth century brought the Jewish legal system into line with non-Jewish majority societies. Although these processes were subject to regional variation, they entailed in all cases a loss of Jewish organizational and practical autonomy regarding the development of the law. On the development within the Russian empire, see Miller, *The Romanov Empire*, pp. 95–7; Rest, *Die russische Judengesetzgebung*. With reference to Polish Jewry, see, e.g., Guesnet, *Polnische Juden*. In the German-speaking countries, legal assimilation followed in the wake of emancipation. See, e.g., Schoeps, *Die missglückte Emanzipation*. On this issue more generally, see Birnbaum, *Paths of Emancipation*.

109 ŻIH, RG 302/129, Pamiętnik Józefa Rode.

110 Arad, *Ghetto in Flames*, p. 291

111 YIVO, RG 223/327. In the same period, a further forty-three sentences were imposed by the ghetto court in civil cases, YIVO, RG 223/326.

112 The juvenile court likewise only resumed its activities on 11 June 1942, "after a long interruption." Feuchert, *Chronik* 1942, p. 290.

113 USHMM, RG 05.008, 27/65 for 1944, public prosecutor of the Court of the Eldest of the Jews to the Criminal Police, 25.4–25.5.1944, fol. 102. For the period from 26 February to 25 March 1944, twenty-one criminal offences had been recorded. RG 05.008, 27/65 for 1944, public prosecutor of the Court of the Eldest of the Jews to the Criminal Police, 25.3.1944, fol. 23. For the period from 26 January to 26 February 1944, forty-seven criminal offences. RG 05.008, 27/65 for 1944, public prosecutor of the Court of the Eldest of the Jews to the Criminal Police, 25.2.1944, fol. 81.

114 See Löw, *Juden im Getto*, p. 112. The oath sworn by judges at their inauguration in December 1941 was accordingly drawn up in Hebrew, Yiddish, German, and Polish. Feuchert, *Chronik* 1941, 2.12.1941, p. 280f.

115 In the case of Vilna, this is apparent from the ghetto court verdicts, which are exclusively in Yiddish. In Warsaw, the majority of the legal personnel and Order Service functionaries were non-Yiddish-speaking Polish converts.

116 It is, admittedly, unclear how representative the documented trials are. Since the verdicts are often unavailable in the original, but are mentioned in chronicles or diaries, the cases in question were presumably those that struck the writers as the most "sensational."

117 USHMM, RG 05.008, 25/58, Lodz Criminal Police department to Lodz Criminal Police directorate, 10.10.1941, fol. 36. This assessment rested on Rumkowski's adherence to German precepts in his ghetto-internal definitions of criminality and law.

118 Straightforward "illegal border crossings" were rarely dealt with by the court, being usually punished directly by the German police or the Jewish Order Service on the instructions of the German Criminal Police. A few cases in which "leaving the residential area without authorization" was dealt with in combination with smuggling can be found mainly in the period from 1941 to late summer 1942: see, e.g., USHMM, RG 05.008, 25/59, verdict Analewicz Icek, 13.2.1941, for violation of the police regulation of 8.2.1940 concerning the Jewish residential area, fol. 60.

119 USHMM, RG 05.008, 25/59, verdict, fol. 43, 44, 45: submission of verdict to the State Criminal Police department in Lodz, 22.4.1941. Similar proceedings are recorded in relation to the sale of smuggled goods: USHMM, RG 05.008, 25/59, verdict Binsztok, 1.4.1941, fol. 58, 59.

120 USHMM, RG 05.008, 27/64, verdict Nusbaum/Zeligman, 21.6.1941, fol. 296, 297.

121 USHMM, RG 05.008, 25/59, verdict Kaliński, Silberszac, Frajlich, and Strusik, 9.4.1941, for violation of the ghetto curfew, fol. 53.

122 Ibid.

123 The accusation of resistance referred to her "violent" attempt to prevent the responsible OS foreman from seizing her son, who had been arrested for smuggling. USHMM, RG 05.008, 25/59, verdict Ester Chlebolub, 14.4.1941, fol. 49, 50, submission to the Lodz State Criminal Police department, fol. 51.

124 Ibid.

125 USHMM, RG 05.008, 25/58, Lodz Criminal Police department to Lodz Criminal Police directorate, 10.10.1941, fol. 36f.

126 The ethnic categorization here is that used by the Nazis.

127 USHMM, RG 05.008, 27/64, verdict Anna Kozlowska, 13.8.1942, fol. 81, 82.

128 Such conclusions should be treated with caution, given the source material constraints, but a change in this direction is nevertheless noticeable.

129 USHMM, RG 05.008, 27/64, Criminal Police to the public prosecutor of the Court of the Eldest of the Jews, 22.12.1942, fol. 30: order for punishment to be imposed by the ghetto court. The term "crimes against the wartime economy" was used from 4 September 1939 to describe violations of the so-called wartime economy regulation, which were mostly dealt with by German Special Courts. The regulation was intended to prevent "conduct detrimental to the war." In addition to "trafficking," offences such as slaughter without official approval and "hoarding" of raw materials and foodstuffs were also prosecuted.

130 For an example from the Vilna ghetto, see Kruk, *The Last Days*, 18.11.1942, p. 416: arrest of two residents for rumour-mongering.

131 APŁ, 278/1076, *Geto-Tsaytung* no. 15, 1.8.1941, p. 4 (emphasis orig.).

132 Kruk, *The Last Days*, 13.12.1942, p. 425.

133 APŁ, 278/1076, *Geto-Tsaytung* no. 3, 21.3.1941, p. 12.

134 Feuchert, *Chronik* 1941, 6.4.1941, p. 110.

135 Ibid., p. 110f.

136 Ibid., 12.4.1941, p. 122.

137 Ibid., 26–30.6.1941, p. 166.

138 The baker Manes Bruks, for example, was sentenced to four months' imprisonment with hard labour for stealing from the bakery at 34 Lutomierska Street, three other employees to two months' imprisonment and hard labour each for "complicity to theft," and Tajko Fajwisz to one month in prison for "keeping flour for the purpose of resale." GFH, Collections Section, 345, verdict 18.7.1941, fol. 2. On this case, see also ŻIH, RG 205/300, fol. 7. On the same day, six other people were sentenced via summary administrative proceedings to between three and six months' imprisonment in combination with hard labour for "organized" flour theft from another bakery, complicity to theft, attempted bribery, and keeping of flour for the purpose of resale. ŻIH, RG 205/300, fol. 1.

139 Feuchert, *Chronik* 1941, 6.4.1941, p. 110.

140 Ibid., p. 137. See also a case from July 1942, in which eight employees from the economics department were sentenced to imprisonment and fines for issuing falsified waste disposal confirmation documents "for mercenary motives." The accused had received 50 pfennings and a portion of soup from the factories for each confirmed disposal trip. Feuchert, *Chronik* 1942, 3.7.1942, p. 345.

141 Feuchert, *Chronik* 1943, 1.4.1943, p. 129.

142 APŁ, 278/1076, *Geto-Tsaytung* no. 6, 11.4.1941, p. 11f.

143 Ibid.

144 Feuchert, *Chronik* 1943, 2.5.1943, p. 181.

145 Ibid., p. 182.

146 Feuchert, *Chronik* 1943, 2.5.1943, pp. 181, 186.

147 Ibid., pp. 181, 187.

148 See Goldfine, *Einführung*, p. 66.

149 Feuchert, *Chronik* 1944, 2.1.1944, p. 17f. At the trial of 23 January 1944, Garfinkel was also accused of embezzling benefits he had received for his workers, profiting from goods deliveries to the workshop, and "furthermore, having a cobbler make him a free pair of shoes in return for transferring the cobbler's wife – an employee of the carpet factory – to the bakery" (ibid., 23.1.1944, p. 70). On 4 January 1944, a further "soup scandal" was reported, in which Rajzla Unterrecht, from the vocational courses section of the tailoring workshop, was charged with misappropriating extra soup allowances earmarked for sick children (ibid., 4.1.1944, p. 24). On this, see also ibid., 14.2.1944, p. 138.

150 Feuchert, *Chronik* 1944, 26.1.1944, p. 75; see also ibid., 30.1.1944, "list of resettled persons," p. 87f.

151 There are no details available on the amount of support received. APŁ, 278/1076, *Geto-Tsaytung* no. 14, 15.7.1941, orig. p. 2; similarly, see the verdicts of June 1941: APŁ, 278/1076, *Geto-Tsaytung* no. 13, 20.6.1941, p. 9.

152 Majer was sentenced to a fine and made to repay the money. APŁ, 278/1076, *Geto-Tsaytung* no. 14, 15.7.1941, orig. p. 2.

153 Feuchert, *Chronik* 1941, 25.3.1941, p. 97f. Similar cases also occurred in the Warsaw ghetto: Czerniaków writes of mothers who kept their dead children hidden under the beds for eight days in order to continue receiving their rations, for instance. Czerniaków, *Warsaw Diary*, 19.11.1941, p. 300.

154 No verdicts relating to electricity theft are recorded in the Chronicle. Whether such cases were only tried by the courts in July 1941 remains open to question. All we know is that the chairman of the court reported to Rumkowski on 16 November 1941 that the total of seven cases constituted "all the instances of electricity theft … that were tried in court and reported by the power station." GFH, Collections Section, 345, Holdings Registry no. C VIII/11 557, letter of 16.11.1941 from the chairman of the court to Rumkowski.

155 In July 1941, the Chronicle notes an increase in "electricity theft," mainly due to fuel shortages. Feuchert, *Chronik* 1941, 24.7.1941, p. 189, and entry 15–31.10.1941, p. 246.

156 GFH, Collections Section, 345, Holdings Registry no. C VIII/11 557, in the former case: verdicts of 6.7, 17.7, 25.7, and 31.7.1941; quote: ibid., verdict of 25.7.1941.

157 YIVO, RG 223/318.5, verdict of 14.12.1941, fol. 286, 287; YIVO, RG 223/318.6, court ruling of 15.1.1942, fol. 312.

158 USHMM, 1999.A.0105, 9/98, verdict on the trial of 5.3.1942, fol. 1/0.

159 Ibid., point 4.

160 Ibid., point 2.

161 Kruk, *The Last Days*, 4.4.1943, p. 500. On 2 April 1943, Kruk noted in the Chronicle that the library had requested the ghetto court to punish fifteen people for failing to return their books (ibid., 4.2.1942, p. 459; YIVO, RG 223/374).

162 The significance and function of education in Nazi ghettos has been studied in depth in a doctoral project by Hanna Schmidt Holländer.

163 Kruk, *The Last Days*, 10.7.1943, p. 587. Which specific actions were defined as "resistance" in this context remains unclear, however. The explicit reference to "nights" rather than "days" may mean that residents still had to go about their work in the daytime.

164 Adler, *In the Warsaw Ghetto*, p. 111.

165 Ibid.

166 Feuchert, *Chronik* 1941, 25.3.1941, p. 98.

167 Ibid., 4.8.1941, p. 210.

168 Ibid.

169 Ibid.

170 YIVO, RG 223/318.5. Through a letter of appeal to the Jewish Council, Chaim Leib Kriszański succeeded in getting the detention period reduced to three weeks. YIVO, RG 223/318.6, fol. 301.

171 USHMM, 1999.A 0105, 8/95, 6.1.1943, fol. 1035.

172 Kruk, *The Last Days*, 29.9.1942, p. 368.

173 Ibid., 9.2.1942, p. 201.

174 Ibid.

175 USHMM, RG 05.008, 27/64, verdict of the Court of the Eldest of the Jews, 18.8.1942, fol. 47ff.

176 He was also condemned for entering the ghetto without official authorization. USHMM, RG 05.008, 27/64, verdict of the Court of the Eldest of the Jews versus Adler, Lubliński, Tułob, Szuf, 18.8.1942, fol. 47ff.

177 USHMM, RG 05.008, 27/64, chairman of the court to the ghetto criminal investigation department, 12.8.1942, fol. 51.

178 USHMM, RG 05.008, 27/64, Ghetto Commissariat report 16.9.1942, fol. 52.

179 Adler, *In the Warsaw Ghetto*, p. 258. Unfortunately neither the sentence imposed nor the date is known.

180 Feuchert, *Chronik* 1943, 14.3.1943, p. 102. It is not clear from the report on the trial what kind of alleged criminal activities the youngsters had in mind.

181 Ibid.

182 Ibid.

183 GFH, Collections Section, 554, *Geto-Yedies* no. 30, 14.3.1943, fol. 6.

184 Ibid.

185 See, e.g. (albeit in relation to a late phase), Jakub Hiller's diary entry of 4 July 1944, in which he writes that Jewish police officers were reported by a woman from the ghetto to have raped young girls awaiting deportation from the central prison instead of releasing them as promised. ŻIH, 302/10, fol. 16, quoted in Feuchert, *Chronik* 1944, 4.7.1944, p. 404, n. 19.

186 GFH, Collections Section, 360 (C VIII/11 140), fol. 4.

187 Feuchert, *Chronik* 1943, 24.9.1943, p. 458.

188 GFH, Collections Section, 360 (C VIII/11 140), fol. 4.

189 According to the Chronicle, this was the third case of murder in the ghetto. The second was perpetrated on a woman named Tauba Hermann in September 1941. Feuchert, *Chronik* 1941, September 1941, pp. 221, 407.

190 Feuchert, *Chronik* 1941, 11.12.1941, p. 297. The accused, who was nicknamed Szlojma Stryczek (a Yiddish/Polish word for string) in the ghetto, was in receipt of financial support. He claimed to have been a door-to-door salesman before the war, and had already been convicted of theft and blackmail three times by the local authorities. Feuchert, *Chronik* 1941, 1–15.10.1941, p. 239. According to his statement, the brawl

had started after Bernstein accused his brother-in-law Litwak of stealing 30 marks from his jacket, while the latter claimed to have lent him the money previously. Feuchert, *Chronik* 1941, 24.12.1941, p. 324f.

191 Ibid., p. 323.

192 Before the war, the district of Bałuty had been known as the poor quarter and home of the "criminal underworld." This was where the Germans had chosen to establish the ghetto.

193 Feuchert, *Chronik* 1941, 24.12.1941, p. 323ff.

194 Ibid., p. 326.

195 Ibid., p. 325.

196 Ibid. It is hard to say how far this allusion to Rumkowski's words reflects a genuinely shared attitude; alternatively, it may have been an empty phrase and the reference to the authority of the Eldest of the Jews obligatory for anyone occupying a position in the ghetto administration.

197 Ibid., p. 326. The verdict forwarded to the German Criminal Police only mentioned the prison sentence: USHMM, RG 05.008, verdict Birensztajn Szlama, 24.12.1941, fol. 303f.; submission of court verdict to Lodz Criminal Police: USHMM, RG 05.008, 11.1.1942, fol. 302.

198 Kruk, *The Last Days*, 4.6.1942, p. 300; ibid., 5.6.1942, p. 302. See also Arad, *Ghetto in Flames*, p. 293.

199 According to Kruk, Gerstein had prepared to hand over the money because his future murderers had promised to sell him food on cheap terms (*The Last Days*, 3.6.1942, p. 300). Arad writes that the victim had been involved in trading and black market activities, which was how he had come into contact with the perpetrators. On the murder of Hertsl Lides, see also Arad, *Ghetto in Flames*, p. 292.

200 Kruk, *The Last Days*, 5.6.1942, p. 301.

201 Arad, *Ghetto in Flames*, p. 292f.; Trunk, *Judenrat*, p. 185, makes brief reference to the case, but classes it indiscriminately as a "murder trial" without mentioning the danger to the ghetto community feared by the Jewish Council.

202 Kruk, *The Last Days*, 14.3.1942, p. 236.

203 Ibid., 5.6.1942, p. 302f.; Arad is in no doubt that Avidon was responsible for the murder of the priest in Lida (*Ghetto in Flames*, p. 292f.).

204 Kruk, *The Last Days*, 4.6.1941, p. 300.

205 Ibid., p. 620.

206 Ibid.

207 Adler, *In the Warsaw Ghetto*, pp. 48, 257, 259.

208 YVA, O-6/102, fol. 202, quoted in Gutman, *Jews of Warsaw*, p. 275.

209 ŻIH, Bernard Mark Collection/482, author unknown, report of 7.12.1941.

210 YVA, JM-1440, verdict of Lodz ghetto court, Szmul Dimantsztajn, re smuggling, 9.8.1942, fol. 297ff.

211 USHMM, RG 05.008, 25/59, verdict of Lodz ghetto court, Majer Lajbman, re smuggling, 25.3.1941, fol. 56; USHMM, RG 05.008, 25/59, verdict of Lodz ghetto court, Ester Chlebolub, re smuggling and resistance, 14.4.1941, fol. 49, 50.

212 USHMM, 1999.A.0105, 9/98, verdict of Vilna ghetto court, 5.3.1942, Fania Pulkin, Efraim Spokoini, re use of stolen food ration cards, fol. 1/0, point 5.

213 USHMM, RG 05.008, 25/59, verdict of Lodz ghetto court, Kaliński, Silberszac, Frajlich, Strusik, 9.4.1941, re smuggling, fol. 53.

214 ŻIH, RG 205/68, verdict of Lodz ghetto court, Hecht, Moszek and Kawelblum, Lajzor, 12.3.1941, re smuggling, fol. 9; USHMM, RG 05.008, 25/59, verdict of Lodz ghetto court, Analewicz Icek, re smuggling, 13.2.1941, fol. 61.

215 YVA, M-1451, verdict of Lodz ghetto court, Icek Adler, re robbery and theft, 18.8.1942, fol. 40ff.; USHMM, RG 05.008, 25/59, verdict of Lodz ghetto court, Ester Chlebolub, re "aiding and abetting the escape of a prisoner and resisting OS officers," 14.4.1941, fol. 49, 50. USHMM, RG 05.008, 25/59, verdict of Lodz ghetto court, Kaliński, Silberszac, Frajlich, Strusik, 9.4.1941, re smuggling, fol. 52, 53 (here: Kaliński's "criminal activity" in the "pre-ghetto period").

216 E.g., USHMM, RG 15.083, 113/364, OS to the public prosecutor in the Lodz ghetto, submission of character reference for Gitla Ehrlich, 6.4.1941, fol. 628, "Opinia," fol. 630.

217 USHMM, RG 05.008, 25/59, verdict Kaliński, Silberszac, Frajlich, Strusik, 9.4.1941; mitigating circumstances for Fraijlich because of his young age, fol. 53.

218 GFH, Collections Section, 365, minutes of 15.6 (year unidentifiable, but probably 1941). The fact that Jacobson was then already attending as chairman of the court he had been entrusted to set up in August 1940 suggests that the relevant meeting took place in June 1941.

219 Ibid.

220 Ibid.

221 Ibid.

222 USHMM, RG 15.083, 38/118, Rumkowski to Neftalin re the creation of a juvenile court, 22.7.1941, fol. 33.

223 GFH, Collections Section, 353, project of the trustee group regarding the treatment of young offenders, undated. The *Geto-Tsaytung* carried a report on the creation of a suitable guardianship panel. APŁ, 278/1076, *Geto-Tsaytung* no. 16, 17.8.1941, p. 2.

224 GFH, Collections Section, 353, project of the trustee group regarding the treatment of young offenders, undated, fol. 2.

225 Ibid.

226 Kruk, *The Last Days*, 7.3.1942, p. 224f. The chronicler gives no indication of which "crimes" the children were guilty of. Here again, they can be assumed to have been minor food thefts, such as those described by Yaakov Shvartsberg, who lived in the Vilna ghetto as a child. As he explains, part of the reason why children joined "child gangs" was that their parents had to go to work in factories or outside the ghetto. YVA, O-3/10906, Testimony of Yaakov Shvartsberg, fol. 30.

227 Kruk, *The Last Days*, 23.10.1942, p. 384.

228 In the Lodz ghetto, this also meant that the various authorities – from family to school – were assigned some responsibility for the supervision of the young. GFH, Collections Section, 353, project of the trustee group regarding the treatment of young offenders, undated, fol. 3.

229 Daily Chronicle, 5.7.1942, "Jugendliche im Gefängnis," quoted in Feuchert, *Chronik 1941*, p. 102; APŁ, 278/1076, *Geto-Tsaytung* no. 3, 21.3.1941, p. 14, "Erziehungsanstalt für minderjährige Unehrliche," fol. 35.

230 APŁ, 278/1076, *Geto-Tsaytung* no. 16, 17.8.1941, "Schaffung einer Vormundschaft zum Schutze für Minderjährige," p. 4.

231 Feuchert, *Chronik 1941*, September 1941, p. 223. In the case of sentences of up to one month, the court chairman adjudicated on behalf of the public prosecutor. The parties concerned could appeal against the amnesty within seven days. See also APŁ, 278/1076, *Geto-Tsaytung* no. 18, 21.9.1941, entry of 19.9.1941, "Amnestieverordnung aus Anlass der Neujahrsfeiertage 1941," p. 2.

232 Feuchert, *Chronik 1941*, 16.12.1941, p. 305f.

233 Feuchert, *Chronik 1943*, 20.4.1943, p. 162, and ibid., 30.10.1943, p. 531. In the case of the Lodz ghetto, a distinction must be made between general and individual amnesties: in a general amnesty, the group of beneficiaries was defined via the sentences imposed on them, whereas an individual amnesty only applied to certain selected "delinquents."

234 The phrase used in an address to heads of department and senior community officials on 1 February 1942. The punishment named by Rumkowski in this context was "deportation," which he took at that time to mean "hard labour." Feuchert, *Chronik 1941*, 1.2.1941, p. 57. A similar threat was issued in a speech of 17 January 1942 at the anniversary celebration of the linen workshop: "I will resettle people from the ghetto for the slightest offence." Feuchert, *Chronik 1942*, 14–31.1.1942, p. 50.

235 The mitigations applied to both prison sentences and hard labour. The number of benefit withdrawals was also halved. Feuchert, *Chronik 1941*, September 1941, p. 223. With regard to the Passover amnesty, see Feuchert, *Chronik 1943*, 20.4.1943, p. 162: in this case, all prison sentences of up to six weeks were cancelled.

236 Feuchert, *Chronik* 1941, September 1941, p. 223.
237 Feuchert, *Chronik* 1943, 30.10.1943, p. 531.
238 Feuchert, *Chronik* 1941, September 1941, p. 223.
239 Feuchert, *Chronik* 1943, 20.4.1943, p. 162.
240 Ibid., 30.10.1943, p. 531
241 YIVO, RG 223/11, Jewish Council chairman and Police Chief Gens, 15.7.1942.
242 Ibid., fol. 1.
243 Ibid.
244 Ibid., fol. 2.
245 Ibid., fol. 1 (emphasis orig.).
246 Adler, *In the Warsaw Ghetto*, p. 164.
247 Ibid.
248 Opoczyński, *Reportaże*, p. 96.
249 Adler, *In the Warsaw Ghetto*, p. 164. This did not apply to the members of the Jewish Council, however, against whom disciplinary proceedings could be brought. Possible reasons for this phenomenon were the improvised nature of the Jewish self-administration organs and their lack of acceptance by the ghetto population.
250 USHMM, 1999.A.0105, 4/63, judicial panel notification, penalty order Motel, Rudninku for non-appearance in the case of Berson, Elias, for forwarding by Police District I, 19.2.1942, fol. 517.
251 Adler, *In the Warsaw Ghetto*, p. 161.
252 The chronicler states that many of the witnesses had belonged to the "darkest underworld of Bałuty." Feuchert, *Chronik* 1941, 24.12.1941, p. 323. As inmates of the ghetto prison, they were among the first to be "made available" for deportation by Rumkowski.
253 USHMM, RG 05.008, 27/64, court of the Eldest of the Jews to the Criminal Police department, 8.1.1943, fol. 32 (re the defendants Abram Krul, Kira Herzberg, and Feiwel Ojzerowicz).
254 E.g., Feuchert, *Chronik* 1941, 25.3.1941, p. 97f., and Feuchert, *Chronik* 1943, trial of 3.5.1943, p. 188.
255 USHMM, RG 05.008, 27/64, public prosecutor of the court of the Eldest of the Jews to Criminal Police, 10.11.1942, fol. 33.
256 YIVO, RG 223/324, art. 4, fol. 1.
257 YIVO, RG 223/326.
258 On 31 October 1942, the so-called *Sonderkommando* ("Special Unit"), which was officially responsible to the Order Service, had been renamed the *Sonderabteilung* ("Special Department"). Its powers had been steadily increasing since the German deportations of September 1942; from then on, the *Sonderabteilung* also had its own investigation department. Feuchert, *Chronik* 1943, 17.4.1943, p. 155; Feuchert, *Chronik* 1942, 11.10.1942, p. 499.

259 Ibid., 25.10.1942, p. 518.
260 Feuchert, *Chronik* 1943, 10.7.1943, amendment to hearing of 5.7.1943, p. 307.
261 Ibid., 14.3.1943, p. 98.
262 Ibid.
263 In one case, a resident accused of stealing a bag of sago was sentenced by the *Sonderabteilung* to sewage removal duty. Feuchert, *Chronik* 1943, April 1943, p. 154. See also ibid., *Sonderabteilung* police report, 1–10.4.1943, p. 146, "Festnahmen durch die Untersuchungskanzlei der Sonderabteilung," 11–20.4.1943, p. 172; ibid., 14.5.1943, p. 205; ibid., 1–26.6.1943, p. 283; ibid., 17.8.1943, p. 380.
264 Ibid., 18.4.1943, p. 157.
265 See Porat, "The Justice System," p. 49f.

5 The Ghetto Penal System

1 Feuchert, *Chronik* 1941, 20.12.1941, p. 311.
2 Ibid., p. 314.
3 In the Lodz ghetto, this was documented as early as 1940 in the "Criminal law procedure in the ghetto" (1940), reprinted in Trunk, *Łódź Ghetto*, p. 74.
4 As in Rumkowski's speech regarding the "resettlements" in December 1941: see Feuchert, *Chronik* 1941, 20.12.1941, p. 314ff. Similarly, his address of 18 January 1941 on the anniversary of the linen workshop: see Feuchert, *Chronik* 1942, 14–31.1.1942, p. 50.
5 On the declining importance of money in the Lodz ghetto, see, e.g., the account by Poznański, *Tagebuch*, 18.4.1943, p. 93, where he refers to a cobbler who would only work for food, not money. This change is also evident from the fact that money was replaced by food as the "object of desire" in most crimes.
6 For Vilna, see, e.g., USHMM, 1999.A.0105, 4/63, police station to detention centre, 20.1.1942, fol. 407: wood theft to be punished with one day's detention in case of non-payment of 2.50 reichsmarks; USHMM, 1999.A.0105, 4/63, judicial panel to Police District 1 (re appropriation of stolen property), 1.2.1942, fol. 509: in case of non-payment of 20-reichsmark fine, conversion to one day per 5 reichsmarks.
7 YVA, O-34/233, Proclamation, 2.3.1941 (emphasis orig.).
8 E.g., YVA, O-34/185, Proclamation no. 176, 8.12.1940; YVA, O-34/274, Proclamation no. 273, 25.5.1941. At a conference of the economics department on 25 May 1942, Rumkowski stipulated that those renting plots of land, e.g., in Marysin, were obliged to hand over the vegetables grown there to the Jewish Council's authorized stores, who would sell them on the open market and give the tenants a share; from then on, "trading" outside these stores was prohibited. Feuchert, *Chronik* 1942, 26.5.1942, p. 233.

9 APŁ, 278/1076, *Geto-Tsaytung* no. 4, 28.3.1941, p. 9: threat of loss of relief aid in the event of wood theft; APŁ, 278/1076, *Geto-Tsaytung* no. 15, 1.8.1941: for "illegal candy production": loss of two weeks' relief aid.

10 See, e.g., APŁ, 278/1076, *Geto-Tsaytung* no. 11–12, 30.5.1941, p. 5: threatened in case of "theft, swindling, and abuses" in workshops, institutions, and offices.

11 APŁ, 278/1076, *Geto-Tsaytung* no. 14, 15.7.1941, p. 2/189, orig. p. 1; see also APŁ, 278/1076, *Geto-Tsaytung* no. 11–12, 30.5.1941, p. 5; APŁ, 278/1076, *Geto-Tsaytung* no. 16, 17.8.1941, p. 2.

12 GFH, Collections Section, 271, report on the preparatory meeting regarding the establishment of the summary court, 14.3.1941, fol. 1.

13 Reprinted in APŁ, 278/1076, *Geto-Tsaytung* no. 16, 17.8.1941, orig. p. 2. As mentioned earlier, after the dissolution of the summary court, all Rumkowski needed was the countersignature of the lawyer Henryk Neftalin.

14 In the Marysin district, fruit and vegetables were cultivated on small plots of land and in gardens at the initiative of the Jewish Council as well as by private tenants. Feuchert, *Chronik* 1941, 21.7.1941, p. 183. Another schoolchild, on receiving a similar punishment, threw himself from the second floor of an apartment block, but survived unhurt (ibid.). In 1940, the German Criminal Police had handed over two underage smugglers to the Jewish Council with instructions to deliver them to their parents. Here too, the parents were held liable and punished with eight days' detention. USHMM, RG 05.008, 9/23, re Ghetto Special Commissariat to the Eldest of the Jews, Order Service Department, 10.7.1940, fol. 434.

15 Feuchert, *Chronik* 1941, 10–24.3.1941, p. 90. On other dismissals, see, e.g., APŁ, 278/1076, *Geto-Tsaytung* no. 17, 14.9.1941, quoted in Feuchert, *Chronik* 1941, p. 233f.

16 Sewage was transported on a hand-drawn cart loaded with buckets. For more detail, see Feuchert, *Chronik* 1941, p. 388, n. 68.

17 As explicitly justified, for instance, in the speech of 4.1.1942: APŁ, 278/1192, fol. 273f. See also Löw, *Juden im Getto*, p. 266.

18 APŁ, 278/1076, *Geto-Tsaytung* no. 15, 1.8.1941, orig. p. 2. This punishment was also imposed for other offences such as illegal bread trading (ibid.).

19 APŁ, 278/1076, *Geto-Tsaytung* no. 8, 25.4.1941, orig. p. 2.

20 Ibid.

21 Feuchert, *Chronik* 1941, 7–9.6.1941, p. 161.

22 In this context, Rumkowski recalled the case of a ghetto resident named Bekerman, whom the Germans had sentenced to death on 13 September 1943 for "sabotage" after he stole a leather strap from a leather and saddlery workshop. Feuchert, *Chronik* 1943, 9.9.1943, p. 428; ibid., 13.9.1943, p. 437.

23 Ibid., 27.9.1943, p. 463; ibid., 29.9.1943, p. 469.

24 ŻIH, RG 205/219, Order no. 7, 26.3.1940, fol. 20.
25 APŁ, 278/1076, *Geto-Tsaytung* no. 4, 28.3.1941, p. 9.
26 APŁ, 278/1076, *Geto-Tsaytung* no. 17, 14.9.1941, orig. p. 1. This declaration was likewise occasioned by damage to buildings and objects in the ghetto as a result of "wood theft," for which Rumkowski sought to hold the "house administrators" accountable.
27 APŁ, 278/1076, *Geto-Tsaytung* no. 13, 20.6.1941, p. 11.
28 ŻIH, 52. RING II/186, The Jewish Council in Warsaw, Proclamation, 22.7.1942, fol. 2.
29 Appeals to report criminal activities by other ghetto residents were based on similar premises.
30 Kruk, *The Last Days*, 23.10.1942, p. 384.
31 ŻIH, RG 302/129, Pamiętnik Józefa Rode. The camps provided temporary accommodation for those newly deported to the ghetto before they were assigned lodgings. On "creative" punishments, see also Adler, *In the Warsaw Ghetto*, p. 111.
32 Speech by Rumkowski, 30.8.1941, Feuchert, *Chronik* 1941, p. 219.
33 APŁ, 278/1076, *Geto-Tsaytung* no. 3, 21.3.1941, report on the "reformatory for dishonest juveniles," p. 14.
34 Feuchert, *Chronik* 1941, November 1941, p. 262.
35 Feuchert, *Chronik* 1943, February 1943, p. 39.
36 Ibid., 7.9.1943, p. 425. This can, however, also be read as an implicit criticism of corporal punishment in general.
37 Ibid.
38 Kruk, *The Last Days*, 16.9.1941, p. 113.
39 Ibid., 21.1.1943, p. 453.
40 Ibid., 5.7.1942, p. 320.
41 YVA, O-3/10906, Testimony of Yaakov Shvartsberg (Vilna), p. 31f.
42 Kruk, *The Last Days*, 18.2.1943, p. 46
43 Engelking and Leociak, *Warsaw Ghetto*, p. 204
44 Feuchert, *Chronik* 1941, 4.8.1941, p. 210.
45 Abraham Feldman, ŻIH, 301/2797, fol. 11; Hershkovitch, "The Ghetto in Litzmannstadt," p. 106; on this, see also Poznański, *Tagebuch*, p. 98, and Feuchert, *Chronik* 1941, p. 405, n.7.
46 The following resigned at the meeting: Aleksander Binsztok, Natan Byteński, Romana Byteńska, Józef Fjdlic, Albert Merlender, Wilhelm Mrówka, Jakub Najman, Jakub Rapner, Bencjon Wajskop, and Aleksander Wolk. See Feuchert, *Chronik* 1941, p. 413, n. 19.
47 Ibid., 4.8.1941, p. 210.
48 Whether the shots were actually fired is uncertain. Szmul Rozensztajn reports in his diary on Rumkowski's negotiations with the Germans in this matter. ŻIH, 302/115, fol. 65, quoted in Feuchert, *Chronik* 1941, p. 394, n. 11.
49 ŻIH, RG 205/276, Rumkowski to the Gestapo, 2.6.1941, fol. 1.

50 Ibid.
51 Feuchert, *Chronik* 1941, 7–9.6.1941, p. 161. Further criminal acts are reported to have taken place in this context, when two ghetto residents resisted OS functionaries after refusing to submit to the curfew (ibid.).
52 Rumkowski sent the plea by the arrested subject's mother to the Special Court and interceded personally for the doctor's release by the end of the investigation. USHMM, RG 05008 M 6/73, Rumkowski to the senior medical officer of the Special Court in Lodz, 29.6.1940, fol. 111.
53 Kruk, *The Last Days*, 25.7.1942, p. 337. Prior to deportations, the Jewish Council sometimes released inmates guilty of only "minor offences" on a temporary basis to prevent them from falling victim to the Germans. In rare cases, Gens "replaced" them all with elderly residents who were no longer fit for work.
54 Ibid., 31.10.1942, p. 398.
55 Ibid., 17.1.1943, p. 450. See the earlier release of thirty-seven inmates from the Lukiszki prison which Dessler managed to procure (ibid., 5.6.1942, p. 303f.).
56 Even before the sealing of the ghetto, Czerniaków had tried repeatedly to ward off brutal German punishments. In January 1940, the Gestapo had announced its intention to shoot 100 Jews after a mentally ill Jewish woman struck a German paramedic during a house disinfection. He succeeded in getting the sentence commuted to a "fine" of 100,000 złoty, but it had to be paid without fail by the following day: Czerniaków, *Warsaw Diary*, 26.1.1940, p. 111.
57 Ibid., 30.6.1942, p. 372.
58 Ibid., 17.1.1942, p. 316; ibid., 13.2.1942, p. 325; ibid., 11.3.1942, p. 331.
59 See Engelking and Leociak, *Warsaw Ghetto*, p. 202f.
60 For more on this involvement of the Polish police, see Szymańska-Smolkin, "Fateful Decisions," p. 108f.
61 For Warsaw, see, e.g., Adler, *In the Warsaw Ghetto*, p. 142; for Lodz, see, e.g., Poznański, *Tagebuch*, p. 231, and USHMM, RG 15.083, 5/24, Rumkowski to the German Criminal Police, 21.11.1941, fol. 107. In Vilna, these cells were also used for those detained by the Jewish Police for a few hours only.
62 This applied in particular to the Lodz ghetto. For the years 1940 to 1944, there are lists detailing the prisoners convicted under "German law" and subsequently sent to the ghetto central prison: USHMM, RG 05.008 M, Lodz municipal authority, fol. 27, 64.
63 This was noted on committal to the ghetto prison. For Vilna, see, e.g., YIVO, RG 223/318.4, police station to detention guard, 12.12.1941; YIVO, RG 223/318.5, 29.12.1941, fol. 297; YIVO, RG 223/318.7, 21.1.1942, fol. 394, 395.
64 Instructions regarding criminal punishment for Jews in the Wartheland, 30.8.1941, AGV/IV/53, quoted in Trunk, *Judenrat*, p. 184
65 USHMM, RG 05.008, 27/64, letter of 3.4.1942 from the higher state prosecutor in Lodz to Frankfurt district court, fol. 338.

66 See Galiński, "Centralne więzienie"; Löw, *Juden im Getto*, p. 111f., and
    Poznański, *Tagebuch*, p. 49, n. 15; Feuchert, *Chronik* 1942, 17.3.1942, p. 90.
67 This happened, for instance, to those brought to the ghetto from labour
    camps in June 1942: Feuchert, *Chronik* 1942, 25.6.1942, p. 319; to seventy-
    seven Jews from Turek in August 1942 (ibid., 4.8.1942, p. 407); and to
    forty-two people from a labour camp in Neustadt in December 1942 (ibid.,
    15.12.1942, p. 598).
68 See Feuchert, *Chronik* 1941, p. 380, n. 136. See also Feuchert, *Chronik* 1942,
    entry "Jugendliche im Gefängnis," 5.7.1942, p. 346f.; APŁ, 278/1076,
    Geto-Tsaytung no. 3, "Erziehungsanstalt für minderjährige Unehrliche,"
    21.3.1941, p. 14; and the report on the juvenile court, whose chairman was
    responsible for the "reformatory." APŁ, 278/1076, *Geto-Tsaytung* no. 15,
    1.8.1941, p. 1.
69 APŁ, 278/1076, *Geto-Tsaytung* no. 3, 21.3.1941, p. 14, fol. 35.
70 Feuchert, *Chronik* 1943, April 1943, p. 136.
71 Czerniaków, *Warsaw Diary*, 6.6.1941, pp. 246–7; Szymańska-Smolkin,
    "Fateful Decisions," p. 80.
72 See Engelking and Grabowski, *Żydów łamiących*, p. 78 (only referenced
    from summer 1941), p. 86; see also Adler, *In the Warsaw Ghetto*, p. 142,
    and an account of the prison by a ghetto resident: 7: ARI/J.M./1209/3,
    "The Jewish Jail on Gęsia Street," in Kermish, *To Live with Honor*, p. 157;
    Weiss, "Ha'mishtara hayehudit," p. 71; Szymańska-Smolkin, "Fateful
    Decisions," p. 81.
73 ŻIH, RG 221/1, The Jewish Residential District in Warsaw (facts and
    figures), June 1942, fol. 7.
74 On this prison and the torture methods used there by the Germans, see
    Sutzkever, *Wilner Ghetto*, p. 35f.
75 YIVO, RG 223/286.1, statistics of the ghetto prison in Vilna for the first half
    of 1942; Kruk, *The Last Days*, 15.4.1942, p. 262: account of a murder and the
    arrest of the suspects; Sutzkever, *Wilner Getto*, p. 55.
76 The Chronicle recorded the gender of the inmates and whether they were
    detained "at the disposal of the German authorities." Adolescents and
    children as well as inmates held in the prison "sickroom" were also noted.
    E.g., Feuchert, *Chronik* 1941, 7.12.1941, p. 291; ibid., 17.12.1941, p. 306;
    Feuchert, *Chronik* 1942, 20.7.1942, p. 370.
77 YIVO, Hersch Wasser Coll., RG 225/43.1 (date and author unknown).
78 See, e.g., USHMM, RG 05.008, 27/64, "Lists of inmates serving sentences
    imposed by the German court in the Jewish central prison 1940–1944."
    The governor of the central prison kept the chairman of the Order
    Service informed of incoming prisoners delivered by the Criminal Police.
    USHMM, RG 05.008, 25/59, fol. 46, 47; USHMM, RG 15.083, 5/24, Gestapo
    to the Eldest of the Jews in Lodz, 18.11.1942, fol. 44, re enforcement of the
    sentence against Julian Weinberg in the central prison.

79 USHMM RG 05.008, 27/64, Lodz Criminal Police department to the governor of the central prison, 24.2.1943, fol. 13.

80 USHMM RG 05.008, 27/64, public prosecutor to the Criminal Police, 19.3.1943, fol. 15.

81 USHMM, RG 05.008, 27/64, Lodz Criminal Police department to the governor of the central prison, 28.4.1943, fol. 6.

82 USHMM, RG 05.008, 27/64, Lodz Criminal Police department to the governor of the central prison, 5.2.1942, fol. 16. For further examples, see ibid., 11.2.1942, fol. 25 (Szajndla Gwireman); ibid., 4.4.1942, fol. 43 (Friede Sara Reppen).

83 USHMM, RG 15.083, 28/118, governor of the central prison to the Eldest of the Jews in Lodz, 3.7.1941, fol. 774; similarly, ibid., 27.6.1941, fol. 780.

84 USHMM, RG 05.008, 27/64, governor of the central prison to the Lodz Criminal Police department, 9.1.1942, fol. 246.

85 USHMM, RG 15.083, 5/24, Jewish Hospital in Lodz to the Eldest of the Jews, 31.10.1940, fol. 4; similarly, ibid., 21.7.1940, fol. 13.

86 USHMM, RG 05.008, 27/64, governor of the central prison to the Lodz Criminal Police department, 10.3.1942, fol. 253, 254. Similar lists of inmates imprisoned for "German offences" had already been compiled for the Criminal Police in 1941. USHMM, RG 05.008, 27/64, central prison to the State Criminal Police, Lodz Ghetto *Sonderkommando*, 24.4.1941, fol. 300, 301.

87 USHMM, RG 15.083, 41/129, governor of the central prison to the Gestapo in Lodz, 3.4.1942, "evacuation" of Malcia Gross from the central prison, fol. 1. USHMM, RG 15.083, 41/129, governor of central prison to Gestapo, "the following inmates, detained at the central prison at your disposal, evacuated," 13.3.1942, fol. 87.

88 Rumkowski's address on the anniversary of the founding of the linen workshop, 18.1.1942, reprinted in Feuchert, *Chronik* 1942, 14–31.1.1942, p. 50.

89 Kruk, *The Last Days*, 7.5.1942, p. 285f.

90 This theory is supported by the fact that the number of offenders was relatively small compared with the total of those sent to Ponary. The number of murder victims for the period from the beginning of September to the end of December 1941 was approximately 26,000. Ibid., 7.5.1942, p. 286.

91 Ibid., 15.6.1942, p. 307. It remains unclear who was authorized to take decisions in this case. It may be that the Jewish police were already responsible at this stage as administrators of the ghetto prison, or possibly Anatol Fried as the Jewish Council chairman before July 1942.

92 Kruk reports that rumours to this effect had been circulating in the ghetto for some days. Ibid., 12.5.1943, p. 538.

93 Ibid. The ten consisted of nine elderly people plus the previously mentioned Jewish police "informer," who had already been held in the ghetto prison for two weeks.

94 Report on the address by the ghetto chairman, ibid., 21.1.1943, p. 453.
95 ŻIH, 44. RING II/140, Auerswald to the head of the Jewish Council, 12.2.1942, fol. 5, requiring a report on the prison occupants to be submitted in a standard format. In the case of those who had attempted to leave the ghetto, the date of their offence had to be stated.
96 ŻIH, 63. RING II/150, 25.3.1942.
97 See Engelking and Grabowski, *Żydów łamiących*, pp. 76, 78, 83. On this episode, see also Gombiński, *Wspomnienia*, p. 74.
98 ŻIH, RING I/130, undated; also Kermish, *To Live with Honor*, p. 157; ŻIH, 427. RING I/95, and YIVO, RG 225/43.1, date and author unknown; see also the entry by Czerniaków, *Warsaw Diary*, 31.7.1941, p. 263, reporting prisoners' complaints of a bread shortage.
99 ŻIH, 61. RING II/148, program, preparation of a literary and artistic evening in the ghetto prison on 24.12.1941.
100 Gorodecka, *Hana*, p. 38.
101 Feuchert, *Chronik* 1941, 14.4.1941, p. 124, and ibid., September 1941, p. 223. According to the Chronicle, 60 prisoners were granted leave in April 1941. Twenty-seven prisoners "at the disposal of the Criminal Police" and a few "serious criminals" had to remain in prison. In September 1941, a counterfeiter who was still under investigation was denied leave. On the return of the inmates, see ibid., 25.4.1941, p. 134.
102 Ibid.
103 See Löw, *Juden im Getto*, p. 266.
104 USHMM, RG 05.008, 27/64, 28.3.1942 fol. 35; similarly ibid., Criminal Police notice, 5.2.1942, fol. 27; ibid., Criminal Police notice, 27.1.1942, fol. 29; ibid., fol. 45: notice of death of a Jewish prisoner "due to heart failure."
105 USHMM RG 05.008, 27/64, Criminal Police notice, 30.6.1942, fol. 68: re Szymon Kaschub, sudden death due to heart attack.
106 On the people imprisoned in the Warsaw ghetto, see, e.g., Engelking and Grabowski, *Żydów łamiących*, p. 86.
107 USHMM, RG 15.083, 41/129, report by central prison governor Hercberg re 24.7.1941, fol. 61. How the plotters were subsequently dealt with within the prison is not clear from the report.
108 YIVO, RG 223/318.6, 9.1.1942, fol. 312: notice of authorization of lawyer's visit for purposes of defence; RG 223/318.8, 9.2.1942, fol. 422: notice of authorization of lawyer's visit for discussion of defence.
109 E.g., YIVO, RG 223/318.8, letter to detention guard, 29.1.1942, fol. 422.
110 USHMM, RG 15.083, 38/118, 11.6.1941, letter from the ghetto hospital to Rumkowski, fol. 67.
111 YIVO, RG 223/318.5, 27.12.1941, fol. 276. The police station wrote to the detention guard instructing them to release the arrested subject Dawid Kinkulin pending a court ruling in return for payment of a fixed bail.

112 Forced labour does not appear to have been a common punishment here, as in the Lodz ghetto.
113 ŻIH, 62. RING II/151, telegram from the governor of the central prison to the Jewish Council, 11.3.1942. The release was occasioned by an amnesty declared by the Germans on 10.3.1942. ŻIH, 44. RING II/140, Auerswald to the Jewish Council chairman re pardoning of Jews, 10.3.1942, fol. 7.

6 Ordinary Ghetto Residents and Their Relationship with Internal and External Authorities

1 USHMM, RG 15.083, 113/363, 27.8.1941, fol. 84. For another reported home theft, see USHMM, RG 15.083, 113/363, 10.8.1941, fol. 94; USHMM, RG 15.083, 113/364, 30.7.1940, fol. 6: reported theft of headscarves; USHMM, RG 15.083, 113/364, 7.7.1941, fol. 99: reported theft of daughter's shoes in the street.
2 Feuchert, *Chronik* 1941, 29.1.1941, p. 48.
3 YVA, JM-1455, verdict against Ester Chlebolub, 14.4.1941, fol. 34.
4 Ibid. Also USHMM, RG 05.008, 25/59, verdict against Ester Chlebolub, 14.4.1941, fol. 49, 50.
5 USHMM, RG. 05.008, 27/64, head of OS to State Criminal Police, Ghetto *Sonderkommando*, 31.7.1942, fol. 66.
6 The point here is not what the offender's true motives were, but how he justified himself before which authorities. The severity of the imposed sentence is not known.
7 Feuchert, *Chronik* 1941, 28.2.1941, p. 66: classed as a "most heinous crime."
8 USHMM, RG 05.008, 9/23, hearing of ghetto resident Abram Gecelew at the Ghetto Special Commissariat, 6.7.1940, fol. 454; another resident named Wenger attempted similarly to clear himself of any suspicion of being a "professional smuggler." USHMM, 05.008, 9/23. Ghetto Special Commissariat to the Eldest of the Jews, citing Wenger's statement, 1.7.1940, fol. 341.
9 USHMM, RG 15.083, 113/363, fol. 39. See also RG 15.083, 113/363, fol. 39: report by a ghetto resident that her cobbler had kept her shoes for himself.
10 USHMM, RG 15.083, 113/363, 20.6.1941, fol. 137. Reported theft of child's trousers; ibid., report 4.6.1941, fol. 164: theft of child's coat; ibid., report of May 1941, fol. 186: theft of suit.
11 USHMM, RG 15.083, 113/364, report 27.7.1941, fol. 13.
12 USHMM, RG 15.083, 113/364, report by house watchman Cielski, 18.7.1941, fol. 47: boards removed from attic, offender unknown; USHMM, RG 15.083, 113/364, report 30.5.1941, fol. 318: boards removed from apartment by neighbour; the reason for reporting the incident was that the victim's wife had fallen through the floor to the storey below.
13 USHMM, RG 15.083, 113/364, 25.4.1941, fol. 512.

14 USHMM, RG 15.083, 113/364, statement by Ida Anszołowska, 27.6.1941, fol. 138f.
15 On 26 June 1941, Halle reported that his daughter had been raped by Suken Weischen. USHMM, RG 15.083, 113/364, 26.6.1941, fol. 175. The possibility that this was a denunciation cannot be ruled out. Precisely because such crimes were not the main focus of interest for the legal authorities, the resident reporting the crime is unlikely to have expected negative consequences to ensue for the accused. For other reports by house watchmen and ordinary ghetto residents, see also the log book of the Order Service in Lodz: USHMM, RG 15.083, 120/396, 1940–2.
16 USHMM, RG 15.083, 113/364, 25.6.1941, fol. 161ff.
17 The first ghetto residents had in fact already been deported in December 1941. It was not until January 1942 that the Germans gave orders to Rumkowski for the Order Service to assist with preparations for the "resettlements." See Feuchert, *Chronik* 1941, p. 337, n. 11.
18 How far this is due to source material availability cannot be conclusively determined. The wealth of earlier material suggests, however, that fewer letters were written after this time.
19 E.g., USHMM, 1999.A.0105, 3/62, transcript of theft report by Josef Matikanski (all documents), signed by chief of police, 23.1.1942, fol. 292; USHMM, 1999.A.0105, 3/62, transcript of report by Eschel Wilion, 2.3.1942, fol. 172: reported loss of yellow skilled worker permit, Lithuanian passport, manual worker certificate; also ibid., fol. 175.
20 USHMM, 1999.A.0105, 4/64, re incident of 22.3.1942, fol. 74, 75.
21 Of the mass of ghetto residents, only a few came into direct contact with the courts as defendants or witnesses. Moreover, most of the writing was done by members of the "intellectual class," who were less likely to come before the courts.
22 Speech by Kitz on his appointment as a ghetto court judge, reprinted in Feuchert, *Chronik* 1941, 2.12.1941, p. 281.
23 ŻIH, RING I/702, *Gazeta Żydowska* no. 36, 6.5.1941, p. 2. See Person, *Policjanci*, p. 80.
24 Nirenberg, *Memoirs of the Ghetto*, p. 20; see also the contemporary critique by Leon Hurwicz and Józef Zełkowicz, Feuchert, *Chronik* 1941, p. 432, n. 24.
25 Hershkovitch, "The Ghetto in Litzmannstadt," p. 106.
26 Zełkowicz, *In Those Terrible Days*, esp. the section "Dura Lex, Sed Lex," pp. 129–39, p. 135f.
27 Feuchert, *Chronik* 1943, 2.5.1943, pp. 181, 187.
28 Ibid., p. 186f. On the case and subsequent proceedings, see ibid., pp. 181–7, as well as Poznański's diary entry of 2.5.1943 (*Tagebuch*, p. 98), and the report on Ratner's "resettlement" from prison citing his offence (ibid., 25.6.1943, p. 117; ibid., 27.6.1943, p. 118f).

29 Feuchert, *Chronik* 1943, 10.8.1943, p. 139. This view of court officials as privileged members of the Jewish Council is also highlighted by a report by Poznański on the court chairman, whose wife had apparently caught him *in flagrante* with his secretary. Poznański comments that every "dignitary" had a mistress (*Tagebuch*, 6.7.1943, p. 122).

30 278/1076, *Geto-Tsaytung* no. 3, 21.3.1941, orig. p. 4.

31 YIVO, RG 241, 537.3/898, images and impressions of the court (undated), fol. 1.

32 Feuchert, *Chronik* 1941, 24.12.1941, p. 326.

33 Kruk, *The Last Days*, p. 602f.

34 Adler, *In the Warsaw Ghetto*, p. 164. Adler points out that examining the witnesses was especially difficult – if not impossible – in cases where the accused was thought to have "good connections" with the Germans (ibid.).

35 Opoczyński, *Reportaże*, p. 96f. The case in question related to rent disputes between two tenants; the witness had been asked to give the house committee an account of the background to the conflict.

36 Adler, *In the Warsaw Ghetto*, p. 199.

37 USHMM, RG 15.083, 113/364, OS to the public prosecutor of the Lodz ghetto, 4.6.1941, fol. 303.

38 USHMM, RG 15.083, 113/364, 22.6.1941, OS to the public prosecutor of the Lodz ghetto, fol. 264.

39 For a retrospective view of this, see APŁ, 278/1076, *Geto-Tsaytung* no. 9, 2.5.1941, p. 1. The Jewish Council did not begin systematizing the Secretariat until after November 1940. On this aspect, see also Polit, who devotes a chapter to the topic of "Rumkowski as an addressee for correspondence." See Polit, *"Moja żydowska dusza"*, p. 108ff.

40 APŁ, 278/1076, *Geto-Tsaytung* no. 9, 2.5.1941, p. 1.

41 APŁ, 278/1076, *Geto-Tsaytung* no. 11–12, 30.5.1941, Proclamation no. 275. On 30.5.1941, Rumkowski delegated responsibility for reports of "dishonesty, abuse and swindling" in departments and workshops to the lawyer Neftalin. "Re: Reports of dishonesty, abuse and swindling of all kinds," p. 13.

42 APŁ 278/1076, *Geto-Tsaytung* no. 1, 7.3.1941, p. 3.

43 APŁ, 278/1076, *Geto-Tsaytung* no. 9, 2.5.1941, p. 3. On the procedures involved, see also Polit, *"Moja żydowska dusza"*, p. 110f.

44 APŁ, 278/1076, *Geto-Tsaytung* no. 1, 7.3.1941, p. 3. The relevant procedures were described by Rumkowski in the *Geto-Tsaytung*: every morning, hundreds of requests and proposals were scrutinized, sorted according to their content and nature, and pre-screened by his team of supervisors (ibid.). There are no replies from Rumkowski among the viewed collections.

45 See Polit, *"Moja żydowska dusza"*, pp. 112–16. Other letters sent to Rumkowski contained greetings or praise on occasions such as public holidays, his birthday, and also his wedding. See ibid., pp. 127–49. For more on the petitions in the Lodz ghetto, see also Bethke, "Attempts."

46 The letters written in German in particular often contain numerous grammatical errors. Ghetto residents probably wrote in German, even though it was not in most cases their native language, in order to gain the attention of the Jewish Council chairman, on whom German had been imposed by the occupiers as the official language.

47 ŻIH, RG 205/288, Rumkowski, The Eldest of the Jews in Lodz, Supreme Control Chamber, 20.8.1942, Circular no.1, re complaints, fol. 1.

48 Feuchert, *Chronik* 1944, 11.3.1944, p. 203. On 29 May 1944, the Chronicle reported Rumkowski's intention to reconstruct the office on a smaller scale (ibid., 29.5.1944).

49 On this subject, see Adler, *In the Warsaw Ghetto*, p. 157, as well as the account of the office's activities during the six months of its existence in the *Gazeta Żydowska* of 4.6.1941.

50 ŻIH, RING I/702, *Gazeta Żydowska* of 4.6.1941.

51 USHMM, 1999/0105, 3/62, 1942: re furs; with regard to armed resistance fighters, see Jakub Gens's address to the foremen of forced labour gangs, 15.5.1943, reprinted in Arad and Gutman, *Documents on the Holocaust*, p. 451ff.

52 USHMM, RG 15.083, 93/283, 5.2.1943, fol. 18f.; forwarded by the petitions office to the ghetto court on 18.2.1943.

53 USHMM, RG 15.083, 93/283, 1.12.1942, fol. 26.

54 USHMM, RG 15.083, 93/283, 16.12.1942, fol. 28: citing illness, among other factors.

55 USHMM, RG 15.083, 93/283, Chaim Welzmann, 10.10.1942, fol. 40ff.

56 YIVO, RG 223/300.1, letter from the prisoner Avidon to chief of police and ghetto chairman Gens, 21.5.1941.

57 USHMM, RG 15.083, 93/283, 14.8.1943, fol. 4: request for release of arrested husband; RG 15.083, 93/283, 12.2.1941, fol. 79: request for release of husband Icek Rypstein; USHMM, RG 15.083, 93/283, 22.2.1941, fol. 76ff.: Miriam Fajtlowicz, request for release of father from prison, citing illness; USHMM, RG 15.083, 93/283, 19.2.1941, fol. 87: M. Kirschbaum, request for release of husband from prison, citing the hardship facing her and her children. For writers asserting innocence, see, e.g., USHMM, RG 15.083, 93/283, 21.1.1941, fol. 85: request by Minia Popowska re the wrongful arrest of her husband, who she claimed had been tricked; USHMM, RG 15.083, 93/283, fol. 82: Chawa Wageman, request for release of her husband and assertion of his innocence, 22.1.1941, USHMM, RG 15.083, 93/283, 17.3.1943, fol. 10f.: request from Fela Lomska, aged fourteen, for the release of her sister Regina, being her only caregiver.

58 Nevertheless, women also played a central role in all ghetto communities when it came to criminal activities such as smuggling, which required illegal border crossings. This was because they – unlike (circumcised) Jewish men – were not immediately identifiable as "Jewish." On this subject more generally, see Weitzman, "Living on the Aryan Side," p. 201.

59 USHMM, RG 15.083, 93/283, Symona Korman, 28.3.1941, fol. 97.
60 USHMM, RG 15.083, 93/283, 10.5.1943, fol. 9.
61 USHMM, RG 15.083, 93/283, 12.5.1943, fol. 15.
62 USHMM, RG 15.083, 93/283, Chaja Faiflowiak, 23.2.1941, fol. 90ff.
63 ŻIH, 289. RING I/1197, undated, pre-July 1942. Winter's chief criticism was that such conduct showed the Jewish Council in a bad light and would discourage people from taking on the role of house committee chairman in future.
64 ŻIH, 263. RING I/230, undated.
65 ŻIH, 292. RING I/215, Letter 1, worker from szopa 12, ul. Prosta 14/II, 26.6.1941 (not sent), fol. 1, 2.
66 ŻIH, 292. RING I/215, Letter 2, 6.7.1941.
67 On this point, see also Polit, *"Moja żydowska dusza"*, p. 151.
68 Feuchert, *Chronik* 1941, 16.1.1941, p. 29.
69 Monika Polit devotes a short section to denunciations in the Lodz ghetto, but without placing them in the context of the ghetto's legal sphere. See Polit, *"Moja żydowska dusza"*, pp. 150–6.
70 The message was forwarded by the director to the Order Service: USHMM, RG 15.083, 113/363, copy of Notification no. 1013, 23.8.1941, fol. 83.
71 Feuchert, *Chronik* 1941, 29.1.1941, p. 48.
72 Ibid., 12.1.1941, p. 21
73 USHMM, RG 05.008, 25/59, verdict against Kaliński, Silberszac, Frajlich, and Strusik for violation of the ghetto curfew regulation, 9.4.1941, fol. 52, 53; submission to the State Criminal Police department: ibid., fol. 54; quotation, ibid., fol. 53.
74 ŻIH, RG 205/68, ghetto court verdict in the case of Moszek Hecht and Lajzor Kawelblum, 12.3.1941, fol. 8, 9.
75 Ibid.
76 USHMM, RG 15.083, 113/364, OS to the public prosecutor of the Lodz ghetto, submission of character reference for Gitla Ehrlich, 6.4.1941, fol. 628.
77 Opoczyński, *Reportaże*, p. 96f. The names of the people concerned cannot be ascertained.
78 USHMM, 1999/0105, 3/62, 1942.
79 Kruk, *The Last Days*, 4.4.1943, p. 497. This report should be treated with caution precisely because Kozik was an acquaintance of the chronicler. Nevertheless, it does support the general impression that emerges with regard to denunciations within the Vilna ghetto community.
00 USHMM, RG 05.008, 27/64, to the commissar of the Criminal Police, Lodz ghetto division, re son Chaim Jankiel Reichman, undated, fol. 276.
81 See, e.g., YVA, JM-839, verdict re Olszer, Abbe, and Walfisz, 15.10.1940: accusation regarding import of goods and food to Warsaw following ghettoization (smuggling), subsequent requests by wife to stagger payment of husband's fine and release him from prison, pleading inability

to feed her family by herself; appeals by imprisoned subjects to be granted leniency on health grounds (requests refused: ibid., fol. 252); YVA, JM-1483, fol. 213: request by mother (Rywka Fajdlowicz, aged sixty-five) to release daughter from prison, pleading inability to look after her babies.

82 As in the case of the seventeen-year-old tailor Michel Brand, for example, after being caught leaving the ghetto: USHMM, RG 05.008, 27/64, 2.12.1941, fol. 280, 281; similarly, the declaration of Izrael Slodkiewicz, aged fourteen, re the same offence: USHMM, RG 05.008, 27/64, police department transcript, declaration 14.10.1941, fol. 282.

83 Case of Slodkiewicz and Brand: USHMM, RG 05.008, 27/64, 14.10.1941, fol. 282: note by Criminal Police, 2.12.1941, ibid., fol. 284, Eldest of the Jews to keep the children's details on file.

84 USHMM, RG 05.008, 9/23, notification of Ghetto Special Commissariat, 27.6.1940, fol. 273. Fol. 274: goods seized, 28.6.1940. Other reports: YVA, JM-1483, e.g., confidential messages to Criminal Police, 17.7.1941, fol. 108: location of hidden silk; ibid., 11.7.1941, fol. 111: location of hidden fur coats; ibid., 11.7.1941, fol. 112: location of hidden crude oil engine and dynamos; ibid., 5.6.1941, fol. 142: buried "Jewish gold and diamonds." See also ŻIH, RG 205/158, fol. 43: notification of hidden furs and trading activities.

85 YVA, JM-1483, anonymous letter, translation of letter by Criminal Police, 14.10.1941, fol. 38.

86 Ibid. The enclosed Criminal Police report of 11 October 1941 indicates that the search failed to uncover anything, leading the police to attribute a revenge motive to the anonymous correspondent.

87 YVA, JM-1483, report by Lodz Criminal Police, 24.4.1941, fol. 230. Such letters were to be ignored in future. Similarly, YVA, JM-1483, anonymous letter and incrimination of ghetto resident Finkelstein and subsequent Criminal Police report, 21.2.1941, fol. 442f.: "This can be assumed to be a case of personal animosity between the letter writer and the F."

88 Sprawozdanie Sonderkommissariat w getcie, VI–VII 1940, Zespół Gettokommissariat w Łodzi (ŻIH), YVA, JM-1496, confidential message to Ghetto Sonderkommando, 31.5.1940, fol. 218.

89 YVA, JM-1483, anonymous letter, 23.5.1941, fol. 172, note by Criminal Police, 24.5.1941, fol. 174.

90 YVA, JM-1483, report subsequent to "confidential information" re alleged smuggling by an escaped resident, 22.4.1941, fol. 274.

91 USHMM, RG 05.008, 30/81, Lodz Criminal Police Department, Meldunki o drobnych przestępstwach dokonanych na terenie getta żydowskiego w Łodzi, 1941–2, e.g., Notification no. 6: Chaim Wajeman, accuses Majlich of stealing his wallet; Notification no. 64, 9.1.1941: informant suspects security guard Kucharska Ruchla of stealing her gold watch; 22.3.1941, Notification no. 391: Kuczer, Icek "reports that his stepson Mojsze Kaufman is (persistently) stealing from him."

92 These are part of a collection of surviving letters of denunciation sent by residents of the city of Warsaw to the Gestapo in 1940 and 1941. The letters were intercepted by underground groups and did not reach the Germans. They can be viewed at IPN, Warsaw, Commander of Security Police and Security Service for the Warsaw district. For an analysis of the letters, see Engelking, *Szanowny panie gestapo*. Some of the results are published in Engelking, "Sehr geehrter Herr Gestapo."

93 IPN, Commander of the Security Police and Security Service for the Warsaw District, Letter no. 205. This act did not become a capital offence in Warsaw until 10 November 1941.

94 YVA, JM-836, extract from the criminal records of the public prosecution department in Warsaw, re Lodz, e.g., Bittermann smuggling case, 29.4.1941, fol. 187; see also the trial of a "Polish/Jewish smuggling gang": YVA, JM-834, 9.9.1941, report of Police District 6 to Ghetto Criminal Police, e.g., fol. 68.

95 Ibid., fol. 2; quotation fol. 45.

96 YVA, JM-845, charge of 6.3.1941 against Mendel Goldberg, brought by Wolf Breitmann, fol. 2.

97 See, e.g., Battrick, "Smuggling." Boneh writes with similar force on the Pinsk ghetto: "Every little bit of fat smuggled through the gates or under the fence at risk of life, every piece of bread or handful of potatoes a Jewish child brought from the next village, crawling under the barbed wire ... all these were great deeds of heroism, acts of resistance against the satanic Nazi plan to destroy the Jews by hunger and disease" (*The Holocaust and the Revolt*, p. 117); see also Bauer, *Rethinking*, p. 120.

98 See, e.g., Engelking and Grabowski, *Żydów łamiących*, p. 8.

99 See Bauer, *Rethinking*, p. 120.

100 For a general introduction to the discussions on Jewish resistance from the 1960s onwards, see Dawidowicz, *The Holocaust*; Bauer, *Rethinking*; Michman, *Holocaust Historiography*.

101 See, for example, Adler's descriptions of the Warsaw ghetto, *In the Warsaw Ghetto*, pp. 146, 149. Bauer argues likewise against classifying the activities of "big-time smugglers" as resistance, since their main aim was to make money (*Rethinking*, pp. 119–66).

102 YVA, O-3/10906, Testimony of Yaakov Shvartsberg, p. 30.

103 Feuchert, *Chronik 1943*, 14.3.1943, p. 102.

104 Adler, *In the Warsaw Ghetto*, p. 126 [translation of original adjusted by Sharon Howe].

105 Feuchert, *Chronik 1941*, 29.7.1941, p. 205.

106 Following Ofer's argument, professionally organized smugglers can be classified as part of a new, better-off "elite" in the ghetto ("Everyday Life," p. 52).

107 This is also evident from the fact that the term "smuggler" was sometimes used as an insult in the Warsaw ghetto. On this aspect, see Opoczyński, *Reportaże*, p. 97; on the distinction between types of smuggler, see also Szpilman, *The Pianist*, p. 13.

108 Adler, *In the Warsaw Ghetto*, p. 47.

109 Kruk, *The Last Days*, 19.1.1943, p. 451. Kruk is not cited here as an ordinary resident because he occupied a post in the Jewish self-administration. Since he was extremely critical of the Jewish Council chairman's strategy, however, we can assume that his view was shared by a number of those within the ghetto community.

110 YIVO, RG 225/17.3, fol. 1. The date of authorship is unknown. The report is part of the Hersch Wasser Collection, which suggests that it was written in the ghetto. The fact that the writer refers to Tofel in the past tense means it was presumably written after his execution in early June 1944.

111 YIVO, RG 225/17.3, fol. 1. The author reports that Mojsze Tofel, along with other "radio listeners," was hanged by the Germans in the prison on Sterlinga Street in June 1944. YIVO, RG 225/17.3, fol. 1. Poznański also used a radio to obtain information on the course of the war. A conspiratorial group of radio listeners had been organized by the Zionist activist Chaim Widawski. Its members were arrested at the same time as Mojsze Tofel following a denunciation on 6 June 1944. Widawski committed suicide after the Germans threated to murder hostages in his place. On this subject, see Poznański, *Tagebuch*, p. 207f.; also nn. 101, 102, 103, and entry of 9.6.1944, p. 219f.

112 On the role played by radio listeners in disseminating news in the Lodz ghetto, see Löw, *Juden im Getto*, p. 448f.

113 Even here, an influence was exerted by the existence of a real audience as opposed to an imagined one, e.g., in the form of oral history interviewers, who inevitably also represent a time-specific sociological interest.

114 YVA, O-3/10906, Testimony of Yaakov Shvartsberg, p. 30.

115 YVA, O-33, Collection of Various Testimonies, Diaries, Memoirs, 1072, Testimony of Symcha Binem Motyl, quoted in Engelking and Leociak, *Warsaw Ghetto*, p. 385. Scrap metal dealers enjoyed a privileged status in the ghetto communities, since they were allowed to leave the ghetto.

Conclusion: Criminality and Law between the Poles of External Power and Internal Autonomy

1 Gringauz, "The Ghetto as an Experiment," p. 6.

2 On "Nazi ethics and morality" more generally, see Bialas, *Moralische Ordnungen*; Bialas, "Nazi Ethics." On German jurisdiction in Nazi-occupied Poland, see, e.g., Jan Grabowski, "Jewish Criminality"; Maximilian Becker, *Mitstreiter*.

3 Judith Vöcker is currently writing a PhD thesis at the Stanley Burton Centre for Holocaust and Genocide Studies at the University of Leicester entitled "'In the Name of the German Nation' – The German Jurisdiction during the Nazi Occupation of Warsaw and Cracow."

4 See, e.g., Jan Grabowski, "Jewish Defendants" and "Żydzi."

5 Trunk, "Note.".

6 Feuchert, *Chronik* 1941, 24.12.1941, p. 325

7 Kruk, *The Last Days*, 9.9.1942, p. 353.

8 See, e.g., Engel, "Who Is"; Finder, "Jewish Collaborators"; Finder, "Sweep Out"; Finder and Jockusch, *Jewish Honor Courts*.

Bibliography

Archival Sources

APŁ – Archiwum Państwowe w Łodzi, Łódź

– 278, Przełożony Starszeństwa Żydów w Getcie Łódzkim (PSŻ)
– 278/1075, 1076, *Geto-Tsaytung*

GFH – Beit Lohamei Ha-Getaot/Ghetto Fighter House, Western Galilee

– Collections Section
– Collections Section, 554, *Geto-Yedies*
– Registry Holdings

IPN – Instytut Pamięci Narodowej, Warsaw

– 165/367, Commander of the Security Police and Security Service for the Warsaw District, Raporty dzienne KSP dla niemieckiego komisarza o planowanych czynnościach służbowych i stwierdzonych uchybieniach porządkowych w getcie

USHMM – United States Holocaust Memorial Museum, Washington, DC

– RG 05.008, Akta Miasta Łodzi, Stadtverwaltung Litzmannstadt (originals in Archiwum Państwowe w Łodzi [APŁ])
– RG 15.083, Przełożony Starszeństwa Żydów w Getcie Łódzkim (PSŻ) (originals in Archiwum Państwowe w Łodzi [APŁ])
– Acc. 1999.A.0105, Vilnius Ghetto Records, 1941–4 (originals in lietuvos vaizdo ir garso archyvas, Vilnius)

YIVO – Institute for Jewish Research, New York

– RG 225, Hersch Wasser Collection, 1939 46
– RG 223, Abraham Sutzkever-Szmerke Kaczerginski Collection, 1806–1945
– RG 241, Nachman Zonabend Collection

YVA – Yad Vashem Archives, Jerusalem

Kriminalkommissariat w Łodzi:
– JM-1440
– JM-1454
– JM-1455
– JM-1483
– JM-1496
Lodz Special Court:
– JM-834
– JM-836
– JM-839
– JM-845
M-41, Archives of Belarus (originals in Gosudarstvenny Arkhiv Brestskoy
    Oblasti-Belarus, Brest)
O-3, Testimonies
O-33, Collection of Various Testimonies, Diaries, Memoirs
O-34, Nachman Zonabend Collection

ŻIH –Żydowski Instytut Historyczny, Warsaw

– RING I, Archiwum Ringelbluma I
– RING I/702, Gazeta Żydowska
– RING II, Archiwum Ringelbluma II
– RG 205, Getto Łódź
– RG 205/349, Getto-Enzyklopädie – Zbiór Materiałów do dziejów ludności
    Żydowskiej w Łodzi 1939–44
– RG 221, Judenraty
– RG 241, Obwieszczenia
– RG 302, Pamiętniki
– Bernard Mark Collection
– Ekspertyzy Korespondencja ŻIH, sąd społeczny

Primary Sources

Adler, Stanisław. *In the Warsaw Ghetto 1940–1943. An Account of a Witness.*
    Jerusalem: Yad Vashem, 1982.

Arad, Yitzhak, and Yisrael Gutman, eds. *Documents on the Holocaust: Selected Sources on the Destruction of the Jews of Germany and Austria, Poland, and the Soviet Union*. Jerusalem: Yad Vashem, 1987.

Balberyszski, Mendl. *Stronger Than Iron: The Destruction of Vilna Jewry 1941– 1945. An Eyewitness Account*. Jerusalem: Gefen Publishing House, 2010. Orig. Yiddish: *Shtarker fun ayzn*. Tel Aviv: Hamenora, 1967.

Berenstein, Tatiana, and Artur Eisenbach, eds. *Faschismus – Getto – Massenmord. Dokumentation über Ausrottung und Widerstand der Juden in Polen während des Zweiten Weltkrieges*. Berlin: Rütten & Loening, 1961.

Berg, Mary. *Warsaw Ghetto*. New York: L.B. Fischer, 1945.

Bryskier, Henryk. *Żydzi pod swastyką, czyli getto w Warszawie w XX wieku*. Warsaw: Oficyna Wydawnicza "Aspra-JR," 2006.

Czerniaków, Adam. *The Warsaw Diary of Adam Czerniaków 1939–1942*. New York: Stein and Day, 1979.

Dworzecki, Mark. *Yerushaleyim de Lite, in kamf un umkum: zichroines fun Wilner geṭo*. Paris: Yidisher Folksfarband in Frankreich un Yidisher Nazionaln Arbeter-Farband in Amerike, 1948.

Eichenbaum, Ray. "A Memorial for Bronia." In Eichenbaum, *Romeks Odyssee. Jugend im Holocaust*. Vienna: Verlag für Gesellschaftskritik, 1996, 11–115.

Eisenbach, Arthur. *Dokumenty i Materiały do Dziejów Okupacji Niemieckiej w Polsce*. Warsaw: Centralna Żydowska Komisja Historyczna, 1946. Vol. 3: *Getto Łódzkie*.

Feuchert, Sascha, ed. *Die Chronik des Gettos Lodz/Litzmannstadt*. 1941. Göttingen: Wallstein, 2007.

– *Die Chronik des Gettos Lodz/Litzmannstadt*. 1942. Göttingen: Wallstein, 2007.

– *Die Chronik des Gettos Lodz/Litzmannstadt*. 1943. Göttingen: Wallstein, 2007.

– *Die Chronik des Gettos Lodz/Litzmannstadt*. 1944. Göttingen: Wallstein, 2007.

– *Die Chronik des Gettos Lodz/Litzmannstadt. Supplemente und Anhang*. Göttingen: Wallstein, 2007.

Goldstein, Bernard. *The Stars Bear Witness*. New York: Viking Press, 1949.

Gombiński, Stanisław. *Wspomnienia policjanta z warszawskiego getta*. Warsaw: Centrum Badań nad Zagładą Żydów/Żydowski Instytut Historyczny, 2010.

Gorodecka, Chana. *Hana. Pamiętnik polskiej Żydówki*. Gdańsk: Atext, 1992.

Kaplan, Chaim. *Scroll of Agony: The Warsaw Diary of Chaim A. Kaplan*. New York: Macmillan Publishers, 1965.

Kermish, Joseph, ed. *To Live with Honor and Die with Honor! Selected Documents from the Warsaw Ghetto Underground Archives "O.S." (Oneg Shabbat)*. Jerusalem: Yad Vashem, 1986.

Kruk, Herman. *The Last Days of the Jerusalem of Lithuania: Chronicle from the Vilna Ghetto and the Camps*. New Haven: Yale University Press, 2002.

– *Togbuch fun Wilner Geto*. New York: YIVO, 1961.

Lewin, Abraham. *A Cup of Tears: A Diary of the Warsaw Ghetto*. Ed. Anthony Polonsky. London: Fontana, 1990.

Nirenberg, Yankl (Jakub). *Memoirs of the Ghetto* ("Di Geshikhte fun Lodzher Geto"). In Nirenberg, *In di yorn fun yiddishen khorbn.* New York 1948, 211–94; Toronto: Lugus Libros, 2003.

Opoczyński, Perec. *Reportaże z warszawskiego getta.* Ed. Monika Polit. Warsaw: Stowarzyszenie Centrum Badań nad Zagładą Żydów/Żydowski Instytut Historyczny, 2009.

Poster: https://www.dhm.de/lemo/Bestand/objekt/xp991312 [accessed 22.4.2015]

Poznański, Jakub. *Tagebuch aus dem Ghetto Litzmannstadt.* Ed. Ingo Loose. Berlin: Metropol-Verlag, 2011.

Ringelblum, Emmanuel. *Notes from the Warsaw Ghetto: The Journal of Emmanuel Ringelblum.* New York: Schocken, 1974.

Rosenfeld, Oskar. *In the Beginning Was the Ghetto: Notebooks from Lodz.* Ed. Hanno Loewy. Evanston: Northwestern University Press, 2002.

Sierakowiak, David. *The Diary of Dawid Sierakowiak: Five Notebooks from the Lodz Ghetto.* Trans. Kamil Turowski. New York: Oxford University Press, 1996.

Sutzkever, Abraham. *Wilner Ghetto 1941–1944.* Zürich: Ammann, 2009.

Szpilman, Wladyslaw. *The Pianist: The Extraordinary Story of One Man's Survival in Warsaw, 1939–45.* London: Victor Gollancz, 1999.

Weh, Albert, ed. *Das Recht des Generalgouvernements: die Verordnungen des Generalgouverneurs für die besetzten polnischen Gebiete und die Durchführungsbestimmungen hierzu, nach Sachgebieten geordnet: Stand vom 1. Mai 1940.* Krakow: Burgverlag, 1940.

Zełkowicz, Josef (Józef). *In Those Terrible Days: Writings from the Lodz Ghetto.* Ed. Michal Unger. Jerusalem: Yad Vashem, 2002.

Secondary Sources

Alberti, Michael. *Die Anfänge und die Durchführung der "Endlösung". Die Verfolgung und Vernichtung der Juden im Reichsgau Wartheland 1939–1945.* Wiesbaden: Harrassowitz, 2006.

Aly, Götz. *"Final Solution": Nazi Population Policy and the Murder of the European Jews.* London: Arnold, 1999.

Arad, Yitzhak. *Ghetto in Flames: The Struggle and Destruction of the Jews in Vilna in the Holocaust.* New York: Holocaust Library, 1982.

Arendt, Hannah. *Eichmann in Jerusalem: A Report on the Banality of Evil.* New York: Viking Press, 1963.

Atamuk, Solomon. *Juden in Litauen. Ein geschichtlicher Überblick.* Konstanz: Hartung-Gorre, 2000.

Baranowski, Julian. *The Łódź Ghetto 1940–1944: Vademecum = Łódzkie getto 1940–1944.* Lodz: Archiwum Państwowe w Łodzi/Bilbo, 2003.

– "Utworzenie i organizacja getta w Łodzi." In Paweł Samuś and Wiesław Puś, eds., *Fenomen getta łódzkiego 1940–1944.* Lodz: Wydawnictwo Uniwersytetu Łódzkiego, 2006, 115–28.

– *Zigeunerlager in Litzmannstadt 1941–1942/The Gypsy Camp in Lodz/Obóz cygański w Łodzi 1941–1942.* Lodz: Archiwum Państwowe w Łodzi/Bilbo, 2003.

Battrick, Carol. "Smuggling as a Form of Resistance in the Warsaw Ghetto." *British Journal of Holocaust Education* 4.2 (1995): 199–224.

Bauer, Yehuda. "Forms of Jewish Resistance during the Holocaust." In *The Jewish Emergence from Powerlessness.* Toronto: University of Toronto Press, 1979, 26–40.

– *Rethinking the Holocaust.* New Haven: Yale University Press, 2001.

Becker, Howard. *Outsiders. Studies in the Sociology of Deviance.* New York/ London: Free Press, 1963.

Becker, Maximilian. *Mitstreiter im Volkstumskampf. Deutsche Justiz in den eingegliederten Ostgebieten 1939–1945.* Berlin: De Gruyter, 2014.

Bender, Sara. "Judenräte and Other Representative Bodies." In *YIVO Encyclopedia of Jews in Eastern Europe.* www.yivoencyclopedia.org/article .aspx/Judenrate_and_Other_Representative_Bodies [accessed 1.4.2015].

Benney, Mark. "Gramsci on Law, Morality, and Power." *International Journal of the Sociology of Law* 11 (1983): 191–208.

Ben-Sasson, Havi. "Christians in the Ghetto: All Saint's Church, Birth of the Holy Virgin Mary Church and the Jews of the Warsaw Ghetto." *Yad Vashem Studies* 31 (2003): 153–73.

Ben-Sefer, Ellen. "Forced Sterilization and Abortion as Sexual Abuse." In Sonja Hedgepeth and Rochelle Saidel, eds., *Sexual Violence against Jewish Women during the Holocaust.* Waltham: Brandeis University Press, 2010, 156–75.

Benz, Wolfgang, ed. *Dimension des Völkermords. Die Zahl der jüdischen Opfer des Nationalsozialismus.* Berlin: De Gruyter, 1991.

Bergen, Doris, Anna Hájková, and Andrea Löw, eds. *Alltag im Holocaust. Jüdisches Leben im Großdeutschen Reich 1941–1945.* Munich: Oldenbourg, 2013.

Bergen, Doris L., Anna Hájková, and Andrea Löw. "Warum eine Alltagsgeschichte des Holocaust?" In Bergen, Hájková, and Löw, eds., *Alltag im Holocaust. Jüdisches Leben im Großdeutschen Reich 1941–1945.* Munich: Oldenbourg, 2013, 1–12.

Bergmann, Werner. *Geschichte des Antisemitismus.* Munich: Beck, 2004.

Berkowitz, Michael. *The Crime of My Very Existence: Nazism and the Myth of Jewish Criminality.* Berkeley: University of California Press, 2007.

Bethke, Svenja. "Attempts to Take Action in a Coerced Community: Petitions to the Jewish Council in the Lodz Ghetto during World War II." In Thomas Pegelow Kaplan and Wolf Gruner, eds., *Resisting Persecution: Jews and Their*

Petitions during the Holocaust. New York/Oxford: Berghahn Books, 2020, 114–37.

– "Crime and Punishment in Emergency Situations: The Jewish Ghetto Courts in Lodz, Warsaw and Vilna in World War II – A Comparative Study." *Dapim, Studies on the Holocaust* 28.3 (2014): 173–89.

– "Regeln und Sanktionen im Getto Litzmannstadt. Die Bekanntmachungen des Judenratsvorsitzenden Rumkowski." *Journal for Genocide Studies* 13.1/2 (2012): 30–52.

– *Tanz auf Messers Schneide: Kriminalität und Recht in den Ghettos Warschau, Litzmannstadt und Wilna*. Hamburg: Hamburger Edition, 2015.

Bethke, Svenja, and Hanna Schmidt Holländer. "Lebenswelt Ghetto. Raumtheorie und interpretatives Paradigma als Bereicherung für die Erforschung jüdischer Ghettos im Nationalsozialismus." *PaRDeS. Journal of the Association of Jewish Studies* 17 (2011): 35–51.

Bialas, Wolfgang. *Moralische Ordnungen des Nationalsozialismus*. Göttingen: Vandenhoeck & Ruprecht, 2014.

– "Nazi Ethics: Perpetrators with a Clear Conscience." *Dapim* 27.1 (2013): 3–25.

Birnbaum, Pierre, ed. *Paths of Emancipation: Jews, States, and Citizenship*. Princeton: Princeton University Press, 1995.

Bloom, Solomon. "Dictator of the Lodz Ghetto: The Strange History of Mordechai Chaim Rumkowski." *Commentary* 7 (1949): 111–22.

– "Towards the Ghetto Dictator." *Jewish Social Studies* 12 (1950): 73–8.

Blumer, Herbert. *Symbolic Interactionism: Perspective and Method*. Englewood Cliffs, NJ: Prentice-Hall, 1969.

Boneh, Nahum. *The Holocaust and the Revolt in Pinsk 1941–1942*. Vol. 1, part 2. Tel Aviv: Irgun yots'e *Pinsk*-Karlin be'Medinat Israel, 1977.

Browning, Christopher. "Nazi Ghettoization Policy in Poland: 1939–41." *Central European History* 19.4 (1986): 343–68.

– *The Origins of the Final Solution: The Evolution of Nazi Jewish Policy, September 1939–March 1942*. Lincoln: University of Nebraska Press, 2004.

Broyde, Michael, and Michael Ausubel. "Legal Institutions." In Gershon David Hundert, ed., *The YIVO Encyclopedia of Jews in Eastern Europe*. New Haven: Yale University Press, 2008, 1007–10.

Buckel, Sonja, and Andreas Fischer-Lescano. "Gramsci Reconsidered: Hegemony in Global Law." *Leiden Journal of International Law* 22 (2009): 437–54.

Chapoutot, Johann. "Eradiquer le typhus: imaginaire médical et discours sanitaire nazi dans le Gouvernement Général de Pologne (1939–1944)." *Revue historique* 1 (2014): 157–78.

Chu, Winson. "'Wir sind keine Deutschen nur dem Volke nach': Multiethnic Pasts and Ethnic Germans in the German Criminal Police in Lodz during the Second World War." *Zeitschrift für Genozidforschung* 16.1 (2018): 35–56.

Cohen, Boaz. *Israeli Holocaust Research: Birth and Evolution*. London: Routledge, 2013.

Cohn, Haim Hermann, and Isaac Levitats. "Bet Din and Judges." In Fred Skolnik and Michael Berenbaum, eds., *Encyclopedia Judaica*. 2nd edition. Detroit: Macmillan Publishers, 2007, 512–24.

Cole, Tim. "Ghettoization." In Dan Stone, ed., *The Historiography of the Holocaust*. London: Palgrave, 2004, 67–77.

– *Holocaust City: The Making of a Jewish Ghetto*. New York: Routledge, 2003.

Corni, Gustavo. *Hitler's Ghettos: Voices from a Beleagered Society, 1939–1944*. London: Arnold, 2002.

Dąbrowska, Danuta. "Administracja żydowska w Łodzi i jej agendy w okresie od początku okupacji do zamknięcia getta (8 IX 1939 r.–30 IV 1940 r.)." *Biuletyn ŻIH* 45.46 (1963): 110–37.

– "Struktura i funkcje administracji żydowskiej w getcie łódzkim (maj–grudzień 1940), Part 1." *Biuletyn ŻIH* 51 (1964): 41–57.

– "Struktura i funkcje administracji żydowskiej w getcie łódzkim (maj–grudzień 1940), Part 2." *Biuletyn ŻIH* 52 (1964): 35–48.

Dawidowicz, Lucy. *The Holocaust and the Historians*. Cambridge, MA: Harvard University Press, 1981.

Dehnel, Jacek. "Wszystkie procesy Eleazara Grünbauma." *Zagłada Żydów: studia i materiały* 12 (2016): 410–24.

Dieckmann, Christoph. *Deutsche Besatzungspolitik in Litauen 1941–1944*. 2 vols. Göttingen: Wallstein, 2011.

– "Die Zivilverwaltung in Litauen." In Wolf Kaiser, ed., *Täter im Vernichtungskrieg. Der Überfall auf die Sowjetunion und der Völkermord an den Juden*. Berlin/Munich: Propyläen-Verlag, 2002, 96–109.

Dieckmann, Christoph, and Babette Quinkert. "Einleitung." In Dieckmann and Quinkert, eds., *Im Ghetto 1939–1945. Neue Forschungen zu Alltag und Umfeld*. Göttingen: Wallstein, 2009.

Diner, Dan. "'Rupture in Civilization': On the Genesis and Meaning of a Concept in Understanding." In Moshe Zimmermann, ed., *On Germans and Jews under the Nazi Regime: Essays by Three Generations of Historians*. Jerusalem: Hebrew University Magnes Press, 2006, 33–48.

Diner, Dan, ed. *Beyond the Conceivable: Studies on Germany, Nazism and the Holocaust*. Berkeley: University of California Press, 2000.

Dreifuss, Havi. "Warsaw." In Guy Miron, ed., *The Yad Vashem Encyclopedia of the Ghettos during the Holocaust*. Jerusalem: Yad Vashem, 2009, 897–921.

Durkheim, Émile. "Kriminalität als normales Phänomen." In Fritz Sack and René König, eds., *Kriminalsoziologie*. Frankfurt am Main: Akademische Verlags-Gesellschaft, 1968.

Edelman, Marek. *The Ghetto Fights: Warsaw 1941–43*. New York: American Representation of the General Jewish Workers' Union of Poland, 1946.

Elon, Menahem. *Jewish Law: History, Sources, Principles (ha'mishpat ha'ivri).* 4 vols. Philadelphia: Jewish Publication Society, 1994.

Engel, David. "Who Is a Collaborator? The Trials of Michał Weichert." In Sławomir Kapralski, ed., *The Jews in Poland.* Vol. 2. Krakow: Judaica Foundation, 1999.

Engelking, Barbara. "Sehr geehrter Herr Gestapo. Denunziationen im deutsch besetzten Polen 1940/41." In Klaus-Michael Mallmann and Bogdan Musiał, eds., *Genesis des Genozids. Polen 1939–1941.* Darmstadt: Wissenschaftliche Buchgesellschaft, 2004, 206–20.

– *Szanowny panie gestapo: donosy do władz niemieckich w Warszawie i okolicach w latach 1940–1941.* Warsaw: Wydawnictwo IFiS PAN, 2003.

Engelking, Barbara, and Jan Grabowski. *"Żydów łamiących prawo należy karać śmiercią!" "Przestępczość" Żydów w Warszawie.* Warsaw: Stowarzyszenie Centrum Badań nad Zagładą Żydów, 2010.

Engelking, Barbara, and Jacek Leociak. *The Warsaw Ghetto: A Guide to the Perished City.* New Haven: Yale University Press, 2009.

Engelking, Barbara, Jacek Leociak, and Dariusz Libionka, eds. *Prowincja noc. Życie i zagłada Żydów w dystrykcie warszawskim.* Warsaw: Wydawnictwo IFiS PAN, 2007.

Feuchert, Sascha. "Die Getto-Chronik: Entstehung und Überlieferung. Eine Projektskizze." In Sascha Feuchert, ed., *Die Chronik des Gettos Lodz/Litzmannstadt. Supplemente und Anhang.* Göttingen: Wallstein, 2007, 168–90.

Finder, Gabriel N. "Jewish Collaborators on Trial in Poland." *Polin. Studies in Polish Jewry* 20 (2008): 122–48.

– "'Sweep Out Evil from Your Midst': The Jewish People's Court in Post-War Poland." In Johannes-Dieter Steinert and Inge Weber-Newth, eds., *Beyond Camps and Forced Labour: Current International Research on Survivors of Nazi Persecution.* Osnabrück: Secolo Verlag, 2005, 269–79.

– The Trial of Shepsl Rotholc and the Politics of Retribution in the Aftermath of the Holocaust." *Gal-Ed* 20 (2006): 63–89.

Finder, Gabriel N., and Laura Jockusch. *Jewish Honor Courts: Revenge, Retribution, and Reconciliation in Europe and Israel after the Holocaust.* Detroit: Wayne State University Press, 2015.

Florin, Moritz. "Tagungsbericht: *Lebenswelt Ghetto.*" H-Soz-u-Kult, H-Net Reviews. November 2009. http://www.h-net.org/reviews/showrev.php?id=29130; [accessed 1.7.2015].

Fox, Frank. "The Jewish Ghetto Police: Some Reflexions." *East European Jewish Affairs* 25.2 (1995): 41–7.

Fraenkel, Ernst. *The Dual State: A Contribution to the Theory of Dictatorship.* New York: Oxford University Press, 1941.

Freund, Florian, Bertrand Perz, and Karl Stuhlpfarrer. "Das Getto in Litzmannstadt." In *"Unser einziger Weg ist Arbeit." Das Getto in Lodz*

1940–1944. Exhibition catalogue of the Jewish Museum Frankfurt. Vienna: Löcker, 1990, 17–31.

Friedländer, Saul. "An Integrated History of the Holocaust: Some Methodological Challenges." In Dan Stone, ed., *The Holocaust and Historical Methodology*. New York/Oxford: Berghahn Books, 2012, 181–9.

– "Eine integrierte Geschichte des Holocaust." *Aus Politik und Zeitgeschichte* 14–15 (2007): 7–14.

– *Nazi Germany and the Jews, Vol. 1: The Years of Persecution, 1933–1939*. New York: HarperCollins, 1997.

– *Nazi Germany and the Jews, Vol. 2: The Years of Extermination, 1939–1945*. New York: HarperCollins, 2007.

Friedman, Philip. "American Jewish Research and Literature on the Jewish Catastrophe of 1939–1945." *Jewish Social Studies* 13 (1951): 135–250.

– "Jacob Gens: 'Commandant' of the Vilna Ghetto." In Friedman, *Roads to Extinction: Essays on the Holocaust*. New York/Philadelphia: Jewish Publication Society of America, 1980, 365–80.

– "The Jewish Ghettos of the Nazi Era." *Jewish Social Studies* 16.1 (January 1954): 61–88.

– "Pseudo-Saviors in the Polish Ghettos: Mordechai Chaim Rumkowski of Lodz." In Friedman, *Roads to Extinction: Essays on the Holocaust*. New York/ Philadelphia: Jewish Publication Society of America, 1980, 333–52.

– "Research and Literature on the Recent Jewish Tragedy." *Jewish Social Studies* 12 (1950): 17–26.

Furła-Buszek, Joanna. "Charakteristika der Bekanntmachungen des Białystoker Judenrats." In Freia Anders and Katrin Stoll, eds., *Der Judenrat von Białystok*. Paderborn/Munich: Schöningh, 2010, 417–26.

Galiński, Antoni. "Centralne więzienie dla Żydów w getcie łódzkim." In Wiesław Puś and Stanisław Liszewski, eds., *Dzieje Żydów w Łodzi 1820–1944. Wybrane Problemy*. Lodz: Wydawnictwo Uniwersytetu Łódzkiego, 1991, 324–37.

– "Policja w getcie." In Okręgowa Komisja Badania Zbrodni Hitlerowskich w Łodzi Instytutu Pamięci Narodowej [OKBZHŁIPN], ed., *Getto w Łodzi 1940–1944. Materiały z sesji naukowej*. Lodz: Instytut Pamięci Narodowej 1988, 27–49.

Geertz, Clifford. *Local Knowledge: Further Essays in Interpretative Anthropology*. New York: Basic Books, 1983.

Gehlen, Arnold. *Moral und Hypermoral. Eine pluralistische Ethik*. Frankfurt am Main: Athenäum-Verlag, 1969.

Geiger, Theodor. *Vorstudien zu einer Soziologie des Rechts*. Berlin: Duncker & Humblot, 1987.

Gerlach, Christian. *Kalkulierte Morde. Die deutsche Wirtschafts- und Vernichtungspolitik in Weißrußland 1941–1944*. Hamburg: Hamburger Edition, 1999.

– "The Wannsee Conference, the Fate of German Jews, and Hitler's Decision in Principle to Exterminate All European Jews." *Journal of Modern History* 70.4 (1998): 759–812.

Gilman, Sander L. *Jewish Self-Hatred: Anti-Semitism and the Hidden Language of the Jews.* Baltimore: Johns Hopkins University Press, 1986.

Goldberg, Amos. "The History of the Jews in the Ghettos: A Cultural Perspective." In Dan Stone, ed., *The Holocaust and Historical Methodology.* New York/Oxford: Berghahn Books, 2012, 79–100.

Goldfine, Yitzhak. *Einführung in das jüdische Recht. Eine historische und analytische Untersuchung des jüdischen Rechts und seiner Institutionen.* Hamburg: Hamburger Gesellschaft für Völkerrecht und Auswärtige Politik, 1973.

Gotzmann, Andreas. "Die Grenzen der Autonomie. Der jüdische Bann im Heiligen Römischen Reich." In Andreas Gotzmann and Stefan Wendehorst, eds., *Juden im Recht. Neue Zugänge zur Rechtsgeschichte der Juden im Alten Reich.* Stuttgart: Duncker u. Humblot, 2007, 41–80.

– *Jüdische Autonomie in der Frühen Neuzeit. Recht und Gemeinschaft im deutschen Judentum.* Göttingen: Wallstein, 2008.

– *Jüdisches Recht im kulturellen Prozess. Die Wahrnehmung der Halacha im Deutschland des 19. Jahrhunderts.* Tübingen: Mohr Siebeck, 1997.

Grabowski, Hans-Ludwig. *Das Geld des Terrors. Geld und Geldersatz in deutschen Konzentrationslagern und Gettos 1933 bis 1945.* Regenstauf: Battenberg Gietl Verlag, 2008.

Grabowski, Jan. *Hunt for the Jews: Betrayal and Murder in German-Occupied Poland.* Bloomington: Indiana University Press, 2013.

– "'Jewish Criminality and Jewish Criminals' in the Warsaw Ghetto: German Courts, Jews and the New German Order in Warsaw, 1939–1942." In Imke Hansen, Katrin Steffen, and Joachim Tauber, eds., *Lebenswelt Ghetto. Alltag und soziales Umfeld während der nationalsozialistischen Verfolgung.* Wiesbaden: Harrassowitz, 2013, 117–29.

– "Jewish Defendants in German and Polish Courts in the Warsaw District." *Yad Vashem Studies* 35.1 (2007): 49–81.

– "Żydzi przed obliczem niemieckich i polskich sądów w dystrykcie warszawskim Generalnego Gubernatorstwa. 1939–1942." In Barbara Engelking, Jacek Leociak, and Dariusz Libionka, eds., *Prowincja noc. Życie i zagłada Żydów w dystrykcie warszawskim.* Warsaw: Wydawnictwo IFiS PAN, 2007, 75–119.

Gregorowicz, Justyna. "Komunikacja telefoniczna w życiu społeczności getta warszawskiego." *Zagłada Żydów: studia i materiały* 10.1 (2014): 409–27.

Gringauz, Samuel. "The Ghetto as an Experiment of Jewish Social Organization (Three Years of Kovno Ghetto)." *Jewish Social Studies* 11 (1949): 3–20.

– "Some Methodological Problems in the Study of the Ghetto." *Jewish Social Studies* 12 (1950): 65–72.

Guesnet, François. *Polnische Juden im 19. Jahrhundert. Lebensbedingungen, Rechtsnormen und Organisation im Wandel.* Cologne: Böhlau, 1998.

Gutman, Yisrael, ed. *Encyclopaedia of the Holocaust.* New York: Macmillan Publishers, 1990.

– *The Jews of Warsaw. 1939–1943. Ghetto, Underground, Revolt.* Bloomington: Indiana University Press, 1982.

Hájková, Anna. *The Last Ghetto: An Everyday History of Theresienstadt.* Oxford: Oxford University Press, 2020.

– "Sexual Barter in Times of Genocide: Negotiating the Sexual Economy of the Theresienstadt Ghetto." *Signs: Journal of Women in Culture and Society* 38.3 (2013): 503–33.

Hansen, Imke, Katrin Steffen, and Joachim Tauber, eds. *Lebenswelt Ghetto. Alltag und soziales Umfeld während der nationalsozialistischen Verfolgung.* Wiesbaden: Harrassowitz, 2013.

Harshav, Benjamin. "Introduction: Herman Kruk's Holocaust Writings." In Kruk, *The Last Days*, xxi–lii.

Hartglas, Apolinary. "How Did Czerniakow Become Head of the Warsaw Judenrat?" *Yad Vashem Bulletin* no. 15, 8 (1964): 4–7.

Hershkovitch, Bendet. "The Ghetto in Litzmannstadt (Lodz)." *YIVO Annual of Jewish Social Science* 5 (1950): 85–122.

Heuer, Hans-Joachim. *Geheime Staatspolizei. Über das Töten und die Entzivilisierung.* Berlin: De Gruyter, 1995.

Hilberg, Raul. *The Destruction of the European Jews.* Vol. 1. New Haven: Yale University Press, 2003.

Holz, Klaus. *Nationaler Antisemitismus: Wissenssoziologie einer Weltanschauung.* Hamburg: Hamburger Edition, 2010.

Horwitz, Gordon. *Ghettostadt: Łódź and the Making of a Nazi City.* Cambridge, MA: Belknap Press of Harvard University Press, 2008.

Huppert, Shmuel. "King of the Ghetto: Mordecai Haim Rumkowski, the Elder of Lodz Ghetto." *Yad Vashem Studies* 15 (1983): 125–57.

Husserl, Edmund. *The Crisis of European Sciences and Transcendental Phenomenology.* Evanston: Northwestern University Press, 1970 (*Husserliana VI*).

– *Ideas Pertaining to a Pure Phenomenology and to a Phenomenological Philosophy – Second Book: Studies in the Phenomenology of Constitution.* Dordrecht: Springer Netherlands, 1989.

Jacobs, Louis. "Halakhah." In Fred Skolnik and Michael Berenbaum, eds., *Encyclopedia Judaica.* 2nd edition. Detroit: Macmillan Publishers, 2007, 251–8.

Kant, Immanuel. *The Metaphysical Elements of Justice; Part I of the Metaphysics of Morals.* Indianapolis: Bobbs-Merrill Company, 1965.

Kassow, Samuel D. "Vilna and Warsaw, Two Ghetto Diaries: Herman Kruk and Emanuel Ringelblum." In Robert Moses Shapiro, ed., *Holocaust Chronicles: Individualizing the Holocaust through Diaries and Other Contemporaneous Personal Accounts*. New York: Ktav Publishing, 1999, 171–215.

– *Who Will Write Our History? Emanuel Ringelblum, the Warsaw Ghetto, and the Oyneg Shabes Archive*. Bloomington: Indiana University Press, 2007.

Katz, Jacob. *From Prejudice to Destruction: Anti-Semitism 1700–1933*. Cambridge, MA: Harvard University Press, 1980.

Kaufmann, Arthur. "Gustav Radbruch und die Radbruchsche Formel. Brief an meinen Enkel Finn Baumann." *Rechtshistorisches Journal* 19 (2000): 604–7.

Keckeisen, Wolfgang. *Die gesellschaftliche Definition abweichenden Verhaltens. Perspektiven und Grenzen des labeling approach*. Munich: Juventa-Verlag, 1974.

Kennedy, Duncan. *A Critique of Adjudication*. Cambridge, MA: Harvard University Press, 1997.

Klein, Peter. *Die "Gettoverwaltung Litzmannstadt" 1940–1944. Eine Dienststelle im Spannungsfeld von Kommunalbürokratie und staatlicher Verfolgungspolitik*. Hamburg: Hamburger Edition, 2009.

Klier, John. "Crime and Criminals." In Gershon David Hundert, ed., *The YIVO Encyclopedia of Jews in Eastern Europe*. New Haven: Yale University Press, 2008, 364–7.

Kunz, Karl Ludwig. *Die wissenschaftliche Zugänglichkeit von Kriminalität. Ein Beitrag zur Erkenntnistheorie der Sozialwissenschaften*. Wiesbaden: Dt. Universitäts-Verl., 2008.

Lehnstaedt, Stephan. *Geschichte und Gesetzesauslegung. Zu Kontinuität und Wandel des bundesdeutschen Wiedergutmachungsdiskurses am Beispiel der Ghettorenten*. Osnabrück: Fibre, 2011.

Levi, Primo. *The Drowned and the Saved*. New York: Summit Books, 1988.

Levin, Dov. "How the Jewish Police in the Kovno Ghetto Saw Itself." *Yad Vashem Studies* 29 (2001): 183–240.

Liang, Oliver. *Criminal-Biological Theory, Discourse, and Practice in Germany, 1918–1945*. Baltimore: UMI Publisher, 1999.

Libionka, Dariusz. *Zagłada Żydów w Generalnym Gubernatorstwie: zarys problematyki*. Lublin: Państwowe Muzeum na Majdanku, 2017.

Longerich, Peter. *Holocaust: The Nazi Persecution and Murder of the Jews*. Oxford: Oxford University Press, 2010.

Löw, Andrea. "Das Getto Litzmannstadt – eine historische Einführung." In Sascha Feuchert, ed., *Die Chronik des Gettos Lodz/Litzmannstadt. Supplemente und Anhang*. Göttingen: Wallstein, 2007, 145–65.

– *Juden im Getto Litzmannstadt. Lebensbedingungen, Selbstwahrnehmung, Verhalten*. Göttingen: Wallstein, 2006.

– "Ordnungsdienst im Getto Litzmannstadt." In Paweł Samuś and Wiesław Puś, eds., *Fenomen getta łódzkiego 1940–1944*. Lodz: Wydawnictwo Uniwersytetu Łódzkiego, 2006, 155–67.

Luhmann, Niklas. *A Sociological Theory of Law*. London: Routledge & Kegan Paul, 1985.

Majewska, Justyna. "'Czym wytłumaczy Pan ...?': inteligencja żydowska o polonizacji i asymilacji w getcie warszawskim." *Zagłada Żydów: studia i materiały* 11 (2015): 325–46.

Marrus, Michael R. "Jewish Resistance to the Holocaust." *Journal of Contemporary History* 30.1 (1995): 83–110.

Meyer, Beate. *Tödliche Gratwanderung. Die Reichsvereinigung der Juden in Deutschland zwischen Hoffnung, Zwang, Selbstbehauptung und Verstrickung (1939–1945)*. Göttingen: Wallstein, 2011.

Michman, Dan. *The Emergence of Jewish Ghettos during the Holocaust*. Cambridge: Cambridge University Press, 2011.

– *Holocaust Historiography. A Jewish Perspective. Conceptualizations, Terminology, Approaches and Fundamental Issues*. London/Portland: Vallentine Mitchell, 2003.

– "Kontroversen über die Judenräte in der jüdischen Welt 1945–2005. Das Ineinandergreifen von öffentlichem Gedächtnis und Geschichtsschreibung." In Freia Anders and Katrin Stoll, eds., *Der Judenrat von Białystok*. Paderborn/Munich: Schöningh, 2010, 311–17.

– "Reevaluating the Emergence, Function, and Form of the Jewish Councils Phenomenon." In *Ghettos 1939–1945: New Research and Perspectives on Definition, Daily Life, and Survival. Symposium Presentations*. Washington, DC: Center for Advanced Holocaust Studies, United States Holocaust Memorial Museum, 2005, 67–83.

– "Why Did Heydrich Write the Schnellbrief? A Remark on the Reason and on Its Significance." *Yad Vashem Studies* 32 (2004): 433–47.

Miller, Alexei. *The Romanov Empire and Nationalism*. Budapest: Central European University Press, 2008.

Miron, Guy, and Shlomit Shulhani, eds. *The Yad Vashem Encyclopaedia of the Ghettos during the Holocaust*. 2 vols. Jerusalem: Yad Vashem, 2014.

Mostowicz, Arnold. "Alltagsleben im Getto. Die Perspektive der Eingeschlossenen." In Doron Kiesel, ed., *"Wer zum Leben, wer zum Tod ..." Strategien jüdischen Überlebens im Getto*. Frankfurt am Main: Campus-Verlag, 1992, 37–50.

Musiał, Bogdan. *"Aktion Reinhardt"; der Völkermord an den Juden im Generalgouvernement 1941–1944*. Osnabrück: Fibre-Verlag, 2004.

– "The Origins of 'Operation Reinhardt': The Decision-Making Process for the Mass Murder of the Jews in the Generalgouvernement." *Yad Vashem Studies* 28 (2000): 113–53.

Novak, David. "Modern Responsa: 1800 to the Present." In Neil Hecht, ed., *An Introduction to the History and Sources of Jewish Law*. Boston: Clarendon Press, 1996, 379–95.

Ofer, Dalia. "Everyday Life of Jews under Nazi Occupation: Methodological Issues." *Holocaust and Genocide Studies* 9.1 (1995): 42–69.

Ostrowska, Joanna. "Prostytucja w Polsce w czasie II Wojny Światowej/ przypadek gett." In *Krytyka Polityczna*, czerwiec 2008, http://www .krytykapolityczna.pl/Teksty-poza-KP/Ostrowska-Piostytucja-w-gettach /menu-id-129.html [accessed 1.4.2015].

Passenstein, Marek. "Szmugiel w getcie warszawskim." *Biuletyn Żydowskiego Instytutu Historycznego* 26.2 (1958): 42–72.

Person, Katarzyna. *Policjanci: wizerunek Żydowskiej Służby Porządkowej w getcie warszawskim.* Warsaw: Żydowski Instytut Historyczny im. Emanuela Ringelbluma, 2018.

– "Sexual Violence during the Holocaust – the Case of 'Prostitution' in the Warsaw Ghetto." *Shofar* 33.2 (2015): 103–21.

Petropoulos, Jonathan, and John Roth, eds. *Gray Zones: Ambiguity and Compromise in the Holocaust and Its Aftermath.* New York/Oxford: Berghahn Books, 2006.

Pingel, Falk. "Social Life in an Unsocial Environment: The Inmates' Struggle for Survival." In Nikolaus Wachsmann and Jane Caplan, eds., *Concentration Camps in Nazi Germany: The New Histories.* London: Routledge, 2009, 70–93.

Podolska, Aldona. *Służba Porządkowa w getcie warszawskim w latach 1940–1943.* Warsaw: Wydawnictwo Fundacji Historia Pro Futuro, 1996.

Podolska, Joanna. "Nie w naszej mocy przebaczać. Chaim Mordechaj Rumkowski, Przełożony Starszeństwa Żydów w łodzkim getcie." In Paweł Samuś and Wiesław Puś, eds., *Fenomen getta łódzkiego 1940–1944.* Lodz: Wydawnictwo Uniwersytetu Łódzkiego, 2006, 205–34.

Pohl, Dieter. "Ghettos im Holocaust. Zum Stand der Historischen Forschung." In Jürgen Zarusky, ed., *Ghettorenten. Entschädigungspolitik, Rechtsprechung und historische Forschung.* Munich: Oldenbourg, 2010, 39–50.

– *Von der "Judenpolitik" zum Judenmord. Der Distrikt Lublin des Generalgouvernements 1939–1944.* Frankfurt am Main: Lang, 1993.

Polit, Monika. *"Moja żydowska dusza nie obawia się dnia sądu." Mordechaj Chaim Rumkowski. Prawda i zmyślenie.* Warsaw: Centrum Badań nad Zagładą Żydów IFiS PAN, 2012.

– "Mordechaj Chaim Rumkowski – literackie oceny i interpretacje." *Zagłada Żydów: studia i materiały* 7 (2011): 373–92.

Porat, Dina. "The Justice System and Courts of Law in the Ghettos of Lithuania." *Holocaust and Genocide Studies* 12.1 (1998): 49–65.

Preiss, Leah. "Women's Health in the Ghettos of Eastern Europe." http://jwa .org/encyclopedia/article/womens-health-in-ghettos-of-eastern -europe#bibliography [accessed 1.2.2013].

Rabinovici, Doron. *Eichman's Jews: The Jewish Administration of Holocaust Vienna 1938–45.* Cambridge: Polity Press, 2011.

Rest, Matthias. *Die russische Judengesetzgebung von der ersten polnischen Teilung bis zum "Položenie dlja evreev".* 1804. Wiesbaden: Harrassowitz, 1975.

Robinson, Jacob. *And the Crooked Shall Be Made Straight: The Eichmann Trial, the Jewish Catastrophe, and Hannah Arendt's Narrative.* New York/London: Macmillan Publishers, 1965.

– *Discontinuity or Continuity in the Jewish Councils during the Nazi Era* (written in Hebrew). Jerusalem: Institute for Contemporary Jewry, Hebrew University of Jerusalem, 1967.

– "Introduction: Some Basic Issues That Faced the Jewish Councils." In Trunk, *Judenrat,* xxv–xxxv.

Roth, Markus, and Andrea Löw. *Das Warschauer Ghetto. Alltag und Widerstand im Angesicht der Vernichtung.* Munich: Beck, 2013.

Rubin, Henryk. *Żydzi w Łodzi pod niemiecką okupacją* ("Jews in Lodz under Nazi Occupation"). London: Kontra, 1988.

Sack, Fritz. *Probleme der Kriminalsoziologie.* In René König, ed., *Handbuch der empirischen Sozialforschung. Wahlverhalten, Vorurteile, Kriminalität.* Stuttgart: Dt. Taschenbuch-Verl., 1978, 192–492.

Sakowska, Ruta. "Komitety domowe w getcie warszawskim." *Biuletyn ŻIH* 61 (1967): 59–86.

– *Menschen im Ghetto. Die jüdische Bevölkerung im besetzten Warschau 1939–1943.* Osnabrück: Fibre, 1999.

Schlüter, Holger. *"… für die Menschlichkeit im Strafmaß bekannt …": Das Sondergericht Litzmannstadt und sein Vorsitzender Richter.* Düsseldorf: Justizministerium des Landes NRW, 2006.

Schoeps, Julius H. *Die missglückte Emanzipation. Wege und Irrwege deutsch-jüdischer Geschichte.* Hildesheim: Olms, 2010.

Schroeter, Gudrun. *Worte aus einer zerstörten Welt. Das Ghetto in Wilna.* St Ingbert: Röhrig, 2008.

Schütz, Alfred, and Thomas Luckmann. *The Structures of the Life-World.* Vol. 1. Trans. Richard M. Zaner and H. Tristan Engelhardt, Jr. Evanston: Northwestern University Press, 1973.

Schwerhoff, Gerd. *Aktenkundig und gerichtsnotorisch. Einführung in die historische Kriminalitätsforschung.* Tübingen: Diskord, 1999.

Shneidman, N.N. *The Three Tragic Heroes of the Vilnius Ghetto: Witenberg, Sheinbaum, Gens.* Oakville, ON: Mosaic Press, 2002.

Sitarek, Adam. "W obliczu 'trudnej konieczności'. Administracja żydowska getta łódzkiego wobec wsiedleń Żydów z Rzeszy i Protektoratu (październik-listopad 1941 r.)." *Zagłada Żydów: studia i materiały* 8 (2012): 331–47.

– "Wire Bound State": Structure and Functions of the Jewish Administration of the Łódź Ghetto. Lodz: Warszawa Instytut Pamięci Narodowej, 2017.

Skibińska, Alina. "Życie codzienne Żydów w Kozienicach pod okupacją niemiecką (1939–1943)." *Zagłada Żydów: studia i materiały* 3 (2007): 64–86.

Stanisławski, Michael. "Kahal (*kehilah*)." In Gershon David Hundert, ed., *The YIVO Encyclopedia of Jews in Eastern Europe.* New Haven: Yale University Press, 2008, 845–8.

Steffen, Katrin. "Connotations of Exclusion: 'Ostjuden', 'Ghettos', and Other Markings." *Simon-Dubnow Institute Yearbook* 4 (2005): 459–79.

Suderland, Maja. *Inside Concentration Camps: Social Life at the Extremes.* Hoboken, NJ: John Wiley & Sons, 2014.

Szymańska-Smolkin, Sylwia. "Fateful Decisions: The Polish Policemen and the Jewish Population of Occupied Poland, 1939–1945." PhD dissertation, University of Toronto, 2017.

Ta-Shma, Israel Moses, Shlomo Tal, and Menahem Slae. "Responsa." In Fred Skolnik and Michael Berenbaum, eds., *Encyclopedia Judaica*. 2nd edition. Detroit: Macmillan Publishers, 2007, 228–39.

Trunk, Isaiah. "The Attitude of the Judenrats to the Problems of Armed Resistance against the Nazis." In Yisrael Gutman and Livia Rothkirchen, eds., *The Catastrophe of European Jewry: Antecedents – History – Reflections.* Jerusalem: Yad Vashem, 1976.

– *Judenrat: The Jewish Councils in Eastern Europe under Nazi Occupation.* New York: Macmillan Publishers, 1972.

– "The Judenrat and Jewish Responses (Discussion)." In Yehuda Bauer and Nathan Rotenstreich, eds., *The Holocaust as Historical Experience*. London: Holmes & Meier, 1981, 223–71.

– *Łódź Ghetto: A History*. Ed. Robert Moses Shapiro. Bloomington: Indiana University Press, 2006.

– "Note: Why Was There No Armed Resistance against the Nazis in the Lodz Ghetto?" *Jewish Social Studies* 43.3/4 (1981): 329–34.

– "The Opposition to the Jewish Councils and the Ghetto Police." In Shmuel Yeivin, ed., *Studies in Jewish History: Presented to Professor Raphael Mahler on His Seventy-Fifth Birthday*. Tel Aviv: Sifriat Poalim, 1974, 137–62.

Turk, Austin T. "Prospects for Theories of Criminal Behaviour." *Journal of Criminal Law, Criminology, and Political Science* 55 (1964): 454–61.

Unger, Michal. "Łódź." In Guy Miron, ed., *The Yad Vashem Encyclopedia of the Ghettos during the Holocaust*. Vol. 1. Jerusalem: Yad Vashem, 2009.

– *Reassessment of the Image of Mordechai Chaim Rumkowski*. Jerusalem: Yad Vashem, 2004.

The United States Holocaust Memorial Museum, ed. *Encyclopedia of Camps and Ghettos, 1933–1945, Vol. II, Ghettos in German Occupied Eastern Europe, Part A.* Bloomington: Indiana University Press, 2012.

van Pelt, Jan. *Łódź and Getto Litzmannstadt: Promised Land and Croaking Hole of Europe*. Toronto: Art Gallery of Ontario, 2015.

Vyleta, Dan. "Jewish Crimes and Misdemeanours: In Search of Jewish Criminality in Germany and Austria, 1890–1914." *European History Quarterly* 35 (2005): 299–325.

Wachsmann, Nikolaus. *KL: A History of the Nazi Concentration Camps*. London: Little, Brown Book Group, 2015.

Weber, Max. *Economy and Society: An Outline of Interpretive Sociology*. New York: Bedminster Press, 1968.

Weiss, Aharon. "Ha'mishtara hayehudit be'general gouvernement u'ba'shlezia ilit bi'tekufat ha'shoa" ("The Jewish Police in the General Gouvernement and Upper Silesia during the Holocaust"). PhD dissertation, Hebrew University of Jerusalem, 1973.

– "Jewish Leadership in Occupied Poland – Postures and Attitudes." *Yad Vashem Studies* 12 (1977): 335–66.

– "Jüdischer Ordnungsdienst." In Israel Gutman, ed., *Encyclopedia of the Holocaust*. Vol. 2. New York: Macmillan Publishing, 1990, 771–4.

– "The Relations between the Judenrat and the Jewish Police." In Israel Gutman and Cynthia J. Haft, eds., *Patterns of Jewish Leadership in Nazi Europe 1933–1945: Proceedings of the Third Yad Vashem International Historical Conference, Jerusalem, April 4–7, 1977*. Jerusalem: Yad Vashem, 1979, 201–18.

Weitzman, Leonore J. "Living on the Aryan Side in Poland." In Dalia Ofer and Leonore J. Weitzman, eds., *Women in the Holocaust*. New Haven: Yale University Press, 1998, 187–222.

Wetzell, Richard. *Inventing the Criminal: A History of German Criminology, 1880–1945*. Chapel Hill: University of North Carolina Press, 2000.

Wiesner, Jonas. *Der Bann in seiner gesellschaftlichen Entwicklung auf dem Boden des Judenthumes*. Leipzig: O. Leiner, 1864.

Wildt, Michael. "Die Transformation des Ausnahmezustands. Ernst Fraenkels Analyse der NS-Herrschaft und ihre politische Aktualität." In Jürgen Danyel, ed., *50 Klassiker der Zeitgeschichte*. Göttingen: Vandenhoeck & Ruprecht, 2007, 19–23.

– *An Uncompromising Generation: The Nazi Leadership of the Reich Security Main Office*. Madison: University of Wisconsin Press, 2009.

Zarusky, Jürgen, ed. *Ghettorenten. Entschädigungspolitik, Rechtsprechung und historische Forschung*. Munich: Oldenbourg, 2010.

Zippelius, Reinhold. *Rechtsphilosophie. Ein Studienbuch*. Munich: Beck, 2011.

Index

Gestapo, 40, 72, 82, 83, 120, 136.
See also German Criminal Police;
German intervention/interference
Geto-Tsaytung reporting, 3, 20, 52, 53,
60, 185n90; ghetto courts, 91, 104,
105, 106, 147, 150
Geto-Yedies reporting, 20, 52, 185n91
. Ghetto Chronicle: ghetto courts, 95,
98, 115, 147; Jewish Police, 79, 84;
penal system, 241n76
ghetto courts, 90–123; amnesties,
117–19, 235n231, 235n233; appeal
courts, 93, 223n29; appeals,
requests, and complaints, 149–50,
151, 154, 157–8, 246n41, 246n44,
246n45; arbitration tribunals, 92,
97, 223n25; border crossings, 91,
93, 102, 229n118; bribery, 104,
105–6, 230n138; candy production,
104, 118, 119; "classical" crime,
109–10, 112, 115–16; death
sentences, 94, 96, 106–7, 113,
114–15, 148, 224n41; deportation,
118, 120–1; food smuggling, 103,
105; food supplies, 106–7, 230n149;
German Criminal Police, 93, 95,
103, 111; German intervention,
94, 104; German offences, 102–3,
229n118; house committees,
92, 120; instructors, 92, 222n18;
Jewish Councils, 97–8, 104–9,
110, 123, 168, 236n249; judges,
12, 90, 95; juvenile courts, 91,
117, 228n112; language use in,
101, 228n114, 228n115; legal
experience, 95–9; legal problems,
120–3; legal procedures, 97,
98, 99; Lodz, 90–1, 93, 98, 101,
104–8, 118, 146, 147, 228n113;
mitigation, 116–19, 235n235;
murder, 94, 112–13, 114–15, 148;
oaths, 98, 228n114; profiteering,
103, 107–8; prosecutors, 90,

221n4; "rescue through labour,"
97, 104; residents' reporting
and actions, 146, 148, 149–59,
245n21; smuggling, 91, 102, 103,
105, 224n36, 229n118, 229n129;
summary courts, 91, 93, 104–5,
147, 223n30; survival in ghettos,
109, 110, 122; theft, 94, 104, 105,
108, 110, 119, 224n44; tried cases,
101–16, 228n111; Vilna, 90, 92–7,
101, 104, 108–12, 114–17, 119–22,
223n28, 228n111, 235n226; Warsaw,
90, 92, 94, 97, 119, 120, 146, 222n17;
witnesses, 120–1, 148, 156–7, 159,
246n34; women, 95, 152, 247n58.
See also Lodz ghetto; Vilna ghetto;
Warsaw ghetto
ghettoization, 10, 23–8
ghettos, open, 19, 184n77
Gliksman, Sról, 142, 155
Gojchbarg, Miriam, 145
Goldberg, Mendl, 159
Goldberg, offender, 47
Goldfarb, Judge, 120
Goldsztejn, Cyrla, 112
Gordon, Chaim-Majer, 35
Göring, Hermann, 25
Gorodecka, Chana, 138
Gramsci, Antonio, 16
Great Provocation, 36
Greenfeld, Yankl, 114
greetings, 45, 54–5
Greiser, Gauleiter Arthur, 34
Gringauz, Samuel, 8, 9, 166, 169, 175
guilt, confessions of, 116, 121
Gutgestalt, Miriam, 117
Gutman, Israel, 31
"gypsies," 33, 34

halakha, 99, 106, 173, 226n86
Halle, Szmul, 145
Hanoar Hatzioni movement, 39,
197n180

labour, 33, 35, 42, 55–6, 97, 152, 206n43; Jewish Police, 68, 69–73, 75, 76, 81–3, 84–5; juvenile crime, 116–17, 228n112, 235n228; legal experience, 96, 97; legal problems, 120, 121–2; living conditions, 33, 143–4, 154, 159; mitigation, 116–17, 143–4, 149, 151, 152–3; moral standards, 3–4, 78, 79, 173; murder, 49, 82–3, 93, 113, 115, 148, 232n189; "objects of value," 55–6, 71–2, 206n38; penal system, 124–8, 129, 130, 131–2, 134, 135–6, 138–9, 140, 241n76; proclamations, 53, 54; profiteering, 60, 103, 107–8; public order, 62–3, 70; punishment, 105–6, 126, 136, 151, 230n140; radio listeners, 251n111; regulations and sanctions, 3, 172–3; relief aid, 58, 60, 107, 125, 128, 208n61; "rescue through labour," 22, 55–6, 58, 64, 126–7, 152, 164, 168, 186n100, 206n43; resettlement, 34, 56, 57, 194n122, 194n123; residents' reporting and actions, 142, 143–5, 146, 149, 154, 162; resistance, 16, 172–3; Secretariat for Complaints and Requests, 149, 150, 247n48; sewage transportation duties, 105–6, 126, 151, 230n140; smuggling, 44, 47–8, 53, 158, 159; *Sonderkommando*, 71–2, 78, 121–2, 206n38, 236n258, 237n263; suicide, 45, 200n220; summary courts, 91, 104–5, 147; survival in ghettos, 35, 52, 54, 55, 76, 91; theft, 72, 94, 104, 110, 143–5, 158, 213n33; theft of bread/from bakers, 105, 119, 230n138; theft of food, 111, 122, 142, 143–4, 151, 157, 161, 237n263; theft of wood, 60, 72, 119, 127, 128, 142, 144–5, 149, 244n44;

vandalism, 3, 61, 177n1; women, 73, 95. See also *Geto-Tsaytung* reporting; Ghetto Chronicle; Rumkowski, Mordechaj Chaim
Lohse, Heinrich, 36
looting, 41
Lublin, 24

Madagascar, 24
Majer, Aleksander, 107–8, 231n152
Markowiszin, offender, 126
Maślanko, Judge, 120
massacres, 30, 36–7, 39, 49, 195n143, 196n151. See also extermination/annihilation of Jews
Merenleder, Judge, 102
messages, receipt of, 45
Millet, Zygmunt, 92
Mishnah, 100
mitigation, 138; ghetto courts, 116–19, 235n235; health and wellbeing, 151, 152–3, 248n81; Lodz, 116–17, 143–4, 149, 151, 152; "rescue through labour," 151–2; residents' reporting and actions, 143–4, 149
money, value of, 125, 237n5
moral standards, 4, 7–8, 9, 122, 169–76; Jewish Councils, 15–16, 166, 172, 173–6; Jewish morality, 101, 172; Jewish Police, 77–9, 80; Lodz, 3–4, 78, 79, 172–3; Nazism, 169, 175–6; residents' reporting and actions, 156, 161–2, 164; survival in ghettos, 164, 172; Vilna, 4, 78, 79–80, 173
Mostowicz, Arnold, 74
Moszkowicz, ghetto resident, 142
Motyl, Judge, 103
Motyl, Symcha Binem, 163–4
murder, 113–16; ghetto courts, 94, 112–13, 114–15, 148; Lodz, 49, 82–3, 93, 113, 115, 148, 232n189; Vilna, 36–40, 94, 114–15, 148, 151–2

Murer, Franz: deportation, 132, 137;
food smuggling, 44, 86; Jewish
Councils, 36, 37, 38, 40, 44, 55,
Jewish labour, 56, 132; Jewish
Police, 68, 69, 70, 83, 86; penal
system, 132, 137

naming publicly, 128
Nazism/National Socialism, 5–6,
23–50; moral standards, 169,
175–6. *See also* German Criminal
Police; German intervention/
interference
Neftalin, Henryk, 91, 98, 126, 150,
246n41
Neuhaus, offender, 111–12
New Year amnesty, 118
newspapers, 20, 45, 47, 49, 52,
168. See also *Gazeta Żydowska*
reporting; *Geto-Tsaytung* reporting;
Geto-Yedies reporting; Ghetto
Chronicle
norms, social, 17
Novak, David, 101
Nowacki, Kazimierz, 158
Nuremberg Laws, 24
Nusbaum, Berek, 102

oaths, 98, 228n114
"objects of value": food supply,
46, 202n233; furs, 55, 156, 204n8;
Lodz, 55–6, 71–2, 158, 206n38;
Vilna, 40, 198n196
offences: German, 102–3, 229n118;
labour, 7, 73, 87
Okladek, Nacha, 152
Olicki, Mojsze, 117
Oneg Shabbat. See Ringelblum,
Emanuel
Opoczyński, Perec, 120, 149, 156
order, public/social, 15, 17, 44–5,
62–3, 70, 87, 183n67

Order Service. *See* Jewish Police/
Order Service
Urdynans, offender, 112
orphans, 73, 117, 160
Orzech, Moritu, 30
Oshemene ghetto, 198n185
Oszmiana ghetto, 39
Owsiana, offender, 110

Palfinger, Alexander, 42
penal system, 124–41; bail, 139,
243n111; children, 126, 130, 134,
238n14; deportation, 124–5, 136–7,
138, 242n90, 242n93; families of
offenders, 125–6, 238n14; Gens,
129–30, 131, 132, 140; German
intervention, 127, 130, 131–2,
133, 139–40, 238n22, 240n56;
German quotas, 132, 240n53;
house committees, 127–8, 239n26;
hygiene, 128, 137; Jewish Councils,
129, 140; Jewish labour, 135–6, 139;
living conditions in prisons, 137–8,
140; Lodz, 124–8, 129, 130, 131–2,
134, 135–6, 138–9, 140, 241n76;
prisons, 135, 136–7, 240n62;
"rescue through labour," 126–7,
132; Vilna, 128–31, 132, 135, 136–7,
139, 240n53, 242n90, 243n111;
Warsaw, 128, 133, 135, 137, 140,
240n56. *See also* punishment
Person, Katarzyna, 181n43
Pinsk ghetto, 250n97
Piotrków Trybunalski ghetto,
183n65, 188n20
Podolska, Aldona, 181n43
Poland: exclusion of the Jews,
24–5, 187n17; ghettoization, 24–5,
188n20
police. *See* German Criminal Police;
Jewish Police/Order Service;
Polish police ("Blue Police")

German and European Studies

General Editor: Jennifer L. Jenkins